A Guide to HIPAA Security
and the Law
Second Edition

Stephen S. Wu

Cover by Lachina Publishing Services, Inc.

Printed in the United States of America.

20 19 18 17 16   5 4 3 2 1

Library of Congress Cataloging-in-Publication Data

Names: Wu, Stephen S., editor
Title: A guide to HIPAA security and the law / [editied] by stephen wu.
Description: Second Edition. | Chicago : American Bar Association, [2016] | Includes bibliographical references and index.
Identifiers: LCCN 2016029675 | ISBN 9781627228350 (print : alk. paper)
Subjects: LCSH: Medical records—Law and legislation—United States. | Medical records—Access control—United States. | Medical records—Secutiry measures— United States. | Data protection—Law and legislation—United States. | United States. Health Insurance Portability and Accountability Act of 1996.
Classiciation: LCC KF3827.R4 G85 2016 | DDC 344.7304/1—dc23
LC record available at https://lccn.loc.gov/2016029675

www.ShopABA.org

Contents

CHAPTER 5
The Security Rule   59

CHAPTER 8
Litigation and Risk Management   219

CHAPTER 9
Emerging Technologies   255

CHAPTER 10
Conclusion

APPENDIX 1
HIPAA Administrative Simplification Provisions

APPENDIX 2
HITECH Act Privacy Provisions

APPENDIX 3
Regulations Establishing General Administrative Requirements

APPENDIX 4
Regulations Comprising the Security Rule, Breach Notification Rule, and Privacy Rule 45 C.F.R. Part 164

Index

To my wife, Mary Wu, for all of her love and support.

To my children, Katherine, Michael, and Elizabeth Wu,
for their love and inspiration.

To Sandra Wu, Helen Wu, and Jussi Saukkonen for their wisdom.

About the Author

Stephen S. Wu is an of counsel attorney with Silicon Valley Law Group in San Jose, California. He advises clients concerning legal matters relating to information security and privacy. These matters include regulatory compliance, negotiating security-related transactions, incident response and investigations, security breach notification, and litigation arising from security incidents. In addition, he advises clients on compliance, liability, security, and privacy matters regarding the latest technologies, including health tech, robotics, artificial intelligence, Big Data, the Internet of Things, and augmented and virtual reality.

Mr. Wu served as the 2010–2011 Chair of the ABA Section of Science & Technology Law and served as Co-Chair of the Section's Information Security Committee from 2001 to 2004. He helped found other committees in the Section, including the Homeland Security Committee, Artificial Intelligence and Robotics Committee, Big Data Committee, and Internet of Things Committee. He is also a member of the Section's Healthcare Technology Committee and the ABA Health Law Section and Section of Litigation.

Mr. Wu has authored or coauthored six books on information security and the law, including his 2013 book on enterprise mobile device management, as well as chapters in other publications. The Daimler & Benz Foundation and ABA recently published his book chapters on driverless car and drone product liability. He is a frequent speaker on information security, robotics, and Internet of Things legal topics.

Before his work in private practice, Mr. Wu was in charge of VeriSign, Inc.'s worldwide policies and practices governing its digital certification security services. Prior to his work at VeriSign, Mr. Wu practiced in the areas of intellectual property, technology transactions, and general commercial litigation for Kirkpatrick & Lockhart LLP (now K&L Gates) and Jones Day. Mr. Wu was a law clerk to the Hon. Joseph P. Kinneary of the United States District Court for the Southern District of Ohio. He received his B.A., summa cum laude, from the University of Pittsburgh in 1985, and received his J.D., cum laude, from Harvard Law School in 1988.

Preface

The Health Insurance Portability and Accountability Act (HIPAA) Security Rule introduced industry-standard information technology security practices to the healthcare field. It provides needed security protections for vital and sensitive health information. The Security Rule, however, poses a challenge for people charged with implementing it, or advising those who must implement it. On one hand, attorneys in the healthcare field may be unfamiliar with information security practices, especially technical security controls. On the other hand, information security professionals may have no formal training in the law.

This book attempts to bridge the gap between the law and information security practices. HIPAA and the Security Rule are sources of law, but the Security Rule also acts as a source of information security practices. The Health Information Technology for Economic and Clinical Health Act, also called the HITECH Act, imposes additional security requirements. This book serves as a reference to a wide audience: healthcare and information security professionals implementing the HIPAA Security Rule and Breach Notification Rule, as well as attorneys and business professionals advising them. It is dedicated to healthcare professionals who struggle every day with meeting their obligations to provide care and services for patients and at the same time are seeking to protect the security of patients' health information. I hope that this book provides vital guidance and information for those involved in compliance with the Security Rule and Breach Notification Rule.

Chapter 1 serves as an introduction to the topic of HIPAA security and the Security Rule. Chapter 2 discusses the reasons for the enactment of the HIPAA legislation and its mandate to develop regulations, including the Security Rule. It also discusses more recent health information technology initiatives. Chapter 3 clarifies the relationship between HIPAA's Privacy Rule and Security Rule. Chapter 3 also describes how the HIPAA legislation and the Privacy Rule themselves call for the security of health information. In addition, it discusses the HITECH Act and its requirements. Chapter 4 covers the scope of the HIPAA Security Rule. Specifically, chapter 4 establishes what information the Security Rule protects and which entities are covered by the Security Rule.

Chapter 5 is the core of this book. Chapter 5 serves as a section-by-section analysis of the HIPAA Security Rule. The section-by-section treatment of the Security Rule is to provide a comprehensive set of guidelines for implementing the Security Rule. Chapter 5 distinguishes between requirements under the law and other so-called "addressable" practices that are not required. A covered entity or business associate must analyze addressable practices in a risk assessment and management process and determine whether they are reasonable and appropriate to implement under its particular circumstances.

Chapter 6 addresses the breach notification requirements for covered entities and business associates. Chapter 7 covers compliance and enforcement. First, it discusses the state of the industry's implementation of the Security Rule. Second, it describes the enforcement of the Security Rule, including the Department of Health and Human Services Office for Civil Rights investigations, the imposition of civil money penalties, and state attorney general enforcement actions. Chapter 8 reports on private plaintiff litigation arising out of the Security Rule. Chapter 9 focuses on particular newer and emerging technologies. It explains these technologies, as well as their security and resulting HIPAA security issues. I present some conclusions in chapter 10.

The appendices to this book contain useful reference materials. Appendix 1 sets forth the administrative simplification provisions of the HIPAA legislation. Appendix 2 contains HITECH Act provisions that supplement HIPAA security and set the stage for the HIPAA Final Omnibus Rule. Appendix 3 contains general administrative requirements from title 45 of the Code of Federal Regulations, part 160, which includes the regulations concerning enforcement. Finally, Appendix 4 contains the HIPAA Security Rule, Breach Notification Rule, and Privacy Rule.

I received assistance on the first edition of this book and inspiration for my work in the area since the first edition from the Information Security Committee (ISC) and the Healthcare Technology Committee of the ABA Section of Science & Technology Law. The ISC is an interdisciplinary group of lawyers, technologists, and other professionals that explores legal, business, and technical aspects of securing information and critical infrastructures within computer systems and networks, such as the Internet. The Healthcare Technology Committee explores information technology issues, such as privacy and security, in the healthcare field. If you wish to delve further into HIPAA security, and discuss healthcare security issues with other professionals, I recommend joining these two committees. Both attorneys and nonattorneys are welcome to join.

For attorneys in the Health Law Section, I recommend exploring the eHealth, Privacy & Security Interest Group. This interest group focuses on cutting edge issues dealing with technology, privacy, and security as they relate to health care. Its website includes a number of member benefit resources.

Stephen S. Wu

Acknowledgements

I wish to thank the following individuals for supporting my work on this book.

- **Michael McAlpen** and **Mehdi Salour**, 8x8, Inc., San Jose, California, for our continued fruitful collaboration over the years.
- **Dan Weirich** and **Michele Caramello**, Treasure Data, Inc., Mountain View, California, for their practical insights into security management.
- **Benjamin Rose, Jim Carden, David Townsend, Paul Starrett**, and **Joshua Gilliland**, Carden Rose, Inc., Cupertino, California, for our long friendship and work together on information security.
- **Benjamin Wilson**, DigiCert, Salt Lake City, Utah, for his assistance in reviewing the book.
- **Kathryn Coburn**, Murphy Cooke & Kobrick LLP, Santa Monica, California, for providing invaluable information and guidance in writing the book.
- **Caryn Hawk, Julia Passamani**, and **Barbara Mitchell**, staff members of the ABA Section of Science & Technology Law, Chicago, Illinois, for our many years together exploring the intersection of law and technology.
- **Sarah Orwig**, ABA Publishing, Chicago, Illinois, for her patience and dedication in support of the book.
- **Molly Montanaro** and **Jenni Claydon**, Lachina Publishing Services, Cleveland, Ohio, for their tireless efforts in helping me complete this book.

Stephen S. Wu
San Jose, California
July 11, 2016

CHAPTER 1

Introduction

Data security breaches are an everyday occurrence. The news media constantly publicize data breaches, especially those involving retailers in which hackers steal the payment card information from millions of consumers. Perhaps of more concern, though, are data breaches in the healthcare field.

In February 2015, Anthem, Inc., the country's second-largest health insurer, announced a massive data breach involving unauthorized access to its database of personal information concerning current and former Anthem members. Victims around the country have experienced identity theft incidents. At the time of this writing, a class action pending in the US District Court for the Northern District of California now seeks compensation for the victims. Also, from 2004 to 2008, former California First Lady Maria Shriver, the late actress Farrah Fawcett, singer Britney Spears, and *Cheers* actress Shelley Long were all victims of breaches involving the unauthorized access to their medical records at the UCLA Medical Center. In the past several months, news reports surfaced regarding hospitals that have fallen victim to "ransomware" attacks. Ransomware is a form of malicious software that, when it infects a computer system, quickly encrypts data on the system and sometimes network storage or other computers. The victim receives a message demanding ransom money to provide a key to decrypt the user's files. If the user fails to pay the ransom, the user could lose access to his or her data. Recent ransomware attacks have locked up electronic medical records of entire hospitals, disabling their information systems and potentially endangering patients.

Health records are among the most sensitive sets of information about us. The results of an unauthorized disclosure of health records could be devastating. Leakage of health records could lead to victims' embarrassment, stigma, job loss, and even identity theft. Following concerns about the privacy and security of health records in the 1990s, the public began to demand protection to ensure that the healthcare industry would implement controls over what information was gathered from patients, how the information could be shared, and the secure management of that information. This public concern prompted Congress to enact legislation in 1996 calling for safeguards over the privacy and security of health information.

The 1996 legislation, called the Health Insurance Portability and Accountability Act of 1996 (HIPAA),[1] has had a broad impact on the healthcare industry since its enactment, transforming practices for creating, storing, managing, transmitting, and disclosing health information in this country. HIPAA called for federal standards for the privacy and security of certain health information (called protected health information under HIPAA, and PHI here). The privacy and security portions of HIPAA appear in the Administrative Simplification subtitle of HIPAA, and later regulations create the standards for privacy and security. The Department of Health and Human Services (HHS) promulgated these regulations in the form of a Privacy Rule[2] and a Security Rule.[3]

In general, HHS intended the administrative simplification provisions in HIPAA to increase the ease and efficiency of exchanging health information and conducting healthcare transactions electronically. Specifically, HIPAA contemplated the use of electronic data interchange (EDI) to accelerate electronic processing of transactions in the healthcare industry. HHS hoped standardizing the formats for many of the most common EDI exchanges of health information would mean the end of much of the confusion in claims submission and payment caused by inconsistent formats and forms, under the Medicare and Medicaid Programs, and beyond. Since the enactment of HIPAA, the healthcare field has seen the proliferation of Internet-based services and cloud computing in addition to EDI. Nonetheless, the Privacy Rule and Security Rule have continued to govern the creation, receipt, use, processing, maintenance, and transmission of electronic PHI regardless of the technology used by businesses in the healthcare field.

The American Bar Association Section of Science & Technology Law published the first edition of this book in 2007. Since then, two important sets of changes to the law have taken place. First, Congress

---

1. Health Insurance Portability and Accountability Act of 1996, Pub. L. No. 104-191, 110 Stat. 1936 (1996) [hereinafter HIPAA].

2. Standards for Privacy of Individually Identifiable Health Information; Final Rule, 65 Fed. Reg. 82,462 (2000) (codified as amended at 45 C.F.R. pts. 160, 164).

3. Health Insurance Reform: Security Standards; Final Rule, 68 Fed. Reg. 8334 (2003) (codified at 45 C.F.R. pts. 160, 162, 164).

passed the Health Information Technology for Economic and Clinical Health Act, also called the HITECH Act. The HITECH Act is part of a larger piece of stimulus legislation enacted during the financial crisis that started in the late 2000s.[4] The HITECH Act made certain changes to HIPAA security and privacy provisions, called for notification of data security breaches to affected individuals, and strengthened HIPAA's enforcement provisions.

Second, HHS issued interim and later final regulations to flesh out the provisions of the HITECH Act, to strengthen HIPAA enforcement, and to somewhat simplify the HIPAA Security Rule and the HIPAA Privacy Rule. The final set of regulations emerging from the HITECH Act is commonly referred to as the HIPAA Final Omnibus Rule.[5] The compliance deadline for the HIPAA Final Omnibus Rule was in September 2013.

Unlike other books on HIPAA, the focus of this book is the HIPAA Security Rule, as modified by the HITECH Act and the HIPAA Final Omnibus Rule. This publication discusses the Security Rule's role in the broader context of HIPAA, the HITECH Act, and their regulations. At the heart of this publication is a detailed section-by-section analysis of each provision in the Security Rule covering a security safeguard. This analysis explains the security topic and what organizations can do to comply. This publication also covers the legal risks of noncompliance by describing the applicable enforcement mechanisms that apply, reporting on past enforcement actions, and describing the body of case law emerging from litigation relating to HIPAA/HITECH security. The intended audience of this book is healthcare and information security professionals, lawyers specializing in these fields, administrators, compliance officers, chief information security officers, and security personnel. Hopefully, the book will provide the reader with useful guidance in meeting security requirements related to PHI.

The Security Rule focuses on PHI in electronic form. The HIPAA Privacy Rule also requires covered entities to implement "appropriate administrative, technical and physical safeguards" for the privacy of PHI,

---

4. Health Information Technology for Economic and Clinical Health Act within the American Recovery and Reinvestment Act of 2009, Pub. L. No. 111-5, 123 Stat. 115 (2009).

5. Modifications to the HIPAA Privacy, Security, Enforcement, and Breach Notification Rules under the Health Information Technology for Economic and Clinical Health Act and the Genetic Information Nondiscrimination Act; Other Modifications to the HIPAA Rules; Final Rule, 78 Fed. Reg. 5566 (2013).

in all its forms, including paper records.[6] At a highlevel, The safeguards described in the Privacy Rule are the same as those in the security Rule: adminstrative, technical, and physical safeguards. They also seek to protect PHI against unauthorized use or disclosure, as the Security Rule does.[7]

Specifically, the Security Rule is designed to protect the confidentiality, integrity, and availability of *electronic* protected health information. In the first edition, we emphasized the difference between PHI addressed in the Privacy Rule by using "ePHI" for electronic PHI, which is specifically addressed in the Security Rule. In this edition, we have decided to abandon the use of "ePHI" in favor of the more commonly used generic term, PHI, because as a practical matter, HIPAA entities need to protect PHI in whatever form, and from an information security perspective, most readers will understand that the type of PHI discussed in this book is electronic PHI. This is also the approach taken in most business associate agreements.

The Security Rule requires entities covered by HIPAA (i.e., covered entities)[8] to implement reasonable and appropriate administrative, physical, and technical safeguards to protect PHI. The HITECH Act and the HIPAA Final Omnibus Rule apply the Security Rule to "business associates" of covered entities, which perform HIPAA-covered functions on behalf of their covered entity customers or clients. Moreover, the HIPAA Final Omnibus Rule covers a broad range of technology vendors and service providers, many of which may offer general-purpose services, may have no intention of focusing on the healthcare market, and may even be unaware that their customers are using their services to store PHI on their systems. Accordingly, the breadth of the HIPAA Final Omnibus Rule has been a surprise to many vendors and service providers.

HIPAA/HITECH safeguards must secure PHI while in the custody of covered entities and business associates, as well as during transmission to or from these businesses. Such safeguards must be adequate to ensure the confidentiality of the information. They must also protect against any reasonably anticipated threats or hazards to the security and integrity of the PHI and protect against unauthorized use or disclosure of the PHI.

Assessing and managing risks are the primary challenges posed by HIPAA security compliance. Risk assessment is the first step in identifying the security threats and hazards that a given covered entity or business

---

6. 45 C.F.R. § 164.530(c)(i).

7. Compare id. § 164.530(c)(2)(i) to id. § 164.306(a)(3).

8. Covered entities are health plans, healthcare providers, and healthcare clearinghouses. 45 C.F.R. § 160.103.

associate can reasonably anticipate, as well as the costs that will be reasonable and appropriate in addressing those risks. Risk assessment includes prioritizing and quantifying the risks. Mitigation and remediating threats that pose risks should follow the risk assessment. If mitigation and remediation are not reasonable and appropriate, it may be necessary to transfer risks (using insurance or third-party indemnification, for instance) or to simply accept and plan on handling risks that cannot otherwise be mitigated. Regardless, the Security Rule requires ongoing monitoring and periodic review to facilitate an ongoing assessment and reevaluation of risks.

Secure electronic transmission of health information offers opportunities to improve the quality and efficiency of healthcare delivery by improving access to information. Specifically, access by healthcare professionals, health plan administrators, and patients will improve. In addition, secure transmission of electronic health information will foster opportunities to implement cost savings as a result of standardized healthcare transactions and the use of the Internet and cloud service providers. Secure electronic transmission of health information can create opportunities to identify and treat those who are at risk for specific diseases, to conduct medical research, and to detect fraud and abuse.

Moreover, the distribution of electronic data can extend far beyond the community where the patient is physically located. Prior to the promulgation of national standards for the confidentiality, security, and electronic exchange of PHI, disparate state laws were a source of confusion and inconsistency. By contrast, comprehensive minimum national standards[9] for the privacy and security of PHI will encourage increased and appropriate use of electronic information while protecting a patient's need for privacy.[10]

Another important health information trend has been the proliferation of non-PC mobile devices. Electronic health data is becoming increasingly mobile as more information becomes available in electronic form. Since the first edition of this book, a revolution in mobile computing has taken place, and mobile computing holds the promise

---

9. HIPAA does not establish comprehensive standards. Rather, it sets a national uniform "floor" of standards. HIPAA expressly preserves state privacy laws that are in conflict with HIPAA if the state provision is "more stringent" than the federal provisions. 45 C.F.R. § 160.203. Consequently, there could potentially be different versions of privacy rules for each of the states, the District of Columbia, Puerto Rico, and U.S. possessions and territories.

10. State laws requiring the protection of personal information of citizens are becoming increasingly common. One example is California's AB 1950. Cal. Civil Code § 1798.81.5. AB 1950, however, does not apply to covered entities, perhaps to avoid disturbing the national standard created by the Security Rule. *Id.* § 1798.81.5(e)(3).

for significant changes in the way professionals provide healthcare services. Healthcare professionals are commonly using smartphones and tablet computers for their everyday work. In addition, special hardware and software applications allow healthcare professionals and patients to use their general-purpose mobile devices for a wide variety of diagnostic, imaging, and wellness applications. Covered entities and business associates must now account for mobile computing in their Security Rule and Privacy Rule compliance programs. Managing mobile health initiatives will not be easy, and mobile devices raise a host of general and healthcare-specific legal issues.[11]

Emerging technologies will pose even greater HIPAA security challenges. For instance, smart devices, wearable computers, Internet of Things devices and systems, augmented and virtual reality systems, telemedicine, 3D printing, new types of mobile devices (even automobiles), and surgical and service robots may create, receive, maintain, or transmit PHI. Covered entities and business associates will need to secure PHI on these new kinds of devices as well. Future decades will see far greater security challenges in the healthcare field. Accordingly, organizations should continuously anticipate future security threats and opportunities as they adopt emerging technologies. Hopefully, this book will assist in those efforts.

---

11. Author Stephen Wu has also written on the general legal issues concerning mobile device management in his August 2013 book, *A Legal Guide to Enterprise Mobile Device Management: Managing Bring Your Own Device (BYOD) and Employer-Issued Device Programs*, also published by the American Bar Association Section of Science & Technology Law.

CHAPTER 2

Background and History of HIPAA, HITECH, and Beyond

A. HIPAA AND THE HITECH ACT

President Clinton signed the Health Insurance Portability and Accountability Act into law on August 21, 1996. The bill that became HIPAA (HR 3103) was initially introduced to solve a social problem commonly referred to as "job lock." Group health insurers were imposing exclusions from coverage for up to one year for preexisting medical conditions when employees and others changed jobs or otherwise obtained new coverage. In the course of the legislative process, the bill became a magnet for a variety of issues. For instance, an entire chapter was added to strengthen the laws regulating fraud and abuse in healthcare and certain other insurance matters.

In addition, many of the parties that pay for healthcare (insurers and health plans) went to Congress to seek "administrative simplification" of healthcare business transactions. Specifically, they sought simplification through the standardization of healthcare information and processing. They proposed legislation to establish mandatory and Internet-friendly uniform rules and formats for electronic transmission of those types of healthcare transactions among healthcare providers, health plans, and healthcare clearinghouses that were perceived to be most important.[1]

---

1. The ten transactions covered by HIPAA are (1) health claims and equivalent encounter information; (2) health claims attachments; (3) enrollment and disenrollment in a health plan; (4) eligibility for a health plan; (5) healthcare payment and remittance advice; (6) health plan premium payments; (7) first report of injury; (8) health claim status; (9) referral certification and authorization; and (10) electronic funds transfers. 42 U.S.C. § 1320d-2(a)(2). HHS later added details about HIPAA transactions, via implementation specifications in regulations.

Supporters contended that uniform standards would facilitate the move from proprietary electronic data interchange networks to the Internet for the transmission of healthcare transactions. The proposals also sought to standardize the code sets used to describe the procedures performed or the services rendered. While Medicare and Medicaid had standardized their forms and transaction formats long ago, over 450 different claim forms and transaction formats remained in use in the United States. Consequently, standardization was an important goal. Backers claimed that this standardization process could save many tens of billions of dollars.

The resulting legislation was the "administrative simplification provisions," which were added to HIPAA at the last moment.[2] Their stated goal was "to improve the . . . efficiency and effectiveness of the healthcare system, by encouraging the development of a health information system through the establishment of standards and requirements for the electronic transmission of certain health information."[3]

At the same time, privacy advocates sought enhanced privacy and security protections for this soon-to-be readily accessible, but highly confidential, health information. As enacted, the administrative simplification provisions not only established a new system for certain healthcare information transactions, but also called for the creation of new standards for the privacy and security of that information. According to the Department of Health and Human Services (HHS), the law protects and enhances the rights of patients by providing them with federally assured access to their health information. It seeks to improve the quality of healthcare by restoring trust in the healthcare system, and it improves the efficiency and effectiveness of healthcare delivery.[4]

HIPAA required the development of specific areas of interrelated regulation. These areas are:

- Standards for Electronic Transactions, 45 C.F.R. part 162 (subparts A, I–R)
- Standards for Privacy of Individually Identifiable Health Information, 45 C.F.R. parts 160 and 164 (subparts A, E)
- National Employer Identification Standard, 45 C.F.R. parts 160, 162 (subparts B, F)
- Security Standards, 45 C.F.R. part 164 (subparts A, C)

---

2. HIPAA, tit. II, subtit. F (codified at 42 U.S.C. § 1320d *et seq.*).
3. HIPAA § 261 (codified at 42 U.S.C. § 1320d note).
4. Standards for Privacy of Individually Identifiable Health Information; Final Rule, 65 Fed. Reg. 82,462 (2000).

- National Provider Identification Standard, 45 C.F.R. part 162 (subparts D, F)
- Enforcement Rule, 45 C.F.R. parts 160 (subparts C–E)

The Security Rule brought significant changes to healthcare. The healthcare industry began to grasp security concepts as part of the effort to comply with a core set of security principles in the Privacy Rule (the "mini" security requirements).[5] The Security Rule complements the Privacy Rule and provides additional substantive guidance for the industry. Essentially, HIPAA introduced industry-standard information technology security practices to the healthcare field.[6]

Also, security requirements extend beyond covered entities to the "business associates" of covered entities. Business associates are described in the HIPAA Rules as those who provide services involving protected health information (PHI) to covered entities and may create and access PHI for their own activities and operations. The Health Information Technology for Economic and Clinical Health Act[7] (HITECH Act) and the HIPAA Final Omnibus Rule broadened the scope of the Security Rule. Not only did they make business associates *directly* responsible for compliance with the Security Rule, but they also expanded the definition of "business associate" to include specific categories of service providers, as well as generally including service providers that create, receive, maintain, or transmit PHI on behalf of a covered entity or other business associate. Subcontractors of business associates performing these functions are themselves considered business associates. In fact, there may be a multitiered chain of business associates, starting with the vendor performing services for a covered entity and including a chain of subcontractors below it.

The Security Rule, like the Privacy Rule, requires that covered entities have agreements with their business associates, frequently referred to as "business associate agreements" or "BAAs" for short. In the case of the Security Rule, covered entities must use BAAs to flow down security

---

5. See the discussion in section 3.C below. *See also* 45 C.F.R. § 164.530(c).

6. This is clear from the references in the HHS's references in the Security Rule's background to standard security resources such as *For the Record: Protecting Electronic Health Information* (Nat'l Res. Council 1997). Health Insurance Reform: Security Standards, 68 Fed. Reg. 8334, 8336–37 (2003).

7. The Health Information Technology for Economic and Clinical Health Act [hereinafter HITECH Act] within the American Recovery and Reinvestment Act of 2009, Pub. L. No. 111-5, 123 Stat. 115 (2009) [hereinafter ARRA].

and other requirements to business associates. Nonetheless, starting with the HITECH Act, and continuing with the HIPAA Final Omnibus Rule, business associates are directly required to comply with the Security Rule and some provisions of the Privacy Rule, separate and apart from any effect of a BAA. In fact, a vendor may be a business associate under the law, even if a covered entity or higher-tier business associate fails to bind the vendor to a BAA or even if the vendor's agreement with its customer disclaims business associate status.

A BAA must require a downstream business associate to:

1. Comply with the Security Rule;
2. Flow down business associate requirements to subcontractors; and
3. Require the business associate to report to the applicable covered entity concerning any "security incident" of which it becomes aware including breaches of unsecured PHI.[8]

The Security Rule defines "security incident" as "the attempted or successful unauthorized access, use, disclosure, modification, or destruction of information or interference with system operations in an information system."[9] Similarly, the Privacy Rule says that BAAs must, among other things, require business associates to:

1. Not use or further disclose PHI other than as permitted or required by the BAA or as required by law;
2. Use appropriate safeguards under the Security Rule to prevent use or disclosure of PHI in violation of the BAA; and
3. Require the business associate to report to the covered entity any use or disclosure of PHI not provided for by the BAA of which it becomes aware including breaches of unsecured PHI.[10]

The policy reflected in the HITECH Act and HIPAA Final Omnibus Rule extending security awareness and implementation beyond covered entities to a potentially multitiered chain of business associates provides both the hope of greater security and the risk of an unrealistic standard for many small organizations. In order to implement a practical compliance program, covered entities and business associates will need

---

8. 45 C.F.R. § 164.314(a)(2)(i). For a discussion of the required content of business associate agreements, see *infra* section 5.B.9.c.

9. *Id.* § 164.304.

10. *Id.* § 164.504(e)(2)(ii).

to distinguish between what are reasonable and appropriate security safeguards on one hand from unrealistic measures on the other. They will need to flow down security requirements in their BAAs that make sense for what may be smaller subcontracting downstream entities. With emerging technologies, they will also have to learn how to manage data in an environment composed of public, private and hybrid clouds, mobile devices, telemedicine, and even robots, as well as sharing of PHI among covered entities and business associates for improving quality of care, treatment outcomes, and overall patient health.

B. HIPAA AND THE FEDERAL INFORMATION TECHNOLOGY STRATEGIC PLAN

The Federal Health Information Technology Strategic Plan 2011–2015[11] (2011 Strategic Plan) sets forth a national strategy for health information security. The 2011 Strategic Plan was developed by the Office of the National Coordinator for Health Information Technology (ONC), an office created by executive order in 2004 and mandated under the HITECH Act.[12] The overall aim of the 2011 Strategic Plan is to promote safe, secure, convenient, interoperable, electronic transmission of health information among patients, healthcare providers, health plans, and public health entities through a nationwide electronic network. The 2011 Strategic Plan has five goals:

1. To achieve adoption of electronic health records (EHRs) and information exchange through the "meaningful use" of health information technology;
2. To improve healthcare and population health and reduce healthcare costs through the use of health information technology;
3. To inspire confidence and trust in health information technology, by improving privacy and security of health information transmissions and improving patient safety;

---

11. Office of the Nat'l Coordinator for Health Info. Tech., Federal Health Information Technology Strategic Plan 2011–2015, *reprinted at* https://www.healthit.gov/sites/default/files/utility/final-federal-health-it-strategic-plan-0911.pdf.

12. HITECH Act, *supra* note 7, div. A, tit. XIII (Health Information Technology); *id.* div. B, tit. IV (Medicare and Medicaid Health Information Technology). Title IV of Division B establishes financial incentives for entities making "meaningful use" of certified health information technology, through electronic health record systems.

4. To empower individuals to improve their own health and the healthcare system through health information technology; and

5. To achieve rapid learning and technological advancement in the use of health information technology.

Trust is the keystone of any successful electronic healthcare system. ONC has initiated several programs and initiatives to increase confidence and trust in secure electronic transmission of healthcare information. First, HHS initiated a program to analyze healthcare data from HHS breach reports in order to identify trends in security vulnerabilities. When HHS identifies a trend concerning a particular vulnerability, the issue is addressed through a modification of the Software Certification Criteria published by the ONC. The use of federally certified software is required to qualify for the Medicare and Medicaid incentive program (also referred to as the "Meaningful Use" program), under the HITECH Act. The vulnerability data enables HHS to follow up and develop Best Practices for HIPAA security.

The Data Segmentation for Privacy (DS4P) Initiative is another federal strategy to promote confidence and trust in a nationwide network for transmission of healthcare information under the 2011 Strategic Plan. Pursuant to the DS4P Initiative, cross-industry partners, such as Health Level 7 International and others, have explored the HIPAA standards that prohibit inappropriate sharing of health information. Health industry partners used the initiative to draft an implementation guide to serve as an exemplar for software developers to use. The guide will assist developers and help healthcare providers withhold sensitive information in situations where disclosure is prohibited by law or regulation. For example, the guide will help software developers create EHRs that will help healthcare providers comply with the "minimum necessary" requirements under the HIPAA Privacy Rule.[13]

As an additional strategy to promote confidence and trust in an electronic healthcare system, HHS's Office for Civil Rights (OCR) investigates complaints, develops policy, and enforces the HIPAA Privacy Rule and Security Rule. OCR initiated an audit program to assess HIPAA organizations' compliance with the HIPAA Privacy Rule and the HIPAA Security Rule.

---

13. 45 C.F.R. § 164.514(d). Providers should limit uses and disclousures of PHI so they are using or disclosing only the minimum amount or extent of PHI reasonably necessary to achieve their purpose.

Furthermore, ONC continues to develop privacy and security technical assistance materials. ONC writes these materials for entities receiving grants from ONC to implement EHR technology and other stakeholders.

Another initiative concerns the breach notification program set in motion by the HITECH Act. Covered entities and business associates must make a notification when a breach of unsecured PHI has occured. Chapter 6 discusses the breach notification initiative in more detail and describes the current breach notification requirements.

The HITECH Act created a federal advisory committee, known as the Health Information Technology (HIT) Policy Committee.[14] The HIT Policy Committee has broad representation from all major healthcare constituencies and provides recommendations to the ONC[15] on issues relating to the implementation of an interoperable, nationwide health information infrastructure. The HIT Policy Committee seeks to identify barriers to the adoption and use of health information technology and to advise the ONC about them.

HHS will continue to modify the HIPAA Security and Privacy Rules, after considering the concerns of the HIT Policy Committee, when HHS deems it necessary to accomplish the goal of a secure, trusted nationwide network for PHI or when modifications are deemed necessary to remove barriers to the exchange of PHI and the adoption of EHRs. For instance, HHS promulgated the HIPAA Final Omnibus Rule[16] through the OCR, on January 13, 2013. The Compliance Date of the HIPAA Final Omnibus Rule was September 23, 2013, and business associate agreements were to be updated as of September 23, 2014.

The HIPAA Final Omnibus Rule is an "omnibus" rule because it combines amendments to four sets of rules. These four rules implement the HITECH Act, modify the HIPAA Privacy Rule, modify the HIPAA Security Rule, and increase privacy protection for genetic information, as required by the Genetic Information Nondiscrimination Act of 2008. The HIPAA Final Omnibus Rule operates to remove barriers to the meaningful adoption of HIT by both individual consumers and covered entities.

---

14. ARRA, *supra* note 7, § 3002(a).

15. *Id.* § 3001(a).

16. Modifications to the HIPAA Privacy, Security, Enforcement, and Breach Notification Rules under the Health Information Technology for Economic and Clinical Health Act and the Genetic Information Nondiscrimination Act; Other Modifications to the HIPAA Rules, 78 Fed. Reg. 5566 (2013).

Significantly, the HIPAA Final Omnibus Rule imposes direct liability for HIPAA compliance on business associates, vastly expanding the jurisdiction of HHS over all entities that create, receive, maintain, or transmit PHI. The requirements of the HIPAA Final Omnibus Rule and its effect on business associates are both discussed in more detail in chapters 4 and 5.

On February 6, 2014, HHS published new regulations concerning patients' access to test reports.[17] The Patients' Access to Test Reports Rule was the result of concerns expressed by the HIT Policy Committee. The HIT Policy Committee was concerned that impeding individual access to an individual's own records of laboratory tests was a barrier to the adoption of EHRs. The Patients' Access to Test Reports Rule authorizes a clinical laboratory to release completed test reports to "authorized persons" and their representatives, upon request, with certain exceptions. Patients are among the "authorized persons" to whom the laboratory may release completed test results, when the patient is authenticated using the laboratory's authentication process.[18]

Other strategies of the ONC, in implementing the HIT 2011 Strategic Plan, have been ongoing development of policies and standards for the Nationwide Health Information Network,[19] the Blue Button Initiative for patients to download and share their health records,[20] and the Direct Project for secure transmission and sharing of health records.[21] The United States has established each of these initiatives and projects for the purpose of facilitating and implementing convenient, cost-effective, secure transmission of PHI across the nation. Along with financial incentives for healthcare providers, information security is the key to creating a trusted system and achieving the goals of the 2011 Strategic Plan.

---

17. CLIA Program and HIPAA Privacy Rule; Patients' Access to Test Reports, 79 Fed. Reg. 7290 (2014) (amending 42 C.F.R. pt. 493 and 45 C.F.R. § 164.524).

18. *Id.* at 7316 (showing amendments to 42 C.F.R. § 493.1291).

19. HHS, Nationwide Health Information Network, https://www.healthit.gov /policy-researchers-implementers/nationwide-health-information-network-nwhin (last visited Apr. 24, 2016).

20. HHS, About Blue Button, https://www.healthit.gov/patients-families/blue-button /about-blue-button (last visited Apr. 24, 2016).

21. *See generally* Direct Project, The Direct Project Overview (Oct. 11, 2010), *reprinted at* http://wiki.directproject.org/file/view/DirectProjectOverview.pdf.

More recently, ONC published a newer strategic plan in 2015[22] (2015 Strategic Plan). The 2015 Strategic Plan extends the original 2011 Strategic Plan's mandate by "continu[ing] to work towards widespread use of all forms of health IT [information technology]."[23] The 2015 Strategic Plan "aims to remain flexible to evolving definitions of health, health care, and the technology developments that support them."[24] The 2015 Strategic Plan has four goals:

1. To advance person-centered and self-managed health through empowerment of individuals, families, and caregivers, as well as partnerships;
2. To transform healthcare delivery and community health through person-centered care, delivery of high-value healthcare, and promoting public health and healthy communities;
3. To foster research, scientific knowledge, and innovation by increasing access to electronic health information and services, accelerate innovative technologies, and promote research on how health information technology can improve health and healthcare; and
4. To enhance the nation's health information technology infrastructure through a Nationwide Interoperability Roadmap, protecting privacy and security, advancing technical standards for interoperable health IT, increasing market confidence in the safety of health IT products, systems and services, and advancing a national communications infrastructure supporting healthcare.[25]

The 2015 Strategic Plan "aims to modernize the U.S. health IT infrastructure so that individuals, their providers, and communities can use it to help achieve health and wellness goals."[26] ONC's hope is that the initiatives in the plan will "promot[e] trustworthy, accessible, and readily available information and technology that helps individuals across the nation achieve their full health potential."[27]

---

22. Office of the Nat'l Coordinator for Health Info. Tech., Federal Health Information Technology Strategic Plan 2015–2020, *reprinted at* https://www.healthit.gov/sites/default/files/9-5-federalhealthitstratplanfinal_0.pdf.

23. *Id.* at 4.

24. *Id.*

25. *Id.* at 9.

26. *Id.* at 5.

27. *Id.* at 6.

CHAPTER 3

HIPAA/HITECH Privacy and Security

Security and privacy are intertwined under HIPAA, and the HIPAA Final Omnibus Rule[1] attempted to coordinate these two policy interests even further. Security is a foundation for privacy. A covered entity or business associate cannot protect the privacy of protected health information (PHI) in its possession unless it maintains the security of the PHI. Covered entities and business associates must protect PHI against both intentional disclosure of PHI in violation of a patient's privacy rights and inadvertent disclosure because of an attacker's unauthorized access to PHI. This chapter discusses the origins of the HIPAA Privacy Rule, the Security Rule, and their relationship to each other. It also covers statutory security requirements in HIPAA and the HITECH Act, as well as security requirements in the Privacy Rule.

A. RELATIONSHIP AMONG HIPAA, THE PRIVACY RULE, AND THE SECURITY RULE

Congress placed HIPAA within the framework of the Social Security Act. Section 261 of HIPAA called for standards and requirements for the electronic transmission of health data. Specifically, HIPAA added an "administrative simplification" part to the Social Security Act,

---

1. Modifications to the HIPAA Privacy, Security, Enforcement, and Breach Notification Rules under the Health Information Technology for Economic and Clinical Health Act and the Genetic Information Nondiscrimination Act; Other Modifications to the HIPAA Rules, 78 Fed. Reg. 5566 (2013).

titled Part C—Administrative Simplification—Sections 1171 to 1179.[2] Section 1173[3] required the creation of the following standards:

1. Standards for transactions and data elements for such transactions, to enable electronic exchange of health information;
2. Unique health identifiers for use in the healthcare system;
3. Code sets for appropriate data elements for electronic transactions in the healthcare system;
4. Security standards for health information;
5. Standards specifying procedures for electronic transmissions and the authentication of electronic signatures; and
6. Standards for the transfer among health plans of information needed for the coordination of benefits, the sequential processing of claims, and other data.[4]

Section 264 called on the Secretary of the Department of Health and Human Services (HHS) to make recommendations to Congress concerning the privacy of individually identifiable health information. The recommendations were to cover the privacy rights of patients, procedures to exercise those rights, and the authorized and required disclosures of individually identifiable health information. Congress had a deadline of 36 months after HIPAA's enactment to create privacy legislation. If Congress failed to pass privacy legislation, section 264 required HHS to promulgate privacy standards within 42 months after the enactment of HIPAA. As it turns out, Congress did not pass privacy legislation within the 36-month time limit. Accordingly, HHS did in fact create privacy standards. Specifically, HHS promulgated the Privacy Rule[5] in August 2002. Later, in February 2003, HHS created final security standards as required in HIPAA.[6] HHS promulgated these security standards as the Security Rule.[7]

---

2. 42 U.S.C. §§ 1320d to 1320d-8. Later, the Genetic Information Nondiscrimination Act of 2008 added an additional section, codified as section 1180 of the Social Security Act at 42 U.S.C. § 1320d-9. Genetic Information Nondiscrimination Act of 2008, Pub. L. No. 110-233, 122 Stat. 881 (2008).

3. 42 U.S.C. § 1320d-2.

4. Later the Patient Protection and Affordable Care Act, Pub. L. No. 111-148, §1104 124 Stat. 119, 149-50 (2010), among other things, called for health plans to certify that their information systems are in compliance with applicable standards for certain HIPAA standard transactions. 42 U.S.C. § 1320d-2(h).

5. 45 C.F.R. pt. 160; *id.* pt. 164 subpt. E.

6. 42 U.S.C. § 1320d-2

7. 45 C.F.R. pt. 160; *id.* pt. 164 subpt. C.

B. HIPAA STATUTORY REQUIREMENT FOR SECURITY

HIPAA promoted the security of health information in two ways. First, HIPAA called for HHS to create "security standards" for the protection of health information.[8] Second, HIPAA required covered entities to implement "safeguards" to protect health information.

More specifically, section 262 of HIPAA says that HHS must adopt security standards that take into account:

- The technical capabilities of records systems used to maintain health information;
- The costs of security measures;
- The need for training persons who have access to health information;
- The value of audit trails in computerized records systems; and
- The needs and capabilities of small heathcare providers and rural healthcare providers.[9]

Section 262 also required security standards to ensure that healthcare clearinghouses that are part of larger organizations have policies and security procedures to isolate their healthcare activities to prevent unauthorized access to health information by the larger organizations.[10] These measures help to prevent unauthorized access to health information by other divisions or affiliates outside the healthcare clearinghouse portion of the organization.

In addition to security standards, HIPAA imposes security requirements on covered entities that maintain or transmit health information.

---

8. The concept of "standard" has different meanings. It may be a general reference to the group of regulations promulgated under HIPAA to address a particular subject. Thus, a reference to the "privacy standard" or "security standard" refers to the groups of HHS regulations on these subjects. Used in this sense, "privacy standard" and "security standard" would be synonymous with the Privacy Rule and the Security Rule respectively. A "standard" within the Security Rule also has a special meaning, as described in more detail in section 5.A.2 *infra*. A "standard" in this context refers to a high-level requirement that covered entities or business associates must meet. Both of these meanings differ from the definition of "standard" that engineers and information security professionals use. The word "standard" adopted by engineers and security professionals refers to technical specifications agreed to by committees to permit developers to build hardware or software components that are interoperable with other components.

9. 42 U.S.C. § 1320d-2(d)(1)(A).

10. *Id.* § 1320d-2(d)(1)(B).

Covered entities must maintain reasonable and appropriate administrative, technical, and physical safeguards to:

- Ensure the integrity and confidentiality of the health information;
- Protect against any reasonably anticipated—
  - Threats or hazards to the security or integrity of the health information, and
  - Unauthorized uses or disclosures of the health information; and
- Ensure compliance with HIPAA by the officers and employees of the covered entity.[11]

Although section 262 uses the word "ensure," HIPAA does not mandate protection of health information, "no matter how expensive."[12] Instead, the covered entity (and now business associates) must analyze the risks to health information and balance the costs of security safeguards against their benefits. "[W]hen [the regulations] state that a covered entity must ensure the safety of the information in its keeping, . . . a covered entity [must] take steps, to the best of its ability, to protect that information. This will involve establishing a balance between the information's identifiable risks and vulnerabilities, and the cost of various protective measures, and will also be dependent upon the size, complexity, and capabilities of the covered entity. . . ."[13]

C. SECURITY REQUIREMENTS IN THE PRIVACY RULE

Discussions about HIPAA security focus mainly on the Security Rule. As mentioned in the previous section, however, the HIPAA statutory language itself imposes high-level security requirements. Moreover, the administrative requirements of the Privacy Rule also contain a security requirement for covered entities to protect the privacy of protected health information. More specifically, under 45 C.F.R. 164.530(c):

> (c)(1) *Standard: Safeguards.* A covered entity must have in place appropriate administrative, technical, and physical safeguards to protect the privacy of protected health information.

---

11. Section 262(a) of HIPAA, codified at 42 U.S.C. § 1320d-2(d)(2).
12. Health Insurance Reform: Security Standards; Final Rule, 68 Fed. Reg. 8334, 8346 (2003) (comments).
13. *Id.*

(2) *Implementation specification: Safeguards.* A covered entity must reasonably safeguard protected health information from any intentional or unintentional use or disclosure that is in violation of the standards, implementation specifications or other requirements of this subpart.

This section of the Privacy Rule implicitly recognizes the principle that security is a foundation for privacy. Like the HIPAA statutory language, the language of section 164.530(c) is high level. Regardless, it is important to keep in mind that a security violation may not only violate the Security Rule, it may also violate the Privacy Rule and the HIPAA statutory requirements.

The one area where section 164.530(c) may come into play concerns the compromise of paper PHI. It could also cover PHI in the form of film and other tangible objects. For instance, the Office for Civil Rights (OCR) sought civil money penalties for violating section 164.530(c)(2) when the respondent failed to safeguard paper PHI.[14] OCR did not seek civil money penalties for violating the Security Rule, presumably because it applies only to electronic PHI. A compromise of electronic PHI in violation of the Security Rule could also constitute a violation of section 164.530(c).

D. SECURITY REQUIREMENTS IN THE HITECH ACT

The Health Information Technology for Economic and Clinical Health Act (HITECH Act) followed HIPAA and supplemented HIPAA's security requirements. The HITECH Act established Title XIII within the American Recovery and Reinvestment Act of 2009.[15] The act established new security principles, which HHS further developed in the HIPAA Final Omnibus Rule. The HITECH Act's two most important security-related changes concern business associates and the creation of a HIPAA/HITECH security breach notification requirement.[16]

Under the original HIPAA requirements, the Security Rule applied only to covered entities, and not business associates. The Security Rule required covered entities to flow down security requirements to

---

14. Dir. of the Office for Civil Rights v. Lincare, Inc., No. C-14-1056, Decision No. CR4505 (Jan. 13, 2016), *reprinted at* http://www.hhs.gov/sites/default/files/lincare _decision_remediated.pdf.

15. Pub. L. No. 111-5, 123 Stat. 115 (2009).

16. The HITECH Act also strengthened HIPAA privacy and enforcement requirements. Chapter 7 covers HIPAA enforcement and discusses the current enforcement provisions.

business associates by contract using business associate agreements. A business associate's violation of these security requirements would constitute only a breach of contract, rather than a violation of law that could trigger civil money penalties. Under the HITECH Act, however, the Security Rule now applies directly to a business associate of a covered entity in the same manner that it applies to the covered entities.[17] In addition to the Security Rule, the HITECH Act's new security requirements also apply to business associates, and covered entities have an obligation to incorporate them into business associate agreements.[18] For the first time, security violations by business associates could trigger liability for civil money penalties.[19]

The HITECH Act's second important change is its creation of a new breach notification requirement for covered entities and business associates. Before the HITECH Act, the states had been in the process of passing breach notification legislation to protect individual state citizens' Social Security numbers, driver's license numbers, and financial account or payment card numbers in combination with a PIN or other security code. The trend began with California's SB 1386 breach notification legislation.[20] Today, almost all of the states have breach notification laws on their books.

Consistent with this trend, Congress created a breach notification requirement for PHI. Under the HITECH Act, covered entities that hold, use, or disclose PHI must notify individuals if their "unsecured" PHI is compromised as a result of a security breach.[21] A business associate of a covered entity also has a breach notification obligation after a breach, but it does not need to notify affected individuals.

---

17. HITECH Act § 13401(a) (codified at 42 U.S.C. § 17931(a)). Note, however, that this section of the act did not apply the Privacy Rule to business associates. Covered entities must use business associate agreements to require business associates to facilitate privacy compliance, but the HITECH Act application of HIPAA directly to business associates covers only the three sections of the Security Rule covering administrative, physical, and technical safeguards, the requirements concerning policies and procedures, and security requirements added by the act. *See id.* ("Sections 164.308, 164.310, 164.312, and 164.316 of title 45, Code of Federal Regulations, shall apply to a business associate of a covered entity in the same manner that such sections apply to the covered entity.").

18. *See id.*

19. *See id.* § 13401(b) (codified at 42 U.S.C. § 17931(b)).

20. An Act to Amend, Renumber, and Add Section 1798.82 of, and to Add Section 1798.29 to, the Civil Code, Relating to Personal Information, 2002 Cal. Legs. Serv. ch. 915 (S.B. 1386) (West) (codified at Cal. Civil Code §§ 1798.29, 1798.82).

21. *See* HITECH Act § 13402(a) (codified at 42 U.S.C. § 17932(a)).

Instead, a business associate need only notify the applicable covered entity of the breach.[22] PHI is "unsecured" if it is not secured through HHS-specified technology described in HHS guidance.[23] The covered entity or business associate has a breach notification obligation if unsecured PHI it holds, uses, or discloses has been, or is reasonably believed to have been, accessed, acquired, or disclosed as a result of a breach.[24]

The detailed breach notification requirements from the HITECH Act and HIPAA Final Omnibus Rule appear in the Breach Notification Rule promulgated by HHS as part of the HIPAA Final Omnibus Rule. The Breach Notification Rule covers the breach notification obligations of covered entities and business associates, the required content of notifications, the timing of notifications, and supplemental or substitute notification. For details concerning the Breach Notification Rule, see chapter 6.[25]

E. "MEANINGFUL USE" INCENTIVE PAYMENTS FOR HEALTH INFORMATION TECHNOLOGY AND ELECTRONIC HEALTH RECORDS

The HITECH Act within the American Recovery and Reinvestment Act of 2009 (ARRA)[26] also established incentive payments to promote the adoption and so-called "meaningful use" of interoperable health information technology (HIT) and qualified electronic heath records (EHR).[27] These provisions appear in title IV of ARRA's division B. "Meaningful use" is the shorthand expression for the policy of promoting real, practical use of HIT to impact patient care, and not simply incentivizing organizations to obtain HIT technology that they do not use. Eligible professionals, eligible hospitals, critical access hospitals, and Medicare Advantage organizations can receive payments under the legislation. Starting in 2011, programs were established to encourage

---

22. *See id.* § 13402(b) (codified at 42 U.S.C. § 17932(b)).

23. *See id.* § 13402(h)(1)(A) (codified at 42 U.S.C. § 17932(h)(1)(A)).

24. *Id.* § 13402(a), (b) (codified at 42 U.S.C. § 17932(a), (b)).

25. The HITECH Act also created a breach notification requirement for vendors of personal health records (PHR). Following a breach of unsecured PHR identifiable information maintained or offered by a PHR vendor, the vendor must notify the affected individual and the Federal Trade Commission. *See id.* § 13407 (codified at 42 U.S.C. § 17937).

26. Pub. L. No. 111-5, 123 Stat. 115 (2009).

27. *See id.* div. B, tit. IV.

the adoption of certified EHR technology. These programs supported three stages of adoption, each with its own criteria for what the eligible organizations needed to demonstrate to show they are making meaningful use of certified EHR technology.[28]

Some of the meaningful use criteria concern information security. In fact, they cross-reference certain sections of the Security Rule that comprise portions of the criteria of the stages of meaningful use. For instance, for Stage 2, eligible professionals must "[c]onduct or review a security risk analysis in accordance with the requirements under 45 CFR 164 308 (a)(1), including addressing the encryption/security of data at rest and implement security updates as necessary and correct identified security deficiencies as part of its risk management process."[29] Stage 3 requires a risk analysis and addressing the encryption of data created or maintained by certified EHR technology.[30]

A full explanation of meaningful use and its information security criteria is beyond the scope of this book.[31] Nonetheless, readers implementing security controls in specific Security Rule sections cross-referenced in meaningful use criteria can find discussions of these controls in chapter 5. These discussions will help eligible entities to implement these criteria in order to demonstrate meaningful use.

---

28. *See generally* Ctrs. for Medicare & Medicaid Servs., Electronic Health Records (EHR) Incentive Programs, https://www.cms.gov/Regulations-and-Guidance/Legislation/EHRIncentivePrograms/index.html (last visited Apr. 14, 2016).

29. Ctrs. for Medicare & Medicaid Servs., Eligible Professional's Guide to Stage 2 of the EHR Incentive Programs 23 (Feb. 2014), *reprinted at* https://www.cms.gov/eHealth/downloads/eHealthU_EPsGuideStage2EHR.pdf; 45 C.F.R. § 495.22(e)(ii).

30. *See* 45 C.F.R. § 495.24(d)(1) (referencing Security Rule sections, *id.* § 164.306(d)(3), 164.308(a)(1), 164.312(a)(2)(iv)).

31. For a thorough discussion of the benefits and risks of EHRs, the standards and certification criteria for meaningful use, a description of the three stages of meaningful use, and calculating the amount of incentive payments, see Arthur E. Peabody Jr., *Electronic Health Records Technology Standards and Incentives for Meaningful Use, in* HEATH CARE IT 177–219 (Arthur E. Peabody Jr. ed., 2013).

CHAPTER 4

Scope and Applicability of the HIPAA Security Rule

Congress originally enacted the HIPAA administrative simplification provisions in order to standardize electronic data transmission formats for healthcare claims and payment transactions.[1] As a result, HIPAA does not authorize the Department of Health and Human Services (HHS) to regulate all uses and disclosures of health information by all persons. The purpose of this chapter is to assist the reader in understanding to whom the HIPAA Security Rule applies and the scope of the information covered by the Security Rule.

A. ENTITIES REGULATED BY THE HIPAA SECURITY RULE

The HIPAA Security Rule applies to two main categories of entities: HIPAA "covered entities" and their "business associates." The covered entities category includes certain "hybrid entities," which are covered entities that have components covered by HIPAA and those that are not. Under section 13408 of the HITECH Act (now codified at 42 U.S.C. § 17938), health information exchange organizations, regional health information organizations, and e-prescribing gateways are also business associates. In addition, the HIPAA Final Omnibus Rule redefines "business associate" to include these organizations and makes it clear that "subcontractors" of HIPAA business associates are covered

---

1. *See* 42 U.S.C. § 1320d-2 (standards for information transactions and data elements). Under section 1320d-2, HHS adopted 45 C.F.R. part 162, which is the HIPAA Standard Transactions Rule.

by the HIPAA Security Rule and, in fact, are themselves considered business associates.[2]

As originally enacted, HIPAA applied directly only to HIPAA covered entities and the healthcare components of hybrid entities. HIPAA covered entities had an obligation under HIPAA to require that business associates implement Security Rule security requirements by contract. Nonetheless, business associates had no obligations under HIPAA or the Security Rule directly to implement security requirements. Consequently, security violations by business associates would, at most, constitute contract breaches, as opposed to violations of the regulations. Business associates would not be subject to enforcement actions for civil money penalties.

The HITECH Act, however, imposed the Security Rule directly on business associates.[3] Nonetheless, the HITECH Act left some uncertainty as to whether subcontractors of business associates had to comply with the Security Rule. The HIPAA Final Omnibus Rule, however, clarified that subcontractors of business associates are themselves business associates and therefore have an obligation to comply with the Security Rule.[4]

1. Covered Entities

Covered entities are (1) healthcare providers, (2) health plans, and (3) healthcare clearinghouses that transmit any health information[5] in electronic form in connection with a HIPAA transaction.[6] "Transaction" is defined in 45 C.F.R. § 160.103 as "the transmission of information between two parties to carry out financial or administrative activities related to health care." The definition includes twelve specific

---

2. 45 C.F.R. § 160.103 (definition of "business associate").

3. 42 U.S.C. § 17931(a).

4. 45 C.F.R. § 160.103(3)(iii) (definition of "business associate"). For an explanation of the inclusion of subcontractors within the scope of HIPAA regulations, see Modifications to the HIPAA Privacy, Security, Enforcement, and Breach Notification Rules under the Health Information Technology for Economic and Clinical Health Act and the Genetic Information Nondiscrimination Act; Other Modifications to the HIPAA Rules; Final Rule, 78 Fed. Reg. 5566, 5572–74 (2013) [hereinafter HIPAA Final Omnibus Rule].

5. For a discussion of the definition of "health information," see section 4.D.1 below.

6. For useful guidance on how to determine whether an organization or individual is a covered entity, see Ctrs. for Medicare & Medicaid Servs., Are You a Covered Entity, https://www.cms.gov/Regulations-and-Guidance/Administrative-Simplification/HIPAA-ACA /AreYouaCoveredEntity.html (last visited Jul. 6, 2016) (linking to a useful "Covered Entity Guidance tool").

types of transmissions, including "First report of injury," which is a HIPAA transaction for the purposes of the Security Rule and the Privacy Rule, under circumstances where workers' health information is in the possession of a healthcare provider. Healthcare[7] "means care, services, or supplies related to the health of an individual."[8]

The HIPAA administrative simplification provisions cover entities only if they transmit electronic health information in one of the standard transactions. Confusion may arise because the Privacy Rule covers all forms of protected health information (PHI), including paper.[9] The Privacy Rule's coverage of paper, however, does not thereby impose HIPAA's security requirements on entities who transmit health information and conduct transactions exclusively in paper form. Instead, the Privacy Rule's coverage of paper merely means that entities conducting electronic transactions must protect both electronic and paper PHI. Entities not transmitting electronic health information are not covered by the administrative simplification provisions at all. These entities have no obligation under HIPAA to protect either paper health information or the electronic health information on local computers. Entities not conducting electronic transactions may have privacy and security obligations under other laws, such as state confidentiality laws, but there are no such obligations under HIPAA.

The common meaning of the term "healthcare providers" includes doctors, hospitals, clinics, psychologists, dentists, chiropractors, nursing homes, and pharmacies.[10] More precisely, however, the term refers to providers of services, as defined in § 1861(u) of the Social Security

---

7. This book uses the spelling "healthcare"; the regulations themselves generally use "health care." When quoting from the regulations, we have followed the spelling used there.

8. 45 C.F.R. § 160.103 (definition of "health care").

Health care includes, but is not limited to, the following:

(1) Preventive, diagnostic, therapeutic, rehabilitative, maintenance, or palliative care, and counseling, service, assessment, or procedure with respect to the physical or mental condition, or functional status, of an individual or that affects the structure or function of the body; and

(2) Sale or dispensing of a drug, device, equipment, or other item in accordance with a prescription.

Id.

9. See section 4.D.1 below.

10. U.S. Dep't of Health & Human Servs. Office for Civil Rights, Covered Entities and Business Associates, http://www.hhs.gov/ocr/privacy/hipaa/understanding/coveredentities/ (last visited Apr. 26, 2016) [hereinafter Covered Entities Website].

Act;[11] providers of medical or health services, as defined in § 1861(s) of the Social Security Act;[12] or any other person or organization that furnishes, bills, or is paid for healthcare in the normal course of business.[13]

"Health plans" are commonly understood to include health insurance companies, health maintenance organizations, company health plans, and government programs that pay for healthcare.[14] More specifically, a health plan is an individual or group plan that provides or pays the cost of medical care, as defined in 42 § U.S.C. 300gg-91(a)(2). Health plans are, singly or in combination:

- Group health plans
- Health insurance issuers
- HMOs
- Part A or Part B of the Medicare Program
- The Medicaid Program
- The Voluntary Prescription Drug Benefit Program set forth at 42 U.S.C. §§ 1395w–101–1395w–152
- Issuers of a Medicare supplemental benefit policy
- Issuers of a long-term care policy, (excluding a nursing home fixed indemnity policy)
- An employee welfare benefit plan and any other arrangement that is established or maintained for the purpose of offering or providing health benefits to the employees of two or more employers
- The healthcare program for the uniformed services under Title 10 of the United States Code
- The veterans healthcare program under 38 U.S.C. chapter 17
- The Indian Health Service Program under 25 U.S.C. § 1601, et seq.
- The Federal Employees Health Benefits Program under 5 U.S.C. § 8902, et seq.
- An approved state child health plan under 42 U.S.C. § 1397, et seq.
- The Medicare Advantage program, set forth in 42 U.S.C. §§ 1395w–21–1395w–28[15]

---

11. 42 U.S.C. § 1395x(u).
12. *Id.* § 1395x(s).
13. 45 C.F.R. § 160.103 (definition of "health care provider").
14. Covered Entities Website, *supra* note 10.
15. HIPAA Final Omnibus Rule, *supra* note 4, at 5664.

- Any high-risk pool that is a mechanism established under state law to provide health insurance coverage or comparable coverage to eligible individuals
- Any other individual or group plan or combination of individual or group plans, that provides or pays for the cost of medical care, as defined in under 42 U.S.C. § 300gg-91(a)(2)[16]

There are, however, some programs that are excluded from the definition of a health plan and that are not subject to the Security Rule. The following plans and programs are excluded from the definition of a health plan under HIPAA and are not obligated to follow the HIPAA Rules:

(i) A particular policy, plan, or program, to the extent that it provides or pays for the cost of designated "excepted benefits," such as liability insurance, disability income insurance, automobile insurance, workers' compensation insurance, and credit-only insurance;[17]

(ii) A government-funded program (other than a high-risk pool that is a mechanism established under State law to provide health insurance coverage or comparable coverage to eligible individuals):

(A) whose principal purpose is other than providing or paying the cost of healthcare (such as food stamps); or

(B) whose principal activity is (1) the direct provision of healthcare to persons (such as community health centers) or (2) the making of grants to fund the direct provision of healthcare to persons;[18] and

(iii) A group health plan with less than fifty participants, administered solely by the employer who establishes and maintains the plan.[19]

Healthcare clearinghouses are public or private entities that enable the transmission of healthcare transactions between covered entities, such as healthcare providers and payers, in the standard formats required by HIPAA. Healthcare clearinghouses are:

1. Billing services, or
2. Repricing companies, or

---

16. *See* 45 C.F.R. § 160.103 (definition of "health plan").
17. *See also* 42 U.S.C. § 300gg-91(c).
18. *Id.*
19. *See* 45 C.F.R. § 160.103 (definition of "health plan" and definition of "group health plan," which does not include plans with fewer than fifty participants).

3. Community health management information systems or community health systems, or
4. "Value-added" networks or telecommunications switches that perform either of the following functions:
    a. processing or facilitating the processing of health information received from another entity in a nonstandard format, or containing nonstandard data content, into standard data elements or a standard transaction or
    b. receiving a standard transaction from another entity and processing or facilitating the processing of health information into nonstandard format or nonstandard data content for the receiving entity.[20]

2. Business Associates

a. Defining Business Associates

Healthcare functions are performed by a wide variety of individuals and organizations. In general, persons and entities that perform these functions and require access to PHI to do so are "business associates."[21] Examples of service providers that may act in this role include entities providing the following services:

- Claims processing or billing
- Data analysis
- Utilization review
- Quality assurance
- Benefit management
- Practice management
- Repricing
- Hardware maintenance
- Actuarial services
- Data aggregation
- Administrative services
- Accreditation
- Financial services[22]

---

20. *See id.* (definition of "health care clearinghouse").

21. *Id.* (definition of "business associate").

22. MATTHEW SCHOLL ET AL., NAT'L INST. OF STANDARDS & TECH., SPECIAL PUBL'N 800-66, AN INTRODUCTORY RESOURCE GUIDE FOR IMPLEMENTING THE HEALTH INSURANCE PORTABILITY AND ACCOUNTABILITY ACT (HIPAA) SECURITY RULE 33 (rev. 1, Oct. 2008), http://csrc.nist.gov/publications/nistpubs/800-66-Rev1/SP-800-66-Revision1.pdf.

The regulations define "business associate" as a person or entity working for a covered entity that:

(i) On behalf of such covered entity or of an organized health care arrangement (as defined in this section) in which the covered entity participates, but other than in the capacity of a member of the workforce of such covered entity or arrangement, *creates, receives, maintains, or transmits protected health information* for a function or activity regulated by this subchapter, including claims processing or administration, data analysis, processing or administration, utilization review, quality assurance, patient safety activities listed at 42 CFR 3.20, billing, benefit management, practice management, and repricing; or

(ii) Provides, other than in the capacity of a member of the workforce of such covered entity, legal, actuarial, accounting, consulting, data aggregation (as defined in § 164.501 of this subchapter), management, administrative, accreditation, or financial services to or for such covered entity, or to or for an organized health care arrangement in which the covered entity participates, where the provision of the service involves the disclosure of protected health information from such covered entity or arrangement, or from another business associate of such covered entity or arrangement, to the person.[23]

Under this definition, even lawyers can be "business associates." Its definition includes "legal . . . services." "In plain English, if" a law "firm represents a covered entity or a business associate of one and it needs to have access to PHI to do its job, such as defending a malpractice claim, business associate status attaches regardless of whether the firm signed a business associate agreement."[24]

A covered entity may be a business associate of another covered entity when the covered entity is acting as a business associate by providing services involving PHI, on behalf of the other covered

---

23. 45 C.F.R. § 160.103(1) (definition of "business associate") (emphasis added). For a definition and discussion of "organized health care arrangement," see *infra* section 4.A.6 "*Workforce* means employees, volunteers, trainees, and other persons whose conduct, in the performance of work for a covered entity or business associate, is under the direct control of such covered entity or business associate, whether or not they are paid by the covered entity or business associate." 45 C.F.R. § 160.103 (definition of "workforce").

24. Gordon J. Apple, *Lawyers as Business Associates under HIPAA: Are You Ready?*, Bench & Bar of Minn., Mar. 11, 2013, *reprinted at* http://mnbenchbar.com/2013/03 /business-associates-under-hipaa/.

entity.[25] In this situation, the covered entity is providing services that are the responsibility of the other covered entity. The covered entity, however, would not be a business associate of the other covered entity if the covered entity providing services is participating in an organized healthcare arrangement (OHCA) with the covered entity receiving the services.

Under the HITECH Act and regulatory amendments made by the HIPAA Final Omnibus Rule, the definition of "business associate" now includes health information organizations, e-prescribing gateways, and other persons that provide data transmission services with respect to PHI to a covered entity, and that require access on a routine basis to such PHI.[26] The HIPAA Final Omnibus Rule also included as business associates persons or entities that offer a personal health record (PHR) to one or more individuals on behalf of a covered entity.[27]

Under the HIPAA Final Omnibus Rule, vendors that are providing PHR collection, viewing, and storage services on behalf of covered entities are "business associates." These PHRs "generally link individuals to, and allow them to view, some or all of the health records maintained about them within the covered entity."[28] In some cases, PHR vendors may provide online accounts linked to wearable heath and fitness devices to collect PHI on behalf of covered entities. The data collected may include metrics such as the steps and distance an individual walks in a day, sleep patterns, swimming laps and distance, calories expended, and heart rate. Healthcare providers can then advise their patients about their health based on the data collected.

By contrast, some PHR vendors are providing similar services directly to individuals or employers (other than the employer's group health plan). When a covered entity is not working with a PHR vendor and the vendor is providing services directly to an individual or employer, the vendor is not a business associate. "Although some of these PHRs may advertise that they are 'HIPAA-compliant,' the Privacy Rule does not apply to or protect the health information within these PHRs. These PHRs are governed by the privacy policies and practices

---

25. 45 C.F.R. § 160.103(2) (definition of "business associate").

26. *Id.* § 160.103(3)(i) (definition of "business associate").

27. *Id.* § 160.103(3)(ii) (definition of "business associate").

28. U.S. Dep't of Health & Human Servs. Office for Civil Rights, Personal Health Records and the HIPAA Privacy Rule 2 (Sept. 3, 2015), *reprinted at* http://www.hhs.gov/sites/default /files/ocr/privacy/hipaa/understanding/special/healthit/phrs.pdf.

of the entities offering or administering the PHRs, as well as by any other applicable laws."[29]

The HIPAA Final Omnibus Rule implemented two additional key changes in the definition of "business associate," which greatly expand the scope of the definition, and thus the scope of HIPAA's coverage. First, the HIPAA Final Omnibus Rule clarifies that subcontractors that create, receive, maintain, or transmit PHI on behalf of a business associate are themselves business associates.[30] Section 4.A.3 below discusses subcontractors in more detail.

Second, the HIPAA Final Omnibus Rule changed the general definition of "business associate." The original language of the definition of "business associate" in the 2003 Security Rule focused on entities that performed functions or activities involving the use or disclosure of individually identifiable health information or other HIPAA-covered functions. The original language left room for vendors to disclaim business associate status.

For example, many vendors argued that they are general service providers and do not focus on the healthcare market. Accordingly, they stated that their functions do not involve use or disclosure of PHI and that they performed no covered functions on behalf of covered entity customers. Also, some vendors claimed that while they stored PHI on behalf of a covered entity, they did not, and did not even want to, access that PHI. Data storage vendors, for instance, said that although they theoretically could have looked at customer data, they did not do that. They simply performed their services without accessing the PHI. Moreover, vendors storing encrypted PHI but who had no access to the encryption/decryption key could have argued that they were not business associates, because they could neither use nor disclose PHI. These vendors would only have access to unintelligible, unusable scrambled information. In these situations, the covered entity customer had sole access to the encryption/decryption key.

The HIPAA Final Omnibus Rule swept away these arguments. The definition of "business associate" includes entities that create, receive, *maintain,* or transmit PHI for a covered entity.[31] In issuing the HIPAA Final Omnibus Rule, HHS drew a distinction between a vendor acting as a "mere conduit" for PHI and a vendor acting as a business associate

---

29. *Id.* at 7.
30. 45 C.F.R. § 160.103(3)(iii) (definition of "business associate").
31. *Id.* § 160.103(3)(i) (definition of "business associate").

by "maintaining" PHI over time. A "conduit" "transports information but does not access it other than on a random or infrequent basis as necessary to perform the transportation service or as required by other law."[32] For instance, the US Postal Service, United Parcel Service, Internet service provider, or a telecommunications company merely moving electronic PHI from Point A to Point B would be a conduit.[33] Occasional random access to service a network, or temporary storage of information as it is moving from Point A to Point B, would not cause an Internet service provider or telecommunications company to become a business associate.[34] If a vendor is a "conduit," it is not a business associate and is exempted from compliance with business associate requirements.

"In contrast, an entity that maintains protected health information on behalf of a covered entity is a business associate and not a conduit, even if the entity does not actually view the protected health information."[35] Thus, HHS rejected arguments based on a vendor's protestations that it does not, and does not want to, access PHI stored by customers on its systems. HHS's position also means that encryption of the PHI does not itself make the vendor a conduit, even though the vendor may not be able to access or use the PHI because of its encrypted state. Of course, if the vendor has access to the encryption/decryption key to access the PHI, it has a harder argument, but HHS's reasoning applies even if the vendor does not have access to the key and, absent breaking the cryptographic protection, has no way to decrypt the PHI to view or access it. Vendors storing encrypted PHI over time are still "maintaining" the PHI on their systems. The key distinction between a conduit and business associate "is the transient versus persistent nature of" the storage of PHI.[36] In other words, a vendor storing PHI persistently and indefinitely over time on behalf of a covered entity means that the vendor is a business associate, and not a conduit, even if it cannot access or use the PHI.

HHS specifically identified data storage companies as an example of business associates.[37] They can maintain PHI indefinitely. Nonetheless, the addition of entities that "maintain" PHI over time to the definition

---

32. HIPAA Final Omnibus Rule, *supra* note 4, at 5571.
33. *See id.*
34. *See id.* at 5571–72.
35. *Id.* at 5572.
36. *Id.*
37. *See id.*

of business associate significantly expands the definition of "business associate." Moreover, because business associates must comply with the Security Rule, this definitional change greatly expands the scope of the Security Rule's coverage to many technology vendors. Starting in 2013, many general technology vendors started facing requests for customers to sign business associate agreements (BAAs), despite claims that they do not access or want to access PHI received from their customer's. Many of these vendors have been surprised when their customers demanded that they sign BAAs. Fortunately, more vendors have recently recognized their business associate status. Ultimately, whether a vendor is a conduit or a business associate is a fact-specific determination.[38]

New categories of business associates include cloud computing service providers with online applications or data storage capabilities. For instance, Amazon Web Services is receiving requests to sign BAAs given its hosting of customer applications and PHI. It was its own form BAA. Moreover, common consumer services like Dropbox, Box, Google Drive, and Microsoft SkyDrive are almost certainly hosting PHI and thus appear to be business associates, too. Colocation and data center services that provide a physical setting for customers to store servers or storage devices containing PHI are physically maintaining PHI over time and thus business associates as well, even if they do not access the PHI on these servers or devices. To the extent covered entities and business associates are storing PHI with these vendors, they must require these vendors to sign a BAA. Vendors are frequently offering their own form BAAs to customers.

Telecommunications companies are an interesting case, since HHS expressly states that they may be a mere conduit to the extent they are merely moving PHI from place to place and have occasional, random access to PHI.[39] Nonetheless, modern telecommunications companies all offer services that involve storage of communications. For instance, if a covered entity obtains desktop or mobile phone service, phones and phone service inevitably come with voicemail. Many services also offer call recording. When users are discussing PHI over the phone and leaving voicemails containing PHI, they are storing PHI with the telecommunications service indefinitely over time. Moreover, since this storage is more than just transitory storage as the voice communication moves from Point A to Point B on the network, even short-term storage

---

38. *See id.* at 5571.
39. *See id.* at 5571–72.

of voicemail makes telecommunications service providers business associates.[40] Like voicemail, call recording features used to facilitate indefinite storage of PHI make the telecommunications vendor a business associate. The same analysis could apply to video conferencing services storing PHI video recordings over time.

In sum, HHS emphasized that the conduit exception is a limited one. It applies only to PHI transmission services, whether the PHI is in paper or electronic form. A conduit's storage of PHI is, by definition, temporary. By contrast, services maintaining PHI over time on behalf of covered entities are business associates.[41] Thus, the new definition of "business associate" in the HIPAA Final Omnibus Rule sweeps in a large swath of vendors that previously never even thought about HIPAA compliance. Accordingly, vendors that might be storing PHI should go through the fact-specific analysis needed to determine whether they are, in fact, business associates.

b. Persons and Entities that Are Not Business Associates

Members of the workforce of an entity, either a covered entity or a business associate, are not business associates of the entity. An organization's workforce includes employees, volunteers, trainees, and others under the control and direction of the organization with regard to the services they provide, even if those persons are not paid for their services.[42] Since they are not business associates, workforce members do not need to sign BAAs with the entity for which they work.

In addition, besides "mere conduits" of PHI discussed in the previous subsection, the definition of "business associate" does not include healthcare providers in relation to treatment, payment, or healthcare operations; health plan sponsors; government agencies administering public benefits programs; and covered entities participating in an OHCA. These entities are not required to sign BAAs.

A covered entity receiving PHI from another covered entity for purposes of treatment, payment, and healthcare operations does not

---

40. It is possible to imagine a voicemail system that deletes a message after the first and only time a recipient hears the message. A covered entity or business associate could argue that such a system only delivers messages and does not store them over time. Nonetheless, voicemail systems do not typically work this way. People would find it very difficult to use a voicemail service like that for fear of losing messages. Accordingly, designing a system like this is probably not a realistic option to avoid business associate status.

41. *See id.* at 5572.

42. *See* 45 C.F.R. § 164.103 (definition of "workforce").

become a business associate of the other covered entity (TPO). Specifically, when one covered entity discloses PHI to another covered entity for treatment of an individual, payment, or for healthcare operations, as defined in the Privacy Rule, the covered entity receiving the PHI is not a business associate of the disclosing covered entity. Therefore, healthcare providers do not require BAAs to disclose PHI to another covered entity for TPO purposes.

Likewise, health plan sponsors, such as employers, labor unions, or entities that they jointly establish,[43] are not business associates of the health plan. Thus, a BAA is not necessary to govern disclosures by a group health plan (or by a health insurance issuer or HMO with respect to a group health plan) to the plan sponsor. For a discussion of health plan sponsors and applicable privacy and information security requirements, see section 4.B. *infra*.

Furthermore, government agencies engaging in legally authorized joint activities to deliver healthcare under a public benefits program are not business associates. "A health plan that is a government program providing public benefits may disclose protected health information relating to eligibility for or enrollment in the health plan to another agency administering a government program providing public benefits. . . ."[44] As a condition of such disclosure, however, "the sharing of eligibility or enrollment information among such government agencies or the maintenance of such information in a single or combined data system accessible to all such government agencies" must be "required or expressly authorized by statute or regulation."[45]

Finally, covered entities collaborating with each other under an OHCA are not acting as business associates with regard to each other. Accordingly, the members of an OHCA do not need BAAs with each other. For more details concerning OHCAs, see section 4.A.6 below.

3. Subcontractors of Business Associates

The regulations define a "subcontractor" as "a person to whom a business associate delegates a function, activity, or service, other than in

---

43. For a definition of "plan sponsor," see 42 U.S.C. § 300gg-91(d)(13) (defining the term by reference to section 3(16)(B) of the Employee Retirement Income Security Act of 1974, 29 U.S.C. § 1002(16)(B)).

44. 45 C.F.R. § 164.512(k)(6)(i).

45. *Id.*

the capacity of a member of the workforce of such business associate."[46] The HIPAA Final Omnibus Rule changed the definition of "business associate" to include subcontractors that create, receive, maintain, or transmit PHI on behalf of a business associate.[47] Thus, subcontractors of business associates performing HIPAA-covered functions are themselves business associates. Before the HIPAA Final Omnibus Rule, there was some debate as to whether subcontractors of business associates were covered by HIPAA. By specifically mentioning "subcontractors," the HIPAA Final Omnibus Rule ended that debate.

The term "subcontractor" under the HIPAA Final Omnibus Rule, however, has a special meaning in that it contemplates the entity is performing a HIPAA-covered function. It does not mean any entity helping a contractor perform services for another. The most obvious example would be vendors that help a business associate deliver services to the covered entity or tiers of business associates above it, but have no need to access PHI.

For instance, assume that a health plan uses a business associate to run a data center for it. The business associate is hosting PHI. The business associate may hire a bookkeeping company to help it manage the finances of the data center, but the bookkeepers have no access to PHI. In a broad sense, the bookkeeping company is a subcontractor of the covered entity, but its functions are not HIPAA-covered functions and so it should not be considered a "subcontractor" within the meaning of 45 C.F.R. § 160.103(3)(iii) and the Security Rule. Accordingly, it would also fall outside the scope of the definition of a "business associate." Thus, the business associate has no obligation to enter into a BAA with the bookkeeping firm.

Given the inclusion of subcontractors within the definition of "business associate," the regulations contemplate a chain of entities starting with a covered entity. The covered entity engages a business associate to perform certain HIPAA-covered functions. The business associate, in turn, engages a subcontractor to perform some or all of the covered functions. The chain may extend to any number of sub-subcontractors below the subcontractor tier.

Subcontractors may include telecommunications providers, mobile device vendors, telemedicine and medical device vendors, or cloud service providers. These entities may be new to HIPAA compliance

---

46. 45 C.F.R. § 160.103 (definition of "subcontractor").
47. *Id.* § 160.103(3)(iii) (definition of "business associate").

and may not be entirely familiar with details of the security and privacy requirements necessary for handling PHI. All business associates should discuss these requirements in some detail with subcontractors. If reasonable and appropriate, business associates should obtain a HIPAA security audit from an independent third-party auditor, or view the results of an independent audit obtained by the subcontractor, prior to entering into a BAA with a subcontractor. Such due diligence is extremely important. HHS has recently confirmed that, in certain circumstances, depending on the degree of control a business associate has over its subcontractor, the subcontractor may be considered to be an agent of the business associate. In a security breach situation, if the subcontractor is determined by HHS to be the agent of a business associate, the business associate, as the principal, might bear full responsibility for the acts of its agent, if those acts were performed within in the scope of the agent's responsibilities under the BAA.

Although the term "subcontractor" implies that there is a contract in place between the business associate and the subcontractor, HHS has clarified, in the description and commentary to the HIPAA Final Omnibus Rule, that the definition of subcontractor applies to an agent or other person who acts on behalf of the business associate, even if the business associate has failed to enter into a business associate contract with that person or agent.[48] Downstream entities that work at the direction of or on behalf of a business associate or subcontractor and handle PHI, are required to comply with the applicable Privacy Rule and Security Rule Provisions in the same manner as the primary business associate. Moreover, downstream business associate subcontractors are directly responsible for the security and privacy of the PHI they receive, create, maintain, or transmit. Finally, downstream business associate subcontractors are all subject to enforcement activities if they fail to comply with the HIPAA Security and Privacy Rules.

Accordingly, the HIPAA Final Omnibus Rule significantly expanded the scope of HIPAA's coverage. As mentioned in section 4.A.2.a above, it expanded the definition of "business associate" to include vendors "maintaining" PHI on behalf of a covered entity over time. Moreover, it extends HIPAA's scope beyond covered entities and the business associate vendors providing services to them to a potentially long chain of subcontractors and sub-subcontractors of such vendors. General

---

48. HIPAA Final Omnibus Rule, *supra* note 4, at 5572–73.

technology vendors should now determine whether their customers are business associates providing services to other business associates or covered entities. If so, they may unknowingly become business associates themselves as a subcontractor.

4. Hybrid Entities with Healthcare Components

Some organizations have, as their primary mission, the performance of a HIPAA-covered function. A "covered function" in this context means performing activity making the organization a health plan, healthcare clearinghouse, or healthcare provider.[49] For instance, a hospital may treat patients in its role as a healthcare provider. It may also administer healthcare payments. These are "covered functions," and they make the hospital a covered entity governed by HIPAA and the Security Rule.

Other organizations, however, focus on activities other than healthcare, but may have groups or departments that perform limited covered functions. For instance, a business may administer its own group health plan. Also, a manufacturer may operate its own clinic for the use of its employees. For these organizations, it would be unreasonable to expect the entire organization to comply with HIPAA and the Security Rule. Only a small part of the organization may be involved with covered functions.

The "hybrid entity" concept addresses the dual nature of these organizations. "Hybrid entity" means "a single entity . . . [t]hat is a covered entity" "[w]hose business activities include both covered and non-covered functions" and that "designates health care components" in writing.[50] The part of the organization performing covered functions is the "health care component." "Health care component means a component or combination of components of a hybrid entity designated by the hybrid entity" as performing covered functions.[51] The written designation must "include any component that would meet the definition of a covered entity or business associate if it were a separate legal entity."[52] The designation may be written or electronic, and the hybrid entity must maintain a copy for six years.[53]

---

49. 45 C.F.R. § 160.103 (definition of "covered entity").
50. *Id.* § 164.103 (definition of "hybrid entity").
51. *Id.* (definition of "health care component").
52. *Id.* § 164.105(a)(2)(iii)(D).
53. *Id.* (citing the requirements in 45 C.F.R. § 164.105(c)(1), (c)(2)).

In general, the Security Rule, Breach Notification Rule, and Privacy Rule "apply only to the health care component(s)" of a hybrid entity.[54] More specifically, this limitation means:

- If one of these rules imposes requirements on "covered entities" (or "health plans," "covered health providers," or "health care clearinghouses"), then the rule applies to the healthcare component of the organization (or component that performs one of the above functions as applicable).[55]
- References to "protected health information" in one of these rules applies to the PHI created or received by or on behalf of the healthcare component of the organization.[56]
- References to "electronic protected health information" in one of these rules applies to the electronic PHI created, received, maintained, or transmitted by or on behalf of the healthcare component of the organization.[57]

None of these rules, however, applies to the nonhealthcare components of the hybrid entity. These nonhealthcare components have no obligation to comply with HIPAA or any of these rules.

In addition to applying the Security Rule, Breach Notification Rule, and Privacy Rule to hybrid entities' healthcare components, hybrid entities must enforce a separation between their healthcare components and the rest of their organizations.

- Their healthcare components must not disclose PHI to another component of the hybrid entity where the Privacy Rule would preclude such disclosure if the healthcare component and the rest of their organizations were separate and distinct legal entities.[58]
- Their healthcare components must protect electronic PHI under the Security Rule just as if they were legally separate from the rest of the organization.[59]

---

54. *Id.* § 164.105(a)(1).
55. *See id.* § 164.105(a)(2)(i)(A)–(a)(2)(i)(B).
56. *See id.* § 164.105(a)(2)(i)(C).
57. *See id.* § 164.105(a)(2)(i)(D).
58. *See id.* § 164.105(a)(2)(ii)(A).
59. *See id.* § 164.105(a)(2)(ii)(B).

- Workers with the same role in both the healthcare component and another component in the organization must not use or disclose PHI created or received in the course of work for the healthcare component in violation of the Privacy Rule.[60]

The regulations also call out specific compliance obligations of hybrid entities. Although only the healthcare component must comply with HIPAA, according to the regulations, the "responsibility of complying," such as cooperating with Office for Civil Rights investigations, rests with the hybrid entity, which is presumably a reference to the top management of the hybrid entity as a whole.[61] The hybrid entity must also have policies and procedures to implement the requirements for BAAs and flowing down privacy and security restrictions on sponsors of group health plans.[62] The hybrid entity is also responsible for its healthcare component's compliance with the Security Rule and the Privacy Rule.

In sum, as long as the hybrid entity actually records and maintains a written designation, the regulations allow the hybrid entity to lower its compliance burden. It need only comply with HIPAA and its rules to the extent they apply to the healthcare component of the organization. Nonetheless, it must enforce an information governance separation from the rest of the organization.

5. Affiliated Covered Entities

Affiliated covered entities (ACEs) are groups of organizations under common control that designate themselves as a single covered entity for purposes of HIPAA compliance. By banding together in this way, they need only have a single set of policies and procedures, a single privacy notice, a single privacy official and staff, a single set of training guidelines, a single form of BAA, and so on. Organizations within a group may be separate legal entities for various business reasons. Nonetheless, affiliated organizations gain efficiencies and reduce administrative burdens by working together in this way.

One example is Stanford University and its ACE. Stanford's ACE includes the university's HIPAA components. Stanford University

---

60. *See id.* § 164.105(a)(2)(ii)(C).

61. *Id.* § 164.105(a)(2)(iii)(A).

62. *Id.* § 164.105(a)(2)(iii)(B) (citing documentation requirements in 45 C.F.R. §§ 164.316, 164.530(i)).

is also a hybrid entity. Its healthcare functions are a minority of its activities, since its main role is serving as an institution of higher learning. The Stanford ACE also includes its main hospital and clinics organization, its children's hospital, and two physician networks—one for each hospital system.[63] All of these entities comprise a single covered entity.

Under the regulations, "[l]egally separate covered entities may designate themselves (including any health care component of such covered entity) as a single, affiliated covered entity, for purposes of" HIPAA compliance "if all of the covered entities designated are under common ownership or control."[64] "Common ownership exists if an entity or entities possess an ownership or equity interest of 5 percent or more in another entity."[65] "Common control exists if an entity has the power, directly or indirectly, significantly to influence or direct the actions or policies of another entity."[66] In order to have an ACE, the members of the ACE must document their designation as an ACE[67] and maintain that documentation in written or electronic form for at least six years.[68]

"An affiliated covered entity must ensure that it complies with the applicable requirements of" the Security Rule, the Breach Notification Rule, and the Security Rule.[69] This compliance obligation includes the provisions concerning isolating healthcare clearinghouse functions and, where the ACE performs multiple functions, complying with Privacy Rule provisions applicable to the functions performed and limiting the access and uses of PHI to those functions.[70] Given the shared nature of authority, responsibility, and potential liability among the members, allocating responsibilities and potential liabilities in a clear written agreement would be helpful.

---

63. Stanford Univ., Covered Entity https://privacy.stanford.edu/covered-entity (last visited July 7, 2016).

64. 45 C.F.R. § 164.105(b)(2)(i)(A).

65. *Id.* § 164.103 (definition of "common ownership") (italics omitted).

66. *Id.* (definition of "common control")

67. *See id.* § 164.105(b)(2)(i)(B).

68. *Id.* (citing the requirements in 45 C.F.R. § 164.105(c)).

69. *Id.* § 164.105(b)(2)(ii).

70. *Id.* (citing *id.* §§ 164.308(a)(4)(ii)(A), 164.504(g)).

6. Organized Healthcare Arrangements

An OHCA[71] gives covered entities the ability to coordinate efforts in an integrated care setting for providing services to common patients without the common ownership or control of an ACE. "For example, an academic medical center often includes university-affiliated physicians and a hospital or health system. Typically, the university is a separate legal entity, but the patients are treated by the faculty within the hospital or health system."[72] Members of an OHCA can use a joint notice of privacy practices and share PHI for purposes of TPO.[73] Use of a joint

---

71. *Organized health care arrangement* means:
   (1) A clinically integrated care setting in which individuals typically receive health care from more than one health care provider;
   (2) An organized system of health care in which more than one covered entity participates and in which the participating covered entities:
      (i) Hold themselves out to the public as participating in a joint arrangement; and
      (ii) Participate in joint activities that include at least one of the following:
         (A) Utilization review, in which health care decisions by participating covered entities are reviewed by other participating covered entities or by a third party on their behalf;
         (B) Quality assessment and improvement activities, in which treatment provided by participating covered entities is assessed by other participating covered entities or by a third party on their behalf; or
         (C) Payment activities, if the financial risk for delivering health care is shared, in part or in whole, by participating covered entities through the joint arrangement and if protected health information created or received by a covered entity is reviewed by other participating covered entities or by a third party on their behalf for the purpose of administering the sharing of financial risk.
   (3) A group health plan and a health insurance issuer or HMO with respect to such group health plan, but only with respect to protected health information created or received by such health insurance issuer or HMO that relates to individuals who are or who have been participants or beneficiaries in such group health plan;
   (4) A group health plan and one or more other group health plans each of which are maintained by the same plan sponsor; or
   (5) The group health plans described in paragraph (4) of this definition and health insurance issuers or HMOs with respect to such group health plans, but only with respect to protected health information created or received by such health insurance issuers or HMOs that relates to individuals who are or have been participants or beneficiaries in any of such group health plans.
   45 C.F.R. § 160.103 (definition of "organized health care arrangement").

72. Margaret Amatayakul, *United under HIPAA: A Comparison of Arrangements and Agreements (HIPAA on the Job)*, J. AHIMA (2002), *reprinted at* http://bok.ahima.org /doc?oid=60011#.VyBLpza3WnA).

73. 45 C.F.R. § 164.506(c)(5).

notice of privacy practice reduces patient confusion and reduces duplication of paperwork.

Unlike an ACE, no written designation is necessary to form an OHCA, although a written record or agreement among the members is a good idea. An agreement would be useful for memorializing the members' respective rights and obligations. At the same time, an agreement could establish common policies, procedures, and standards. In order to operate a single notice of privacy practices, the OHCA members must agree to abide by its terms regarding PHI created or received as part of the OHCA arrangement.[74] The notice must disclose the identity of the covered entities using the notice.[75] The notice must also describe where the services are delivered (exact service delivery sites or classes of sites).[76] If the OHCA members are sharing PHI with each other for TPO purposes, the notice must disclose the fact of that sharing.[77]

B. HEALTH PLAN SPONSORS

While a health plan is a covered entity, the health plan sponsor, such as an employer, labor union, or joint entity, is neither a covered entity nor business associate. Nonetheless, the Privacy Rule requires that the health plan documents contain certain privacy and confidentiality restrictions on the plan sponsor's uses and disclosures of the PHI.[78] Moreover, under the Privacy Rule, a health plan intending to use or disclose PHI for underwriting purposes must notify patients that it is not permitted to disclose, or permit a health insurance issuer or HMO to disclose, PHI that is genetic information.[79] The scope of this restriction on disclosing genetic information includes PHI disclosures to a plan sponsor. Furthermore, the Security Rule requires group health plans to flow down security requirements to plan sponsors, as discussed below.

HIPAA does not directly regulate employers and other plan sponsors,[80] but HIPAA does apply to "group health plans" that are

---

74. *Id.* § 164.520(d)(1).
75. *See id.* § 164.520(d)(2)(i).
76. *See id.* § 164.520(d)(2)(ii).
77. *See id.* § 164.520(d)(2)(iii).
78. 45 C.F.R. § 164.504(f).
79. *Id.* § 164.520(b)(1)(iii)(C).
80. *See* HHS, As an Employer, I Sponsor a Group Health Plan for My Employees. Am I a Covered Entity under HIPAA?, http://www.hhs.gov/hipaa/for-professionals/faq/499/am-i-a-covered-entity-under-hipaa/index.html (last visited Apr. 26, 2016).

sponsored by employers, labor unions, or jointly established entities (except for self-administered plans with fewer than fifty participants).[81] In such cases, the plan sponsor pays a health insurer to provide health benefits under the group health plan. Such group health plans are called "fully insured health plans" and are covered entities. However, the employer or other entity that sponsors the plan is not a covered entity, and the plan sponsor is not directly subject to HIPAA.

Nonetheless, to the extent the plan documents are incorporated into agreements between the group health plan and plan sponsor, the group health plan must enforce security and privacy restrictions by contract.[82] Moreover, HIPAA restricts the flow of PHI from the group health plan to the employer or other plan sponsor, except when summary health information is disclosed to plan sponsors for certain limited administrative purposes.[83]

The Security Rule created a special security standard for group health plans that applies when they disclose PHI to plan sponsors.[84] As a threshold matter, however, this standard does not apply[85] when the only PHI disclosed to a plan sponsor is either:

1. Summary health information, that is, information that summarizes the claims history, claims expenses, or types of claims experienced by individuals for whom a plan sponsor has provided health benefits under the group health plan, and is also information that has been stripped of all individual identifiers, but not necessarily fully "de-identified," as defined by the Privacy Rule;[86] requested for the purpose of obtaining premium bids from health plans for providing health insurance coverage under the group health plan; or requested for purposes of modifying, amending or terminating the group health plan;[87] or

---

81. *See id.*

82. *See* 45 C.F.R. §§ 164.314(b), 504(f).

83. *See id.* § 164.504(f)(1).

84. *Id.* § 164.314(b)(1).

85. The security requirements do not apply "when the only electronic protected health information disclosed to a plan sponsor is disclosed pursuant to § 164.504(f)(1)(ii) or (iii), or as authorized under § 164.508." *Id.*

86. *Id.* § 164.504(a)(1)–(2) (definition of "summary health information").

87. *Id.* § 164.504(f)(1)(ii).

2. Enrollment information, that is, information as to whether an individual is participating in the group health plan or is enrolled in or disenrolled from a health insurance issuer or an HMO offered by the plan;[88] or

3. Information requested pursuant to a valid authorization;[89] such information may be disclosed to the plan sponsor, although the information may contain PHI.

Aside from these exceptions, if a plan sponsor requests any PHI from the group health plan, the Security Rule requires the group health plan to ensure that the plan documents of the plan sponsor impose security requirements on the plan sponsor. Specifically, "a group health plan must ensure that its plan documents provide that the plan sponsor will reasonably and appropriately safeguard electronic protected health information created, received, maintained, or transmitted to or by the plan sponsor on behalf of the group health plan."[90]

In order to implement this standard, group health plans are required to incorporate provisions in their plan documents requiring the plan sponsor to whom the PHI is disclosed, to:

1. Implement administrative, physical, and technical safeguards that reasonably and appropriately protect the confidentiality, integrity, and availability of the PHI that the plan sponsor creates, receives, maintains, or transmits on behalf of the group health plan;

2. Ensure that the adequate separation between the group health plan and the plan sponsor, as required by 45 C.F.R. § 164.504(f)(2)(iii), is supported by "reasonable and appropriate" security measures;

3. Ensure that the agents to which it provides the PHI agree to implement reasonable and appropriate security measures to protect the information; and

4. Report to the group health plan any security incident of which the group health plan becomes aware.[91]

---

88. *Id.* § 164.504(f)(1)(iii).
89. *Id.* § 164.508.
90. *Id.* § 164.314(b)(1).
91. *Id.* § 164.314(b)(2).

C. BUSINESS ASSOCIATE AGREEMENTS

Section 4.A above discusses the different entities that fall within the scope of HIPAA and the Security Rule, such as covered entities, covered entities with nonhealthcare operations designated as hybrid entities, ACEs, OHCAs, business associates, and subcontractors, which are themselves now considered business associates. BAAs are crucial for tying business associates to covered entities and governing their relationships. Covered entities, the healthcare components of hybrid entities, and business associates (including subcontractors) are each responsible for the security and privacy of the PHI that they receive, create, maintain, and/or transmit. Each of them is directly liable, in the event of a failure to comply with the requirements of the Security Rule, the Breach Notification Rule, the Privacy Rule, or obligations under HIPAA or the HITECH Act.

The HIPAA Rules generally require that covered entities enter into contracts—BAAs—with their business associates to ensure that the business associates will appropriately safeguard the PHI they receive, create, transmit, and/or maintain on their behalf. The HIPAA regulations also require business associates to enter into BAAs with their subcontractors to ensure that the subcontractor will appropriately safeguard the PHI. A covered entity is not required to enter into a contract with a subcontractor of a business associate.[92]

BAAs typically contain certain provisions that accomplish the following:

1. Establish the permitted and required uses and disclosures of PHI by the business associate;
2. Provide that the business associate will not use or further disclose the PHI other than as permitted by the contract or as required by law;
3. Require the business associate to implement appropriate safeguards to prevent unauthorized use or disclosure of the PHI, including implementing requirements of the Security Rule with regard to electronic PHI;

---

92. 45 C.F.R. § 308(b)(i); HIPAA Final Omnibus Rule, *supra* note 4, at 5573. "This proposed modification would not require the covered entity to have a contract with the subcontractor; rather, the obligation would remain on each business associate to obtain satisfactory assurances in the form of a written contract or other arrangement that a subcontractor will appropriately safeguard protected health information." *Id.*

4. Require the business associate to report to the covered entity[93] any use or disclosure of the information not provided for by its contract, including security incidents that may include breaches of unsecured PHI;

5. Require the business associate to disclose PHI as specified in its contract to satisfy a covered entity's obligation with respect to individuals' requests for copies of their PHI, as well as make available PHI for amendments (and incorporate any amendments, if required) and accountings;

6. To the extent the business associate is to carry out a covered entity's obligation under the Privacy Rule, require the business associate to comply with the requirements applicable to the obligation;

7. Require the business associate to make available to the Secretary of HHS, the business associate's internal practices, books, and records relating to the use and disclosure of PHI received from, or created or received by the business associate on behalf of the covered entity, for the purpose of determining the covered entity's compliance with the HIPAA Privacy Rule;

8. At termination of the contract, if feasible, require the business associate to return or destroy all PHI received from, or created or received by, the business associate on behalf of the covered entity;

9. Ensure that any subcontractors it may engage on its behalf, that will have access to PHI, agree to the same restrictions and conditions that apply to the business associate with respect to such information; and

10. Authorize termination of the contract by the party receiving services (a covered entity or business associate) if the service provider (a business associate or subcontractor) violates a material term of that contract.[94]

---

93. Note that this provision requires notification to the covered entity, not to the entity in privity with it. Thus, a BAA with a subcontractor must require notification of the covered entity. There is no obligation under this provision to notify the business associate in privity with the subcontractor. HHS may or may not have intended this result after the HIPAA Final Omnibus Rule expressly covered subcontractors. Nonetheless, business associates should ask to include such notification in the BAA as well.

94. 45 C.F.R. §§ 164.314(a), 164.504(e).

Contracts between business associates and other business associates acting as subcontractors are subject to these same requirements.

Although the implementation specification in the Privacy Rule mandates the coverage of the above topics, one open question is whether a BAA must include topics that are completely inapplicable to the services provided by the business associates. For instance, under the Privacy Rule, a BAA must provide that the business associate will make PHI available to facilitate individuals' requests for PHI under 45 C.F.R. § 164.524.[95] Under section 164.524, an individual has a right to inspect and obtain a copy of PHI about the individual. Some business associates, however, never have contact with individual patients. For example, "an entity hired by a business associate to appropriately dispose of documents that contain protected health information is also a business associate and subject to the applicable provisions of the HIPAA Rules."[96] No patient would ever approach a paper shredding company to obtain a copy of his or her medical records. Accordingly, it does not make sense to require a paper shredding company to make PHI available to facilitate individuals' access to PHI. Nonetheless, the Privacy Rule includes it as a mandatory topic for BAAs.

Including inapplicable provisions in a BAA simply because it is on the list of mandatory topics complies with the Privacy Rule, but for vendors, it creates compliance burdens. For example, vendors may need to explain in an audit or assessment why they are not complying with the inapplicable BAA requirements. Moreover, they increase the risk for vendors of facing accusations of contract breaches based on violations of BAA terms they cannot meet. Accordingly, including inapplicable BAA provisions does not seem satisfactory.

One possible solution is to simply leave out inapplicable provisions, which may shorten the BAA and make it simpler, although there is some risk of noncompliance with the Privacy Rule. Another possible solution is to modify the obligation to maintain the spirit of the requirement, even if the letter is inapplicable. Thus, in our example, requiring a paper shredding company to forward any requests for PHI to the covered entity, in the unlikely event an individual patient comes to it looking for access to his or her medical records, may address the requirement without requiring the vendor to do the impossible. This approach may risk technical Privacy Rule noncompliance, although it may minimize that risk. Each vendor

---

95. *Id.* § 164.504(e)(2)(ii)(E).
96. HIPAA Final Omnibus Rule, *supra* note 4, at 5574.

negotiating a BAA will need to make its own judgment about which approach is best under the facts and circumstances of the arrangement.

A BAA should set forth the responsibilities of the business associate in sufficient detail to adequately inform the business associate regarding the expectations of the party receiving the services (a covered entity or upstream business associate) with regard to the privacy and security standards that must be implemented or addressed in order to protect the PHI covered by the BAA. Moreover, BAAs can contain provisions describing how, when, and under what circumstances the party receiving services can assess the business associate's security practices, as implemented, or require an independent third-party audit or other assessment of the security practices and policies of the business associate. If the business associate is a cloud computing service provider or if the business associate maintains, discloses, or transmits any of the covered entity's PHI using a cloud service provider subcontractor, viewing the results of a security audit by an independent third party may be the only way to ensure that the business associate and/or the subcontractor and possible sub-subcontractors are operating their businesses as represented in their respective BAAs. The obligations of each downstream BAA must be consistent with the privacy and security requirements of the covered entity that is disclosing PHI. Accordingly, vendors may ask for notification from their customers in BAAs of possible limits imposed by covered entitles privacy practices.

In January 2013, HHS released an updated sample BAA.[97] The sample BAA describes "Obligations and Activities of Business Associate" and then provides a framework for addressing "Permitted Uses and Disclosures by Business Associate" and additional optional and boilerplate language. However, additional issues during the negotiations of a BAA and/or the related service agreement may include warranties, representations, limitation of liability, and indemnification terms.

Business associates, including subcontractors, are required to notify the covered entity for whom they are directly or indirectly performing services or activities, in the event of a breach of unsecured PHI.[98] The idea here is for the business associate to place information about the

---

97. U.S. Dep't of Health & Human Servs. Office for Civil Rights, Sample Business Associate Agreement Provisions (Jan. 25, 2013), http://www.hhs.gov/hipaa/for-professionals/covered-entities/sample-business-associate-agreement-provisions/index.html (last visited Apr. 26, 2016).

98. 45 C.F.R. § 164.410(a)(1).

breach in the hands of the party with the obligation to notify affected individuals. Only the covered entity is required by law to provide the notice to affected individuals in the event the security of their PHI has been compromised. However, BAAs with subcontractors typically require that the subcontractor also notify the business associate receiving services of the breach.

Recovering from a data breach, including providing notification of a breach of unsecured PHI to affected individuals, is expensive. A recent report of the Ponemon Institute estimates that the cost of HIPAA breaches to the healthcare industry in 2015 may have reached $6.2 billion.[99] Covered entities often desire to shift the burden of paying for breach notification to a business associate in BAAs when the breaches occur on the systems of the business associate or on a system used or controlled by a subcontractor of the business associate, possibly a cloud services provider. The burden of payment and providing notice (but not the potential liability of the covered entity to ensure that the notice is provided) may be shifted to the business associate by a promise of the business associate to "indemnify, defend and hold harmless the Covered Entity" for "any and all costs, claims and expenses in the event of a material breach of this Agreement by Business Associate" or other similar indemnification language.

In view of the large amount of potential liability assumed by a business associate who agrees to indemnification, from a vendor perspective, any and all agreements to indemnify should either be negotiated out of BAAs or be carefully drafted and limited via negotiations. Indemnification clauses are not inconsequential boilerplate to be accepted for the sake of striking a quick deal. To the contrary, given the frequency of breaches, and the magnitude of the potential liability, they raise significant risk for the vendor and, if triggered, may result in liability that could threaten the existence of the vendor. Covered entities and business associates who desire indemnification should assure themselves that the would-be indemnitor is contractually obligated to carry insurance and evidence such coverage by a certificate of insurance in the desired amount, from a best-rated insurer.

Many potential business associates, particularly cloud services providers, may ask to add a clause to the contract limiting their liability under the BAA to a specified amount. This clause adds risk for a

---

99. Ponemon Inst. LLC, Sixth Annual Benchmark Study on Privacy & Security of Healthcare Data, at 1 (May 2016), *reprinted at* https://www2.idexpertscorp.com/sixth-annual-ponemon-benchmark-study-on-privacy-security-of-healthcare-data-incidents

covered entity, given that the covered entity will be surrendering control over the security and privacy of the PHI to the business associate. Both the vendor and the party receiving services can manage their risk through third- and first-party insurance coverage. Many cyber risk insurance policies include coverage for the cost of breach notification, which addresses one of the major costs arising from a breach.

The time allotted for the covered entity to provide notice of a breach to affected individuals is generally "without unreasonable delay" but no later than sixty days after the breach is discovered.[100] On the other hand, business associates are required under the Security Rule to provide the covered entity with notice of any "security incident"[101] of which the business associate becomes aware (which may include a breach) within the time specified in the BAA between the covered entity and the business associate.[102] State breach notification laws often allow a considerably shorter time to provide notice of a security breach then sixty days. Moreover, breach notices must include a considerable amount of information, such as the name of the individual whose information was disclosed, the nature of the information disclosed, the time and place of the breach, how the breach occurred, what the covered entity will do to mitigate the breach, and so forth.[103] Therefore, it is advisable to draft BAAs to require the vendor to provide notice of a security incident within a specified number of days, in order to allow the covered entity a reasonable time to collect all the necessary information that must be provided in the notice of breach and to comply with any applicable state laws.

Vendors will need to balance the demands of their covered entity or business associate customers for prompt notice against the need to leave reasonable time to investigate possible breaches. Commonly, subcontractors negotiating BAAs will need to commit to notice within time periods closer to state breach notification laws than sixty days.

HHS's sample BAA includes an optional "Permitted Uses and Disclosures" provision stating, "Option 1—Provide a specific list of permissible purposes." It is important that covered entities and business associates pay close attention to what is listed as a permitted or allowed

---

100. 45 C.F.R. § 164.404(b).

101. "Security Incident" "means the attempted or successful unauthorized access, use disclosure, modification or destruction of information or interference with system operations in an information system." *Id.* § 164.304 (definition of "security incident").

102. *Id.* § 164.314(a)(2)(i)(C).

103. *See id.* § 164.404(c)(1).

use of the PHI. In other words, if it is used, the language in this section should be specifically tailored for the work with the PHI that the business associate is contracted to perform. For instance, it would be a mistake for it to say, "Business Associate may use the PHI only as set forth in this Agreement" and then not specify further what those allowed or permitted uses are. However, the BAA may define "The Agreement" as the service agreement into which the BAA is incorporated by reference or to which it is otherwise related, thereby limiting the uses and disclosures of PHI to the subject matter of the master services agreement, that is, the specific work the business associate has contracted to perform. In any case, when using such a provision, the BAA must define the restrictions and limitations on the uses and disclosures of PHI by the business associate or subcontractor.

D. INFORMATION COVERED UNDER THE HIPAA SECURITY RULE

1. Protection of Electronic Protected Health Information

HIPAA and the Security Rule contain numerous defined terms about the information they cover. Understanding these defined terms is key to understanding the scope of HIPAA and the Security Rule. In this section, we discuss the following terms, which are defined in more detail below:

- "Health information"—the broadest category of information discussed in HIPAA and its regulation.
- "Individually identifiable health information" or "IIHI"—a subcategory of "health information" that identifies an individual.
- "Protected health information" or "PHI"—a subcategory of individually identifiable health information, which excludes IIHI governed by certain other laws or relates to a person who has been deceased for more than fifty years.
- "Electronic protected health information" or "ePHI"—a subcategory of PHI. ePHI refers to PHI in electronic form.

"Health information" is broadly defined and

> means any information, including genetic information, whether oral or recorded in any form or medium, that:

(1) Is created or received by a health care provider, health plan, public health authority, employer, life insurer, school or university, or health care clearinghouse; and

(2) Relates to the past, present, or future physical or mental health or condition of an individual; the provision of health care to an individual; or the past, present, or future payment for the provision of health care to an individual.[104]

As noted above, "individually identifiable health information" is a narrower category. IIHI is a subset of "health information" and includes demographic information collected from an individual.[105] IIHI:

(1) Is created or received by a health care provider, health plan, employer, or health care clearinghouse; and

(2) Relates to the past, present, or future physical or mental health or condition of an individual; the provision of health care to an individual; or the past, present, or future payment for the provision of health care to an individual; and

   (i) That identifies the individual; or

   (ii) With respect to which there is a reasonable basis to believe the information can be used to identify the individual.[106]

"Protected health information" is the information protected by HIPAA and the HIPAA Privacy Rule.

Protected health information means individually identifiable health information:

(1) . . . that is:

   (i) Transmitted by electronic media;

   (ii) Maintained in electronic media; or

   (iii) Transmitted or maintained in any other form or medium.[107]

"Electronic media" is a term that includes electronic storage and transmission. Storage electronic media include memory devices in computers (e.g., hard drives or solid state drives) and any removable/transportable digital memory medium, such as magnetic tape or disk, optical disk, or digital memory card.[108] Transmission electronic media are those used to exchange information already in electronic storage media. Transmission

---

104. 45 C.F.R. § 160.103 (definition of "health information").

105. *See id.* (definition of "individually identifiable health information").

106. *Id.*

107. *Id.* (definition of "protected health information").

108. *Id.* § 160.103(1) (definition of "electronic media").

media include, for example, the Internet (which is open and public), an extranet (using Internet technology to link a business with information accessible only to collaborating parties), leased lines, dial-up lines, private networks, and the physical movement of removable/transportable electronic storage media. Certain transmissions, including transmissions of paper records via facsimile and transmission of voice via telephone, are not considered to be transmissions via electronic media, because the information did not exist in electronic form before the transmission.[109]

The definition of "PHI" excludes certain categories of individually identifiable health information, namely:

1. IIHI in education records covered by the Family Educational Rights and Privacy Act (FERPA), as amended;
2. IIHI in 20 U.S.C. § 1232g records, described at 20 U.S.C. § 1232g(a)(4)(B)(iv) (education records regarding individuals with disabilities in federally funded educational agencies or institutions subject to FERPA);
3. IIHI in employment records held by a covered entity in its role as employer; and
4. IIHI regarding a person who has been deceased for more than fifty years.[110]

Finally, the Security Rule defines electronic protected health information as follows: "*Electronic protected health information* means information that comes within paragraphs (1)(i) or (1)(ii) of the definition of *protected health information* as specified in this section."[111] In other words, ePHI is PHI that is transmitted by electronic media or maintained in electronic media.

It is important to note that the text of the Security Rule focuses on the protection of *electronic* protected health information, and not PHI generally. The Security Rule requires covered entities and business associates to ensure the confidentiality, integrity, and availability of electronic PHI that they create, receive, maintain, or transmit.[112] By contrast, the Privacy Rule speaks of protecting the privacy of PHI generally, since it covers paper as well as electronic PHI.

---

109. *Id.* § 160.103(2) (definition of "electronic media").
110. *Id.* § 160.103 (definition of "protected heath information").
111. *Id.* § 160.103 (definition of "electronic protected heath information").
112. *Id.* § 164.306(a)(1).

Notwithstanding this distinction, in this book, we refer in chapter 5 and elsewhere to the protection of "PHI." We use the term "PHI" rather than "ePHI" since BAAs commonly require protection of PHI generally, given that BAAs implement both the Privacy and Security Rule requirements. Moreover, in common discourse about HIPAA, people more often refer to PHI than ePHI. Part of the reason for this use of the term PHI in discussions of the Security Rule reflects the reality that the Security Rule and the Privacy Rule together require protecting the security of all PHI.[113] Specifically, the Privacy Rule requires administrative, technical, and physical safeguards (i.e., security controls) to protect the privacy of PHI.[114] Thus, the combined effect of the Security Rule and Privacy Rule is to implement security safeguards for all PHI for organizations conducting standard electronic transactions.

2. Status of De-identified Protected Health Information

It is possible to change PHI to remove its ability to identify individual patients in a process called "de-identification."[115] Once it has gone through that process, de-identified PHI is no longer considered to be IIHI or PHI.[116] De-identified PHI is not subject to protections under either the Privacy Rule or the Security Rule. The process of de-identification involves converting the PHI to health information that does not identify an individual and with respect to which there is no reasonable basis to believe that the information can be used to identify an individual.

The de-identification process must meet certain regulatory requirements. A covered entity may determine that PHI is de-identified and is no longer PHI, in either of two ways:

1. The covered entity may strip the information of each of eighteen listed identifiers and have no actual knowledge that the information could be used, alone or in combination with other information, to identify an individual who is the subject of the information, or

---

113. The Privacy and Security Rules apply if the organization is conducting standard electronic transactions involving PHI. If the organization conducts no electronic transactions at all, it is not subject to the Privacy or Security Rule. See *supra* section 4.A.1.

114. *Id.* § 164.530(c)(1).

115. 45 C.F.R. § 164.514.

116. *See id.* § 164.514(a)(1).

2. The covered entity may engage a person with appropriate knowledge and experience with generally accepted statistical and scientific principles and methods for rendering information not individually identifiable. That person must, by applying such principles and methods, determine that the risk is very small that the information could be used, alone or in combination with other reasonably available information, to identify an individual who is the subject of the information, and the person must document the methods and results of the analysis that justify that determination.[117]

De-identification of PHI may be accomplished by using an encryption key to scramble the health information. Encryption is sometimes reversible. Decrypting the information may allow for re-identification of the PHI, in which case HIPAA Privacy and Security Rules will again apply to the re-identified information. If an encryption method is used, then secure de-identification of PHI goes hand-in-hand with control over the encryption key that was used to de-identify the PHI (as well as the activation data for the key, such as a password, PIN, or other code). Covered entities and their business associates should implement reasonably appropriate procedures for secure key management and adequately train their employees concerning these procedures to avoid unintentional or unauthorized re-identification of the PHI and its compromise.

---

117. *See id.* § 164.514(b).

CHAPTER 5

The Security Rule

A. GENERAL RULES

In general, the Security Rule ensures that covered entities and business associates protect the confidentiality, integrity, and availability of electronic protected health information (ePHI).[1] For a definition of "protected health information" (PHI) and "electronic protected health information," see section 4.D.1 above. As mentioned in that section, this book uses the term "PHI" rather than "ePHI," because PHI is more commonly used in practice. Nonetheless, the reader should understand that references to PHI in the Security Rule are actually to ePHI. Also, any quotations to provisions of the Security Rule reflect the exact language of the regulations, including references to ePHI. Finally, the standards and implementation specifications described in this chapter apply to both covered entities and business associates. Sometimes this book uses the term "organization" as a shorthand term for the applicable covered entity or business associate seeking to comply with the Security Rule.

1. Security Requirements in General

Information security professionals commonly refer to the protection of confidentiality, integrity, and availability of information. The Security Rule's language stating its high-level requirement of security reflects these goals.[2] "Confidentiality" means that data or information are not made available or disclosed to unauthorized persons or processes.[3] In other words, organizations must protect PHI against interception and other unauthorized access or use by people or processes, such as software applications. The term "integrity" refers to the prevention of

---

1. 45 C.F.R. § 164.306(a)(1). As mentioned in section 4.C.1, the security of paper PHI falls under the Privacy Rule, rather than the Security Rule. *See id.* § 164.530(c)(1).

2. *See id.* § 164.306(a)(1).

3. *Id.* § 164.304 (definition of "confidentiality").

unauthorized alteration or destruction of data or information.[4] That is, integrity safeguards should provide assurances that no information has been tampered with or corrupted. At least, integrity safeguards can provide assurances that if tampering or corruption occurs, it can be detected. "Availability" refers to data or information being accessible and usable upon demand by an authorized person.[5] The availability concept provides assurances that information is there when it is needed. An illustration of this concept is the "denial of service" attack in which the attacker makes a website or other application or system inaccessible by flooding it with bogus transactions or requests for information. Assurances of availability to fight denial of service attacks help to ensure that the website, application, or other service is available when users wish to access it.

In addition to these general principles, the Security Rule requires organizations to:

- Protect against reasonably anticipated security threats;
- Protect against reasonably anticipated uses or disclosures that violate the Privacy Rule;
- Ensure that its workforce complies with the Security Rule;[6] and
- Periodically review and modify security measures and update security documentation to maintain continuing compliance.[7]

Note that the Security Rule refers to members of an organization's "workforce." The Security Rule does not limit its coverage to employees. Accordingly, the Security Rule contemplates that some members of an organization's workforce may be independent contractors, workers placed with the organization by a staffing agency, trainees, or volunteers.[8] In this chapter, the terms "worker" and "workforce" broadly

---

4. *See id.* (definition of "integrity").
5. *See id.* (definition of "availability").
6. *See id.* § 164.306(a)(2)–(a)(4).
7. *See id.* § 164.306(e).
8. We substituted the term "workforce members" for the statutory term "employees" because "workforce member" is a defined term for purposes of the HIPAA Rules and means employees, volunteers, trainees, and other persons whose conduct, in the performance of work for a covered entity or business associate, is under the direct control of such covered entity or business associate.

Modifications to the HIPAA Privacy, Security, Enforcement, and Breach Notification Rules under the Health Information Technology for Economic and Clinical Health Act and the Genetic Information Nondiscrimination Act; Other Modifications to the HIPAA Rules; Final Rule, 78 Fed. Reg. 5566, 5640 (2013) [hereinafter HIPAA Final Omnibus Rule].

cover employees, independent contractors, workers placed with an organization by a staffing agency, trainees, and volunteers.

2. Flexibility in Implementation: Standards and Implementation Specifications

The Security Rule recognizes that there is no "one size fits all" method of securing information and systems. The rule does not require a single set of security measures for all organizations. To the contrary, the Security Rule permits a great deal of flexibility. In deciding on which specific security measures to implement, organizations have some discretion to select security measures that "reasonably and appropriately" implement the regulations.[9] The regulations permit organizations to make this decision by considering the following factors:

- The size, complexity, and capabilities of the covered entity or business associate;
- The covered entity's or the business associate's technical infrastructure, hardware, and software security capabilities;
- The cost of security measures; and
- The probability and criticality (likelihood of occurrence and magnitude of harm) of potential risks to the PHI.[10]

The structure of the regulations comprising the Security Rule consists of numerous security "standards" that are, in essence, a series of high-level requirements that organizations *must* meet.[11] To flesh out the details of the Security Rule and its standards, the regulations present a series of "implementation specifications." Two types of implementation specifications appear in the Security Rule. First, some implementation specifications are called "required." [12] An organization *must* implement required implementation specifications.[13] The exact mechanisms to do this are not specified because, as mentioned above, organizations have the flexibility to choose security measures that "reasonably and appropriately" implement the required implementation specifications.

The second type of implementation specification is called "addressable."[14] Addressable implementation specifications *are not*

---

9. 45 C.F.R. § 164.306(b)(1).

10. *Id.* § 164.306(b)(2)(i)–(b)(2)(iv).

11. *See id.* § 164.306(c).

12. *Id.* § 164.306(d)(1).

13. *Id.* § 164.306(d)(2).

14. *Id.* § 164.306(d)(1).

requirements and need be implemented by all organizations in all circumstances. Instead, organizations must go through a process by which they analyze whether a particular addressable implementation specification is reasonable and appropriate in view of its likely contribution to the security of PHI.[15] If the addressable implementation specification is reasonable and appropriate under the circumstances, then the covered entity or business associate *must* implement it.[16] If it is not reasonable and appropriate, then the covered entity or business associate must instead:

- Document why it would not be reasonable and appropriate to implement it; and
- Implement an equivalent alternative safeguard, if it is reasonable and appropriate.[17]

B. ADMINISTRATIVE SAFEGUARDS—SECTION 164.308

Administrative safeguards are administrative actions, and policies and procedures, to manage the selection, development, implementation, and maintenance of security measures to protect electronic protected health information and to manage the conduct of the covered entity's or business associate's workforce in relation to the protection of that information.[18]

Administrative safeguards are the nontechnical measures that a covered entity or business associate's management establishes regarding acceptable employee conduct, personnel procedures, and correct technology usage within the enterprise. Information security professionals memorialize and explain safeguards with various kinds of documentation. Common forms of documentation include:

- Policies—Management's documented statement of intent.
- Standards—Policy-mandated technical measures the organization will use to solve specific problems. Standards often specify the appropriate use of technology.[19]
- Guidelines—Suggested, usually strongly suggested, behavior recommendations that usually will be followed.

---

15. *Id.* § 164.306(d)(3)(i).
16. *Id.* § 164.306(d)(3)(ii)(A).
17. *Id.* § 164.306(d)(3)(ii)(B)(1)–(d)(1)(ii)(B)(2).
18. 45 C.F.R. § 164.304 (definition of "administrative safeguards").
19. This use of the word "standard" is in the engineering sense of the word, and is different from references to regulations or groups of regulations. See section 3.B n.8 *supra*.

- Procedures—Documented methods for implementing mandated processes.

These safeguards range from policies, which are the most general, to procedures, which are the most specific. Standards and guidelines are in between. Addressable implementation specifications are akin to guidelines in the sense that both are not mandatory, but they are not identical. The Security Rule has a specific definition for, and procedures for applying, addressable implementation specifications.[20]

The Security Rule requires the organization to establish (through its management's approved documentation) and implement (carry out and enforce) policies and procedures for administrative safeguards in these areas:[21]

- Security management process;
- Assigned security responsibility;
- Workforce security;
- Information access management;
- Security awareness and training;
- Security incident procedures;
- Contingency plans; and
- Evaluation.

The subsections of this section (5.B) discuss each of these areas in turn.

1. Security Management Process (Standard)—Section 164.308(a)(1)(i)

Implement policies and procedures to prevent, detect, contain, and correct security violations.

The security management process section and its implementation requirements below are the foundation of all of the administrative security safeguards. Keys to the management process are:

- Management support at the highest levels;
- Initially defining policies and procedures;
- Execution and enforcement of policies and procedures; and
- Maintenance, periodic update, and diligent refinement of policies and procedures.

---

20. See section 5.A.2 *supra.*
21. 45 C.F.R. § 164.308(a).

No single policy will fit all covered entities and business associates, and the Security Rule specifically recognizes that security policies must align with business imperatives.[22] Protecting the security of PHI is part of overall covered entity or business associate healthcare business management. Moreover, an organization should coordinate its HIPAA compliance effort with its overall security function, especially hybrid entities. A healthcare-focused organization may have a single HIPAA-compliant security policy. Other entities, including hybrid entities, may have a general overall security policy supplemented by a HIPAA-compliant subordinate policy covering healthcare operations and components. These subordinate HIPAA security policies can augment the organization's general security policy and enhance the organization's security infrastructure.

A Security Rule-compliant security policy must contain at least the following four required sections: risk analysis, risk management, sanction policy, and information system activity review. The policy containing the process and results of the risk assessment should be in writing, which may be in electronic form.[23]

a. Risk Analysis (Required)—Section 164.308(a)(1)(ii)(A)

Conduct an accurate and thorough assessment of the potential risks and vulnerabilities to the confidentiality, integrity, and availability of electronic protected health information held by the covered entity or business associate.

At the heart of HIPAA compliance is an assessment of confidentiality, integrity, and availability risks to PHI. A risk assessment is the foundation of all future compliance efforts. Indeed, the Office for Civil Rights (OCR) has cited the lack of a risk assessment as a basis for enforcement activity.[24] An organization cannot know what information or data it needs to protect and what safeguards to implement until it has completed a thorough risk assessment. The first part of this section discusses who should conduct a risk assessment for an organization, and the second part discusses the content of a risk analysis.

---

22. *See id.* § 164.306(b)(2) (permitting consideration of various business factors in a decision concerning which security measures to use).

23. *Id.* § 164.316(b)(1)(i).

24. See section 7.F *infra.*

i. Who Should Conduct a Risk Assessment?

The threshold consideration for any covered entity or business associate conducting a risk assessment should be the identity of the team or person who will conduct it. Larger entities may have internal auditors or security professionals with the expertise, time, and resources to conduct their own risk assessments. These larger entities may believe that maintaining a team of internal auditors or security professionals is the most cost-effective way to conduct risk assessments. The money spent on hiring auditors or security professionals as full time employees may, over time, be much less than the fees charged by outside consulting firms. Moreover, internal auditors or security professionals have greater knowledge of their own organizations than outside consultants and therefore are likely to be more efficient in conducting their risk assessments.

Nonetheless, larger entities may wish to obtain a risk assessment from an outside consulting firm for various reasons. First, the organization may not want to devote internal resources to conducting risk assessments. Some entities maintain lean information technology and security staffing, and spending the time and effort to conduct a risk assessment may prevent staff members from performing their critical daily activities. Second, the organization may believe that an independent risk assessment places it in a better position to defend the risk assessment later. An independent risk assessment may have more credibility to regulators or triers of fact questioning the security decisions made by the organization in an investigation, audit, enforcement action, or lawsuit. Third, entities with knowledge of potential or actual critical vulnerabilities may want to use outside counsel to hire an outside consulting firm to conduct the risk assessment. Entities can seek to protect communications between the outside consulting firm, acting as an extension of outside counsel, and the organization's personnel discussing the critical vulnerabilities with the attorney-client privilege. The facts and data about the underlying vulnerabilities are not protected by the privilege, but the communications may be protected.

Smaller entities conducting risk assessments have more resource constraints concerning risk assessments and therefore should give careful thought to who will conduct their risk assessments. Smaller entities are much less likely than larger entities to have internal resources with the expertise, time, and resources to conduct a thorough risk assessment. As shown in the next subsection, a risk assessment may involve complicated and time-consuming activities. Many smaller entities will want to outsource the risk assessment to an outside consulting firm. There are many smaller consulting firms charging reasonable rates capable of conducting thorough risk assessments.

Some small organizations may want or need to conduct a risk assessment themselves. They may have a very simple information technology infrastructure and may be unable or unwilling to spend the money to hire an outside consulting firm. Such entities should carefully consider their situations before making the decision to conduct their own risk assessments. Although a great deal of data security and HIPAA compliance information is freely available or available at low cost, these smaller entities are taking a considerable risk that their knowledge and experience are insufficient for the job. Moreover, conducting a risk assessment would distract staff members from their daily activities and may not be worth the money saved. Entities with so few resources that they cannot afford an outside consulting firm to perform a risk assessment, however, may be taking on so great a level of risk in the HIPAA compliance and other areas of operations that they should question whether or not they should be in business at all or at least should consider not conducting standard HIPAA electronic transactions and thereby remain outside the scope of the HIPAA Security Rule.

ii. What Should a Risk Assessment Contain?

The Security Rule does not state what a compliant risk analysis contains, leaving the content of the risk analysis to the discretion of the covered entity or business associate. The covered entity or business associate may benefit from reviewing previous risk analyses, security audits, and other assessments to compare the current risk profile with previous ones.

Information security professionals, however, generally use four components for their risk analyses: asset identification and valuation, threat identification, vulnerability identification, and risk identification.

Asset Identification and Valuation. The term "assets" refers to items of value to the covered entity or business associate. Assets include (among other things) computer hardware, software, records, PHI, and other information. Asset identification and valuation involve inventorying and listing assets to be considered within the scope of the risk assessment. Under the Security Rule, the focus is on inventorying PHI and those assets containing, processing, or transmitting PHI. In short, the covered entity or business associate must know what PHI it possesses and where it is located and communicated.

In order to identify the risks to PHI accurately and limit the scope of the risk assessment, the assets analyzed should be limited to avoid sweeping in threats and vulnerabilities relevant to the larger organization, system, or application but not to PHI. Once identified, the covered entity or business associate needs to assign the appropriate value to each asset, which can be monetary or simply a qualitative measure of the asset's value (e.g., high, medium, or low). The value of the information should account for its sensitivity.

Threat Identification. The covered entity or business associate should determine the threats facing its PHI-related assets. A threat is a possible future negative event that can damage an asset vulnerable to such a threat. Information security threats have the potential to compromise the confidentiality, integrity, or availability of information. Threats may be intentional, such as a hacker attempting to break into a network. Likewise, terrorist attacks may affect physical facilities hosting information systems processing or storing PHI. Additionally, though, threats may also be inadvertent, such as the mistyping of an e-mail address, which may be attributable to natural human carelessness or fatigue. Threats may extend beyond human conduct, whether intentional or not, to natural or physical phenomena. For instance, hurricanes, tsunamis, floods, fires, and earthquakes pose threats to the availability of information when they strike data centers, offices, and the equipment operating in them.

In identifying threats, risk assessors may be able to identify a large range of threats. Some will be severe and likely threats. Others will be more remote, unlikely, and insignificant in impact. The threats that are reasonably anticipated are the ones on which risk assessors should focus most of their attention.

Vulnerability Identification. The covered entity or business associate should next ascertain the extent to which it is vulnerable to certain threats. The covered entity or business associate should determine what safeguards are currently in place to address specific threats. They should also assess the strengths and weaknesses of their safeguards.

A vulnerability is a weakness in an asset that allows a threat to damage that asset. This weakness can stem from the lack of a safeguard designed to protect the asset, a weakness in the safeguard, or in a characteristic of the asset itself. Threats have the potential of exploiting these weaknesses to damage the confidentiality, integrity, or availability of the asset. Vulnerabilities, however, only exist in the context of specific threats. Thus, the covered entity or business associate must carefully consider which threats are relevant to it and its PHI when assessing the vulnerability of an asset to a particular threat.

Risk Identification. The risk identification step analyzes risk based on the likelihood that a threat will exploit a vulnerability and the impact that event would have on the vulnerable asset. The covered entity or business associate can use existing questionnaires, interviews with experts, past history, and other means to determine the risks the organization may encounter. The covered entity or business associate should document potential risk elements as part of its risk management process. High risks are those involving threats that occur frequently and/or exploit vulnerabilities of high-value assets. Low risks are those where a minor vulnerability may expose a low-value asset to unlikely or infrequent compromise or loss. Even when the risk identification step is completed there is a remaining "unidentified risk." That is, risks may arise from threats that assessors cannot reasonably discover or identify.

In the process of identifying risks, it may become apparent to risk assessors that the covered entity or business associate should implement or strengthen certain safeguards. These recommendations can inform the risk management process described below.[25] Risk assessors may also be able to identify areas where risk is likely to remain, even after reasonable and appropriate safeguards are put into place.

Security professionals use two analytic methodologies used to quantify risk: qualitative and quantitative risk analysis.

Qualitative Risk Analysis. Not only does risk analysis involve the evaluation of the probability and frequency that an identified threat will exploit a vulnerability, but it also involves measuring the anticipated impact that exploiting the vulnerability will have on the organization. Each risk is analyzed in terms of its anticipated impact (severity) and its probability or frequency (occurrence). Qualitative risk analysis classifies risk into categories of severity and occurrence such as "low," "medium," and "high." The outcome of this risk analysis may be represented in table 5.1.

The table shows one example of how assessors can categorize different types of risks. It is merely an example. Note also that the numbers 1 through 9 are categories and do not necessarily connote a ranking

---

25. See section 5.B.1.b *infra*.

Table 5.1. Qualitative Risk Analysis

Risk	Severity	Occurrence
1	Low	Low
2	Low	Medium
3	Low	High
4	Medium	Low
5	Medium	Medium
6	Medium	High
7	High	Low
8	High	Medium
9	High	High

of risk. At times, for instance, addressing a very high-frequency, low-severity threat (e.g., spam not containing malicious code) may take precedence over addressing a high-severity, rare threat (e.g., a meteor destroying a facility).

The risk-managed organization will categorize possible risks and then focus its energy first on the high-severity, high-occurrence risks. Once the most significant risks are addressed, it can move on to lower risks.

This approach, while conceptually straightforward, is very subjective. In the absence of objective information, senior management often relies heavily upon its judgment to classify risk, making its decisions potentially difficult to justify to auditors, regulators, and other managers. The covered entity or business associate should carefully document all the objective information, subjective judgment, and other rationales underlying a qualitative risk analysis.

Quantitative Risk Analysis. Some risks lend themselves to an analysis that estimates loss in financial terms. This kind of analysis assesses:

F—the expected or estimated Frequency (events per year) of occurrence of the threat

L—the anticipated Loss from the vulnerable asset of each successful occurrence

V—the probability that the threat successfully exploits a Vulnerability

E—the Expected Loss each year from the identified risk

The expected loss each year, E, can be calculated by using the following formula:

$$E = F \times L \times V$$

An organization should prioritize risks according to its expected losses. It can address the high-risk threats first and move on to lower-risk threats later. Some security professionals, however, point out limitations inherent in a quantitative risk analysis. Obtaining reliable data on the frequency and probability that a threat will exploit a vulnerability can be difficult. Because threats and vulnerabilities vary by organization, widely aggregated risk data may not be useful. Moreover, information security threats, while essentially independent variables, can be influenced by the value of an asset or its vulnerabilities to attack. Consequently, even reliable threat data may not yield accurate estimates of expected losses. Accordingly, in situations where quantitative risk analysis is not possible or meaningful, an organization may be limited to analyzing its risk in a qualitative fashion.

As mentioned earlier, the Security Rule does not define how an organization must conduct its risk analysis. No matter what approach the covered entity or business associate takes in analyzing its PHI security risk, whether qualitative or quantitative, it should carefully document all elements of the analysis and understand that auditors, regulators, business managers, and opposing counsel may challenge the results sometime in the future.

Risk assessment is complete once the above steps for asset identification and valuation, threat identification, vulnerability identification, and risk identification have been completed.

b. Risk Management (Required)—Section 164.308(a)(1)(ii)(B)

Implement security measures sufficient to reduce risks and vulnerabilities to a reasonable and appropriate level to comply with § 164.306(a).

Risk management describes the continuous, iterative process of:

1. Reviewing the results of the organization's risk analysis to assess the effectiveness of current safeguards to provide assurances of confidentiality, integrity, and availability of PHI in light of reasonably anticipated threats, and to identify any gaps in effectiveness that create risk;
2. Analyzing recent changes to the organization's environment, including such factors as (a) implementation of new technology and associated vulnerabilities; (b) developments in new threat technology; (c) changes to organizational structure and business goals; and (d) changes in applicable law;

3. Measuring and prioritizing risks and corresponding mitigation safeguards and other measures, and incorporating them into a risk management plan; and

4. Implementing those mitigation measures defined in the risk management plan. As mentioned above, the Security Rule permits flexibility in implementing security measures that are "reasonable and appropriate." Accordingly, the covered entity or business associate must apply its business judgment in managing existing and new risks.

The risk management plan should address how each identified risk is to be managed to an acceptable level. Risks may be prioritized on the basis of degree of risk, magnitude of harm that a threat could cause, the cost to mitigate a vulnerability, business and operational goals and critical needs, and expected effectiveness of mitigation measures. This requirement's objective is to eliminate as much expected loss as is "reasonable and appropriate." The covered entity or business associate can address any residual expected loss in its security documentation. The organization may shift risk via insurance coverage or indemnities. Finally, it may decide to accept certain risks. The risk management plan identifies the specific mitigation measures that are taken to address the risks to the confidentiality, integrity, and availability of the covered entity or business associate's PHI.

In determining what safeguards are necessary to reduce risks and vulnerabilities to a "reasonable and appropriate" level, the covered entity or business associate should consider the following factors:

- The size, complexity, and capabilities of the covered entity or business associate;
- The covered entity's or the business associate's technical infrastructure, hardware, and software security capabilities;
- The cost of security measures; and
- The probability and criticality of potential risks to PHI.[26]

The risk management process results will drive the organization's further efforts to manage PHI security. The covered entity or business associate is not expected to eliminate all risks. Instead, the Security Rule requires the covered entity or business associate only to manage the risks to a reasonable and appropriate level, based upon its risk analysis.

---

26. 45 C.F.R. § 164.306(b)(2).

When risk management requires the procurement of new hardware, software, or services to implement or strengthen safeguards, the covered entity or business associate should determine whether the costs are worth the benefits of those new products or services. In addition, the covered entity or business associate will have to integrate any new purchases with its existing technology, systems, and personnel. Security solutions that address a vulnerability, but disrupt other systems and services, may create more problems than they solve.

Moreover, new technology procurements are not a panacea for complying with the Security Rule, though. Some security threats may require changes to policy or procedures or more extensive training programs for the organization's personnel. To comply with the Security Rule, the covered entity or business associate must consider all sources of risk, including those sources stemming from its people and processes and not just from its technology. In short, there is no "security in a box" that an organization can simply purchase to have instant compliance with the Security Rule.

c. Sanction Policy (Required)—Section 164.308(a)(1)(ii)(C)

Apply appropriate sanctions against workforce members who fail to comply with the security policies and procedures of the covered entity or business associate.

The covered entity or business associate must have the policies and accompanying procedures in place to take action against individuals who violate its documented security policy. The rule does not state what those sanctions must be, but instead requires them to be reasonable and appropriate. For instance, an organization may impose various disciplinary measures for security violations up to and including termination. The purpose of the Sanction Policy is to hold employees and contractors accountable for their actions.

Implementing a sanctions policy involves several steps. First, the policy should be in writing and should address the different types of sanctions imposed for different types of security violations. The policy should also address procedures for investigating, reporting, and resolving security violations. The covered entity or business associate should plan in advance what sanctions are appropriate for what kinds of conduct. Second, the covered entity or business associate must inform its staff of the sanctions policy to set expectations of appropriate conduct, deter violations of security policies, and provide fair, advance warning of sanctions that security violations may trigger. Some organizations include a discussion of sanctions in their security training programs. Third, organizations should actually implement the sanctions policy as violations occur, and implement the policy in a consistent, even-handed manner.

Some organizations integrate accountability for security compliance into their human resources practices. For instance, managers may consider security compliance as one topic on which workers are reviewed as part of an annual or other work performance or compensation review process. A worker's failure to comply with security requirements may lead to consequences during the review process, such as lower compensation or taking other corrective actions. Entities including security as a review topic show that they are taking security requirements seriously, and workers understand that security compliance becomes a pocketbook issue.

d. Information System Activity Review (Required)—Section 164.308(a)(1)(ii)(D)

> Implement procedures to regularly review records of information system activity, such as audit logs, access reports, and security incident tracking reports.

This requirement specifies that the covered entity or business associate must set up its information system monitoring or audit function and also must review the data collected. The procedures in the organization's security policy should define what information is collected and when and now it is to be reviewed. The sanction policy should describe what the implications are for discovered abuse/misuse. The purpose of this requirement is to detect security incidents and breaches and provide the evidence needed to take remedial actions.

Organizations should consider the following factors when establishing policies concerning the review of information system activity. First, they should designate a person or group to take charge of the review process for various items of activity information. Second, they should determine how often personnel should review activity information and how much of the information personnel can review practically. If the activity information, such as log files, is too voluminous to review in total, organizations may be able to use automated tools to alert responsible staff members of especially serious events. Finally, organizations should address the need to retain in a secure fashion activity information that may become evidence in later legal proceedings to provide assurances against falsification, tampering, and corruption and to maintain a chain of custody.[27]

2. Assigned Security Responsibility (Standard)—Section 164.308(a)(2)

Identify the security official who is responsible for the development and implementation of the policies and procedures required by this subpart for the covered entity or business associate.

One of the required administrative safeguards is the organization's documented appointment of a responsible official who has direct, accountable responsibility for Security Rule-required policies and procedures. In larger entities, this official will frequently have a chief security officer, chief information security officer, or chief privacy officer title. In smaller entities, an office manager might serve this role. Note that this official is not required to have policy approval responsibilities, but rather just policy development and implementation responsibilities. This official need not be the same individual who serves as chief privacy officer or is otherwise responsible for compliance with the Privacy Rule.

The organization's documentation should include a description of the security official's responsibilities and tasks. The covered entity or business associate should, in turn, notify its staff and downstream business associates of the security official's role. Business associates should inform their covered entity and business associate customers of the security official's role. Finally, the covered entity or business associate should tell staff and these other entities of the security official's contact information to ensure proper and timely reporting of security incidents to the security official and to coordinate responsive actions. Staff, upstream entities, and downstream entities should know what and how they should communicate with the security official.

3. Workforce Security (Standard)—Section 164.308(a)(3)(i)

Implement policies and procedures to ensure that all members of its workforce have appropriate access to electronic protected health information, as provided under paragraph (a)(4) of this section, and to prevent those workforce members who do not have access under

---

27. In many jurisdictions, parties have an obligation under applicable law to preserve evidence relevant to reasonably anticipated litigation. The reasonable anticipation of litigation triggers the evidence preservation obligation, and logs and other records of information system activity may be some of the evidence an organization would need to preserve.

paragraph (a)(4) of this section from obtaining access to electronic protected health information.

People are both the weakest link and greatest threat in any security program. Information security professionals frequently discuss mitigating the "insider threat" to information systems. High-profile cases of medical records "snooping" underscore the need to limit PHI access to individuals authorized and having a need to access PHI. In one particular case, a nurse at Ronald Reagan UCLA Medical Center accessed Farah Fawcett's medical records and sold the records to the *National Enquirer.* Other celebrities at UCLA Health Systems Hospitals affected by similar snooping incidents include Michael Jackson, former California First Lady Maria Shriver, and singer Britney Spears. UCLA Health System ended up paying $865,500 as part of a settlement of a federal investigation arising out of these incidents.[28]

To address this combined vulnerability and threat, the covered entity or business associate must institute policies, procedures, and standards for ensuring that the security risk of the workforce itself is managed. Only workers with a need to access PHI should have that access. Those workers without the need to access PHI should not be given access rights, and workers without explicit access rights must be denied access to PHI. To comply with these administrative safeguards, the organization, through administrative procedures, should meet the following three specifications: authorization and/or supervision, workforce clearance procedure, and termination procedures.

a. Authorization and/or Supervision (Addressable)—Section 164.308(a)(3)(ii)(A)

> Implement procedures for the authorization and/or supervision of workforce members who work with electronic protected health information or in locations where it might be accessed.

This specification calls for the implementation of workforce security procedures that define and address allowable access, such as which workers should have authorization to view and change PHI, where such procedures are reasonable and appropriate. Under the standard of the previous subsection, management must document the procedure for

---

28. *See* Molly Hennessy-Fiske, *UCLA Hospitals to Pay $865,500 for Breaches of Celebrities' Privacy,* L.A. Times, Jul. 8, 2011, http://articles.latimes.com/print/2011/jul/08/local/la-me -celebrity-snooping-20110708.

granting access to PHI. This specification addresses how an organization grants access rights to PHI. Further, organizations should properly supervise those who do have access.

For instance, the covered entity or business associate should have a clear reporting structure to establish who has authority to make what decisions about staff access to PHI under what circumstances, and who has the responsibility to supervise staff. The covered entity or business associate should train staff members concerning that reporting structure and the authorization process. A helpful step to having a clear reporting structure is having written job descriptions for each position that identify and define levels of access to PHI to be granted to that position. Descriptions of levels of access should address the appropriateness of granting rights such as reviewing records, creating new records, modifying records, and deleting records; the circumstances for exercising these rights; the purposes for proper exercise of these rights; and the types of records to which these rights should apply.

Procedures should cover the process by which a new member of an organization's workforce gains access to PHI. Frequently, an organization's job requisition to be filled by a new worker will correspond to a job description that references appropriate access to PHI. The covered entity or business associate should consider whether a worker's role requires access to PHI and, if so, which categories of PHI. Once the new worker starts his or her job or role, his or her supervisor may need to give approval to the worker's access to information systems resources, including access to the PHI appropriate to the worker's function.

Managers can supervise workforce members by monitoring access to PHI, providing continuing oversight and training concerning appropriate PHI access, evaluating their performance of security responsibilities, and holding them accountable for violations. As mentioned in section 5.B.1.c above, some entities are including security responsibilities as a topic of annual compensation and performance reviews. Making security a part of general oversight and management demonstrates the organization's commitment to security.

b. Workforce Clearance Procedure (Addressable)—Section 164.308(a)(3)(ii)(B)

> Implement procedures to determine that the access of a workforce member to electronic protected health information is appropriate.

Under the workforce security standard, management must define and document the criteria and procedures for granting PHI access to those workers who need it as part of their job responsibilities. Under this addressable implementation specification, an organization must (if reasonable and appropriate) implement procedures to ensure that it hires trustworthy and competent staff members for a position whose job description entails access to PHI. An organization can more efficiently make a determination of the appropriateness of access to PHI before hiring a staff member, in contrast to hiring the person and making a later determination about the appropriateness of access, which may result in the need to terminate an unqualified new hire. Making this threshold determination involves comparing the potential hire's skills, qualifications, background, and experience against the job description to determine whether the potential hire is competent. Checking qualifications can (if reasonable and appropriate) involve checking references and objective sources of information, such as transcripts from educational institutions and certifications, to make sure that the potential hire does, in fact, possess the qualifications he or she purports to have.

Determining appropriate hires also might include background screenings and other assessments to determine whether a particular individual should have access to PHI. For instance, a criminal background check may be reasonable and appropriate for certain positions. Such background checks could reveal that a candidate for a position with access to PHI has convictions for fraud, suggesting that the candidate is not trustworthy. The covered entity or business associate can use that information in deciding which candidate to choose for a position.

c. Termination Procedures (Addressable)—Section 164.308(a)(3)(ii)(C)

Implement procedures for terminating access to electronic protected health information when the employment of, or other arrangement with, a workforce member ends or as required by determinations made as specified in paragraph (a)(3)(ii)(B) of this section.

This specification aims to prevent the situation of an employee or contract worker who is terminated or otherwise leaves an organization but is still able to access PHI. This situation may occur because the information technology (IT) security staff is not advised of the termination, or if aware, fails to disable the departing worker's information system access. Failing to terminate departing workers' access leaves the organization's systems vulnerable to the departing workers' misuse and abuse at a particularly risky time—right after termination. This addressable specification calls for the covered entity or business associate to have procedures to manage this risk if reasonable and appropriate. One example is a set of procedures to notify security staff promptly of a termination so that access to PHI can be revoked in a timely manner.

The covered entity or business associate should have a standard set of termination procedures for returning property of the covered entity or business associate, including company-owned computing devices, keys, identification badges, cards used for physical access to a facility, and tokens for access to IT resources. In addition, the covered entity or business associate should have backups of business information including PHI so that the covered entity or business associate does not lose information if the termination does not smoothly transition the departing worker's information. There may be circumstances where some information, which may include PHI, is unavoidably under the sole control of the departing worker. One example may be information on the mobile device or portable media of a worker who has left the office before backups were made. The covered entity or business associate should have procedures to obtain and transition such information to staff members who are staying. Transitioning the information helps to avoid its loss. Finally, the organization's procedures should include provisions to terminate user accounts for accessing IT systems containing PHI. Procedures may need to vary based on the circumstances of the termination. That is, the risk of misuse following a voluntary departure or retirement is lower than in situations where a worker is laid off or fired for cause. Whatever standard procedures the covered entity or business associate establishes, the covered entity or business associate should apply them consistently and even-handedly when terminating workers.

As mentioned in section 5.A.1 above, the terms "worker" and "workforce" broadly cover employees, independent contractors, workers placed with an organization by a staffing agency, trainees, and volunteers. This specification speaks of "employment of a workforce member," which seems to imply an employer-employee relationship between the covered entity or business associate and the workforce member. Nonetheless, the word "employment" does not imply that a "workforce member" must be an employee. Moreover, organizations should apply the practices described in this subsection to all departing workers who have access to PHI, including independent contractors, workers placed by staffing agencies, trainees, and volunteers.[29]

---

29. See section 5.A.1 n.8 *supra*.

4. Information Access Management (Standard)—Section 164.308(a)(4)(i)

Implement policies and procedures for authorizing access to electronic protected health information that are consistent with the applicable requirements of subpart E of this part.[30]

This section directs an organization's management to develop, document, and implement policies and procedures for authorized access to PHI. The policies and procedures must be consistent with the applicable requirements of subpart E of 45 C.F.R. part 164, which refers to the Privacy Rule. Implementation specifications cover three specific areas, one required and two addressable, as discussed in the sections below.

a. *Isolating Health Care Clearinghouse Functions (Required)—Section 164.308(a)(4)(ii)(A)*

If a health care clearinghouse is part of a larger organization, the clearinghouse must implement policies and procedures that protect the electronic protected health information of the clearinghouse from unauthorized access by the larger organization.

Healthcare clearinghouses are covered entities. At the same time, they may be part of a larger organization that may or may not be related to healthcare. If a healthcare clearinghouse is part of a larger organization, it must erect a PHI information flow barrier or "Chinese wall" between the healthcare clearinghouse function and any of the other business functions of the larger organization.

The healthcare clearinghouse should scrutinize areas where overlap or crossover of PHI may occur, such as information systems and resources (including shared cloud computing facilities), physical facilities, and staff members. If reasonable and appropriate, the healthcare clearinghouse may want to isolate the network and information systems resources of the clearinghouse function entirely from systems serving other operations. The healthcare clearinghouse should also include, as a component of its security awareness training, proper procedures for isolating the PHI of the clearinghouse from the rest of the organization.

b. *Access Authorization (Addressable)—Section 164.308(a)(4)(ii)(B)*

Implement policies and procedures for granting access to electronic protected health information, for example, through access to a work station, transaction, program, process, or other mechanism.

---

30. Subpart E is the Privacy Rule, 45 C.F.R. §§ 164.500–164.534.

The administrative procedures described in this implementation specification govern how organizations grant and control access privileges for PHI to authorized people in the organization. They must be implemented if they are reasonable and appropriate. When determining who in the organization should access applications, workstations, networks, systems, databases, or other intermediaries to PHI, management should consider policies that make access rights commensurate with the level of access needed to perform workers' job functions. The policies should limit access to the minimum number of people and minimum extent necessary for workers to perform their jobs.

Granting privileges that exceed the minimum required for proper job performance can add risk to PHI security and privacy. As discussed in sections 5.B.3 and 7.A.1, unauthorized access by insiders in healthcare facilities is a significant issue. High-profile stories about "snooping" into the medical records of celebrities underscore the need to control access to PHI to only those authorized to have such access and only to the extent permitted.

Under some circumstances, an organization may need to share PHI with an outside party that may have a need to know PHI concerning the patient. The covered entity or business associate should make an assessment as to whether that access is appropriate and permitted under the Privacy Rule. Even if granting access to a user is appropriate, the covered entity or business associate should limit that access to the minimum level necessary for the outsider to perform needed or desired functions.[31]

Part of the determination of whether access is appropriate involves "authenticating" the user, process, or device seeking to access PHI: ensuring that the person, entity, application, or process seeking access is who he, she, or it purports to be. "Authentication" means "[v]erifying the identity of a user, process, or device, often as a prerequisite to allowing access to resources in an information system."[32] The authentication process of an individual, for instance a member of a workforce, often has two separate steps, depending on the need for rigor in the authentication process.

---

31. The procedures for determining levels of access appropriate for certain roles is described in section 5.B.3 *supra*.

32. NAT'L INST. OF STANDARDS & TECH., NIST SPECIAL PUBL'N 800-53, SECURITY AND PRIVACY CONTROLS FOR FEDERAL INFORMATION SYSTEMS AND ORGANIZATIONS, at B-2 (Rev. 4, Apr. 2013), http://nvlpubs.nist.gov/nistpubs/SpecialPublications/NIST.SP.800-53r4.pdf.

First, an organization may verify the identity of the individual typically using identification documents to ensure that the individual to be granted access corresponds to a real-world identity. For instance, if an organization in the United States wishes to hire a new physician purporting to be Jane Smith, the organization will be required by immigration laws to check identification credentials during the hiring process to complete the U.S. Citizenship and Immigration Services Form I-9—Employment Eligibility Verification. Government-issued identification credentials allow the organization to determine whether there is, in fact, a real Jane Smith. Further authentication steps can link the Jane Smith job applicant to her credentials as a physician. This type of authentication process prevents people from using a fictitious identity.

Second, assuming that a real-world identity exists, the authentication process can ensure that an applicant or person seeking PHI access does, in fact, correspond to the previously identified real-world identity. For instance, in the example of physician Jane Smith, comparing the identification credentials to the person appearing before the organization to apply for the physician job can confirm that the person seeking the position is, in fact, Jane Smith. The organization would match the photo on the identification credential with the person presenting it. The purpose of this kind of authentication is to prevent the impersonation of a real person.

In addition, even if the covered entity or business associate hires and sets up an account for the real Jane Smith, the covered entity or business associate should have procedures to ensure that a person seeking access to PHI on its information systems at a given time is, in fact, the same Jane Smith. Again, the organization is controlling access to PHI by determining if the person seeking access to PHI is, in fact, who he or she purports to be and to prevent impersonation of an authorized user. Technical safeguards should be in place to control access. Technical safeguards can control access to a given workstation, program, process, or other system. Organizations can use technical safeguards to ensure that only authorized users can complete certain kinds of transactions.

If individuals, processes, or devices outside the organization are permitted access to PHI or information systems containing PHI, the organization will need to determine how to authenticate them. In the case of an outside individual whose employer is permitted PHI access, the organization could require the employer to authenticate the individual. Alternatively, the organization may want to reauthenticate the individual itself. The organization will need to determine whether or not it should reauthenticate the individual based on its risk assessment.

Various technical measures are available to control access to individuals. They include user name-password combinations, access tokens such as one-time password devices and smart cards, digital certificates,[33] and biometric devices such as fingerprint readers. Technical access control safeguards are discussed in more detail below in section 5.D.1.[34]

Finally, an organization can also authenticate a process or device. Various technical mechanisms can be used to authenticate a process or device, including Transport Layer Security, Secure Sockets Layer, and digital signatures. The organization may also authenticate the human sponsor seeking to establish the access and verify the authorization of the individual controlling the process or device to obtain that access.

c. Access Establishment and Modification (Addressable)—Section 164.308(a)(4)(ii)(C)

Implement policies and procedures that, based upon the covered entity's or the business associate's access authorization policies, establish, document, review, and modify a user's right of access to a workstation, transaction, program, or process.

People who move from job to job within an organization tend to accumulate information-access privileges along the way. This addressable provision calls for polices for the documented establishment and periodic review of a worker's PHI access privileges to ensure that the worker has appropriate access privileges to perform his or her current functions. These policies and procedures must be implemented if they are reasonable and appropriate. Granted privileges should be the minimum needed for a worker to perform his or her job.

From time to time, the covered entity or business associate should review the worker's access privileges. When discovered, unnecessary privileges should be removed. By contrast, promotions or increases in responsibilities may require increasing a worker's access privileges. The covered

---

33. For example, the Direct Address Certificate, which is used in conjunction with the Direct protocol, similar to e-mail, *see* Federal Health Architecture Program Mgmt. Office, Office of the Nat'l Coordinator for Health IT, Certificate Issuance and Assurance in Direct Messaging 14–15 (Mar. 25, 2015), *reprinted at* https://www.healthit.gov/sites/default/files /certificate_issuance_and_assurance_in_direct_messaging_final_4915.pdf

34. *See* 45 C.F.R. § 164.312(a).

entity or business associate should maintain records concerning which staff members have what access privileges and should protect these records against unauthorized alteration, corruption, or tampering.

5. Security Awareness and Training (Standard)—Section 164.308(a)(5)(i)

Implement a security awareness and training program for all members of its workforce (including management).

An organization must have a comprehensive security awareness and training program. The organization must provide security training to all new workers having access to PHI. People cannot perform their duties securely unless they are familiar with the organization's security policies and procedures. Awareness allows workers to grasp the importance of security and its role in protecting privacy. Training focuses on how to use the security features and maintain a secure information-processing environment.

Even after a new worker has received training, the new worker should know how to access instructional material on security procedures for later reference and people to whom the new worker can direct security questions or report incidents. Moreover, the covered entity or business associate should apply and enforce policies and procedures covered in the security awareness and training program consistently and in an even-handed fashion.

Recent trends confirm the importance of security awareness and training. First, OCR enforcement has focused on lost and stolen laptops and portable devices as the top threat addressed by enforcement activity.[35] The loss and theft of mobile devices are generally preventable threats with proper training. The second most common subject of enforcement activity has been improper disposal of PHI.[36] Again, training can eliminate most of the risk of improper disposal. The organization can train workers on the proper way to dispose of media containing PHI. Finally, training can help prevent the recent threats stemming from ransomware and other malicious software caused by users falling victim to phishing, spear phishing, and infection from websites.

Implementation of this requirement consists of four specifications as described below.

---

35. See *infra* section 7.F.
36. *See id.*

a. Security Reminders (Addressable)—Section 164.308(a)(5)(ii)(A)

Periodic security updates.

Training and awareness are continuous, not one-time events. The covered entity or business associate must, where reasonable and appropriate, have an ongoing program of periodic security awareness and training. Its goal should be to keep staff up-to-date on the latest risks and threats the organization is facing, as well as any changes in the organization's security programs, policies, or procedures. As mentioned in the previous section, the loss or theft of mobile devices, proper disposal of PHI, and preventing infection by malicious software, especially through phishing and ransomware, deserve particular attention in an organization's training program.

The covered entity or business associate should schedule periodic refresher courses on security awareness. It may also use informal security reminders and updates. For instance, some organizations display security training information on screen savers that users see on a daily basis when using their workstations. Other organizations use "gamification" to make use of security training software that includes an element of gaming competition and fun to promote interest and retention of information. E-mail "penetration tests" using social engineering can also be used to identify workers more likely to fall victim to phishing and malware (discussed in section 5.B.5.b below). The results of such tests can help organizations train workers how to avoid these threats. In addition, the organization may, from time to time, uncover an unusually urgent emerging threat. In that case, it may be reasonable and appropriate to hold immediate training in methods to address vulnerabilities exploitable by the threat.

The covered entity or business associate can also make use of refresher training sessions to make adjustments in the type and scope of training provided. The organization should assess the effectiveness of its training. If deficiencies appear in its training program, it should supplement its instruction at the next appropriate opportunity for refresher training.

b. Protection from Malicious Software (Addressable)—Section 164.308(a)(5)(ii)(B)

Procedures for guarding against, detecting, and reporting malicious software.

If reasonable and appropriate, the organization must have a policy and procedures on how it will protect itself from malicious software.

Given the frequency of recent attacks in the news, it is apparent that absent unusual circumstances, training workers on preventing malicious software will be reasonable and appropriate. Malicious software can be anything that affects PHI confidentiality, integrity, and availability. Examples of malicious software include viruses, worms, and Trojan horses. More recently, phishing and ransomware (discussed below) have emerged as particularly acute threats for infection by malicious software. Software can enter the environment from many sources including e-mail, employee-installed software, and websites.

The organization's security awareness and training should include instruction on avoiding harm from malicious software. Many of the sources of malicious software rely on "social engineering," that is, nontechnical means of bypassing security safeguards by prompting some response by a legitimate user. For instance, some virus-laden e-mails recite that their attachments contain images of a popular celebrity. These messages trick users who want to see the images into clicking on the attachment. Clicking on the attachment then executes code that installs the malicious software. Some training may also be important to prompt users to seek out patches and updates to antivirus software, or at least not defeat or obstruct automated processes to install patches and updates.

"Phishing" attacks are another means of social engineering and are a significant threat to information systems. "Phishing" refers to an attacker impersonating a legitimate business by sending an e-mail or other message appearing to come from the business. The e-mail urges the user to click on a link to a website. Sometimes, the website causes malicious software to infect a user's computer. In addition, the website may appear to be the business's legitimate log-in page and urge users to put in their log-in credentials—e.g., a user name and password. The attacker then harvests the log-in credentials provided by users and uses them to log into the website of the business, impersonate users, and steal money or conduct other illegal activities. While this section does not expressly mention phishing, it is arguably broad enough to encompass guarding against phishing in addition to ransomware, viruses, worms, and Trojan horses.

The organization can train workers to avoid phishing. For instance, they can talk about how legitimate organizations do not request personal information by e-mail and how users should be skeptical about misspelled links and requests to update personal information. Organizations can train workers about keeping filtering software updated.

Finally, organizations can train workers about "spear phishing," which is a specific kind of phishing in which attackers send e-mails appearing to be from specific legitimate sources to targeted individuals.[37]

More recently, a series of news stories have appeared concerning hospitals that have fallen victim to ransomware attacks.[38] "Ransomware is a form of malware that targets both human and technical weaknesses in organizations in an effort to deny the availability of critical data and/or systems."[39] Commonly spread via phishing or spear phishing attacks, ransomware is software that rapidly encrypts files or folders containing critical data. The organization is then unable to access its own critical data. The attacker demands payment of a ransom to provide the organization with the decryption key or other means to recover its data.[40]

To address the threat of ransomware, an organization should train its workers on how ransomware attacks occur and how they can be prevented. In addition, the organization can update its operating system software, application software, and antivirus or other security software to detect and prevent the latest types of ransomware. The organization should also regularly back up its data and ensure backups are not connected to the computers and networks they are backing up. Backups may be the only way an organization can recover its data following a ransomware attack.[41] The FBI guidance on ransomware contains a number of additional security controls that can help contain the threat.[42]

While some organizations have made ransom payments to attackers, the FBI does not recommend paying ransom demands.[43]

> Paying a ransom does not guarantee an organization will regain access to their data. In fact, some individuals or organizations were never provided with decryption keys after paying a ransom. Paying a ransom emboldens the adversary to target other organizations

---

37. Many resources are available to discuss steps an organization can take to prevent phishing attacks. *See, e.g.,* Fed. Bureau of Investigation, *Spear Phishers: Angling to Steal Your Financial Info* (Apr. 1, 2009), https://www.fbi.gov/news/stories/2009/april /spearphishing_040109.

38. *See Three US Hospitals Hit by Ransomware*, BBC NEWS, Mar. 23, 2016, http://www .bbc.com/news/technology-35880610.

39. FBI Cyber Div., Ransomware, at 1 [hereinafter Ransomware Data sheet], *reprinted at* http://www.americanbar.org/content/dam/aba/administrative/cyberalert/ransomware .authcheckdam.pdf (last visited Apr. 21, 2016) (log-in required).

40. *See generally id.*

41. *See id.* at 2.

42. *See generally id.*

43. *See id.*

for profit and provides a lucrative environment for other criminals to become involved. Finally, by paying a ransom, an organization is funding illicit activity associated with criminal groups, including potential terrorist groups, who likely will continue to target an organization.[44]

Nonetheless, the FBI recognizes the reality that sometimes businesses will pay the ransom because they feel they have no choice. "While the FBI does not advocate paying a ransom, there is an understanding that when businesses are faced with an inability to function, executives will evaluate all options to protect their shareholders, employees, and customers."[45] Indeed, some cyber-risk insurance policies provide first-party coverage for responding to ransomware attacks, which may include coverage for ransom payments themselves.

The best response to a ransomware threat is prevention. If the organization has taken steps to train workers to prevent attacks, it can avoid the threat altogether. If an attack has occurred, the organization may be able to resume operations by restoring data from backups. Since the Security Rule requires backups,[46] a compliant organization should be able to recover from a ransomware attack. The organization, however, may lose some amount of data. Nonetheless, if backups are unavailable or cannot be restored, an organization will need to make its own decision about whether to pay the ransom or not. Consulting IT consultants, forensic experts, and experts supplied by an insurance carrier will help an organization respond to a ransomware attack. In any case, an organization should plan for a possible attack pursuant to its security incident procedures.[47]

Finally, an organization's security program should include the topics of detecting and reporting malicious software. Antivirus and other security software provides alerts to users when scanning systems. Server software and network hardware devices can similarly detect malicious software and alert the organization to malware threats. The Security Rule does not contain an express requirement to use antivirus or other security software or hardware. Nonetheless, given the significant threat from malicious software, requiring the use of antivirus or other security

---

44. *Id.*
45. *Id.*
46. See section 5.B.7.a *infra.*
47. See section 5.B.6 *infra.*

software or hardware will likely be reasonable and appropriate.[48] The organization should obtain security software or hardware that covers the threats identified during its risk assessment.

The organization should also have procedures to cover reporting malicious software attacks. Section 5.B.6 below covers security incident handling. The organization should include malicious attacks among the threats addressed by its incident-handling procedures. Workers should report all malicious software detected using the systems discussed above in accordance with these procedures. More serious attacks, such as ransomware attacks, require immediate attention and responses.

c. Log-in Monitoring (Addressable)—Section 164.308(a)(5)(ii)(C)

Procedures for monitoring log-in attempts and reporting discrepancies.

The covered entity or business associate must, where reasonable and appropriate, have appropriate procedures for monitoring attempts to log into systems or applications that contain or can access PHI and for reporting anomalous events. Examples of these events include:

- Unusual times for a workstation to be active or logged in (such as well after business hours or during an employee's off time), which may indicate that an employee may be trying to obtain access to PHI outside of the scrutiny of his or her supervisor, or an attacker may be attempting to gain unauthorized access.
- Unusually high numbers of failed log-in attempts, which might indicate that an attacker is trying to log in but does not know the password, and is attempting to guess it.

Each organization, however, has different operations and working environments. For some entities, workers frequently travel to other countries in other time zones. Thus, it may be quite plausible that a remote worker traveling abroad might access system resources in the middle of the night in the time zone of the worker's principal office.

---

48. The discussion of malicious software appears in the administrative safeguards section on security awareness and training. The use of antivirus and other security software, however, is a technical security safeguard and perhaps HHS should have added a section to the technical safeguards section to cover it. The technical safeguards section does have provisions concerning integrity. See *infra* section 5.D.3. Arguably, the integrity requirement to prevent improper alteration or destruction includes protecting against systems becoming infected by malicious software. Nonetheless, a discussion of the use of security software and hardware appears here in the administrative safeguards section, because this is where HHS placed the topic of malicious software.

Each organization will need to configure its program to detect security incidents while minimizing false positive reports of anomalies.

Training is helpful in the area of log-on monitoring to inform users how to report log-on anomalies. One example of an anomaly is a user arriving at work and seeing that someone has already gained access to the user's account on the user's workstation. Personnel should also report anomalies pursuant to the organization's security incident procedures.[49]

d. Password Management (Addressable)—Section 164.308(a)(5)(ii)(D)

Procedures for creating, changing, and safeguarding passwords.

Organizations must, where reasonable and appropriate, implement password security procedures. These procedures will likely require all personnel to bear the responsibility for maintaining secure passwords. Passwords may have security standards themselves, such as:

- Minimum length
- Complexity (e.g., required numeric and nonalphabetical characters, lower and upper case letters, etc.)
- Difficulty of guessing (e.g., avoidance of dictionary words, maiden names, pets' names, spouse's name, etc.)
- Minimum and maximum usage time dictating when they must be changed
- Precluding a user from reusing a previous password (at least within a certain number of change cycles)

Password management and password confidentiality policies and procedures directly affect the security of the accessed system or application. If the covered entity or business associate makes use of passwords for access control, it should train its workforce concerning the choice and updating of passwords that are hard to compromise. If reasonable and appropriate, the organization may wish to make use of automated tools to enforce secure password use. For instance, some tools require users to change passwords after a defined time has elapsed.

Likewise, the organization may wish to require the use of password management applications. These applications generate complex passwords automatically and secure them in encrypted form on a workstation or mobile device. The user does not need to remember all the

---

49. See section 5.B.6 *infra*.

complex passwords used on his or her various accounts. Instead, the user remembers a single master password that unlocks the individual passwords for the user's accounts.

6. Security Incident Procedures and Responses—Section 164.308(a)(6)

a. Security Incident Procedures (Standard)—Section 164.308(a)(6)(i)

Implement policies and procedures to address security incidents.

The first step in implementing policies and procedures for security incident handling is developing and establishing those policies and procedures. Moreover, the personnel developing the policies and procedures should understand what a "security incident" is. The Security Rule defines "security incident" as follows: "Security incident means the attempted or successful unauthorized access, use, disclosure, modification, or destruction of information or interference with system operations in an information system."[50]

The organization should establish a person or team of people to develop incident-handling policies and procedures. Team members should have sufficient experience and training in incident response to create sound documentation. Further, the policies and procedures resulting from the team's work should have the support and priority from management to ensure their smooth implementation.

In addition to the team of people to *develop* the incident-handling policies and procedures, the policies and procedures should identify the team of people to *implement* the procedures and *respond* to incidents. For instance, organizations should consider the roles of management, operational personnel, IT personnel, public relations, and in-house or outside attorneys when establishing policies and procedures. Smaller organizations may have individual workers who are responsible for more than one of these roles.

When considering the composition of the team to investigate and report on security incidents, the organization should consider using outside counsel in combination with outside computer forensic and other investigative experts. Investigations from counsel and investigative personnel outside the organization typically have more credibility than strictly internal investigations. For instance, it may help in negotiations with government regulators looking into a breach to be able to

---

50. 45 C.F.R. § 164.304 (definition of "security incident").

report that the organization hired outside firms to conduct a thorough investigation of the breach.

Moreover, using outside counsel and investigators may help protect communications using the attorney-client privilege. Investigations of an incident may show that the organization had vulnerabilities. Communications between an investigator and workers may include discussions of ways in which the organization failed to take reasonable steps to protect PHI. If an organization uses internal investigators or hires outside investigators directly, all such communications are discoverable in litigation. These communications may constitute admissions of facts that may increase the organization's risk of legal liability.

By contrast, if the organization hires outside counsel and outside counsel in turn hires an investigative firm, the investigative firm can assist outside counsel with gathering information and assessing options. Expert investigators assisting counsel can help counsel understand the terminology, technology, and procedures involved with information security. Investigators can act as an extension of counsel. Structuring the investigative team in this way can maximize the chances that communications between the organization and such experts can be protected by the attorney-client privilege.[51]

Thus, when workers in the organization are discussing with investigators the vulnerabilities and instances in which the organization may have failed to reasonably protect PHI, the organization may be able to protect such communications from disclosure in litigation using the privilege. The underlying facts about the presence, absence, strengths, or weaknesses of safeguards remain fully discoverable. Nonetheless, the privilege may help protect the communications about the underlying facts.

In addition to planning the composition of the team to investigate security incidents, the organization should also identify the types of incidents that may occur, and plan and document how it should react to each type of incident. The organization's risk assessment involves identifying threats to PHI. Thus, assessors can help develop incident-handling policies by informing the drafters of the types of security incidents likely to result from these threats.

Some security incidents that require organizational monitoring and response were already specified in the Log-in Monitoring section

---

51. *See, e.g.*, United States v. Kovel, 296 F.2d 918, 922 (2d Cir. 1961) (protecting communications under the attorney-client privilege between a client and accountant retained by an attorney to help the attorney provide legal services).

above.[52] The organization must go further than log-in monitoring, however, and develop procedures to address any security incident it discovers. Procedures should address proper reporting of the incident, determining an appropriate response, communications and implementing the proper response, evidence preservation, and postincident assessment and remediation to detect, deter, and mitigate future similar incidents. Communications may include discussions by management and public relations personnel with affected parties outside the organization and the media to allay concerns and provide information concerning the organization's planned response.

Once personnel develop the policies and procedures, the organization should implement them. It should make personnel aware of its provisions and clearly communicate the incident reporting procedures as part of its overall training program. As incidents occur, personnel should consistently apply the policies and procedures.

In addition, organizations should determine whether a security incident triggers an obligation to notify affected individuals under the HIPAA Breach Notification Rule implemented via the HITECH Act and the HIPAA Final Omnibus Rule. Chapter 6 discusses the details of the HIPAA Breach Notification Rule, such as the triggers for a breach notification obligation, who must receive breach notifications, the logistics and timing of breach notifications, and the required content for notices. Organizations should also determine if a security incident triggers breach notification obligations under other applicable state or foreign breach notification laws. One such breach notification law is California's SB 1386.[53] Almost all of the states have similar notification laws. The organization should also determine if the HIPAA Breach Notification Rule preempts otherwise applicable state breach notification laws.

After the organization implements the policies and procedures and accrues experience in their workability, it should periodically review and update them to ensure they are effective and practical. Periodic testing and exercises to train the organization's workforce on the operation of incident-handling policies and procedures provide valuable insight

---

52. See section 5.B.5.c *supra*. *See also* 45 C.F.R. § 164.308(a)(5)(ii)(C).

53. CAL. CIVIL CODE §§ 1798.82, 1798.84. If a covered entity satisfies the HITECH Act's requirements for notification of affected residents of California, it is deemed to have met the requirements of SB 1386 for breach notification content. *Id.* § 1798.82(e). Nonetheless, making a breach notification under the HITECH Act does not excuse the organization from compliance with any other requirements under SB 1386. *See id.*

into the effectiveness of incident-handling policies and procedures. The policy development team should seek guidance from operational personnel, who may have advice on improving the effectiveness and efficiency of the incident-handling procedures. The organization should maintain documentation concerning how well the policies and procedures worked after testing or actual incidents, any needed improvements, and steps taken to improve policies and procedures.

b. Response and Reporting (Required)—Section 164.308(a)(6)(ii)

Identify and respond to suspected or known security incidents; mitigate, to the extent practicable, harmful effects of security incidents that are known to the covered entity or business associate; and document security incidents and their outcomes.

This section requires an organization to implement a security incident response program. Security awareness and training makes discovery of these kinds of events every worker's responsibility. Organizations must determine when a security incident has occurred, or at least when it suspects an incident has occurred. Moreover, the organization should train workers to follow through with reporting procedures pursuant to its incident-handling policies and procedures.

As a response to incidents, organizations must take steps first to find out exactly what happened. Only when the incident response team has the facts can it make an informed decision on a response. A response must also include reporting of the incident. Personnel should report the incident to management internally. Also, external reporting may be appropriate to allay the concerns of affected parties outside the organization. The organization may want to consider coordination of the investigation with law enforcement personnel. In addition, a breach notification to affected individuals and others may be required by the HIPAA Breach Notification Rule, which is discussed in chapter 6, as well as state or foreign breach laws such as California's SB 1386, as mentioned in the previous section.

The organization should also take steps to mitigate the effect of incidents. Mitigation may take many forms, including closing a vulnerability that caused the incident, changing passwords that had been misused, removing malicious software from systems, seeking to remotely wipe data from a lost or stolen mobile device, retrieving information that was lost or misappropriated, implementing a new security safeguard, or strengthening an existing safeguard. The organization should coordinate the timing of mitigation steps with management and law enforcement personnel. Law enforcement may want to investigate an active breach by leaving a vulnerability open and gathering evidence of an attack. In that case, an organization may need to wait until the investigation is done to close the vulnerability. Nonetheless, if there is no investigative need to keep vulnerabilities open, the organization should promptly close any vulnerabilities revealed by its investigation to mitigate harm.

In any event, organizations must document incident reporting and handling. Documentation can enable the organization to make a record of what happened, assist in managing future efforts to respond to the incident, and facilitate remedial actions to prevent similar incidents in the future. Organizations should also preserve any evidence of the incident that may assist in legal proceedings arising from the incident.

7. Contingency Plan (Standard)—Section 164.308(a)(7)(i)

Establish (and implement as needed) policies and procedures for responding to an emergency or other occurrence (for example, fire, vandalism, system failure, and natural disaster) that damages systems that contain electronic protected health information.

Information security personnel refer to requirements of this type as business continuity planning and/or disaster recovery. The disaster stemming from Hurricane Katrina along the Gulf Coast in the southeastern United States, the earthquake and tsunami that affected Japan, and Hurricane Sandy on the East Coast underscore the importance of implementing effective business continuity and disaster recovery procedures. Business continuity/disaster recovery consists of:

- Conducting business-impact assessment and analysis to identify critical business processes, services, and operations that need disaster recovery protection and to establish priorities and objectives for business continuity.
- Undertaking business continuity plan development to determine how critical business processes will maintain operations during an emergency or after a disaster.
- Determining the maximum allowable downtime of critical business processes, which determines the requirements for contingency planning, subsequent implementation, and disaster recovery; for example, a hospital needs to maintain patient care at all times, but may be able to tolerate some delay in processing administrative tasks.

The contingency plan must continue to maintain the confidentiality, integrity, and availability of PHI despite reasonably anticipated disasters or emergency events. The organization's risk assessment should identify potential disasters or emergencies that would threaten the availability of PHI. Measures to respond to a disaster or emergency should be reasonable and appropriate in light of their costs and feasibility.

As with security incident policies and procedures, an organization should identify a person or assemble a team to develop business continuity/disaster recovery policies and procedures. The personnel responsible for developing and/or implementing the policies and procedures should have the experience and management support necessary to execute their responsibilities. Management, operational personnel, IT personnel, public relations, and in-house or outside attorneys may all have appropriate roles in implementing business continuity/disaster recovery policies and procedures.

In addition, when a disaster or emergency occurs, the organization should put these policies and procedures into action. It should make workers aware of them during security training. Periodic testing of contingency plans is crucial for maintaining preparedness and ascertaining whether contingency plans are effective. Also, the organization should periodically assess and review the effectiveness of its contingency planning policies and procedures in order to incorporate improvements and updates.

a. Data Backup Plan (Required)—Section 164.308(a)(7)(ii)(A)

Establish and implement procedures to create and maintain retrievable exact copies of electronic protected health information.

The loss of PHI can disrupt the operations of an organization. Having backups of PHI available may prevent such disruption. Recent examples of hospitals needing backups to recover from ransomware attacks underscore the importance of an effective data backup plan.[54] Accordingly, the organization should regularly back up its data. The FBI has advised that backups may be the only way an organization can recover its data following a ransomware attack.[55]

---

54. See *supra* section 5.B.5.b.
55. Reasomware Data Sheet, *Supra* note 39, at 2.

Under this implementation specification, the organization must develop policies and procedures governing the backup and retrieval of PHI. Data backup planning and execution involves more than occasionally making a copy of PHI and storing it somewhere. Backup planning and implementation must be a formal process that includes the planning of:

- The location of backups.
  - For instance, the organization will want to consider having both local copies of PHI as well as remote copies. Local backups are frequently easier and faster to restore than remote copies. Nonetheless, a single disaster could affect both production systems and local backups, making it important to have a copy of PHI in a remote geographic location so that a local disaster does not cause the organization to lose all copies of PHI.
  - Backing up PHI using online or cloud computing storage facilities or services also helps mitigate the risk of a disaster affecting a single geographical location.
  - To prevent a ransomware attack affecting backups, the organization should ensure backups are not connected to the computers and networks they are backing up.[56]
- Backup frequency and maximum allowable data loss. The backup frequency (e.g., once per week, once per day, once per hour) and the location of the backup media determine the maximum allowable data loss (the amount of data that was not backed up, but now due to the emergency or other incident, is not retrievable).
- Maximum time to restore. This metric determines how long it will take to move the backup copy into service. Different methods of storage—tape, optical disk, cloud-based, etc.—require different amounts of time to restore.

Policies and procedures should identify people who are responsible for performing or overseeing the backup and retrieval functions. Moreover, security training should include procedures for users to take to make appropriate backups and to prevent the loss, destruction, or corruption of PHI. Many backup systems automatically make backups at configured intervals, thereby minimizing the risk arising from users forgetting to make backups.

---

56. *See id.* at 2.

PHI backups need the same security protection as PHI in its primary (production) systems for normal use. Backup policies and procedures must establish safeguards for backup data that are of equivalent strength to safeguards protecting production services in light of the risks. Note that the physical remoteness of backups stored off-site or in the cloud may reduce the risk of unauthorized access, although management of that physical location by third parties requires supervision by the organization.

All backup copies must be maintained and be recoverable. Maintenance and recoverability include the following:

- Proper backup media storage to ensure recoverability. All storage media have their specific physical (temperature, humidity, etc.) requirements to ensure recoverability years, even decades after initial backup. All backup media must be physically stored in a manner consistent with these requirements.
- Maintenance of restoration technology itself. With the rapid change of storage and retrieval technology, organizations have to plan on how they will maintain recoverability of their backups as storage technology and file formats continue to evolve. Moreover, storage media degrade over time and have limits to their useful lifespans. Information may need to be rotated onto fresh media at defined intervals to mitigate the risk of media degradation. Using cloud-based storage of backup data may offload some of the complexity of media rotation to a cloud service provider, which would be responsible for maintaining data in accessible form.

b. Disaster Recovery Plan (Required)—Section 164.308(a)(7)(ii)(B)

Establish (and implement as needed) procedures to restore any loss of data.

The purpose of maintaining backups of PHI is to have the backup copies available if the data on primary systems are unavailable. The organization can use the backup copy to restore the data to the primary systems or systems established for emergency-mode operation. Restoration of the data permits the organization to continue operations.

This specification requires the organization to document how it restores lost data. The organization's recovery/continuity plan should include how data will be restored on both its primary (production) site and any contingency (emergency) site. Data recovery policies and procedures should work together smoothly with backup policies and procedures.

c. Emergency Mode Operation Plan (Required)—Section 164.308(a)(7)(ii)(C)

Establish (and implement as needed) procedures to enable continuation of critical business processes for protection of the security of electronic protected health information while operating in emergency mode.

The ability to maintain operations during an emergency or ongoing disaster requires substantial planning and preparation. The organization must incorporate these plans into appropriate policies and procedures. Contingency planning should identify and prioritize which operations need to be continued during emergency-mode operation and which operations are not necessary to continue during emergency-mode.

In planning emergency-mode operation, the organization should consider, among others, the following variables:

- Selecting an appropriate site to process and store PHI during emergency-mode operation and configuration of systems at the chosen site.
- Time to load and start service at the site used as a backup (contingency site) to the primary site.
- Security of operations at the contingency site before, during, and after any disaster.
- Operations at the contingency site.
- Transition back to the primary site after the disaster is over, including a PHI backup for restoration at the primary site.
- Disaster plan maintenance—periodic review and any necessary updating.

Large organizations may find it reasonable and appropriate to have a dedicated "hot site" recovery location where backup information systems can provide services to ensure continuity. Smaller organizations may not find it reasonable and appropriate to incur the expense of equipment sitting idle in a dedicated facility waiting for a disaster, but should have plans for emergency-mode operations on-site or off-site, if the organization's primary facility is still usable. For instance, if electric surges damage computer equipment, but the facility is intact, emergency mode may simply involve obtaining new equipment and operating in emergency mode until systems are restored.

Continued operations in the organization's primary facility may not be possible, though. For instance, following a flood or earthquake, it may be appropriate for personnel to move salvaged equipment to temporary or new office space and obtain new or leased equipment to replace damaged systems. Once the primary facility is restored, it may be possible for the organization to transition back to the primary site.

In any case, regardless of whether the organization uses a designated hot site, or simply plans for off-site operations in cases where the primary facility is unavailable, the organization should provide security for PHI stored and used at the temporary facility. All of the administrative, technical, and physical safeguards that should be in place at the organization's primary facility should also be in place at the temporary facility. Policies and procedures should document how systems at the temporary facility provide equivalent levels of security in light of the risks.

d. Testing and Revision Procedures (Addressable)—Section 164.308(a)(7)(ii)(D)

> Implement procedures for periodic testing and revision of contingency plans.

To prove the viability of contingency planning, the organization must periodically test its current contingency plan to verify it will actually work during an emergency. Defining and documenting the proper scope, test frequency, and revisions to the contingency plan is left to the discretion of the organization.

Two types of testing are possible for contingency plans. First, the organization may conduct a "walk-through" exercise, in which staff meet in a meeting room and discuss how personnel would respond to a disaster. Second, the organization can actually simulate a disaster by shutting down systems and/or setting up operations in the temporary site for emergency operations. The second type of test will more accurately reflect how the organization will need to respond to a disaster, but it may not be feasible to conduct that kind of test, or even if feasible, it may not be reasonable or appropriate to conduct that kind of testing in light of the nature of the organization and the expense involved. In any case, the testing process can be part of the training or refresher training program of the organization to ensure that personnel are prepared to handle emergencies.

Following the testing process, an organization will likely gain experience from attempting to replicate the disaster recovery process. That experience should provide useful feedback for updating and improving policies and procedures established for contingency planning. The organization should solicit feedback from personnel involved in the testing and incorporate the feedback into the next version of the documentation. That feedback may cover the effectiveness of a contingency plan or the policies or procedures supporting the contingency plan.

e. Applications and Data Criticality Analysis (Addressable)—Section 164.308(a)(7)(ii)(E)

Assess the relative criticality of specific applications and data in support of other contingency plan components.

As discussed above under "Contingency Plan,"[57] the organization should, if reasonable and appropriate, identify critical business processes, services, and operations involving PHI, and prioritize them as part of the analysis of its business continuity needs. Some processes, services, and operations are more sensitive to downtime than others. For instance, systems for a hospital to access patient records are extremely critical, and the loss of access to patient records would be highly disruptive. By contrast, systems used for marketing are far less critical, and the organization can tolerate longer downtime for these systems. Therefore, the organization's criticality analysis should include a determination of maximum allowable downtime that the organization can permit and still meet its operational requirements and goals.

Keep in mind that information maintained in a noncritical application may be essential to a critical application. A complete business-impact assessment should identify these data dependencies so that the required data can be backed up or otherwise made available to support all critical applications.

8. Evaluation (Standard)—Section 164.308(a)(8)

Perform a periodic technical and nontechnical evaluation, based initially upon the standards implemented under this rule and, subsequently, in response to environmental or operational changes affecting the security of electronic protected health information, that establishes the extent to which a covered entity's or business associate's security policies and procedures meet the requirements of this subpart.

---

57. See section 5.B.7 above.

No policy or procedure lasts forever. Management must ensure that policies and procedures implement the requirements of the Security Rule. Moreover, it must keep policies and procedures current with prevailing security threats, information system vulnerabilities, and security and privacy risks. Management must identify the policy and procedure evaluation frequency (such as once per year, etc.) and document it in the organization's security policies and procedures. Organizations need to maintain version control of all policies and procedures. All employees and regulators should be working with the most recent version of a policy or procedure.

In addition to evaluating periodically the text of the policies and procedures themselves, the organization must also evaluate the implementation of the policies and procedures. That is, the organization must determine whether and to what extent the real-life procedures and operations of the organization implementing the documentation do, in fact, match what the organization describes in its documentation. The organization's auditors will likely do this as well. The organization can evaluate the effectiveness of its policies and procedures by a security assessment.

The purpose of most security assessments will be to maintain the effectiveness of an organization's security program over time. Nonetheless, some organizations may want assurances that they are, in fact, properly complying with the Security Rule. Moreover, organizations may undertake a security assessment to demonstrate the effectiveness of its security program to potential customers and business partners. Unlike security frameworks such as ISO 27001[58] or a Service Organization Control (SOC) 2 assessment,[59] the HIPAA Security Rule does not specify a defined assessment methodology or assessment output similar to an ISO 27001 certification or SOC 2 report.

Indeed, the Department of Health and Human Services (HHS) states, "there is no standard or implementation specification that requires a covered entity to 'certify' compliance."[60] An organization can

---

58. Int'l Org. for Standardization, Information technology—Security techniques—Information security management systems—Requirements, ISO/IEC 27001 (2d ed. Oct. 1, 2013).

59. *See generally* Am. Inst. of CPAs, Service Organization Control (SOC) Reports, http://www.aicpa.org/InterestAreas/FRC/AssuranceAdvisoryServices/Pages/SORHome.aspx (last visited Apr. 23, 2016).

60. HHS, Are We Required to "Certify" Our Organization's Compliance with the Standards of the Security Rule?, http://www.hhs.gov/hipaa/for-professionals/faq/2003/are-we-required-to-certify-our-organizations-compliance-with-the-standards/index.html (last visited Apr. 23, 2016).

use internal resources or an external firm to conduct an assessment.[61] Moreover, "HHS does not endorse or otherwise recognize private organizations' 'certifications' regarding the Security Rule, and such certifications do not absolve covered entities of their legal obligations under the Security Rule."[62]

In the absence of a mandatory assessment methodology or specific output document, one possible means of an organization demonstrating compliance is through the legal opinion of counsel. The organization can use a security consulting or auditing firm to perform a factual investigation concerning the presence, documentation, and effectiveness of specific administrative, physical, and technical safeguards. The firm can produce a report. Management may supplement its report with specific attestations. The attorney can rely on the security report and management attestation to generate a legal opinion. The legal opinion would state whether, based on the facts in the security report and management attestations, the organization is complying with the Security Rule. An organization may find a legal opinion can give it and others additional confidence that it is in compliance with the Security Rule.

The organization can use the Security Rule itself as a source for the initial criteria for a security assessment. Provisions of the Security Rule should act as a checklist to ensure compliance. Environmental and operational changes will then inform what criteria to use in future assessments. For instance, emerging threats and vulnerabilities may make it important to bolster certain assessment criteria.

The standard does not specify who must conduct the security assessment. Larger organizations may find it reasonable and appropriate to hire outside auditors or security consultants to conduct the assessment, while the expense of outside auditors or consultants may not be reasonable for smaller organizations. Smaller organizations may find it more appropriate to use internal personnel to conduct a self-assessment.

In addition to the assessors, it may be useful to include in the assessment process representatives from groups within the organization other than those responsible for the day-to-day operational management of the security function. For instance, management should oversee the process generally. Management should also communicate its support for the process to ensure that operational personnel understand the organization's

---

61. *See id.*
62. *Id.*

commitment to a thorough assessment. Also, larger organizations may have internal security auditors who can perform security assessments. They should be independent of the workers managing the systems and procedures being audited. An internal audit group should report to managers other than those overseeing the operations of the security function. Internal auditors should have the authority from management or a governing board to review and report on the status of the security of the information systems and related activities of the organization.

Moreover, the organization should consider consulting legal counsel to provide advice concerning the assessment and compare the results of the assessment to the Security Rule to make a bottom-line legal judgment as to whether the organization complies with the Security Rule or not. Whether or not an organization complies with the Security Rule is a legal question, which presumably a lawyer should answer, even if the facts and circumstances of what the organization is doing to comply can be described by internal or external security staff. Thus, nonlawyer security consultants who purport to advise organizations whether they are or are not complying with the Security Rule may be engaging in the unauthorized practice of law.

Likewise, it is beyond the competence of most lawyers to assess the adequacy and implementation of various kinds of security controls, especially the technical ones. Lawyers advising their clients about HIPAA security compliance will most likely need the assistance of information security professionals to help them understand information security concepts and controls, as well as their reasonableness. If an assessment is likely to show vulnerabilities and problems with the organization's protection of PHI, the organization should consider using outside counsel to hire outside security assessors. As discussed above in section 5.B.6.a, it may be possible to protect communications between the assessors and the organization under the attorney-client privilege, although the underlying facts about the organization's security posture are discoverable.

Once the organization has planned out how the assessment will occur, and who will undertake the assessment, it must then conduct the assessment. Assessment involves inspecting physical facilities, reviewing outputs from information systems and testing processes to determine the strength of technical controls, and communicating with staff concerning the effectiveness of administrative, physical, and technical security controls. Information systems may yield information via testing tools and system logs.

One issue the organization will need to consider is whether it should conduct some kind of penetration testing (using trusted personnel to attempt to gain unauthorized access to PHI to test the effectiveness of security controls). A penetration test of an online system may involve trying to gain unauthorized access to a website, application, or cloud-based service. A physical penetration test can involve sending an investigator into a facility to see if that person can access rooms, media, systems, and devices without authorization.

If reasonable and appropriate, the organization should undertake penetration testing. If the organization is conducting some kind of penetration testing, it will need to retain trained personnel, which involves the expense of hiring a firm or people to carry out the testing. Alternatively, for websites, online systems, and online applications, the organization may be able to make use of automated tools to conduct testing. Automated tools may involve an upfront expense of licensing the technology to conduct the testing, but ultimately may involve cost savings. The organization could also implement some combination of manual and automated testing for testing online systems.

Once the organization gathers and generates information from the assessment, it should analyze the results to determine if it reveals any weaknesses or vulnerabilities. Vulnerabilities may arise from the absence of a safeguard that should be in place or a weakness in a safeguard. Following the identification of vulnerabilities, the organization should develop a plan to implement any needed or recommended corrective actions.

The organization must document the process of its assessment, its analysis of the results, and plan for taking corrective actions. The organization should then circulate the documentation to key personnel to communicate the results. Since test results reveal vulnerabilities that attackers could exploit, the organization must also protect assessment results from unauthorized disclosure.

Finally, the organization should develop and implement a policy regarding repeating security assessments at designated time intervals. Periodic testing will enable the organization to ensure that changes in the organization and its systems do not degrade the level of its security. In addition, assessment outside the normal cycle of testing may become necessary if emergent new threats appear, if a breach or security incident occurred, or if the organization has made significant changes to its operating environment. Likewise, a new or special assessment may become necessary if amendments to the Security Rule or the creation or amendments of other federal or state healthcare security laws create new or different requirements.

9. Imposing Security Requirements on Business Associates— Section 164.308(b)

a. *Business Associates Contracts and Other Arrangements—Section 164.308(b)(1)*[63]

> A covered entity may permit a business associate to create, receive, maintain, or transmit electronic protected health information on the covered entity's behalf only if the covered entity obtains satisfactory assurances, in accordance with § 164.314(a), that the business associate will appropriately safeguard the information. A covered entity is not required to obtain such satisfactory assurances from a business associate that is a subcontractor.

Section 4.A.2 above discusses business associates—what they are and their roles. Covered entities have an obligation to oversee the activities of its business associates regarding their use of PHI created, received, maintained, or transmitted on behalf of the covered entity. Moreover, a business associate may have subcontractors that assist it in providing services to a covered entity. The subcontractor of a business associate performing HIPAA-covered services is itself a business associate.[64] Business associates have an obligation to oversee the activities of their business associate subcontractors regarding PHI.

This provision requires that the covered entity have, from each business associate with PHI access, formal assurances in a business associate contract (or equivalent documentation) that the business associate has appropriate security safeguards for PHI. The contract or assurances must satisfy the requirements under 45 C.F.R. § 164.314(a). This book uses the term "business associate agreement" (BAA) rather than "business associate contract," because the former is more commonly used in practice. Nonetheless, the reader should understand that references

---

63. HHS designated section 164.308(b)(1), before the Final Omnibus Rule, as a standard. The latest version of section 164.308(b)(1) does not say whether it is a "standard" or something else. The omission is likely an oversight. Accordingly, it would be prudent to assume section 164.308(b)(1) and (b)(2) are standards.

64. *See* 45 C.F.R. § 160.103(3)(iii) (definition of "business associate"). "*Business associate* includes:" "A subcontractor that creates, receives, maintains, or transmits protected health information on behalf of the business associate." *Id.*

to a business associate agreement in the Security Rule are actually to a business associate contract. Also, any quotations to provisions of the Security Rule reflect the exact language of the regulations, including references to business associate contracts.

Where a covered entity uses a business associate, and that business associate uses a subcontractor business associate, the rule expressly states that the covered entity has no obligation to enter into a direct BAA with that subcontractor. Instead, it is left to the business associate to enter into a BAA with its subcontractor. Section 5.B.9.b below discusses the requirements involved with business associates entering into BAAs with their subcontractors. Under this way of flowing down security requirements, there may be a chain of BAAs starting with a covered entity and ending in the lowest-tier subcontractor. It is up to each business associate in the chain to make sure that agreements with subcontractors provide it with the rights it needs to comply with agreements with organizations above it in the chain.

In overseeing the activities of its business associates, a covered entity must identify which entities are, in fact, business associates with access to PHI, and what these entities do for the covered entity. Section 4.A.2 above explains the definition of "business associate" and describes which kinds of service providers are included and which are excluded. The regulatory definition of "business associate" specifically includes certain categories of service providers.[65] They would clearly fall within the definition. Nonetheless, the regulation has a general definition of "business associate" which sweeps in a potentially broad group of service providers.[66] Given the complexity of the definition of a "business associate," it is not always easy for a covered entity to determine which vendors are business associates.

Some vendors may be unaware they are "business associates" within the meaning of HIPAA and the Security Rule. They may also have the mistaken belief that if they can avoid signing a BAA, they are not "business associates" under the law. The requirements on business associates under HIPAA and the Security Rule apply as a matter of law regardless of whether a BAA is in place or not. If a vendor falls under the regulatory definition of "business associate," acknowledging business associate status in a BAA does not make the vendor a business associate

---

65. *Id.* § 160.103(3)(i), (ii).
66. *See id.* 160.103(1)(i), (ii).

where it otherwise would not be one. Likewise, a vendor refusing to sign a BAA does not exclude the vendor from business associate status.

A vendor could argue that its signing a BAA is an implicit admission that it is a business associate. To the vendor's point, if it is truly not a business associate under the law, it may be creating legal risk for itself by signing a BAA unnecessarily. The vendor could argue that it is taking on contractual obligations that are not needed. At a minimum, the fact that the vendor was willing to sign a BAA could leave an impression (even a subconscious one) with a regulator or other fact finder that the vendor is in fact a business associate. A person might assume that the vendor is a business associate if the vendor itself thinks it is one. Nevertheless, the question of whether a vendor is a business associate is a legal question. If there is no question about the services being performed, the only issue is whether it fits the regulatory definition. The vendor's willingness or unwillingness should have no effect on the interpretation of the regulation.

Assuming the covered entity determines that a vendor is a business associate, it must put a BAA into place with the vendor.[67] If a vendor within the definition refuses to sign a BAA, the covered entity would violate 45 C.F.R. § 164.308(b)(1) if it uses that vendor. When faced with a vendor that does not want to sign a BAA, the covered entity must either convince the vendor to sign one, use a different vendor, or perform the functions in question itself.

What happens where the vendor is essential for the covered entity but the vendor refuses to sign a BAA? The covered entity may be unable, as a practical matter, to perform the vendor's functions itself. Moreover, there may be no practical, alternative vendors. In these situations, the only possible way to comply with the BAA requirements is to impose all of the security requirements of the Security Rule in the agreement with the vendor[68] and cover all the required topics under 45 C.F.R. § 164.314(a) without calling the agreement a "Business Associate Agreement" or acknowledging the vendor's business associate status.[69]

---

67. HHS has provided a sample business associate agreement as a template for those covered entities or business associates without one. HHS, Business Associate Contracts, http://www.hhs.gov/ocr/privacy/hipaa/understanding/coveredentities/contractprov.html (Jan. 25, 2013).

68. All of the topics in the Security Rule would have to be set forth verbatim if the vendor refuses to allow the agreement simply to refer to the C.F.R. sections in the Security Rule.

69. The covered entity would also need to include any applicable Privacy Rule requirements in the vendor's agreement as well.

In theory, the title of the agreement is not important as long as the agreement covers all the topics in section 164.314(a).

If the vendor is unwilling to implement all of the security controls described in the Security Rule and use an agreement that includes the terms required by section 164.314(a), then the covered entity would not be able to comply with the BAA requirements. It would need to find another way to perform the functions in question. Nonetheless, the covered entity may be able to convince the vendor to sign an agreement that imposes all of the required terms without calling it a "Business Associate Agreement."

Arguably, HHS should be satisfied with the covered entity if its agreement with a business associate vendor imposes all of the topics required by section 164.314(a) and requires compliance with all of the administrative, physical, and technical safeguards of the Security Rule, even if it is not titled a "Business Associate Agreement" and even if the agreement does not include an express acknowledgement of the vendor's business associate status. Nothing in the regulations require an express acknowledgement of business associate status as long as the vendor agrees to do everything a business associate would be required to do under the Security Rule, including agreeing to the security controls that appear in the Security Rule, flowing down to subcontractors a requirement to implement the same controls, and requiring notification of any security breaches. It would then be between the vendor and the OCR or other litigants as to whether the vendor really is a "business associate" under the law or not. Resolution of the issue of business associate status could be postponed while the covered entity would not be out of compliance.[70]

Nonetheless, there is no authority to support this approach, and it would be better for both parties for the agreement to acknowledge the business associate status of the vendor if it fits within the regulatory definition of "business associate." A regulator or other person scrutinizing the compliance of the covered entity or vendor may be looking to see a document in place titled "Business Associate Agreement." If there is a different kind of agreement in place, there might be greater scrutiny (and skepticism) about whether the agreement meets the requirements.

---

70. A situation in which the agreement disclaims business associate status at the vendor's insistence would be a harder case, but if the agreement meets the other substantive requirements of business associate agreements, any mistake of law about business associate status arguably does not affect the covered entity's compliance with 45 C.F.R. § 164.308(b)(1).

After identifying which service providers are business associates, the covered entity must then ensure that BAAs or other written assurances are in place to flow down security requirements to each of those business associates. A BAA is the most important tool a covered entity can use to oversee activities of a business associate. A covered entity must also ensure that its BAAs satisfy 45 C.F.R. § 164.314(a). A discussion of the required topics of a BAA appears in section 5.B.9.c below.

45 C.F.R. § 164.308(b)(1) does not itself define "satisfactory assurances" to "appropriately safeguard" PHI or specify specific security safeguards. Nonetheless, this section cross-references section 164.314(a), which requires that BAAs include certain topics, including a requirement that the business associate comply with the Security Rule.[71] Business associates have an obligation to comply with the Security Rule regardless of what a BAA might say. Nonetheless, covered entities must also impose on business associates a contractual requirement to comply with the Security Rule. Presumably, HHS thought that enforcement of BAAs by covered entities would supplement HHS's enforcement of the Security Rule directly on business associates and make business associate compliance more likely. BAAs may also impose additional obligations on business associates not required by the Security or Privacy Rule.

b. Business Associate Contracts and Other Arrangements—Section 164.308(b)(2)[72]

> A business associate may permit a business associate that is a subcontractor to create, receive, maintain, or transmit electronic protected health information on its behalf only if the business associate obtains satisfactory assurances, in accordance with § 164.314(a), that the subcontractor will appropriately safeguard the information.

This section sets forth the obligations of business associates to flow down security requirements to subcontractors via BAAs.[73] Business associates have an obligation to oversee the activities of their subcontractors regarding their use of PHI created, received, maintained, or

---

71. *See id.* § 164.314(a)(2)(i)(A).

72. As mentioned in the previous section, it appears that HHS intended for this section to be part of a "standard," although apparently omitted that designation due to an oversight.

73. As mentioned in the previous section, the subcontractor of a business associate performing HIPAA-covered services is itself a business associate. *See* 45 C.F.R. § 160.103(3)(iii) (definition of "business associate"). "*Business associate* includes:" "A subcontractor that creates, receives, maintains, or transmits protected health information on behalf of the business associate." *Id.*

transmitted on their behalf and ultimately on behalf of a covered entity. Subcontractors may have their own subcontractors to assist them in providing services to a business associate. Accordingly, subcontractors have an obligation to oversee the activities of subcontractors in the tiers below them regarding PHI.

45 C.F.R. § 164.308(b)(2) requires that a business associate entity have, from each of its subcontractor business associates with PHI access, formal assurances in a business associate contract (or equivalent documentation) that the subcontractor has appropriate security safeguards for PHI. The contract or assurances must satisfy the requirements under 45 C.F.R. § 164.314(a). A discussion of the required topics of a BAA appears in section 5.B.9.c below. As mentioned in the previous section, this book uses the term "business associate agreement" (BAA) rather than "business associate contract," because the former is more commonly used in practice.

Unlike section 164.308(b)(1), this section does not mention whether a business associate must not only enter into a BAA with a subcontractor, but also enter into direct agreements with sub-subcontractors. The logic of section 164.308(b)(1), requiring covered entities to enter into BAAs with only the tier of business associates directly below it, suggests that business associates need only enter into BAAs with the tier of subcontractors directly below it. It would be up to the subcontractor to enter into an appropriate BAA with the sub-subcontractor in the tier below it. The same logic would apply to tiers below the sub-subcontractor.

The analysis in the previous section concerning covered entities' compliance with BAAs requirements applies here. A business associate must identify which of its vendors are, in fact, subcontractor "business associates." Subcontractors are mentioned by the regulatory definition of "business associate."[74] Nonetheless, some vendors, even ones considered "subcontractors" outside the HIPAA context, may not be business associates. For a discussion of this issue, see section 4.A.3 *supra*.

In overseeing the activities of its subcontractor business associates, a business associate must identify which entities are, in fact, business associate subcontractors with access to PHI, and what these entities do for the business associate. As mentioned in the previous section, some vendors may be unaware that they are, in fact, "business associates"

---

74. *See id.*

within the meaning of HIPAA and the Security Rule. If a business associate wishes to use a vendor "subcontractor" that falls within the definition of a "business associate," the business associate must enter into an appropriate BAA with the subcontractor. If the vendor refuses to sign a BAA, the business associate must either find another vendor or perform the functions itself. Even if the vendor does not want to title the agreement a "Business Associate Agreement," the business associate arguably can satisfy the requirements of section 164.308(b)(2) by using the agreement to impose all of the security requirements appearing in the Security Rule and by covering all of the required topics mentioned in 45 C.F.R. § 164.314(a). Nonetheless, this approach entails some risk for the business associate, and having the subcontractor acknowledge business associate status would be better.

c. Implementation Specifications: Written Contract or Other Arrangement (Required)—Section 164.308(b)(3)

> Document the satisfactory assurances required by paragraph (b)(1) or (b)(2) of this section through a written contract or other arrangement with the business associate that meets the applicable requirements of § 164.314(a).

This provision states that written arrangements for the protection must meet 45 C.F.R. § 164.314(a). It applies to arrangements imposed by covered entities on business associates, as well as arrangements between business associates and their subcontractor business associates. Section 164.314(a) requires that any BAA or other written arrangement must satisfy the requirements in its subsections "as applicable."[75] A BAA is not necessary in all cases; it is possible for the requirements in section 164.314(a) to be satisfied by written arrangements other than a BAA.

Specifically, an arrangement that meets the requirements of 45 C.F.R. § 164.504(e)(3) will satisfy the requirement for a written arrangement.[76] Under that section, when the covered entity or upstream business associate and the business associate are both governmental entities, an "other arrangement" for assuring security may consist of a memorandum of understanding that accomplishes the objectives of a BAA.[77] Additionally, where it can be shown that other provisions of applicable

---

75. 45 C.F.R. § 164.314(a)(1).
76. *Id.* § 164.314(a)(2)(ii).
77. *See generally id.* § 164.504(e)(3)(i)(A).

law accomplish the objectives of the BAA, a signed BAA is not required.[78] The covered entity or business associate should retain copies of such applicable law to document the business associate's assurances of security.

In most cases, however, if a covered entity or business associate is using the services of a business associate vendor, it must enter into a BAA with the vendor. Any organization[79] must include three key terms in its BAA with a business associate:

1. The BAA must provide that the business associate will "comply with the applicable requirements of this subpart,"[80] which means the Security Rule.

2. The business associate must use its own BAA or other written arrangement[81] to flow down Security Rule requirements to any "subcontractors that create, receive, maintain, or transmit" PHI on its behalf.[82] Any such BAA must meet the requirements of 45 C.F.R. § 164.314.[83] Thus, the BAA between the business associate and its subcontractor must include a requirement for the subcontractor to use a BAA with any of its sub-subcontractors.

3. The business associate must notify the covered entity of any security incident of which it becomes aware, including breaches of unsecured PHI as required by 45 C.F.R. § 164.410 of the Breach Notification Rule.[84] If a business associate customer is entering into a BAA with a subcontractor vendor, the BAA will typically require reporting the security incident to

---

78. *See generally id.* § 164.504(e)(3)(i)(B).

79. The requirements in this section apply not only to covered entities' BAAs but also to BAAs imposed by business associates on its subcontractors. 45 C.F.R. § 164.314(a)(2)(iii). Section 164.314(a)(2)(iii) cross-references 45 C.F.R. § 164.308(b)(4) as setting forth business associate requirements for using BAAs, but there is no such section, which is apparently an oversight. HHS apparently intended to refer to section 164.308(b)(2).

80. *Id.* § 164.314(a)(2)(i)(A).

81. Other written arrangements besides a business associate agreement are acceptable in this context. *See id.* § 164.314(a)(2)(ii). See the discussion above regarding "other arrangements."

82. *Id.* § 164.314(a)(2)(i)(B).

83. *See id.* (*referencing* § 164.308(b)(2), which in turn, references § 164.314(a)).

84. *Id.* § 164.314(a)(2)(i)(C).

the customer in addition to or instead of notifying the covered entity.[85]

As mentioned above, each organization in the chain, starting at the covered entity and ending with the penultimate tier subcontractor, must enter into a BAA with the business associate in the tier below it. Each of the three essential elements listed above must appear in the BAA. They will apply in the context of the organization and its arrangement with the business associate in the tier below it.

By requiring the business associate in the next tier to comply with the Security Rule, every business associate in the chain will have a contractual obligation to comply with the Security Rule, in addition to its regulatory compliance obligation. Each must make a notification of security incidents and breaches to the entity above it in the chain. Note that in order to meet time limits on breach notification to the organization above it, a business associate will need to impose a shorter deadline for notifications to the business associate below it, or else coordinate breach notification provisions so that an organization is not in breach simply because it did not find out about a security incident or breach in time to meet its own breach notification deadline. Finally, each organization must flow down the requirement to the business associate in the next tier an obligation to use its own BAA with its subcontractors. This requirement creates a chain of BAAs that further flow down security requirements.

10. Conclusion Regarding Administrative Safeguards

The purpose of the Security Rule is to impose reasonable, cost-effective, and appropriate security standards and requirements upon health plans, healthcare clearinghouses, and healthcare providers. The HITECH Act

---

85. The plain language of section 164.314(a)(2)(i)(C) technically requires a subcontractor in this circumstance to report the security incident to the covered entity, but not the business associate. It does not distinguish between business associates with a direct relationship with the covered entity and subcontractor business associates that have no relationship with the affected covered entity and may not even know its identity. If a security incident occurs, the subcontractor may know which business associate customer's PHI was involved in the security incident, but may not know which covered entity it came from. If a subcontractor knows or can easily find out the identity of a covered entity affected by a security incident, notifying the covered entity makes sense. By contrast, if a subcontractor cannot reasonably be expected to know the identity of an affected covered entity, the reasonable course of action is to notify the business associate customer and then to work together to identify the affected covered entity and notify it. Even if the subcontractor can notify the covered entity, the business associate customer would likely negotiate to receive a notification as well.

and Final Omnibus Rule applied these standards and requirements to business associates. To establish reasonable, cost-effective, and appropriate policies, procedures, and safeguards, management teams of these organizations must implement administrative safeguards as outlined in this section. The risk-managed security policy forms the initial foundation for administrative controls. Continued diligence enhances the ability of initial policies to keep current with the changing vulnerabilities, threats, and risks.

Management has always been responsible for exercising due care and due diligence in securing business assets. Its responsibilities now include, by regulatory mandate, the protection of PHI. Security does not stand by itself; it is just one component of good corporate governance. Therefore, a principal objective of a program to comply with the Security Rule should be coordination with more general security policies and procedures, as well as other compliance and information governance efforts.

C. PHYSICAL SAFEGUARDS—SECTION 164.310

Physical safeguards are physical measures, policies, and procedures to protect a covered entity's or business associate's electronic information systems and related buildings and equipment, from natural and environmental hazards, and unauthorized intrusion.[86]

The physical safeguards section, 45 C.F.R. § 164.310, consists of four parts: facility access control, workstation use, workstation security, and device and media controls. The subsections below address these four areas.

The definition of "physical safeguards" above implies that the Security Rule addresses two general classes of risks to PHI: one from natural and environmental causes such as fire, flood, hurricane, and earthquake, and the second from unauthorized human physical access to PHI. Most of the text in section 164.310 addresses the threat of unauthorized human access to PHI. From an information security perspective, however, it is also important to address natural and environmental hazards. The section does have a discussion of contingency operations following an emergency, which would include a natural disaster, but the discussion does not directly address facility construction and

---

86. 45 C.F.R. § 164.304 (definition of "physical safeguards").

operations before a disaster. Planning for fires, floods, hurricanes, earthquakes, and other natural hazards in advance of an event is critical. This is one lesson from Hurricane Katrina in 2006.

Facility natural disaster planning is not only good information security practice, such planning is also arguably required by HIPAA and the Security Rule. Section 164.310 does not expressly address facility natural disaster planning the way it does facility security planning for unauthorized human access. Nevertheless, HIPAA requires that covered entities maintain "administrative, technical, and physical safeguards" to protect health information.[87] Moreover, the above definition of "physical safeguards" includes protection of "information systems and related buildings and equipment" and specifically protection from "natural and environmental hazards." Consequently, these two provisions imply that covered entities must plan their facilities to address natural disasters and environmental hazards, in addition to man-made threats.

Safeguards to mitigate PHI security risks due to natural and environmental causes can include:

- Judicious site selection for a data center or other facility housing PHI;
- Facility construction techniques, including conformance to applicable building codes;
- Fire prevention, detection, and suppression within the facility;
- Flood control or other water management measures within the facility; and
- Regulated and backup air conditioning and power.

1. Facility Access—Section 164.310(a)

a. *Facility Access Controls (Standard)—Section 164.310(a)(1)*

Implement policies and procedures to limit physical access to its electronic information systems and the facility or facilities in which they are housed, while ensuring that properly authorized access is allowed.

The facility access controls standard establishes a general requirement of physical access control for the physical location in which PHI is gathered, stored, processed, and communicated. As mentioned above, facilities planning is an important component of physical security.

---

87. 42 U.S.C. § 1320d-2(d)(2).

This section and section 164.310(a)(2)(ii) address the threat of unauthorized physical human access to PHI.

In practical terms, the covered entity or business associate should design its facilities to prevent attackers from walking into the facility and stealing or accessing computers, servers, laptops, mobile devices, or media that could contain PHI. Safeguards to mitigate PHI security risks due to unauthorized physical human access to the facility include:

- Doors, locks, secure rooms that enforce physical access controls, allowing authorized people into the facility, and excluding unauthorized people or those without a specific need to access a facility;
- Fences and gates that mediate access to the organization's site and buildings;
- Oversight by the use of guards and other security personnel;
- Within rooms, segregating sensitive items or equipment via locked cabinets, locked drawers, lockers, cages, and safes;
- Lighting in and around parking lots, hallways, and rooms;
- Alarms, cameras, and intrusion detection systems; and
- Antiterrorism safeguards; such as concrete barriers.

For smaller organizations, placing a reception area near the entrance staffed by workers who can watch out for intruders wandering into the facility can help deter and stop the theft of equipment. More sensitive devices should have greater protection. For instance, an organization may operate a server and place it in a locked room in order to physically segregate it from individuals walking through the facility.

The above safeguards, as well as safeguards against natural and environmental hazards, generally represent good business practices, and the organization may already be in compliance with the physical security portions of the Security Rule. Otherwise, compliance might require remediation in one or more of the areas above, commensurate with the determined risk to PHI confidentiality, integrity, and availability and appropriate for the size of the organization. The risk assessment conducted by the organization[88] should include an analysis of any vulnerabilities stemming from physical threats to the organization's facility. Risk management principles[89] then can guide the organization in determining which physical safeguards to implement or strengthen.

---

88. See section 5.B.1.a *supra.*
89. See section 5.B.1.b *supra.*

Policies on physical access to a facility or an information system should also consider safeguards to prevent incidental, unauthorized access to PHI. For example, one kind of vulnerability stems from a physical layout of the facility permitting unnecessarily visible or accessible monitors and keyboards that could expose PHI to casual observers or tampering. Establishing the location of workstations and plans to prevent incidental access should begin in planning the general layout of the facility.

In considering the scope of physical safeguards for "electronic information systems," organizations should address a crucial issue of scope: what is an electronic information system? While the Security Rule does not define this term, certainly a data center, server, or desktop workstation in an office building, hospital, medical office, laboratory, or other facility qualifies as one. Laptops are computers and perform the same functions as desktop computers, so they too need to be considered electronic information systems. In addition, following widespread "consumerization" of IT, mobile devices, such as mobile phones, tablet computers, and digital cameras, can capture, store, communicate, or print PHI. Mobile devices are therefore "electronic information systems" requiring physical safeguards if the organization uses them to process or store PHI.

More recently, a whole host of new smart devices are appearing. Organizations are starting to make use of or access wearable computers; devices connecting to the Internet of Things; information systems in cars, trucks, and other vehicles; 3D printers; and surgical and service robots. For a discussion of these newer and emerging technologies, see chapter 9. To the extent these devices create, receive, maintain, or transmit PHI, they too are "electronic information systems" requiring physical security safeguards to prevent the loss or theft of PHI or tampering for malicious purposes.

Physical security also poses a related scope question: what is a facility? The Security Rule defines it as follows: "Facility means the physical premises and the interior and exterior of a building(s)."[90]

"Facility" generally means the building that houses electronic information systems, such as a healthcare provider's place of business. Although nothing in the rule addresses the issue of mobile information systems, the physical premises, interior, and exterior of a building

---

90. 45 C.F.R 164.304 (definition of a "facility").

that contains PHI could conceivably include a worker's home, an airport, hotel, or other structure outside the general intuitive meaning of a workplace building. Thus, the concept of a regulated facility may extend into these nontraditional areas, and the organization should develop and implement policies on the allowable use of its information systems outside its ordinary physical premises. Given the frequency of lost and stolen mobile devices, especially from automobiles, the organization should include in its training program content concerning awareness of physical surroundings when using mobile devices and safeguards to reduce risks.

In general, the organization should develop and then implement reasonable and appropriate physical security policies and procedures. While the HIPAA Security Rule does not specify standards on how to develop and implement policies and procedures, the organization should use some reasonable and appropriate process to periodically review, update, and check its physical security. An example of the process might be something like the following:

- Analysis of the current environment for vulnerabilities and determination of the physical security "gap" that needs to be filled (Review);
- Identification, development, and updating of the policies and procedures to fill the gap (Update);
- Implementation of the policies and procedures to put them into practice (Implement); and
- Testing and validation of the identified updated policies and procedures to ensure they fill the gap identified during the Review (Check).

b. Facility Access Controls Implementation Specifications—Section 164.310(a)(2)

In addressing facility physical access control safeguards, the rule requires the organization to address contingency operations, facility security planning, access control and validation, and maintenance record keeping.

i. Contingency Operations (Addressable)—Section 164.310(a)(2)(i)

Establish (and implement as needed) procedures that allow facility access in support of restoration of lost data under the disaster recovery plan and emergency-mode operations plan in the event of an emergency.

This subsection addresses disaster recovery and business continuity concerns first discussed in section 5.B.7 above. It focuses on the recovery of data and operations following an emergency.

45 C.F.R. § 164.308(a)(7) (Contingency Plan)[91] requires the organization to have a written disaster recovery plan and procedures to continue operations during an emergency or after a disaster. The physical safeguards relative to this plan would include the logistics of responding to a failure of the facility, equipment, or critical service (e.g., power, Internet, or telecommunications).

This subsection raises the following questions when normal controls and procedures are inoperable:

- Who will have access to the primary and any backup facilities during an emergency?
- How will those authorized people gain access to these facilities?
- How will unauthorized people be denied access to these facilities?

The covered entity must, if reasonable and appropriate, implement access control procedures addressing these issues following an emergency. In other words, this addressable specification calls for the organization to analyze the risk of delay in system restoration (e.g., workers responsible for recovery are locked out of physical facilities) caused by efforts to prevent unauthorized persons from compromising system security. Also, any facilities used specifically for contingency operations to gather, process, store, and transmit PHI following an emergency should have physical safeguards providing equivalent levels of assurances as those in the organization's primary facility.

ii. Facility Security Planning (Addressable)—Section 164.310(a)(2)(ii)

Implement policies and procedures to safeguard the facility and the equipment therein from unauthorized physical access, tampering, and theft.

The organization must, if reasonable and appropriate, document and implement procedures to protect against unauthorized physical access, tampering, or theft of any equipment, devices, or media containing PHI. The organization may find it reasonable and appropriate to

---

91. Section 5.B.7 above discusses this section of the Security Rule.

include in these policies and procedures the physical security controls described in section 5.C.1.a above. In addition, policies and procedures should include:

- Who has site and system access and under what conditions;
- Who is responsible for implementing physical security policies and procedures;
- Controls for unauthorized individuals and people with limited authorization (such as visitors, contractors, and service vendors);
- Property inventory, removal, and tracking of information systems assets (how property and equipment can enter and leave the facility, and for what purposes); and
- Designation of worker responsibility for property while in his or her care outside of the facility.

Procedures should document how organizations will seek to prevent equipment and information access, tampering, and theft. These procedures implement the above policy and could include:

- Visitor and contractor access, sign-in/-out logs, escort procedures, restricted areas, etc.;
- Property removal authorization and tracking systems and procedures;
- Physical access control methods such as security badge or card key access systems; and
- Controlling the issuance of keys and locks to authorized individuals.

Facility security planning is too broad to be comprehensively addressed here. Organizations that do not have a comprehensive facility security plan should create one that complies with this standard.

iii. Access Control and Validation Procedures (Addressable)—Section 164.310(a)(2)(iii)

Implement procedures to control and validate a person's access to facilities based on their role or function, including visitor control, and control of access to software programs for testing and revision.

Organizations must, if reasonable and appropriate, implement procedures that restrict access based on workers' roles or functions. These procedures should be consistent with the organization's PHI access control policy. The rule calls for the use of "roles," or groupings of individuals with similar job responsibilities or access requirements, which the organization assigns to individuals based upon their legitimate job-related facility access requirements and its access control policy. For example, an exterior landscaper does not need, and should not have, access to offices with desktops that display patient information. The organization's policy and procedures should limit the landscaper's facility access to only those areas required for the performance of his or her duties. A document that defines the roles used as the basis for granting access to areas where PHI is available in the facility should include procedures that:

- Sufficiently identify and authenticate individuals before assigning them to their role(s);
- Assign individuals to roles;
- Control access to the facility based upon the individual's role; and
- Verify an individual's identity and role before granting access to restricted areas within the facility.

This section specifically calls out the need for procedures that control physical access to software programs for testing and updating, something often overlooked in facility access control policy and procedure documents. The organization should address how software entry points (USB ports, optical disk drives, and other ports on systems that can be used to install and alter software) are secured and who has access to them.

A full discussion of facility access control policy and procedure cannot be presented within the scope of a publication such as this. Publications of the National Institute of Standards and Technologies are useful references for fleshing out the details of physical access controls.[92] Many organizations have a plan in which the above safeguards have been addressed. If the organization does not have a comprehensive set of

---

92. For NIST resources in the computer security area, see NIST Computer Security Division's CSRC home page at http://csrc.nist.gov. NIST special publications available on that site are particularly useful for providing guidance on various security topics. For instance, special publication 800-66 is a good introduction to safeguards intended for compliance with the Security Rule. MATTHEW SCHOLL ET AL., NAT'L INST. OF STANDARDS & TECH., SPECIAL PUBL'N 800-66, AN INTRODUCTORY RESOURCE GUIDE FOR IMPLEMENTING THE HEALTH INSURANCE PORTABILITY AND ACCOUNTABILITY ACT (HIPAA) SECURITY RULE (rev. 1, Oct. 2008), http://csrc.nist.gov/publications/nistpubs/800-66-Rev1/SP-800-66-Revision1.pdf

physical access control policies and procedures, the organization must (if reasonable and appropriate) develop and maintain one.

iv. Maintenance Records (Addressable)—Section 164.310(a)(2)(iv)

Implement policies and procedures to document repairs and modifications to the physical components of a facility which are related to security (for example, hardware, walls, doors, and locks).

Under this implementation specification, the organization must (if reasonable and appropriate) create and implement policies and procedures to document changes, updates, and repairs to a facility's physical security mechanisms. This documentation may include:

- A policy mandating the documentation of all repairs to facility physical security mechanisms;
- A policy holding identified workers responsible for maintaining such documentation;
- A procedure articulating how the organization will produce the documentation; and
- The change control documentation itself to show ongoing compliance with the policy and procedure.

As a practical matter, this rule will usually apply only to permanent building facilities, such as the organization's primary facility. Changes to a home telecommuting environment would be appropriate to log as well. Nothing in this section explicitly addresses nontraditional locations, such as a car. Nonetheless, organizations should have policies governing how employees physically protect devices storing PHI while traveling.

2. Workstation Use (Standard)—Section 164.310(b)

Implement policies and procedures that specify the proper functions to be performed, the manner in which those functions are to be performed, and the physical attributes of the surroundings of a specific workstation or class of workstations that can access electronic protected health information.

This section requires that organizations protect "workstations." One threshold issue is what constitutes a "workstation." The Security Rule defines "workstation" as follows:

Workstation means an electronic computing device, for example, a laptop or desktop computer, or any other device that performs similar functions, and electronic media stored in its immediate environment.[93]

This definition expressly includes laptops and desktops, but it extends far beyond these devices. It also applies to mobile phones, tablet computers, and e-mail devices, and their associated removable storage devices to the extent they process or store PHI. It may also include other nontraditional computing devices. For instance, some automobiles have in-dash web browsers capable of connecting to any web-based systems that can access PHI. Therefore, even an automobile may contain an "electronic computing device." Even a telepresence robot used for mobile on-site videoconferencing and data collection, could be included.

Given the plethora of new and emerging types of devices, organizations should analyze carefully which devices fall within the definition of "workstation." Also, organizations have an obligation to secure PHI as a general matter. Thus, even if a device is not technically a "workstation," the organization must still secure it. In any case, the organization should track the usage of electronic computing devices through inventory or other records. The organization should have records of which workers are using which devices to process or store PHI.

The organization must develop and implement policies and procedures on the acceptable use and physical environment of a workstation that stores or uses PHI. Security considerations include:

- Physical and electronic openness of the environment. For example, can passersby, walking throughout the facility, see a screen containing PHI? How can others remotely connect to the computing environment, such as through the network or remote dial-in access?
- Security of remote or off-site locations. The organization may, for example, wish to prohibit laptop use to access PHI in a crowded airport, or it may only allow use in a private location such as a hotel room when no one else is around.

These considerations and others can result in a determination that some workstations are not physically secure enough to perform certain functions. These restrictions must be documented by policy and enforced through procedures. Organizations should tailor policies and

---

93. 45 C.F.R. § 164.304 (definition of "workstation").

procedures to the capabilities and vulnerabilities of the different types of workstations used by workers.

The organization has flexibility to address this requirement as it makes sense to the business while maintaining the security of PHI. At a minimum, the organization should, under this implementation specification, prepare:

- A workstation use policy; and
- A workstation use set of procedures.

These policies and procedures should focus particular attention on the loss or theft of mobile devices. A review of OCR enforcement activity shows that lost and stolen laptops have been the top threat addressed by enforcement activity.[94] Also, five out of the nine publicized state attorney general enforcement actions concerned lost laptops or media.[95] Therefore, workstation policies and procedures should include training workers on how to keep track of their mobile devices and protect them from theft.

For instance, thieves commonly break into cars to steal laptops and other computing devices that are visible from the outside. Accordingly, workers should avoid leaving mobile devices stored in a visible location in the passenger compartment of an automobile. If they must leave it in an automobile, they should lock it in the trunk, glove box, or console.

3. Workstation Security (Standard)—Section 164.310(c)

Implement physical safeguards for all workstations that access electronic protected health information, to restrict access to authorized users.

The organization should assess and manage the risk of what work is being done, on what kind of workstations, and where. The organization must consider the security risks to PHI before installing a workstation in a particular physical location. For instance, covered entities should separate patient waiting areas from workstations to the extent they can in order to prevent patients and visitors from viewing PHI about others on workstation screens. If possible, workstations can be placed in a separate room. Workstations that need to be near patients, such as in reception areas, should face away from patients. Cubicle and desk

---

94. See section 7.F *infra*.
95. See section 7.E *infra*.

designs may enhance separation between workstations and patients. Also, organizations should implement protections against the theft of workstations. Reasonable and appropriate safeguards to protect workstations might include doors, locks, screen covers, cable locks to keep a device in place, cameras, and other inventory control and theft deterrent mechanisms.

Administrative and technical safeguards may be taken into account when an organization determines the overall risk to PHI security that a particular location poses. Strong authentication, encryption, and software access controls, for example, *may* mitigate risks of poor physical security. Laptops often contain these kinds of technical safeguards to mitigate risks to confidentiality. However, if despite the combination of all security safeguards, the physical location of the workstation is insufficiently secure for gathering, processing, storing, or transmitting PHI, then that workstation should not be used for those purposes at that location.

4. Device and Media Controls—Section 164.310(d)

a. *Device and Media Controls (Standard)—Section 164.310(d)(1)*

Implement policies and procedures that govern the receipt and removal of hardware and electronic media that contain electronic protected health information into and out of a facility, and the movement of these items within the facility.

This section requires that organizations track and protect "hardware" and "electronic media." A threshold issue, however, is what assets constitute "electronic media." The Security Rule defines "electronic media" as:

(1) Electronic storage material on which data is or may be recorded electronically, including, for example, devices in computers (hard drives) and any removable/transportable digital memory medium, such as magnetic tape or disk, optical disk, or digital memory card;

(2) Transmission media used to exchange information already in electronic storage media. Transmission media include, for example, the Internet, extranet or intranet, leased lines, dial-up lines, private networks, and the physical movement of removable/transportable electronic storage media.[96]

---

96. 45 C.F.R 160.103 (definition of "electronic media").

Under this standard, the organization must track the movement of information-processing and storage devices and media into and out of the facility. The organization must also secure equipment by which the organization receives access to telecommunications services, such as Internet access. Threats an organization faces include:

- The loss of devices or media shipped to another location for transfer or archival purposes. Two of the state attorney general enforcement actions were against covered entities that lost track of backup tapes being shipped from their facilities.[97]
- Unknown import of a storage device containing PHI, which the organization now would be obliged to manage in accordance with the Security Rule or, at worst, might contain malicious software.
- Unknown export of PHI information onto uncontrolled storage devices connected to workstations, either unintentionally or for purposes of theft. With the popularity and availability of large capacity USB drives, users may be able to copy large amounts of PHI onto these devices and remove them without the organization's knowledge. The organization should have acceptable use policies and controls for this kind of storage media.
- Physical removal of media containing PHI from the organization's facility.
- Allowing devices or media to leave the facility for purposes of reuse, transfer, sale, donation, or other disposition without removing unencrypted PHI stored on them.
- Accidental disclosure of PHI by using electronic storage media for multiple purposes.

To cover these and other security threats, the organization must develop written policies and procedures covering four specification areas: disposal, media reuse, accountability, and data backup and storage. The first two of these are required, while the others are addressable.

---

97. See *infra* section 7.E (cases involving South Shore Hospital and Women & Infants Hospital of Rhode Island). With the recent increasing usage of cloud-based storage of data, the need to ship backup tapes will likely decline in the future.

b. Device and Media Controls Implementation Specifications—Section 164.310(d)(2)

i. Disposal (Required)—Section 164.310(d)(2)(i)

Implement policies and procedures to address the final disposition of electronic protected health information, and/or the hardware or electronic media on which it is stored.

The organization must have policies and procedures to ensure that PHI cannot be inadvertently disclosed during or after disposal or reuse of its storage media. Next to the theft or loss of laptops and media, the second most common subject of OCR enforcement has been improper disposal of PHI.[98] For example, in the South Shore Hospital security breach attorney general enforcement action, the hospital retained a data management company to dispose of computer tapes containing PHI, but the tapes were lost in transit. The hospital failed to delete the PHI from the tapes before shipping them.[99] In another case, the OCR forced a health plan to pay over $1.2 million after it returned photocopiers to a leasing company without first removing electronic PHI from them.[100]

Some of the OCR enforcement activities concerned cases involving the improper disposal of paper PHI. As mentioned in section 4.D.1, the security of paper PHI falls under the Privacy Rule, rather than the Security Rule.[101] In one of the OCR cases, workers left boxes of paper medical records on a retiring physician's driveway while he was away.[102] In one attorney general enforcement action, the Massachusetts attorney general sued former owners of a medical billing practice and four pathology groups after they improperly disposed of paper records with sensitive PHI in a public dump, which were found by a *Boston Globe* photographer. The former owners paid $140,000 to settle the claim.[103]

---

98. See section 7.F *infra*.

99. *See* Press Release, Mass. Att'y Gen.'s Office, South Shore Hospital to Pay $750,000 to Settle Data Breach Allegations (May 24, 2012), http://www.mass.gov/ago/news-and-updates /press-releases/2012/2012-05-24-south-shore-hospital-data-breach-settlement.html.

100. See section 7.F Table 7.2 *infra* (Affinity Health Plan case).

101. 45 C.F.R. § 164.530(c)(1).

102. See section 7.F Table 7.2 *infra* (Parkview Health System case).

103. Press Release, Mass. Att'y Gen.'s Office, Former Owners of Medical Billing Practice, Pathology Groups Agree to Pay $140,000 to Settle Claims that Patients' Health Information was Disposed of at Georgetown Dump (Jan. 7, 2013), http://www.mass.gov/ago/news-and -updates/press-releases/2013/140k-settlement-over-medical-info-disposed-of-at-dump.html.

The principle of secure PHI disposal, however, applies both to electronic and paper media. Organizations usually shred PHI in paper form to dispose of it. To securely dispose of electronic PHI, the organization can:

- Securely destroy the storage media. When erasure is impractical, as in the case of a CD-ROM, the organization must physically destroy the electronic media.
- Securely erase the PHI from the storage media using appropriate software or demagnetizing (degaussing) equipment.
- Some mobile devices have "wiping" functions that can securely delete data from them.
- Encrypt all PHI on the device and then delete the encryption/decryption key (or its activation data)[104] to prevent any future decryption of the data.

Safeguards to prevent disclosure should account for reasonably anticipated techniques for recovering erased data, such as unerase utilities, block read utilities, etc.

One particular threat is the reuse or disposal of a workstation or laptop that previously stored or processed PHI. Simple file deletion generally does not permanently erase the information, and many utilities can easily recover these files. The organization must use a secure data destruction methodology to cleanse any storage media before reusing or disposing of them. The organization should also train workers concerning the threat posed by discarded media and the practices and technical standards it utilizes to eliminate PHI from media before discarding it.

ii. Media Re-Use (Required)—Section 164.310(d)(2)(ii)

Implement procedures for removal of electronic protected health information from electronic media before the media are made available for re-use.

Under this section, organizations must address the reuse of media containing electronic PHI. Reusable electronic media such as disk drives, thumb drives, tape media, Zip drives and other high-capacity disks, and rewritable CDs, that have had PHI recorded on them, must be securely and completely erased to protect against unauthorized

---

104. "Activation data" refers to a password or code used to operate an encryption key.

disclosure of PHI when the media are reused. Failing to remove PHI from a device before reuse may trigger an enforcement action, as one health plan found out after it had to pay over $1.2 million to settle an OCR investigation stemming from its return of photocopiers to a leasing company without first removing electronic PHI from them.[105]

The previous section mentions four means of removing electronic PHI from media before they are reused: destruction of the media, erasing software or hardware, making use of a mobile device's "wiping" function, and encrypting PHI and deleting the encryption/decryption key or its activation data. Organizations should train their personnel concerning the risks to PHI from media reuse, as well as the safeguards implemented by the organization to minimize unauthorized disclosure of PHI stemming from media reuse.

iii. Accountability (Addressable)—Section 164.310(d)(2)(iii)

Maintain a record of the movements of hardware and electronic media and any person responsible therefore.[106]

Under this section, when reasonable and appropriate, physical safeguards must include maintaining a record (manual or automated) of all hardware and electronic media movements. The records should include log of disposal and reuse, within the organization and outside it, and the individual or group responsible for hardware and electronic media movement. The intent of this provision is to create strong accountability for protection of PHI on media circulating within and outside the organization.

Procedural controls (e.g., an inventory) and technical controls can help to monitor media movement. With the introduction of small, removable storage devices such as USB drives, users with physical access to standard ports on workstations may be able to move large amounts of information without detection. The organization should consider this risk and, as a part of its overall security awareness program, train workers in the appropriate and inappropriate use of available storage technology on systems storing PHI.

iv. Data Backup and Storage (Addressable)—Section 164.310(d)(2)(iv)

Create a retrievable, exact copy of electronic protected health information, when needed, before movement of equipment.

---

105. See section 7.F Table 7.2 *infra* (Affinity Health Plan case).

106. It appears that the word "therefore" is a typographical error, and should actually be "therefor."

Data integrity and availability are two fundamental goals of the Security Rule. This addressable requirement is intended to prevent accidental data loss from equipment movement, when stored information is at a higher than usual risk of loss. From a practical perspective, this implementation specification includes the requirement that the organization can also restore the exact copy of the PHI onto new media. The organization should make a reasoned, risk-managed decision concerning procedures to back up data as needed to prevent the loss of PHI when the organization moves the equipment containing it.

5. Conclusion Regarding Physical Safeguards

The physical safeguard standards represent long-existing good business practices. Many organizations already have the necessary policies, procedures, and metrics in place to manage physical security in the customary system topology, for example, a central facility with wired desktop workstations and data centers. For these organizations, little additional work beyond compliance verification is required. Other organizations may use cloud service providers to host PHI. Many reputable cloud service providers have robust physical security controls, as shown by industry-standard security certifications. When storing PHI in the cloud, these organizations can concentrate on securing their own facilities, which may actually host very little of the organization's PHI.

Others will have to add missing documentation and implement security procedures. For these organizations, existing security standards and best practices should help them so that they do not have to "reinvent the security wheel." One well-known international standard is ISO 27001, which presents an approach to managing many of the safeguards in the rule. The special publications of the National Institute of Standards and Technology also include useful guidance on physical security controls.

With increasing mobility comes increasing reliance upon the individual to care for his or her workstation. Consumer devices, such as laptops, mobile phones, tablet computers, cameras, and other electronic marvels, increasingly store and process PHI. Emerging categories of devices, such as automotive in-dash information systems, Internet of Things devices, and even various categories of robots may now create, receive, maintain, or transmit PHI. Users of these devices must commit to providing acceptable physical security, to use their devices responsibly and securely, and to invoke sufficient technology expertise to protect PHI should their devices fall into the wrong hands.

With mobility, the definition of "facility" may change to include a worker's home or car, a common carrier, or other building or transportation vehicle. While the Security Rule does not yet expressly cover these alternate types of "facilities," the organization is still responsible for PHI physical security without regard to where a device might be located at any given time. Managing this risk will be a challenge for regulators, organization management, and workers alike.

D. TECHNICAL SAFEGUARDS—SECTION 164.312

This section presents technical requirements with which operators of information systems that store, process, or transmit PHI must comply. How operators comply with these rules, however, is usually *un*specified, so the covered entity or business associate must use risk management and business management judgment to satisfy the requirements. The Security Rule defines "technical safeguards" as follows:

> Technical safeguards means the technology and the policy and procedures for its use that protect electronic protected health information and control access to it.[107]

Technical safeguards are broken down into two major categories:

1. System security safeguards, which apply to the operation of information systems that store or process PHI. Operators must configure and maintain their systems using:
   - Access controls;
   - Audit controls;
   - Data integrity safeguards; and
   - Person (user) or entity identification and authentication mechanisms.
2. Data transmission security safeguards, which protect information while it is in transit (that is, while on the corporate network, an intranet, an extranet, and/or the Internet) between information systems. These safeguards protect information's confidentiality and integrity while it travels between systems.

The Security Rule's technical safeguards section does not require the use of any specific technical solution. Rather, it gives the organization choice and flexibility to meet the requirements.

---

107. 45 C.F.R. § 164.304 (definition of "technical safeguards").

For more information concerning access control, integrity, authentication, and encryption, readers should consult the American Bar Association Section of Science & Technology Law's recent publications in this area:

- Arthur Peabody Jr., *Health Care IT* (2013).
- Stephen S. Wu, *A Legal Guide to Enterprise Mobile Device Management* (2013).
- Lucy L. Thomson, et al., *Data Breach and Encryption Handbook* (2011).
- *Information Security and Privacy* (Thomas J. Shaw ed. 2011).

1. Access Control Safeguards—Section 164.312(a)

a. Access Control (Standard)—Section 164.312(a)(1)

Implement technical policies and procedures for electronic information systems that maintain electronic protected health information to allow access only to those persons or software programs that have been granted access rights as specified in § 164.308(a)(4).

Access controls:

- Allow the right (authorized) people and processes to have access to PHI in a manner that complies with administrative policy and procedures; and
- Prevent the wrong (unauthorized) people and processes from accessing PHI.

The analysis described in sections 5.B.3 and 5.B.4 above describe the process by which an organization determines appropriate access rights for workers and perhaps vendors: who has a need to access which kinds of PHI, by what means should personnel gain access to PHI, and what are the minimum access rights necessary for personnel to perform required job duties. The organization must memorialize its access control practices in policies and procedures. These access control policies and procedures then inform the implementation of policies and procedures for implementing technical safeguards for access control. In any case, the organization should include in its training program both administrative and technical access control policies and procedures. The organization should update and improve these policies and procedures based on its experience in implementing them.

The organization's access control system must identify, authenticate, and authorize people and processes; implement a method of mediating access to information based upon the authenticated entity's authorization; and log information accesses to track user activity upon later review. The organization must develop and implement policies and procedures on how it manages and controls access to PHI. These policies and procedures must meet the following specifications:

- Every user is uniquely identified and authenticated.
- User activity is logged and tied to a unique user.[108]
- Access controls are in place and are effective (e.g., PHI is kept secure from unauthorized access and/or encrypted to ensure its confidentiality).

The following sections specify the implementation standards to achieve these access control objectives. Also, network security systems, such as firewalls, intrusion detection systems, and intrusion prevention systems, help prevent and detect unauthorized access to networked systems containing PHI.

b. Access Control Implementation Specifications—Section 164.312(a)(2)

i. Unique User Identification (Required)—Section 164.312(a)(2)(i)
Assign a unique name and/or number for identifying and tracking user identity.

This section requires an organization to assign unique identifiers to users to identify and track their conduct. The system the organization establishes must uniquely identify each user and track each user's activities while logged on to the system. No two users may share the same user account or other authentication mechanism to access PHI. Users sharing credentials might blame each other for unauthorized activity, and thereby impede the organization's efforts to hold wrongdoers responsible for unauthorized activity. Thus, this requirement creates user accountability when it is used in conjunction with access controls and an audit trail. This requirement may significantly impact those organizations that have multiple systems each with shared IDs.[109]

ii. Emergency Access Procedure (Required)—Section 164.312(a)(2)(ii)
Establish (and implement as needed) procedures for obtaining necessary electronic protected health information during an emergency.

---

108. See also *infra* section 5.D.2.
109. UNIX systems, for example, with the standard UNIX "root" administrative account may require additional policy, procedures, and technology to allow multiple system administrators to manage the system without having to share the single "root" account.

This section's requirement has two parts. The first is a technical requirement for systems to be able to bypass predefined access controls to allow access to PHI during an emergency, such as when an attending physician needs immediate access to patient information during a healthcare emergency. The information system must provide a mechanism to do this. Nonetheless, controls should be in place to ensure that emergency procedures are not used to obtain unauthorized access or access control rights.

The second part requires a contingency data access method to be invoked during times of natural or man-made disaster when the information system itself is unavailable, such as due to an electrical power or telecommunications failure. Section 5.B.7 above covers contingency planning for possible disasters. The organization should include, in its contingency planning, mechanisms to maintain the availability of systems capable of processing PHI during an emergency. Under this requirement, the organization should maintain procedures and technology needed to control access to these systems.

In both of these cases the audit system, discussed below, must log the emergency access.

iii. Automatic Logoff (Addressable)—Section 164.312(a)(2)(iii)

Implement electronic procedures that terminate an electronic session after a predetermined time of inactivity.

The organization must address how it manages the security risk of logged-in users leaving their workstations unattended, where reasonable and appropriate. If a user is logged into a workstation and then leaves it unattended, an attacker could start using the workstation and use the access privileges available to the user. If a workstation suspends or terminates activity after a period of time, then an attacker cannot use the system in the user's absence.

This addressable implementation specification calls for a technical safeguard to address this risk of unattended workstations. The safeguard would either terminate or suspend the session after a set time of inactivity. The functionality to require the user to put in a password or code to resume activity after a period of inactivity frequently appears in operating system software. For instance, it is possible to set a personal computer to invoke a screen saver after a set amount of time, and the user must enter a password to resume activity. Mobile devices have similar functionality. Many online and mobile applications have similar features.

The organization should determine a reasonable and appropriate time period of inactivity, following which workstations would suspend or terminate activity, such as by use of a screen saver. The organization's risk assessment would help it determine an appropriate time period. That time period may depend on the type of device and its physical setting. For instance, desktop computers in an office setting may not need as short a time period to trigger a screen saver compared to a mobile device. Once the organization decides on appropriate time periods, the organization should document inactivity time periods in access control polices and implemented in system administration procedures. System administrators may be able to centrally manage operating systems and applications to set a policy for teams or organization-wide to suspend or terminate a session after a period of user inactivity.

iv. Encryption and Decryption (Addressable)—Section 164.312(a)(2)(iv)
Implement a mechanism to encrypt and decrypt electronic protected health information.

Under this addressable implementation specification, organizations must encrypt PHI, if encryption is reasonable and appropriate. This encryption specification applies to PHI residing on system storage on workstations, mobile devices, or servers, such as disk drives and solid state drives. It also applies to portable media that could contain PHI, including USB drives, portable hard drives, CDs, DVDs, and older types of media, such as tapes and floppy disks. This specification also applies to PHI stored in cloud-hosted accounts. The organization must assess the security risk of PHI stored in "cleartext" (i.e., unencrypted) at rest on these storage media. Likewise, the specification applies to PHI in transit from one device to another. The organization must also assess the risk of interception of PHI that it transmits.

Encryption also helps an organization enforcing access controls. If an organization's system authenticates an authorized user, the user obtains access to the system. By contrast, the system should prevent access to the system and associated data to unauthorized individuals. Encrypting PHI helps to prevent an attacker from bypassing system access controls and accessing PHI directly. With the combination of access control and encryption, authorized users gain access to the system and the underlying data are decrypted while in use. Attackers gaining access to the underlying data without obtaining access to the system would only have access to encrypted data and would not be able compromise its confidentiality.

The Security Rule, as originally promulgated, does not impose an unconditional requirement on organizations to encrypt PHI. Instead, encryption is only an addressable implementation specification, and HHS has not since amended this provision. Thus, if the organization's risk assessment shows an unacceptably high risk associated with unencrypted PHI, and no equivalent alternative measures would provide commensurate security, then the organization must encrypt stored and/or transmitted PHI.

By contrast, because encryption is only an addressable implementation specification, in theory, if the security risks are acceptably low, or if equivalent alternative measures are available, then the organization does not need to encrypt stored and/or transmitted PHI. In making this risk decision, the organization may consider all environmental conditions and security measures—administrative, physical, and technical— in assessing these data security risks. Whether or not the organization encrypts PHI or uses equivalent alternative measures, it should document its reasoning.

Although encryption is only an addressable implementation specification, encryption is, as a practical matter, almost a de facto requirement for all organizations. It is difficult to imagine a scenario in which an organization could claim that it need not use encryption on at least some of its systems or media. Perhaps the risk to PHI on media stored in a locked safe is low enough not to need encryption protection. Nonetheless, for devices used for day-to-day computing purposes, encryption is a key security protection.

For example, an organization would almost certainly find it reasonable and appropriate to encrypt PHI on laptops and other mobile devices. As mentioned in sections 7.E and 7.F below, lost and stolen laptops and portable media are the most frequent incidents giving rise to HIPAA enforcement actions and investigations. The news media are filled with stories about lost laptops and mobile devices. The loss of devices is a top cause of security breaches generally. Moreover, the plaintiffs in the Anthem data breach case asserted the lack of database encryption as evidence of Anthem's liability.[110] Organizations can avoid such claims if they encrypt their databases. Accordingly, taking only one step—encrypting PHI—may do more than any other

---

110. Second Consolidated Amended Class Action Complaint¶ 5, *In re* Anthem, Inc. Data Breach Litig., No. 15-MD-02617-LHK (filed Mar. 11, 2016).

single safeguard to mitigate legal risk associated with potential HIPAA Security Rule violations.

The HIPAA Breach Notification Rule and state breach notification laws add additional impetus for implementing encryption technology. As discussed in chapter 6, the HITECH Act now requires notification to individuals affected by a breach of "unsecured protected health information."[111] As discussed in section 6.C, "unsecured" PHI essentially means PHI not encrypted using one of the methods specified in guidance from the National Institute of Standards and Technology (NIST).[112] HHS has pointed to NIST guidance concerning encrypting PHI stored on devices and PHI being transmitted.[113] For PHI at rest (stored), HHS announced that encryption processes in NIST Special Publication 800-111, *Guide to Storage Encryption Technologies for End User Devices*, satisfy the standard. For PHI data in motion (being transmitted), HHS pointed to Transport Layer Security (TLS), IPsec virtual private networks, and other technology validated under Federal Information Processing Standards (FIPS) 140-2. These methods appear in NIST Special Publications 800-52, *Guidelines for the Selection and Use of Transport Layer Security (TLS) Implementations*; 800-77, *Guide to IPsec VPNs*; and 800-113, *Guide to SSL VPNs*.[114] NIST published FIPS 140-2 on its website.[115]

If an organization encrypts PHI using the NIST guidance, it is not considered "unsecured" PHI. The HITECH Act and the Breach Notification Rule require notifying individuals affected by a breach only if it involves the compromise of "unsecured" PHI.[116] PHI encrypted in accordance with NIST guidance is not "unsecured" PHI. Therefore, if an attacker compromises encrypted PHI, for instance by stealing a laptop with stored PHI, the organization has no obligation to make a breach notification. Because breach notifications trigger scrutiny from

---

111. See section 6.B *infra*.

112. See section 6.C *infra*.

113. HHS, Guidance to Render Unsecured Protected Health Information Unusable, Unreadable, or Indecipherable to Unauthorized Individuals, http://www.hhs.gov/hipaa /for-professionals/breach-notification/guidance/index.html (last visited Apr. 6, 2016).

114. NIST published these documents on the website of its Computer Security Division at http://csrc.nist.gov.

115. Nat'l Inst. of Standards & Tech., FIPS Publ'n 140-2, Security Requirements for Cryptographic Modules (May 25, 2001), http://www.nist.gov/customcf/get_pdf .cfm?pub_id=902003.

116. See section 6.D.1 (breach notification triggers), 6.D.2 (a covered entity's breach notification obligation), 6.D.3 (the breach notification obligation of business associates) *infra*.

the OCR, state attorneys general, and potential private plaintiffs, avoiding the need for a breach notification will greatly reduce the legal risk of potential enforcement actions and litigation.

Encrypting PHI will also help reduce state law claims. In general, state breach notification laws require an organization that owns or licenses certain categories of personal information to inform individuals affected by a breach involving such personal information if it is unencrypted. As with the HITECH Act and Breach Notification Rule, encrypting personal information acts as a safe harbor. The loss or compromise of personal information in encrypted form does not trigger an obligation to notify potentially affected individuals.[117] The states assumed that attackers would not be able to compromise the confidentiality of lost personal information if it is encrypted.[118] Regardless, encrypting PHI will help reduce the legal risk following a breach notification under state law. Moreover, state laws sometimes require taking reasonable care to protect the confidentiality of certain categories of personal information. Encryption would reduce the legal risk based on claims under these laws, since encryption is an industry-standard method of protecting sensitive personal information.

In light of all of these factors, organizations have strong incentives to encrypt PHI. Encryption software and hardware are widely available and cost-effective (or free). Many (although not all) are easy to use. Some encryption capability is even built into the operating systems of common computing and mobile devices, such as Microsoft Windows, Apple Macintosh, Apple iOS,[119] and Google Android. Encryption was

---

117. Depending on the state law, the organization would also need to prevent the compromise of the encryption keys used to encrypt the personal information or any associated activation data (such as a password) needed to access and use the key to decrypt the personal information.

118. That assumption may not always be sound. It is possible to use weak, easily broken cryptographic controls. Accordingly, the states may find it necessary to require minimum standards of encryption to qualify for the safe harbor from notification, similar to the HITECH Act and the Breach Notification Rule's reverences to NIST guidance.

119. Indeed, Apple's iOS encryption was so hard to break, the U.S. government sought court assistance compelling Apple to help it decrypt iPhones it seized in investigations of criminal cases, including the Apple 5C seized in the investigation of the December 2015 San Bernardino, California, terrorist attack. *In re* the Search of an Apple iPhone Seized During the Execution of a Search Warrant on a Black Lexus IS300, California License Plate 35KGD203, No. ED 15-0451M (C.D. Cal. Feb. 16, 2016). Although the government announced it was able to decrypt this phone, the government may not be able to decrypt newer iPhones, and the issue of the government's ability to access encrypted devices is likely to arise again.

harder in 2003, when HHS promulgated the Security Rule. Fewer solutions were available then. Nonetheless, advances since then have removed the main obstacles to adoption. Therefore, when balancing the benefits of encryption described above against the low costs and burdens associated with its use, it is difficult to understand why organizations would now store PHI without encrypting it.[120] The bottom line is that organizations should encrypt the PHI they maintain.

2. Audit Controls (Standard)—Section 164.312(b)

Implement hardware, software, and/or procedural mechanisms that record and examine activity in information systems that contain or use electronic protected health information.

While the Security Rule requires audit controls, it does not specify what form they should take or how much audit data is enough. The organization must have a technical method for logging user activity and a method, automated or procedural, for examining that activity log for unauthorized activity. The overall intent of this requirement is to give the organization a means of monitoring user access to PHI and to hold users accountable for their access behavior. Audit information may also be useful evidence in legal proceedings in the wake of wrongful conduct.

Events since HHS promulgated the Security Rule have proven the need for robust audit controls.

Section 7.A.1 below discusses the high-profile snooping incidents involving celebrities' medical records at UCLA Health Systems. Hospital employees viewed the medical records of celebrities such as Britney Spears, Farrah Fawcett, and then-California First Lady Maria Shriver, without authorization.[121] Presumably, the access logs enabled the hospital to detect the incidents and discipline the employees involved.[122]

The organization should determine how much audit information it needs to collect and the mechanisms by which it will collect the information. It should also ascertain how it should review log

---

120. Some may argue that encrypting PHI stored on servers degrades the performance of networks and access to encrypted PHI in databases. Nonetheless, given the legal risk organizations face, the benefits of encryption seem well worth the performance degradation from the use of encryption. Moreover, there may be means of mitigating the performance degradation.

121. Molly Hennessy-Fiske, *UCLA Hospitals to Pay $865,500 for Breaches of Celebrities' Privacy*, L.A. Times, Jul. 8, 2011, http://articles.latimes.com/print/2011/jul/08/local/la-me -celebrity-snooping-20110708.

122. Moreover, these incidents led California to enact state law protections against medical records snooping. Cal. Health & Safety Code §§ 1280.15(a), 1280.18(a).

information and how frequently reviews will take place. A security information and event management (SIEM) system can help an organization analyze and interpret log data. For instance, a SIEM system may be able to identify advanced persistent threats (APTs), by which attackers attempt to use malicious software to gain unauthorized access to systems. The organization's risk analysis should inform it as to areas in which logging is necessary or desirable and the frequency of review. The organization should then document its audit information gathering and assessment policies and procedures, and train its workforce on its audit program. These policies and procedures should dovetail with the organization policies concerning periodic security assessments.[123]

3. Integrity

a. Integrity (Standard)—Section 164.312(c)(1)

Implement policies and procedures to protect electronic protected health information from improper alteration or destruction.

This standard requires the organization to consider what kind of technology it should apply to prevent improper data alteration (i.e., protect data integrity) and prevent its alteration or destruction from causes such as:

- Equipment failure
- User accidents or other unintentional acts of authorized users
- Malicious authorized and unauthorized user acts
- Malicious software, including ransomware
- Intruder (hacker) acts

The organization's risk assessment[124] should help it determine what integrity safeguards it should use to address the risks and vulnerabilities associated with PHI integrity. Integrity vulnerabilities may arise from attackers seeking to alter or corrupt information. In addition, however, damage to systems may also occur as a side effect of an attacker's conduct. Moreover, the risk assessment may also reveal inadvertent sources of alteration or corruption.

Technologies like RAID (redundant arrays of inexpensive disk), error-correcting memory, and fault tolerant (clustered systems) can reduce the risk of data alteration or loss from equipment failure. Well-designed

---

123. See section 5.B.8 *supra*.
124. See section 5.B.1.a *supra*.

user interfaces to databases and applications can reduce accidental data alteration or loss. File hashing and digital signature technology[125] can provide strong assurances of security in detecting corruption or malicious user data manipulation.[126] If the hash or digital signature on information cannot be verified, the receiving party knows that the information is unreliable and may have been altered. Thus, the recipient knows not to use or rely on information associated with an unverifiable digital signature, and file hashes and checksums[127] can also help identify maliciously altered information. The standard does not specify what, if any, technologies are required. These choices are left to the organization.

In addition to data at rest, this section also covers data in transit. Accordingly, this section overlaps with the integrity controls implementation specification below in section 5.D.5.b.i.[128]

In any case, technologies exist to reduce risks to data integrity. Therefore, the organization must define policies and procedures concerning the use of technology to provide assurances of data integrity. The organization should then communicate its policies and procedures to workers, for instance, in the course of its training programs. Finally, the organization must also reassess its policies and procedures for integrity from time to time in order to account for its experience in implementing them, for changes in technology, and for changes in its operating environment.

b. Implementation Specification: Mechanism to Authenticate Electronic Protected Health Information (Addressable)—Section 164.312(c)(2)

Implement electronic mechanisms to corroborate that electronic protected health information has not been altered or destroyed in an unauthorized manner.

---

125. Digital signatures are secure electronic signatures created using certain encryption technology. For more information about how digital signatures work, see INFO. SEC. COMM., ABA SEC. OF SCI. & TECH. LAW, PUBLIC KEY INFRASTRUCTURE ASSESSMENT GUIDELINES 304–13 (2003) [hereinafter PAG].

126. Hashes in isolation, however, must be secured to prevent tampering. Digital signatures make use of hashing and any alteration of data would be evident when the recipient attempts to verify the signature.

127. A checksum is a value associated with data and communicated with the data to the recipient. The sender and recipient use the same method of generating the checksum from the data. If the recipient sees that the checksum transmitted by the sender with the data and the checksum value generated by the recipient are the same, the recipient has some assurance that the information was not altered in transit. The methods of generating checksums range in the levels of assurance provided to detect corruption and malicious alteration of transmitted information.

128. 45 C.F.R. § 164.312(e)(2)(i).

Once an organization has established its policies and procedures, it must, if reasonable and appropriate, implement the chosen technical approach toward providing assurances of data integrity. Technologies to provide assurances of integrity include the technical solutions mentioned in the previous section. Organizations may find it reasonable and appropriate to adopt several technologies that meet the objective of maintaining PHI integrity in the organization's information systems.

4. Person or Entity Authentication (Standard)—Section 164.312(d)

> Implement procedures to verify that a person or entity seeking access to electronic protected health information is the one claimed.

This provision requires that systems technically verify that the users or devices seeking access to PHI are who they purport to be. Section 5.B.4 above concerns the administrative process of granting, exercising, and updating access privileges: who should have access to what kinds of PHI under what circumstances. Also, section 5.B.4 describes the authentication process and the threats it addresses: ensuring a real-world identity exists for an authorized user and ensuring that a person seeking PHI access with that user's name is, in fact, that authorized user. By contrast, this section concerns the technical mechanisms to enforce access control policies and procedures via authentication. For instance, technical controls can provide assurances that a person seeking to log on to a system is, in fact, the authorized user he or she purports to be.

An organization's risk assessment[129] should determine how vulnerable its systems are to impersonation by unauthorized personnel seeking access to PHI. The risk assessment should also suggest mechanisms for safeguarding against impersonation. Authentication is a key challenge in electronic communications, especially through the Internet, because communicating parties cannot use authentication methods available in a face-to-face setting, such as checking photo identification documents.

Systems commonly use passwords, tokens, biometrics, or dial-back techniques to verify an individual's or entity's identity. The Security Rule requires that the system verify identity; it does not specify any

---

129. See section 5.B.1.a *supra*.

technology for doing so. Sometimes, authentication mechanisms are referred to as "factors" or authentication approaches:

- One kind of authentication relies on something that the user knows, such as a password or PIN. As long as the user, and only the user, knows the password, entering the password confirms that the user is who he or she claims to be.

- Another kind of authentication is based on something that the user possesses, such as a smart card, a device that displays one-time passwords, or even a mobile phone.[130] The user allows the system to read the information on the token (e.g., by inserting it into a reader or entering information displayed by the hardware device). As long as the user has not lost the token, using the token proves the user's identity.

- The final kind of authentication type is based on something that "the user is" (something inherent with the user's body). Biometric identifiers, such as fingerprints, iris patterns, and voice patterns, can authenticate a user. A device reads the user's fingerprint or other identifier to ensure that it matches the identifier in its system. As long as the identifier is unique to the user, it shows the user's identity. For instance, some computers and mobile devices have fingerprint readers. The user can use a finger or thumb to unlock the device instead of or in addition to using a password or one-time code.

Digital signatures supported by a "public key infrastructure" (PKI) can also serve to authenticate users. Digital signatures are a secure form of electronic signature making use of particular cryptographic techniques to provide assurances, for instance, that a signature has originated from an identified person. PKIs frequently make use of "digital certificates," which can serve, among other things, as electronic credentials to identify a user. The use of passwords, tokens, and biometric readers can enhance the security of a PKI authentication mechanism and provide high assurances of identity of known users.[131]

---

130. A mobile phone can act as a security token when a user requests access to a system and the system generates a code sent by SMS to the phone number associated with the phone. The user cannot obtain the code without physical possession of the phone. Therefore, inputting the proper code proves possession of the phone.

131. PAG, *supra* note 125, at 304–13.

The organization's risk assessment should determine whether using one of the above factors or approaches is reasonable and appropriate, or whether more than one is needed to provide adequate authentication. The combination of a user name and password has been considered sufficient for many lower-security applications. By contrast, higher-security applications generally call for two-factor authentication. The risk assessment should account for the tradeoff between the rigor provided by high-security authentication mechanisms and the increased cost and difficulty associated with their use.

Regardless of the authentication mechanism chosen, the organization should train its personnel in the secure method of using the selected authentication mechanism. Training topics include secure establishment of the mechanism, preventing compromise, and notifying the appropriate security personnel if a mechanism is compromised. For instance, if the organization uses passwords, it should instruct users about choosing strong passwords, methods of avoiding compromise of the password, and how to notify the appropriate personnel in case the password is compromised.[132] The organization should assess the effectiveness of its authentication mechanism and adjust its policies, procedures, and authentication methods as it obtains experience in controlling access to PHI, as technology changes, and as its operating environment changes.

5. Transmission Security—Section 164.312(e)

a. Transmission Security (Standard)—Section 164.312(e)(1)

Implement technical security measures to guard against unauthorized access to electronic protected health information that is being transmitted over an electronic communications network.

This section and the subsections below apply to information while in transit over a network such as the Internet or internal network. Security threats addressed include:

- Eavesdropping: an unauthorized person intercepts communications and views, sees, or hears the communications of PHI on an unprotected or open network; and
- Data modification: interception and surreptitious modification of or tampering with PHI by an attacker in a way that the recipient cannot detect.

---

132. See section 5.B.5.d *supra.*

As with other technical mechanisms, the organization's risk assessment[133] should inform the organization as to the various threats that may affect transmitted PHI and possible mechanisms that may provide security to address the threat. The organization must protect PHI while in transit using mechanisms providing security that is commensurate with the transmission security risks and their associated mitigation costs.

Once the organization develops policies and procedures for the use of specific technical safeguards for transmission security, the organization should implement them and train its personnel on their proper use. It should also monitor the use of these safeguards to determine their effectiveness. This experience along with changes in risks and threats facing the organization should provide feedback for changes and updates in the organization's policies and procedures.

One commonly used technical standard for transmission security is Transport Layer Security (TLS), which is a successor to the Secure Sockets Layer (SSL) protocol. TLS and SSL use encryption to protect information in transit from interception. Also, TLS and SSL include the use of a checksum[134] to provide assurances of the integrity of the communications. Finally, TLS and SSL make use of digital certificates to provide assurances of identity concerning the server with which the user is communicating, and optionally to authenticate the user to the server.[135]

In the future, transmission security will become even more important. As Internet of Things devices, smart and network-aware devices, telemedicine sessions, and robots become more common, organizations will need to provide assurances of confidentiality and integrity of the communications with these devices. See chapter 9 for more information about emerging technologies and their security challenges.

---

133. See section 5.B.1.a *supra*.

134. For information concerning checksums, see section 5.D.3.a *supra*.

135. For instance, in the ecommerce context, TLS and SSL protect sessions in which a user purchases products from an online merchant's secure site. TLS and SSL authenticate the merchant to the user's browser, so that the user knows the identity of the merchant whose site he or she has accessed. Also, integrity checks provide protection against corruption of the data being communicated. Finally, TLS and SSL protect a user's communication session with encryption to prevent interception of sensitive information, such as payment card information. TLS and SSL can provide these same capabilities in the context of the transmission of PHI.

b. Transmission Security Implementation Specifications—Section 164.312(e)(2)

i. Integrity Controls (Addressable)—Section 164.312(e)(2)(i)

Implement security measures to ensure that electronically transmitted electronic protected health information is not improperly modified without detection until disposed of.

The organization must address what technology it will use to ensure data it sends are not undetectably changed while in transit over a network. Because data may pass through systems outside of its control, the organization cannot ensure that PHI will arrive at destinations unchanged. It can and must ensure, though, that the recipient can detect any changes or data loss during transmission. Presumably, the recipient can, upon detection of modification or loss, request a retransmission. As mentioned above, SSL/TLS makes use of checksum technology to detect changes or data loss.

ii. Encryption (Addressable)—Section 164.312(e)(2)(ii)

Implement a mechanism to encrypt electronic protected health information whenever deemed appropriate.

As discussed in section 5.D.1.b.iv, organizations almost certainly have an obligation to encrypt PHI. This section focuses on mechanisms to encrypt PHI being transmitted from one device to another. It is one aspect of the encryption discussion in section 5.D.1.b.iv above.

As part of its risk assessment, the organization must evaluate and decide whether encrypting some or all of its PHI transmitted over networks is reasonable and appropriate. If encryption is reasonable and appropriate, the organization must implement encryption for PHI in transit. Considerations going into this decision include:

- The recipients' ability to receive and decrypt encrypted communications;
- The sensitivity of the transmitted PHI;
- The potential impacts of unauthorized PHI disclosure;
- The costs of implementing, managing, and operating the encryption system; and
- The vulnerabilities of the network and overall environment.

This analysis applies to PHI without regard to its particular method or protocol of transmission. Therefore, transmissions such as e-mail, web, and dedicated protocol traffic may all need to be encrypted, to the extent reasonable and appropriate for the organization. For additional details about encryption, see 5.D.1.b.iv. As mentioned there, encryption is now industry standard, reasonably priced, and perhaps one of the most effective security controls an organization can implement to reduce its legal risk of HIPAA violations. Accordingly, an organization is almost certainly going to find that encrypting PHI transmissions is reasonable and appropriate, and therefore required.

6. Conclusion Regarding Technical Safeguards

The HIPAA Security Rule's technical safeguards are intended to catalyze with reasonable, appropriate, and cost-effective measures to ensure the security of PHI. Compliance with the rule will include:

- A full assessment of current PHI security and protection practices
- A reasoned security response commensurate with the discovered security risks
- Cost-effectiveness
- Achievability with available technology
- Consistency with generally accepted sound IT systems management and security philosophy
- Likely influence on future technology purchases

In many respects, the Security Rule represents sound business and IT systems management practices that healthcare and other industries have recognized for many years. Many organizations may already be complying with most, if not all, provisions of the Security Rule. Regardless, however, the organization must assess its compliance with the Security Rule to demonstrate to itself, its business partners, and potentially the OCR that it meets PHI security standards.

HHS intended that generally accessible, commercially available technology would suffice for compliance with the Security Rule. The organization may already have sufficient technology and other resources to comply with the technical portion of the Security Rule, and (at least in theory) any missing technology should be available from multiple vendors at reasonable costs. Compliance, however, must be reviewed periodically. As security threats and reasonable and appropriate technology both constantly change, the organization must reassess its PHI security risks and technical security safeguards.

E. POLICIES, PROCEDURES, AND DOCUMENTATION— SECTION 164.316

1. Policies and Procedures (Standard)—Section 164.316(a)

Implement reasonable and appropriate policies and procedures to comply with the standards, implementation specifications, or other requirements of this subpart, taking into account those factors specified in § 164.306(b)(2)(i), (ii), (iii), and (iv). This standard is not to be construed to permit or excuse an action that violates any other standard, implementation specification, or other requirements of this subpart. A covered entity or business associate may change its policies and procedures at any time, provided that the changes are documented and are implemented in accordance with this subpart.

One of the key components of any security program is documentation. The various sections of the HIPAA Security Rule include a requirement that covered entities and business associates implement "reasonable and appropriate" documentation in the form of policies and procedures to comply with standards and implementation specifications in the regulations.[136] Various sections in the regulations require the implementation of security policies and procedures.

In the development of policies and procedures, organizations should ensure that they are sufficient to cover all of the applicable security criteria. Applicable criteria include the portions of the Security Rule that are mandatory (standards and required implementation specifications) and addressable implementation specifications (or equivalent alternative controls) that reasonably and appropriately apply to the organization. If the policies and procedures are incomplete or do not cover all of the applicable security criteria, then they will not be sufficient for compliance.

Further, organizations should tailor their policies and procedures to the actual practices of the staff and downstream business associates in conducting their day-to-day activities. Organizations that simply copy "off the shelf" policies and procedures from a book or other source risk having documents that are divorced from the reality of their daily activities. Instead, organizations should use their risk assessment procedures to develop policies and procedures that address their individual situations and the risks they face. The end result should be policies

---

136. 45 C.F.R. § 164.316(a).

and procedures that create effective and realistic risk management approaches tied to how an organization really operates.

Also, the scope of the organization's policies and procedures should account for:

- Its size, complexity, and capabilities;
- Its security capabilities regarding its technical infrastructure, hardware, and software;
- The costs of security measures; and
- The probability, impact, and criticality of potential risks to PHI.[137]

Policies and procedures should lay out security targets that readily permit auditing and other assessment. An assessor should be able to look at a policy or procedure document to check to see whether the organization actually does what it says it does in the document. Policies and procedures that are insufficiently clear or set out goals that cannot be measured make it difficult to assess compliance.

Finally, organizations should reexamine their policies and procedures on a periodic basis to make sure that they remain reasonable and appropriate. Threats, vulnerabilities to those threats, security technology, IT, the organization's operating environment, and business needs change over time. Security incidents may also call attention to needed amendments to policies and procedures. Organizations should make amendments as needed to account for these changes. Periodic reexamination and amendment can ensure that policies and procedures remain relevant over time.

When making amendments, organizations should follow the change control procedures set forth in the policies and procedures. For instance, change control procedures can address issues such as:

- Who can propose changes
- Who must approve changes
- Notifications to affected parties
- The process for obtaining approval and finalization
- When documentation becomes effective and when it must be reevaluated

Further, when making changes, organizations should have explanatory documentation, such as the reason for the changes, the nature

---

137. *See id.* § 164.306(b).

of the changes, and how they intend to implement the changes. Organizations may find it helpful to task a team of personnel to solicit input, investigate changed circumstances, and implement amendments to policies and procedures periodically.

2. Documentation—Section 164.316(b)

a. Documentation (Standard)—Section 164.316(b)(1)

1. Maintain the policies and procedures implemented to comply with this subpart in written (which may be electronic) form; and
2. If an action, activity, or assessment is required by this subpart to be documented, maintain a written (which may be electronic) record of the action, activity, or assessment.

Organizations must maintain policies and procedures in written form, which may be in the form of electronic records,[138] such as word processing files. Likewise, some of the regulations require that actions, activities, or assessments be documented. For instance, if an addressable implementation specification is not reasonable or appropriate to implement, the organization must maintain documentation as to why it is not, and should document why any equivalent alternative measure would be appropriate and reasonable.[139] If an organization determines that no alternative measures are reasonable and appropriate, the organization should document the reasoning behind its decision. Where regulations require documentation, organizations must maintain a written record of the action, activity, or assessment. Again, electronic documents are acceptable.[140]

One question that arises is whether the organization should have a general set of security documents, in which HIPAA Security Rule compliance is one component, or whether the organization should maintain a separate set of HIPAA-specific documentation. The regulations do not require one or the other. Therefore, an organization with a general security policy can simply add HIPAA-specific provisions to address the Security Rule. Other organizations may wish to maintain a separate set of HIPAA-specific documents to address the HIPAA Security Rule. For organizations that face requirements from multiple sources, such as health insurers, it may be easier to have a single security policy

---

138. 45 C.F.R. § 164.316(b)(1)(i).
139. *Id.* § 164.306(d)(3)(ii)(B).
140. *Id.* § 164.316(b)(1)(ii).

combining mandates from HIPAA, the Gramm-Leach-Bliley Act, and other requirements, as opposed to having multiple policies, each addressed to one statutory scheme or source. At a minimum, however, HIPAA-specific documentation should not conflict with other security policies and procedures.

b. Documentation Implementation Specification—Section 164.316(b)(2)

1. *Time limit (Required).* Retain the documentation required by paragraph (b)(1) of this section for 6 years from the date of its creation or the date when it last was in effect, whichever is later.
2. *Availability (Required).* Make documentation available to those persons responsible for implementing the procedures to which the documentation pertains.
3. *Updates (Required).* Review documentation periodically, and update as needed, in response to environmental or operational changes affecting the security of the electronic protected health information.

These required implementation specifications for documentation state that organizations must retain the documentation described in the previous section for a period of six years. The six years start to run from the documentation's date of creation or the date when the described program was last in effect, whichever is later.[141] Organizations retaining documentation in electronic form over time should consider:

- Measures to ensure that documentation is not inadvertently lost, destroyed, or corrupted.
- Measures to prevent intentional alteration.
- Maintaining backup copies of the documentation to ensure recovery from loss, destruction, corruption, or malicious alteration.
- Accounting for changes in software and hardware and ensuring that archived documentation is still accessible on currently-used systems. For instance, if an organization migrates from the use of one word processing program to another, the organization may want to retain an old system to access archived word processing documents, or archived documentation may need to be resaved in the new format.

---

141. 45 C.F.R. § 164.316(b)(2)(i).

Organizations must also make their documentation available to the personnel who are responsible for implementation of the procedures documented.[142] Documentation, such as policies, procedures, and their amendments, would do no good unless the personnel implementing them know where to find them and have access to them. One way to make documentation available is to include it in routine, special, or refresher education and security awareness training programs. Another option is to publish it on an internal network or on internal wiki pages.

Finally, organizations must review their documentation from time to time and update it as needed. Updates are required whenever an organization makes changes in its environment (e.g., its facility) or operations (such as the activities it conducts) that affect the security of PHI.[143] Good documentation is also crucial in any audit or enforcement situation to demonstrate the organization's good-faith efforts to comply with the rules.

---

142. *Id.* § 164.316(b)(2)(ii).
143. *Id.* § 164.316(b)(2)(iii).

CHAPTER 6

The Breach Notification Rule and Handling Breaches

Chapter 5 covers the Security Rule and how covered entities and business associates can prevent breaches from occurring. Nonetheless, data breaches involving healthcare organizations are common. For instance, the oft-cited Ponemon Institute's May 2016 survey of healthcare organizations found that 89 percent of covered entity respondents and 61 percent of business associate respondents had experienced a data breach in the previous 24 months. Forty five percent of covered entity respondents and 13 percent of business associate respondents had experienced more than five breaches in that time period.[1] In light of the reality of the frequency of data breaches, covered entities and business associates should not only take actions to prevent breaches, they should also be prepared to handle data breaches when they do occur and minimize the harm from them. This chapter uses the term "organization" as a shorthand term for the applicable covered entity or business associate.

Congress recognized the need for organizations to prepare for breaches and minimize the harm from data breaches when it enacted the HITECH Act. Specifically, it enacted provisions requiring covered entities and business associates to notify those affected by a data breach. In doing so, Congress borrowed the popular idea of breach notification from the states, almost all of which enacted their own breach notification legislation covering sensitive personal information.

This chapter focuses on breach notification requirements in the HITECH Act and the Breach Notification Rule. Section 6.A of this chapter discusses the history and background of the breach notification

---

1. *See* Ponemon Inst. LLC, Sixth Annual Benchmark Study on Privacy & Security of Healthcare Data 19 (May 2016), https://www2.idexpertscorp.com/fifth-annual-ponemon -study-on-privacy-security-incidents-of-healthcare-data.

concept in state law. Section 6.B covers the HITECH Act provisions on breach notification. Section 6.C explains the key concept of "unsecured protected health information," which appears in the HITECH Act and the Breach Notification Rule, and affects the analysis of whether a covered entity or business associate has a breach notification obligation. Section 6.D covers the Breach Notification Rule and describes the scope and details of a covered entity's or a business associate's breach notification obligation.

This chapter covers the breach notification standards appearing in the HIPAA Final Omnibus Rule.[2] The Final Omnibus Rule's breach notification standards supersede the earlier standard in the Interim Final Rule.[3] The Final Omnibus Rule clarified the standard for breach notification. Specifically, when an organization experiences a potential breach, it must conduct a risk assessment focused on objective factors to make a final determination as to whether or not a "breach" has in fact occurred. Second, the Department of Health and Human Services (HHS) created a presumption in favor of finding a "breach": an impermissible use or disclosure of protected health information (PHI) *is presumed to be a breach*. An organization can decide that a breach did not occur only if it demonstrates that there is a low probability that the PHI has been compromised.[4] In other words, in the case of true uncertainty, or when a determination could "go either way," the organization must make a breach notification.

A. BACKGROUND ABOUT BREACH NOTIFICATION

The world's first breach notification law was California's SB 1386 legislation. Throughout recent decades, California has proven to be on the forefront of many trends in the law. The areas of privacy and identity theft are prominent examples. Senator Stephen Peace and my own Assembly Member Joe Simitian coauthored the legislation.[5]

---

2. Modifications to the HIPAA Privacy, Security, Enforcement, and Breach Notification Rules under the Health Information Technology for Economic and Clinical Health Act and the Genetic Information Nondiscrimination Act; Other Modifications to the HIPAA Rules; Final Rule, 78 Fed. Reg. 5566 (2013) [hereinafter Final Omnibus Rule].

3. Breach Notification for Unsecured Protected Health Information, 74 Fed. Reg. 42,740 (2009).

4. Final Omnibus Rule, *supra* note 2, 78 Fed. Reg. at 5641.

5. Senator Peace's Senate bill was SB 1386, while Assembly Member Simitian's companion bill in the Assembly was AB 700. The legislation is generally referred to by its Senate number.

The motivation for SB 1386 was a data breach. On April 5, 2002, hackers exploited vulnerabilities in a server holding a database of personnel information on California's 265,000 state employees. The security breach at California's Stephen P. Teale Data Center in Rancho Cordova compromised names, Social Security numbers, and payroll information. Public outrage soon followed the May 24, 2002 announcement of the breach. For almost two months, the state failed to discover the breach in a timely fashion and tell the affected employees. The victims included then Governor Gray Davis and 120 state legislators.[6]

Following the incident at the Teale Data Center, demands and the perceived need for legislative protection, likely bolstered by the personal impact on the governor and state legislators, led the California legislature to enact SB 1386. Governor Davis signed the bill in September 2002. SB 1386 became effective on July 1, 2003, and was the first breach notification law.[7] The legislature believed that requiring notification would give affected individuals the ability to take steps to prevent identity theft and minimize the impact of a breach.[8] The idea was not to punish custodians of personal information, but rather to help affected individuals.

SB 1386 required businesses to notify California residents of a breach in the security of certain categories of personal information: first name or initial and last name in combination with one of the following:

- Social Security number;
- Driver's license number or California Identification Card number; and
- Financial account or payment card account number in combination with any code or password that would permit access to the account.

---

6. For general background about the Teale Center breach, see Ryan Kim, *Hackers Gain Entry to Key State Database; Personnel Files Were Breached Last Month for 265,000 Workers*, S.F. CHRON., May 25, 2002, http://www.sfgate.com/news/article/Hackers-gain-entry-to-key-state-database-2833196.php.

7. The Senate analysis of SB 1386 cited the Teale Center breach as motivation for the bill. Saskia Kim, SB 1386 Senate Bill—Bill Analysis 3, 4 (hearing held June 18, 2002), http://www.leginfo.ca.gov/pub/01-02/bill/sen/sb_1351-1400/sb_1486_cfa_20020617e_141710_asm_comm.html.

8. *See id.* at 1.

Since the original enactment of SB 1386, the California legislature added "medical information"[9] and "health insurance information"[10] to the categories of data whose compromise triggers a breach notification obligation.[11]

Since California enacted SB 1386, 46 other states, the District of Columbia, Guam, Puerto Rico, and the Virgin Islands have enacted breach notification laws, making the total 47 states. The only states without breach notification laws are Alabama, New Mexico, and South Dakota, although at the time of this writing, a breach notification bills is pending in Alabama.[12] As is apparent by the breadth of adoption, the breach notification concept is popular throughout the United States. Moreover, breach notification legislation is now spreading beyond the United States and informing international law and laws in other countries.[13] The one simple idea of breach notification from California Senator Steve Peace and Assembly Member Joe Simitian of helping individuals prevent identity theft has now spread throughout the world.

---

9. Cal. Civil Code § 1798.82(i)(2). "For purposes of this section, 'medical information' means any information regarding an individual's medical history, mental or physical condition, or medical treatment or diagnosis by a health care professional." *Id.*

10. *Id.* § 1798.82(i)(3). "For purposes of this section, 'health insurance information' means an individual's health insurance policy number or subscriber identification number, any unique identifier used by a health insurer to identify the individual, or any information in an individual's application and claims history, including any appeals records." *Id.*

11. The California law states that a HIPAA covered entity making a HITECH Act-compliant breach notification is deemed to have satisfied the breach notification content requirement of SB 1386, but is not exempted from complying with any other provision of the law. *Id.* § 1798.82(e) ("A covered entity under the federal Health Insurance Portability and Accountability Act of 1996 (42 U.S.C. Sec. 1320d et seq.) will be deemed to have complied with the notice requirements in subdivision (d) if it has complied completely with Section 13402(f) of the federal Health Information Technology for Economic and Clinical Health Act (Public Law 111-5). However, nothing in this subdivision shall be construed to exempt a covered entity from any other provision of this section."). This provision suggests that satisfying the HITECH Act breach notification content requirement is good enough for SB 1386, but the requirement to make the breach notification itself is not excused.

12. H.B. 291, Reg. Sess. (Ala. 2016), http://alisondb.legislature.state.al.us/alison /searchableinstruments/2016rs/bills/HB291.htm and http://www.nmlegis.gov/Sessions/16%20 Regular/bills/house/HB0325.pdf. N.M bill died.

13. *E.g.,* Commission Regulation (EU) No 611/2013, Official J. of the E.U. 173/2 (Jun. 26, 2013) (European Union regulation for breach notification for public electronic communications service providers in the European Union); Directive 2002/58/EC of the European Parliament and of the Council of 12 July 2002 concerning the processing of personal data and the protection of privacy in the electronic communications sector (EU directive harmonizing law concerning public electronic communications services in the EU, including safeguarding subscriber information and informing them about risks from a security breach).

B. HITECH ACT'S BREACH NOTIFICATION REQUIREMENT

The HITECH Act brought the concept of breach notification to healthcare information technology security. The act requires covered entities to notify individuals affected by a breach of unsecured PHI. More precisely, section 13402 of the act, codified at 42 U.S.C. § 17392(a), states:

> A covered entity that accesses, maintains, retains, modifies, records, stores, destroys, or otherwise holds, uses, or discloses unsecured protected health information (as defined in subsection (h)(1)) shall, in the case of a breach of such information that is discovered by the covered entity, notify each individual whose unsecured protected health information has been, or is reasonably believed by the covered entity to have been, accessed, acquired, or disclosed as a result of such breach.[14]

A few observations will assist in understanding this core statutory breach notification requirement. First, the requirement in the act applies to covered entities, not business associates. Business associates have their own breach notification requirement in a separate provision of the act. Second, the concept of "unsecured protected health information" is critical to understanding whether a party has a breach notification obligation. Section 6.C below defines "unsecured protected health information." Third, breach notification is a duty, and not simply a guideline, recommendation, or addressable practice. Section 17932(a) states that covered entities "shall" notify affected individuals.

Fourth, the duty to notify turns on whether a "breach" within the meaning of the act occurred. "The term 'breach' means the unauthorized acquisition, access, use, or disclosure of protected health information which compromises the security or privacy of such information, except where an unauthorized person to whom such information is disclosed would not reasonably have been able to retain such information."[15] As described below in section 6.D.1 and 6.E, determining whether a "breach" occurred is a key step in complying with the act and regulations.

The act has three exceptions to the definition of "breach," which are instances in which Congress imposed no duty to notify. A "breach" does not include:

---

14. 42 U.S.C. § 17932(a).
15. *Id.* § 17921(1)(A).

(i) any unintentional acquisition, access, or use of protected health information by an employee or individual acting under the authority of a covered entity or business associate if—

  (I) such acquisition, access, or use was made in good faith and within the course and scope of the employment or other professional relationship of such employee or individual, respectively, with the covered entity or business associate; and

  (II) such information is not further acquired, accessed, used, or disclosed by any person; or

(ii) any inadvertent disclosure from an individual who is otherwise authorized to access protected health information at a facility operated by a covered entity or business associate to another similarly situated individual at [the] same facility; and

(iii) any such information received as a result of such disclosure is not further acquired, accessed, used, or disclosed without authorization by any person.[16]

Fifth, certain knowledge that a compromise occurred is not necessary to trigger a breach notification. Instead, a covered entity must notify affected individuals not only if it knows that unsecured PHI has been compromised, but also if the unsecured PHI "is reasonably believed" by the covered entity to have been compromised. Under this standard, if the covered entity cannot be certain a compromise occurred, but has evidence of a compromise, and based on the evidence, it would be reasonable to conclude a compromise occurred, the covered entity must make a breach notification.

Finally, section 17932(a) contemplates different forms of possible compromise: access, acquisition, or disclosure. These are not extremely precise concepts, and their boundaries may be uncertain in some cases. For instance, in some instances of "access," an attacker is seeking to obtain PHI, finds it, and views it. In other instances, access may be inadvertent. Information may be sent to an unauthorized recipient without the recipient seeking it out. Likewise, "acquisition" and "disclosure" may be intentional or inadvertent. The plain words of section 17932(a) cover inadvertent conduct and thereby make its scope broader than simply covering situations of intentional attacks.

---

16. *Id.* § 17921(1)(B). Note that (i) is followed by "or" but (ii) is followed by "and," which may lead to some interesting interpretations. One possibility is that (iii) should have been included in (ii), rather than set out separately.

Under the act, "[t]he terms 'disclose' and 'disclosure' have the meaning given the term 'disclosure' in section 160.103 of title 45, Code of Federal Regulations."[17] As defined in section 160.103, "*[d]isclosure* means the release, transfer, provision of access to, or divulging in any manner of information outside the entity holding the information."[18] While this definition adds additional concepts to the idea of "disclosure," these concepts are also somewhat imprecise.

"Disclosure" may occur through different means. "Disclosure" may occur because of a transfer of paper, an e-mail, exfiltration by an attacker from a network, download from a file sharing system, or any number of ways. Its boundary is uncertain where, for instance, an entity inadvertently posts PHI to a location accessible to the public Internet where it is not clear if anyone actually accessed it. Arguably, "disclosure" occurred because it was released outside the entity holding it. The entity provided "access" to it to anyone with a browser. Anyone on the Internet had "access" to it. On the other hand, if no one ever viewed or copied the posted files, and the posting entity promptly took down the files, the access led to no one outside the entity seeing it. Did "disclosure" really occur? The answer is uncertain (unless comprehensive logging of file access can unequivocally establish that the files were not downloaded).

Business associates have their own breach notification obligation. As with covered entities, a breach of unsecured PHI sustained by a business associate triggers the duty to notify. Unlike covered entities, however, a business associate has no obligation under the act to notify affected individuals. Instead, the business associate only has a duty to notify the applicable covered entity. Once notified of the breach by the business associate, it is the covered entity that has the obligation to notify affected individuals. Specifically:

> A business associate of a covered entity that accesses, maintains, retains, modifies, records, stores, destroys, or otherwise holds, uses, or discloses unsecured protected health information shall, following the discovery of a breach of such information, notify the covered entity of such breach. Such notice shall include the identification of each individual whose unsecured protected health information has been, or is reasonably believed by the business associate to have been, accessed, acquired, or disclosed during such breach.[19]

---

17. *Id.* § 17921(4).
18. 45 C.F.R. § 160.103 (definition of "disclosure").
19. 42 U.S.C. § 17932(b).

The remaining provisions of section 17932 describe more details about when the affected entity must make a breach notification, acceptable methods of notice, notifying the Secretary of HHS, what content the notice must contain, delaying notification at the request of law enforcement, and the definition of "law enforcement" and "unsecured protected health information."[20] Section 6.D below integrates the act's detailed requirements with its discussion of the Breach Notification Rule in the regulations. In the event of an investigation or compliance review, the burden of proof is on the organization to show that it made the notifications required by section 17932.[21] In addition, the Secretary of HHS must report to Congress each year on the number and nature of breaches as well as responsive actions.[22] Finally, the act calls for HHS to issue interim final regulations on breach notification,[23] which HHS issued on August 24, 2009.[24] The Final Omnibus Rule then superseded the interim final regulations.

C. UNSECURED PROTECTED HEALTH INFORMATION

The critical question regarding possible breach notification following any security incident is whether a "breach" of "unsecured protected health information" occurred. If a compromise of PHI involves secured PHI, the affected entity has no duty to notify. By contrast, if the compromised PHI was unsecured, a breach of the PHI will trigger a duty to notify. Therefore, it is important to understand the definition of "unsecured protected health information" under the HITECH Act. A full understanding of the concept of "unsecured protected health information" requires several steps, because the definition incorporates guidance outside the act by reference.

The act states, "[F]or purposes of this section, the term 'unsecured protected health information' means protected health information that is not secured through the use of a technology or methodology specified by the Secretary in the guidance issued under paragraph (2)."[25] Thus, to understand if PHI was "unsecured," it is necessary to refer to HHS

---

20. *Id.* §§ 17932(c)–(h).

21. *See id.* § 17932(d)(2).

22. *Id.* § 17932(i).

23. *Id.* § 17932(j).

24. Breach Notification for Unsecured Protected Health Information, 74 Fed. Reg. 42,740 (2009) [hereinafter Interim Final Breach Notification Rule].

25. 42 U.S.C. § 17932(h)(1)(A).

guidance. Paragraph (2) requires HHS to issue such guidance each year. "[T]he Secretary shall, after consultation with stakeholders, issue (and annually update) guidance specifying the technologies and methodologies that render protected health information unusable, unreadable, or indecipherable to unauthorized individuals. . . ."[26] "[M]ethodologies that render" "information unusable, unreadable, or indecipherable" are either encryption or secure disposal techniques. Accordingly, Congress apparently intended that "unsecured" means, as a practical matter, "unencrypted" or not disposed of in a secure fashion.

In 2009, HHS issued guidance on how to render PHI unusable, unreadable, or indecipherable. Information rendered unusable, unreadable, or indecipherable using the recommended methods is secured.[27] "Unsecured protected health information" means any PHI that is not secured using one of these methods. The 2009 guidance specifies two methods of securing PHI that would make breach notification unnecessary.

For PHI still in use, the PHI must be encrypted.

> Electronic PHI has been encrypted as specified in the HIPAA Security Rule by "the use of an algorithmic process to transform data into a form in which there is a low probability of assigning meaning without use of a confidential process or key" and such confidential process or key that might enable decryption has not been breached. To avoid a breach of the confidential process or key, these decryption tools should be stored on a device or at a location separate from the data they are used to encrypt or decrypt.[28]

Note that this guidance calls for sound encryption key management. Encryption is no use if the key used to encrypt and decrypt information has been compromised. Therefore, it is important to protect symmetric cryptographic keys or asymmetric private keys and keep these keys away from systems holding the data.

HHS identified certain publications of the National Institute of Standards and Technology (NIST) that specify encryption processes. HHS said the methods in these publications meet its standard for avoiding breaches. For data at rest, HHS said encryption processes in NIST Special Publication 800-111, *Guide to Storage Encryption*

---

26. *Id.* § 17932(h)(2).
27. Interim Final Breach Notification Rule, *supra* note 24.
28. *Id.*, 74 Fed. Reg. at 42,742 (footnote omitted).

Technologies for End User Devices, satisfies the standard.[29] For data in motion, HHS said Transport Layer Security (TLS), IPsec virtual private networks, and other technology Federal Information Processing Standards (FIPS) 140-2 validated meet the standard: NIST Special Publications 800-52, *Guidelines for the Selection and Use of Transport Layer Security (TLS) Implementations*; 800-77, *Guide to IPsec VPNs*; or 800-113, *Guide to SSL VPNs*, or others that are FIPS 140-2 validated.[30] As of the date of this publication, HHS's website lists these same publications as the current guidance for securing PHI.[31]

For PHI that is no longer to be used, rendering the PHI unusable, unreadable, or indecipherable means disposing of it securely using one of HHS's specified methods. These methods call for destruction of the media on which the PHI has been stored. For physical media, physical destruction satisfies the standard: "Paper, film, or other hard copy media have been shredded or destroyed such that the PHI cannot be read or otherwise cannot be reconstructed."[32] "Redaction is specifically excluded as a means of data destruction."[33] For electronic PHI, the methods in NIST's media sanitization satisfies the standard: "Electronic media have been cleared, purged, or destroyed consistent with NIST Special Publication 800-88, *Guidelines for Media Sanitization*, such that the PHI cannot be retrieved."[34] Again, as with PHI still in use, HHS's current guidance regarding media sanitization is the same as the 2009 guidance.[35]

D. THE BREACH NOTIFICATION RULE

Having discussed the HITECH Act's general breach notification requirements and the key concept of "unsecured protected health information," it is now possible to describe in detail the Breach Notification Rule regulations in 45 C.F.R. part 164. Section 6.D.1 elucidates the definition of a "breach" and what triggers a notification obligation.

---

29. *Id.*
30. *Id.*
31. HHS, Guidance to Render Unsecured Protected Health Information Unusable, Unreadable, or Indecipherable to Unauthorized Individuals, http://www.hhs.gov/hipaa/for-professionals/breach-notification/guidance/index.html (last visited Apr. 6, 2016) [hereinafter HHS Guidance].
32. Interim Final Breach Notification Rule, *supra* note 24, 74 Fed. Reg. at 42,743.
33. *Id.*
34. *Id.* (footnote omitted).
35. HHS Guidance, *supra* note 31.

The definition of "breach" is critical, because in the absence of a "breach," there is no obligation to notify anyone under the HITECH Act or the Breach Notification Rule. Section 6.D.2 explains the breach notification-related obligations of a covered entity. Finally, section 6.D.3 describes the notification-related obligations of a business associate.

1. Definition of a Breach and Breach Notification Triggers

The definition of "breach" in the Breach Notification Rule is similar, but not identical, to that in the HITECH Act. "*Breach* means the acquisition, access, use, or disclosure of protected health information in a manner not permitted under [the Privacy Rule of] subpart E of this part which compromises the security or privacy of the protected health information."[36] This definition places an emphasis on "compromise" as the touchstone of unauthorized acquisition, access, use, or disclosure. Access that does not result in a "compromise," such as a momentary flashing of PHI on a video screen, where there is no way a viewer could retain the information, would not be a "breach."

The Breach Notification Rule also includes exceptions similar but not identical to those in the HITECH Act of access or disclosure that do not constitute a "breach." A "breach" excludes:

(i) Any unintentional acquisition, access, or use of protected health information by a workforce member or person acting under the authority of a covered entity or a business associate, if such acquisition, access, or use was made in good faith and within the scope of authority and does not result in further use or disclosure in a manner not permitted under subpart E of this part.

(ii) Any inadvertent disclosure by a person who is authorized to access protected health information at a covered entity or business associate to another person authorized to access protected health information at the same covered entity or business associate, or organized health care arrangement in which the covered entity participates, and the information received as a result of such disclosure is not further used or disclosed in a manner not permitted under subpart E of this part.

(iii) A disclosure of protected health information where a covered entity or business associate has a good faith belief that an

---

36. 45 C.F.R. § 164.402.

> unauthorized person to whom the disclosure was made would not reasonably have been able to retain such information.[37]

The most significant difference between the HITECH Act and the Breach Notification Rule is that HHS's third exception is more specific and easier to determine if it is met. The act's third exception states that a breach has not occurred if "any such information received as a result of such disclosure is not further acquired, accessed, used, or disclosed without authorization by any person," while the Breach Notification Rule's exception turns on whether a recipient reasonably would have been able to retain the disclosed PHI. The example above in this section of PHI flashing on a screen momentarily would be a good example of information that a recipient would not reasonably have been able to retain.

The Breach Notification Rule's definition of "breach" contains an important addition. The definition presumes a "breach" occurred when a violation of the Privacy Rule occurs.

> Except as provided in paragraph (1) of this definition [providing exceptions to the definition of a "breach"], an acquisition, access, use, or disclosure of protected health information in a manner not permitted under subpart E [the Privacy Rule] *is presumed to be a breach* unless the covered entity or business associate, as applicable, demonstrates that there is a low probability that the protected health information has been compromised based on a risk assessment of at least the following factors:
>
> (i)   The nature and extent of the protected health information involved, including the types of identifiers and the likelihood of re-identification;
>
> (ii) The unauthorized person who used the protected health information or to whom the disclosure was made;
>
> (iii) Whether the protected health information was actually acquired or viewed; and
>
> (iv) The extent to which the risk to the protected health information has been mitigated.[38]

The organization must make a breach notification following a "breach" as defined above. If it wishes to avoid making a notification, it must undertake a risk assessment to weigh these four factors. The organization can avoid notification only if the evidence shows

---

37. *Id.* § 164.402(1).
38. *Id.* § 164.402(2)(emphasis added).

a low probability of compromise, supporting a conclusion that no "breach" occured.

The Breach Notification Rule contains its own definition of "unsecured protected health information." It refers back to the HITECH Act's incorporation of HHS guidance on making PHI unusable, unreadable, or indecipherable. "*Unsecured protected health information* means protected health information that is not rendered unusable, unreadable, or indecipherable to unauthorized persons through the use of a technology or methodology specified by the Secretary in the guidance issued under section 13402(h)(2) of Public Law 111-5."[39]

Having defined "breach" and "unsecured protected health information," it is now possible to establish what triggers a breach notification obligation. Whether a covered entity or a business associate is involved, a "breach" of "unsecured protected health information" triggers a breach notification obligation. Without a "breach," no obligation to notify arises. Moreover, the disclosure of secured PHI triggers no obligation. The information involved in a Privacy Rule violation or security incident must be unsecured and the violation or incident must rise to the level of a "breach."

2. Covered Entity Breach Notification Obligations

The Breach Notification Rule's requirements expand upon the HITECH Act. The core breach notification requirement appears in 45 C.F.R. § 164.404(a)(1). "A covered entity shall, following the discovery of a breach of unsecured protected health information, notify each individual whose unsecured protected health information has been, or is reasonably believed by the covered entity to have been, accessed, acquired, used, or disclosed as a result of such breach."[40]

A covered entity must comply with certain administrative requirements in the Privacy Rule, 45 C.F.R. § 164.530, in connection with the Breach Notification Rule.[41] For instance, the requirements to maintain implementing policies and procedures, create documentation, train its workforce, and impose sanctions for noncompliance all apply to the Breach Notification Rule.

---

39. *Id.* § 164.402(definition of "unsecured protected health information").

40. 45 C.F.R. § 164.404(a)(1).

41. 45 C.F.R. § 164.414(a) (stating that covered entities must comply with section 164.530(b), (d), (e), (g), (h), (i), and (j) with regard to the Breach Notification Rule).

If a covered entity is uncertain as to whether a breach of unsecured PHI occurred, the Breach Notification Rule resolves doubts in favor of making a breach notification. Likewise, if the scope of whom and how to notify recipients is in doubt, the rule weighs in favor of broader or more notice, rather than less. It resolves these doubts by creating a burden of proof that the covered entity must meet. The burden of proof is on the covered entity to either demonstrate that it made all required notifications following a use or disclosure of PHI in violation of the Privacy Rule, or that the use or disclosure did not constitute a "breach" within the meaning of the rule.[42]

Therefore, if a covered entity avoided notifying anyone following a Privacy Rule violation or security incident based on the belief that no "breach" occurred, it would have the burden of proof. Specifically, in the event of an investigation, compliance review, enforcement action, or litigation, it would have the burden to prove no "breach," in fact, took place. If, following a covered entity's investigation of an incident, it has no evidence one way or another that a breach took place, or if the evidence weighs equally in favor and against a finding that a breach occurred, the rule requires the covered entity to make a breach notification. If the covered entity fails to make the required notifications, it would be unable to meet its burden of proof and would be liable for the failure to notify.

This may be the most difficult provision in the Breach Notification Rule to implement. People may have a natural human tendency to not want to make a notification if they have no evidence that anyone viewed or received the PHI at issue, or that a compromise otherwise occurred. Nonetheless, the Breach Notification Rule resolves doubts in favor of notification, and covered entities are risking liability if they fail to make the required notifications.

a. Timing of Breach Notification

A covered entity must make the notification "without unreasonable delay and in no case later than 60 calendar days after discovery of a breach."[43] This timing requirement is the same as the one in the HITECH Act.[44] It does not establish a firm deadline, other than the 60 day outer limit, but instead focuses on what is reasonable. Undertaking an investigation

---

42. *Id.* § 164.414(b).
43. 45 C.F.R. § 164.404(b).
44. 42 U.S.C. § 17932(d)(1).

obtain the facts and circumstances surrounding an incident is likely a reasonable basis for delaying notification.

Delay to avoid premature notification with probably incorrect and ultimately confusing information is likely reasonable as well. Nonetheless, taking too long to investigate would be unreasonable. The covered entity will need to balance the need to obtain correct information in an investigation against the possibility of unreasonable delay in order to decide the right time to make a notification. In almost all cases, sixty days is likely ample time to conduct an investigation to find out the facts surrounding an incident. As a result, it is much more likely that the "without unreasonable delay" requirement is going to set the time limit by which a covered entity must notify individuals, rather than the sixty-day limit.

The time to make a notification begins at the time of "discovery." "[A] breach shall be treated as discovered by a covered entity as of the first day on which such breach is known to the covered entity, or, by exercising reasonable diligence would have been known to the covered entity."[45] The knowledge of workforce members or agents of a covered entity is imputed to the covered entity as to when discovery occurs: "A covered entity shall be deemed to have knowledge of a breach if such breach is known, or by exercising reasonable diligence would have been known, to any person, other than the person committing the breach, who is a workforce member or agent of the covered entity (determined in accordance with the federal common law of agency)."[46]

Despite the requirement for making a breach notification without unreasonable delay, the Breach Notification Rule includes an exception. If a law enforcement official requests that the covered entity delay notification because a notice would "impede a criminal investigation or cause damage to national security," the covered entity must delay notification.[47] The HITECH Act contains a similar provision.[48]

The Breach Notification Rule covers cases in which the law enforcement official communicates a demand or request for delay in writing to the covered entity as well as cases in which the official communicates a request or demand orally. If the official communicates in writing and specifies a time period of delay, the covered entity must delay

---

45. 45 C.F.R. § 164.404(a)(2).
46. *Id.*
47. *Id.* § 164.412.
48. 42 U.S.C. § 17932(g).

the notice until that time period elapses.[49] The rule does not specify what happens if the writing does not specify what happens if the official's written communication does not include a time period. Accordingly, it is a good idea for the covered entity to request that the official specify a time period in the written communication. If the official communicates a request or demand for delay orally, the covered entity must delay notification for thirty days. Nonetheless, if, during this thirty-day period, the official making the oral request later provides a writing specifying a time period for delay, the time period in the later writing will govern how long the covered entity must wait to notify affected individuals.[50]

b. Content of the Notification

The Breach Notification Rule specifies the content of a notification. To the extent possible, a notice must include:

(A) A brief description of what happened, including the date of the breach and the date of the discovery of the breach, if known;

(B) A description of the types of unsecured protected health information that were involved in the breach (such as whether full name, social security number, date of birth, home address, account number, diagnosis, disability code, or other types of information were involved);

(C) Any steps individuals should take to protect themselves from potential harm resulting from the breach;

(D) A brief description of what the covered entity involved is doing to investigate the breach, to mitigate harm to individuals, and to protect against any further breaches; and

(E) Contact procedures for individuals to ask questions or learn additional information, which shall include a toll-free telephone number, an e-mail address, website, or postal address.[51]

This required content is almost the same as the content specified in the HITECH Act.[52] The notification must appear in plain language.[53] The covered entity is not required to use any particular kind of software or system, or provide an affected individual with any specific kind

---

49. 45 C.F.R. § 164.412(a).

50. *Id.* § 164.412(b).

51. 45 C.F.R. § 164.404(c)(1).

52. 42 U.S.C. § 17932(f).

53. 45 C.F.R. § 164.404(c)(2).

of reports, in order to satisfy the content requirements for a breach notification.[54]

c. Who Must Receive a Notice and Methods of Notification

If possible, a covered entity must notify an individual affected by a breach directly in writing by first-class mail or electronic mail.[55] A covered entity may use e-mail only if the individual has affirmatively agreed to receive electronic notice and has not withdrawn that agreement.[56] Thus, as a default, the individual himself or herself should be the person receiving a breach notification, and first-class mail is the default method of providing notification.

i. Alternative Recipients of Notice

The Breach Notification Rule expressly covers the situation where an individual affected by a breach is deceased. If the individual is deceased, the covered entity knows of the individual's death, and has the address of next of kin or a personal representative, the covered entity must provide the notice to such next of kin or personal representative.[57] If the covered entity does not know of an individual's death, nothing in the Breach Notification Rule or the HITECH Act requires the covered entity to provide notice other than in the name of the individual to the last known address of the individual.

The other possible cases in which another person could receive notice is one in which the individual has a personal representative or the individual is an unemancipated minor. A personal representative may be an agent acting under a healthcare directive or healthcare power of attorney. It may also be a conservator or guardian of the person, in case the individual is incapacitated. An adult individual or emancipated minor may have such a personal representative. The parent, guardian of the person, or other person acting in loco parentis of an unemancipated minor may be making healthcare decisions for the minor.

---

54. *See* United States *ex rel.* Sheldon v. Kettering Health Network, No. 1:14-cv-345, 2015 WL 74950, at *4 n.4 (S.D. Ohio Jan. 6, 2015), *aff'd*, 816 F.3d 399, 11 (6th Cir. 2016) (relator in a False Claims Act case failed to adequately plead a "false statement"; a failure to run a specific kind of report following a breach did not support allegations that defendant made a "false statement").

55. 45 C.F.R. § 164.404(d)(1)(i). *Accord* 42 U.S.C. § 17932(e)(1)(A).

56. *See* 45 C.F.R. § 164.404(d)(1)(i). *Accord* 42 U.S.C. § 17932(e)(1)(A).

57. 45 C.F.R. § 164.404(d)(1)(ii). *Accord* 42 U.S.C. § 17932(e)(1)(A).

Under the Privacy Rule, a covered entity must treat a personal representative of an individual as the individual himself or herself, for example for purposes of giving authorization to the covered entity to disclose PHI.[58] A covered entity must treat a parent, guardian, or other person acting in loco parentis of an unemancipated minor as a personal representative.[59] The applicable section in the Privacy Rule states that treating such a person as the individual applies "for purposes of this subchapter."[60] The subchapter in which this provision appears is Subchapter C of Subtitle A in title 45 of the Code of Federal Regulations, which includes all of 45 C.F.R. part 164, including the Security Rule and Breach Notification Rule. Therefore, these provisions apply to a breach notification situation.

Accordingly, if the covered entity is aware that an individual has a personal representative acting on behalf of the individual, the covered entity must send the notice to the personal representative. If the covered entity is not aware of the personal representative, nothing in the Breach Notification Rule or the HITECH Act requires the covered entity to provide notice other than in the name of the individual to the last known address of the individual. For minors, the covered entity must provide notice to the parent, guardian, or other person acting in loco parentis. Presumably, a notice addressed to "the parent(s) or guardian(s) of" an individual sent to the individual's last known address would suffice. If the covered entity is aware the minor individual has been emancipated, the covered entity must send the notice directly to the individual.

ii. Alternative Methods of Notification

The Breach Notification Rule provides for alternative methods of notification if the covered entity has insufficient or out-of-date contact information. The covered entity might, for instance, know that the postal address of an individual is out of date if the Postal Service returns mail sent by the covered entity to the individual at the last known address with a notation saying that no such person is at that address. In such cases, where the insufficiency of information precludes direct written or (if agreed to) electronic notification, the covered entity must provide a substitute form of notice.[61]

---

58. 45 C.F.R. § 164.502(g)(1), (g)(2).
59. *Id.* § 164.502(g)(3)(i).
60. *Id.* § 164.502(g)(1).
61. 45 C.F.R. § 164.404(d)(2). *Accord* 42 U.S.C. § 17932(e)(1)(B).

If there are fewer than ten affected individuals with insufficient contact information, the covered entity has discretion to choose an alternative form of notification "reasonably calculated to reach the individual": alternative written notice, telephone, or any other means.[62] Substitute notice is not necessary if the covered entity knows the individual is deceased and the covered entity has insufficient contact information of next of kin or a personal representative.[63] If ten or more individuals are involved, any substitute notice must be in the form of a notice on the home page of the covered entity's website or conspicuous notice in major print or broadcast media in the geographic areas of the individuals with insufficient contact information. The notice must include a toll-free phone number to accept inquiries. This notification must be viewable for at least ninety days.[64]

iii. Supplemental Methods and Recipients of Notification

Apart from notification to an individual directly in writing by postal mail or e-mail, the Breach Notification Rule provides for additional methods and recipients of notification. First, in urgent situations, because of possible imminent misuse of unsecured PHI, a covered entity may provide telephone or other notification to affected individuals.[65] Second, covered entities affected by a breach involving more than 500 residents of a state or jurisdiction must "notify prominent media outlets serving the State or jurisdiction."[66] For instance, they could issue a press release to media outlets in the relevant geographic area. The requirements for timing and content of the notice are the same as the requirements for individual notification.[67]

Finally, the Breach Notification Rule requires covered entities to report their breaches to HHS.[68] If a breach involves 500 or more individuals, a covered entity must report it immediately to HHS.[69] If a breach involves less than 500 individuals, a covered entity must document it in a log, add it to information about other such smaller breaches during the year, and report to HHS all such breaches at one time.[70]

---

62. 45 C.F.R. § 164.404(d)(2), (d)(2)(i).
63. *See id.* § 164.404(d)(2).
64. *See id.* § 164.404(d)(2)(ii). *Accord* 42 U.S.C. § 17932(e)(1)(B).
65. 45 C.F.R. § 164.404(d)(3). *Accord* 42 U.S.C. § 17932(e)(1)(C).
66. 45 C.F.R. § 164.406(a). *Accord* 42 U.S.C. § 17932(e)(2).
67. *See* 45 C.F.R. § 164.406(b)–(c).
68. 45 C.F.R. § 164.408(a). *Accord* 42 U.S.C. § 17932(e)(3).
69. 45 C.F.R. § 164.408(b). *Accord* 42 U.S.C. § 17932(e)(3).
70. 45 C.F.R. § 164.408(c). *Accord* 42 U.S.C. § 17932(e)(3).

HHS operates a website stating that notifications to HHS must be submitted there electronically.[71] The reporting entity must fill out all of the required fields. One kind of report is for breaches involving 500 or more individuals. Another is for smaller breaches. HHS has also posted an online list of all breach reports.[72] Anyone can download the list in a spreadsheet or as a pdf file. The list provides interesting metrics concerning healthcare data breaches. The data include the name of the reporting entity, the state of the entity, the type of entity (e.g., healthcare provider, health plan, and business associate), the number of affected individuals, the date of the report's submission, the type of breach (e.g., theft of device, loss of device, hacking, and improper disposal), and location of the breached information (e.g., paper or film, laptop, desktop, portable electronic device, or network server). As of the date of this writing, the list has 1,601 rows in it; 1,601 large data breaches appear on the list. The largest reported breach is the Anthem, Inc. breach with the company reporting 78,800,000 affected individuals.

3. Business Associate Breach Notification Obligations

Business associates have their own form of breach notification obligation, but it is not the same as that of a covered entity. Many business associates have no contact with individual patients. They may perform services of which patients are completely unaware. Therefore, placing an obligation on a business associate to notify affected individuals does not make sense in the context of many kinds of services. As a result, the Breach Notification Rule requires only that a business associate notify the applicable covered entity when a breach occurs. "A business associate shall, following the discovery of a breach of unsecured protected health information, notify the covered entity of such breach."[73]

The Breach Notification Rule requires notification "without unreasonable delay and in no case later than 60 calendar days after discovery of a breach."[74] It is common, however, for business associate agreements, by contract, to shorten a business associate's deadline for

---

71. HHS, Submitting Notice of a Breach to the Secretary, http://www.hhs.gov/hipaa/for-professionals/breach-notification/breach-reporting/index.html (last visited Apr. 7, 2016).

72. HHS Office for Civil Rights, Breaches Affecting 500 or More Individuals, https://ocrportal.hhs.gov/ocr/breach/breach_report.jsf (last visited Apr. 7, 2016).

73. 45 C.F.R. § 164.410(a)(1). *Accord* 42 U.S.C. § 17932(b).

74. 45 C.F.R. § 164.410(b).

making a notification. Discovery of a breach occurs when it is known to the business associate or would have been known by exercising reasonable diligence.[75] Knowledge of an employee, officer, or other agent is imputed to the business associate concerning when discovery occurs.[76]

Finally, the rule discusses what content a business associate must include in a notice to a covered entity. The rule has a caveat, though. The business associate need only provide information "to the extent possible"[77] and information that is "available."[78] In other words, the business associate has no obligation to provide information it does not have or that is not possible to obtain. If possible, the business associate must identify individuals whose unsecured PHI has been compromised during the breach.[79] Moreover, the business associate must provide the covered entity with "any other available information" of the kind the covered entity would need to provide to the affected individuals.[80] If information is not available to a business associate, however, the covered entity or upstream business associate customer can nonetheless negotiate a contractual obligation on the part of the business associate to provide reasonable assistance when it tries to identify affected individuals.

E. RESPONDING TO SECURITY INCIDENTS AND BREACHES

Imagine for a moment that you believe your organization may have experienced a data breach. In other words, your security organization has detected or has been notified of some event. What do you do now?

First, take a deep breath. It is important to think clearly and not react instantly based on gut feelings and instinct.

Next, if you have done advance planning, you will have an incident response plan ready to go. It is a matter of executing the plan that you have already created. Initial steps include notification to your breach response team. Depending on the nature of the breach, and the size of your organization, team members include workers performing legal, IT,

---

75. *Id.* § 164.410(a)(2).
76. *See id.*
77. *Id.* § 164.410(c)(1).
78. *Id.* § 164.410(c)(2).
79. *See id.* § 164.410(c)(1). *Accord* 42 U.S.C. § 17932(b).
80. 45 C.F.R. § 164.410(c)(2).

security, HR, marketing, and finance functions. In a large organization, the team may include department heads. In a small medical office or clinic, a single office manager may perform many of these functions. Initial meetings can focus on the nature of the events, the initial take on what happened, understanding the severity of the incident, and identifying affected external parties or participants in the event.

Following initial meetings, the initial days of a breach response include an internal investigation to determine the facts and circumstances surrounding the apparent breach. What really happened? Information begins streaming in, and it may or may not show that a breach occurred. If it is clear that a breach occurred, it might not be clear how it happened, who was responsible, and whether it is still ongoing. The internal investigation phase is to find answers to all of these questions.

At the same time the internal investigation is starting, any internal IT, security, and perhaps external forensic experts should be analyzing systems to determine and implement the best course of action to prevent further exploitation of the breach, minimize the damage from the breach, determine the source and scope of the attack, leave open the possibility of a law enforcement investigation, detect and find evidence of the attacker, and preserve evidence needed for later legal proceedings, including both defensive and offensive actions. It may not be possible to meet all of these goals. Accordingly, the organization may need to decide on the priority of these goals.

During this initial phase, the organization should also consider notifying law enforcement. Collaborating with law enforcement has plusses and minuses beyond the scope of this book. One important plus for involving law enforcement, however, is the fact that under the Breach Notification Rule and many states' breach notification laws, an organization may delay in making required breach notifications if law enforcement believes that such delay is important for its investigation of the breach. Accordingly, working with law enforcement may buy the organization some time when it comes to making decisions about the need for, or the timing of, breach notifications.

While the internal investigation is getting underway, the legal team can determine the legal posture of the organization in light of the breach. The legal team should consider implementing a litigation hold and its scope, as well as taking steps to preserve evidence relevant to possible litigation. It should also start analyzing possible claims that parties could assert against the organization, or possible claims that the organization has against others, arising from the apparent breach.

Keep in mind that if investigations may show that the organization had vulnerabilities, the organization may want to have outside counsel hire the computer forensic experts investigating the breach. Hiring experts in this way makes them an extension of outside counsel. Structuring a relationship with an expert in a certain way can maximize the chances that communications between the organization and such experts can be protected by the attorney-client privilege.[81] Thus, when the organization is discussing vulnerabilities and weaknesses in systems or other information that may tend to indicate liability, it can try to protect such discussions with the privilege.

Upon the completion of an initial internal investigation and a possible additional external investigation, the organization should develop enough information to determine if a breach notification is necessary under the Breach Notification Rule and if it is, whom the organization should notify. As noted above in section 6.D.1, the organization must conduct a risk assessment referencing the factors in the rule that bear on whether a "breach" occurred. If the risk assessment shows a low probability of compromise, the organization can conclude no breach occurred. If, however, a risk assessment shows a high probability of compromise, or it cannot tell one way or another, it must make a breach notification. The organization should also determine if state law would require a notification, even if the Breach Notification Rule does not require one.

In preparing breach notifications, the organization should account for the Breach Notification Rule's requirements about the content of the notices. It should also consider content that may be required under state law. It should also take into account requirements to notify HHS, an attorney general, media or other entities, in addition to the affected individuals. Finally, it should be aware of possible alternative means of notice under certain state laws, in case these means are the only way to inform some of the affected individuals.

Once an investigation is completed and law enforcement has wrapped up its investigation, the organization can change continue to systems, close vulnerabilities, and remediate problems uncovered by the investigation.[82] These steps can prevent the attackers from making

---

81. *See, e.g.*, United States v. Kovel, 296 F.2d 918, 922 (2d Cir. 1961) (protecting communications under the attorney client privilege between a client and accountant retained by an attorney to help the attorney provide legal services).

82. As mentioned above, the initial phase of the response may have already included beginning to close vulnerabilities and mitigate harm.

additional attacks or exploiting the current breach. In addition, these steps will hopefully prevent future breaches by others.

Following the remediation phase, the organization can then "close the loop" and undertake steps to evaluate what happened and make changes to prevent future breaches. For instance, postbreach analysis is a good time to reconsider the controls in the organization's security program to make changes and upgrades to minimize the risk of future breaches. The organization may wish to make changes in its security policies, its procedures, technical standards, training programs, supporting guidelines, or technology.

In addition, the organization may want to undertake a new risk assessment to provide an updated view of the organization's security posture. A risk assessment is a fundamental tool to determine what risks exist, which risks to mitigate, which risks it makes sense to shift (e.g., through insurance or indemnities), and which risks to accept.

Upon completion of these steps, the organization should implement changes to procedures, standards, training, guidelines, and technology based on the information developed in this phase. At the end of this process, the organization will hopefully be in a better position to deter, detect, and prevent security breaches.

CHAPTER 7

Compliance and Enforcement

Chapter 5 and 6 discuss the core requirements of the Security Rule and the Breach Notification Rule. This chapter discusses the state of compliance with the Security Rule and Breach Notification as of spring 2016. Since the Department of Health and Human Services (HHS) enacted the Security Rule, we have had surveys, academic studies, news stories, case examples; and anecdotal experience that permit us to draw some conclusions about compliance. Section 7.A summarizes these experiences. As described in section A, compliance remains a significant challenge for the healthcare field.

The remaining sections of this chapter discuss enforcement. What happens when, as is apparent, covered entities and business associates (referred to in this chapter by the shorthand term "organizations") are not complying with the HIPAA regulations? Section 7.B discusses the statutory penalties for HIPAA violations. Section 7.C covers the Final Enforcement Rule regulatory procedures HHS can use to enforce HIPAA. Section 7.C.1 provides additional details about HHS compliance reviews and investigations following complaints received by the HHS Office for Civil Rights (OCR). Section 7.C.2 explains actions HHS can take following a compliance review or investigation. Section 7.C.3 describes the basis for civil money penalties against organizations, as well as the amount of penalties that can be imposed. Section 7.D provides information about the current state of the OCR auditing program intended to detect violations and promote compliance. Section 7.E covers civil actions state attorneys general can file against organizations pursuant to the HITECH Act. Finally, section 7.F identifies the types of violations seen in enforcement activity. Sections 7.E and 7.F will assist organizations in assessing the legal risks associated with various types of security vulnerabilities and thereby help them prioritize their compliance activities.

A. THE STATE OF COMPLIANCE

As of the spring of 2016, the state of HIPAA compliance in the United States remains, in a word, deficient. Since HHS issued the Security Rule in 2003, Congress enacted the HITECH Act, and HHS issued the Omnibus Final Rule, healthcare journals, professional organizations, and word of mouth raised awareness of security obligations placed on organizations. The good news is that these events prompted many diligent organizations to take the steps necessary to comply. Many skilled and knowledgeable professionals in these organizations, as well as their outside counsel and consultants, have dedicated considerable time, effort, and resources to compliance within their organizations. Many organizations have achieved what can be characterized as a "reasonable and appropriate" level of security.

Large segments of the healthcare field, however, are not complying with HIPAA. Various sources of information are available to assist in determining the state of compliance. They include academic studies and papers, which are the most formal and rigorous; industry surveys, which may not be scientific; news stories based on journalists' investigations; case examples; and anecdotal experiences. Case examples and anecdotes about data breaches and failures to comply are sometimes enlightening, but it is not possible to draw general conclusions from anecdotes alone. If case examples and anecdotes were the only data points showing problems with compliance, a large dose of skepticism would be in order concerning conclusions about widespread noncompliance.

Nonetheless, every one of the sources of information available—academic studies, industry surveys, news stories, case studies, and anecdotes—all point to a dismal state of compliance in spring 2016. Given that all the data points are in agreement, the inevitable conclusion is that HIPAA compliance remains a significant challenge thirteen years after HHS issued the Security Rule. Clearly, organizations must do more to comply. While the legal risks associated with noncompliance have apparently failed to incentivize full compliance to date, the new audit program, increased enforcement activities, and an emerging and growing plaintiff's bar in the data security field mean that legal risks for noncompliant organizations will rise significantly in the future.

1. News Stories, Case Studies, and Anecdotes

The news media are full of stories about data breaches and HIPAA violations. While there are far too many news stories about data breaches to cite in this publication, a few examples will suffice. One writer sums up the state of security by saying, "Data breaches are now inevitable."[1] Another writes, "Cyberattacks have become an ever-increasing threat."[2] Another story discusses the high-profile snooping incident at UCLA Health Systems in which hospital employees viewed the medical records of celebrities such as Britney Spears, Farrah Fawcett, and then-California First Lady Maria Shriver without authorization.[3] "While HIPAA is the legislation (passed in 1996) designed to protect patients against loss, theft or disclosure of their sensitive medical information, the fines and penalties don't appear to be having a discernible effect on either patient privacy or data security."[4] "2015 was the year of the healthcare breach, with many organizations falling victim to malicious attacks."[5] "[W]e should reasonably expect more of the same for 2016."[6]

One of the most striking news stories is an article written by Charles Ornstein about his investigation of medical records.[7] He begins the story by talking about Farrah Fawcett's last media interview before her death. She suspected that an employee at UCLA Medical Center was talking about her cancer treatments with the *National Enquirer*. "To prove her theory, Fawcett set up a sting: In May 2007, she withheld news of her cancer's return from nearly all of her relatives and friends. Within days, the story was in the Enquirer. 'I couldn't believe how fast it came out,' Fawcett said."[8]

---

1. *Crime Leading HIPAA Breach Cause Says Ponemon Data Security Study*, HIPAA J., May 8, 2015, http://www.hipaajournal.com/crime-leading-hipaa-breaches-cause-says-ponemon-data-security-study-4432/.

2. Kevin Granville, *9 Recent Cyberattacks against Big Businesses*, N.Y. TIMES, Feb. 5, 2015, http://www.nytimes.com/interactive/2015/02/05/technology/recent-cyberattacks.html (discussing breaches including those that affected Primera Blue Cross and Anthem).

3. Molly Hennessy-Fiske, *UCLA Hospitals to Pay $865,500 for Breaches of Celebrities' Privacy*, L.A. TIMES, Jul. 8, 2011, http://articles.latimes.com/print/2011/jul/08/local/la-me-celebrity-snooping-20110708.

4. Dan Munro, *Data Breaches in Healthcare Totaled over 112 Million Records in 2015*, FORBES, Dec. 31, 2015, http://www.forbes.com/sites/danmunro/2015/12/31/data-breaches-in-healthcare-total-over-112-million-records-in-2015.

5. *Id.* (quoting Gerry McCracken, VP of Tech, WinMagic).

6. *Id.*

7. Charles Ornstein, *Farrah Fawcett Was Right—We Have Little Medical Privacy*, PROPUBLICA, Dec. 30, 2015, https://www.propublica.org/article/farrah-fawcett-was-right-we-have-little-medical-privacy.

8. *Id.*

Ornstein began investigating breaches, and found that they extended far beyond the world of celebrities. His findings are sobering, and the stories he reports are shocking.

> At the time, I thought that this was a problem largely confined to the People magazine world of celebrities and that this law would quash the prurient interest in their medical records.
>
> I was wrong.
>
> After spending the past year reporting on loopholes and lax enforcement of the Health Insurance Portability and Accountability Act, the federal patient-privacy law known as HIPAA, I've come to realize that it's not just celebrity patients who are at risk. We all are.
>
> Over the course of my reporting, I've talked to hundreds of people who said their medical records were hacked, snooped in, shared or stolen. Some were worried about potential consequences for themselves and their families. For others, the impact has been real and devastating, requiring therapy and medication. It has destroyed their faith in the medical establishment.[9]

Ornstein concludes his article with an indictment of HIPAA. "In each story, a common theme emerged: HIPAA wasn't working the way we expect. And the regulatory agency charged with enforcing it, the HHS Office for Civil Rights, wasn't taking aggressive action against those who violated the law."[10] Indeed, in its February 2016 press release about its case against Lincare, Inc., HHS said, "This is only the second time in its history that OCR has sought [civil money penalties] for HIPAA violations."[11] Ornstein says, "[I]n reality, [HIPAA] is a toothless tiger."[12]

---

9. *Id.*

10. *Id.*

11. HHS Press Office, Administrative Law Judge Rules in Favor of OCR Enforcement, Requiring Lincare, Inc. to Pay $239,800 (Feb. 3, 2016), http://www.hhs.gov/about /news/2016/02/03/administrative-law-judge-rules-favor-ocr-enforcement-requiring-lincare -inc-pay-penalties.html. The other case OCR is referring to was a Privacy Rule case concerning not giving patients a copy of their medical records upon request. Sebelius v. Uplift Med., P.C., No. RWT 11cv2168, 2012 WL 8251345 (D. Md. Aug. 30, 2012) (granting summary judgment to HHS in an action to enforce civil money penalties it imposed after Uplift failed to request an ALJ hearing). Thus, Lincare was the very first action to redress a security violation and, at that, OCR framed the case as a Privacy Rule case under 45 C.F.R. § 164.530(c) apparently because only paper PHI was involved. Accordingly, OCR has never yet instituted formal proceedings to seek civil money penalties for violations of the Security Rule or Breach Notification Rule. The previous payments have been pursuant to settlements.

12. Ornstein, *supra* note 7.

Unless you're famous, most hospitals and clinics don't keep tabs on who looks at your records if you don't complain. And even though the civil rights office can impose large fines, it rarely does: It received nearly 18,000 complaints in 2014 but took only six formal actions that year. A recent report from the HHS inspector general said the office wasn't keeping track of repeat offenders, much less doing anything about them.[13]

Part of the cause in his mind is enforcement, and part is the lack of a private right of action. "[I]f the federal government doesn't enforce the law, there are often no consequences for breaking it."[14]

Sections 7.E and 7.F contain various case examples of enforcement actions against healthcare organizations due to lax security. These actions concerned different individual incidents, including the thefts of laptops and USB drives, improper disposal of protected health information (PHI), posting of PHI to locations accessible by anyone through the public Internet, and attacks resulting from malicious software. The loss or theft of devices was the most common scenario involved with state attorney general actions and HHS resolution agreements.

Discussions with other attorneys and professionals, such as in meetings of the Information Security Committee of the American Bar Association Section of Science & Technology Law, provide additional anecdotes of compliance challenges. Examples include stories of:

- Vendors that are "business associates" under the law refusing to acknowledge their status as such or sign business associate agreements (BAAs).
- Organizations not undertaking formal risk assessments.
- Covered entities not undertaking proper investigations of security incidents.
- Organizations with absolutely no security policies or procedures, or copying documentation found from the Internet without applying it to their individual environments.
- Organizations not funding the security and compliance function properly.
- Organizations hiring untrustworthy personnel and not conducting background checks.

---

13. *Id.*
14. *Id.*

2. Academic Studies and Industry Surveys

Stories from individuals, case studies, and anecdotes about possible or actual individual HIPAA violations are one thing. Academic studies confirm these concerns about the state of compliance. Not many studies are available. Nonetheless, one Dartmouth study reviewed compliance literature and stated that "recent industry report[s], conducted post HIPAA enforcement deadlines, present[] a bleak picture of HIPAA compliance."[15] Based on 2003 data, the researchers looked at the types of covered entities most likely to comply and concluded, "In [the] case of security rules on average larger non-profit hospitals [that are] considered as IT Leader[s] and have [a] higher [electronic medical record] system installed base are more likely to be compliant irrespective of their academic status."[16]

The same Dartmouth researchers later conducted another study and found additional conclusions. They noted, "Unfortunately, recent industry reports indicate low levels of regulatory compliance, thus raising security concerns for the US health IT infrastructure."[17] Their research focused on different factors that facilitated compliance. For example, they found that academic hospitals and for-profit hospitals tend to have higher compliance with privacy and security rules.[18]

Finally, a Nova Southeastern University dissertation investigated factors that bear on HIPAA compliance.[19] "The research problem that the author investigated was that academic medical centers (AMCs) and other covered entities in the U.S. are not fully complying with the Health Insurance Portability and Accountability Act (HIPAA) . . . ."[20] The dissertation found that management support, security awareness,

---

15. Ajit Appari et al., Which Hospitals Are Complying with HIPAA: An Empirical Investigation of US Hospitals 1 (undated manuscript), http://www.ists.dartmouth.edu/library/417.pdf.

16. *Id.* at 12.

17. Ajit Appari et al., HIPAA Compliance: An Examination of Institutional and Market Forces 1 (June 2009), http://apps.himss.org/foundation/docs/appari_etal2009_hipaacompliance_20091023.pdf.

18. *Id.* at 15.

19. James William Brady, An Investigation of Factors That Affect HIPAA Security Compliance in Academic Medical Centers (2010) (Ph.D. dissertation, Nova Southeastern University), http://nsuworks.nova.edu/cgi/viewcontent.cgi?article=1099&context=gscis_etd.

20. *Id.* at 1.

and a culture of security promoted compliance.[21] These studies did not survey or focus on the extent of the noncompliance problem, but rather noted the problem and then tried to explain the factors promoting compliance.

Industry surveys corroborate the anecdotes and observations that compliance is a significant problem. For instance, the oft-cited Ponemon Institute conducts a survey each year of privacy and security in the healthcare field.[22] It surveys both covered entities and business associates. "Despite the increased frequency of breaches, the study found that many organizations lack the money and resources to manage data breaches caused by evolving cyber threats, preventable mistakes, and other dangers."[23] Ponemon stated, "Based on the results of this study, we estimate that data breaches could be costing the healthcare industry $6.2 billion."[24] Ponemon found that 89 percent of covered entity respondents and 61 percent of business associate respondents had experienced a data breach in the previous 24 months. Forty-five percent of covered entity respondents and 13 percent of business associate respondents had experienced more than 5 breaches in that time period.[25]

"Despite the increased frequency of breaches, the study found that many organizations lack the money and resources to manage data breaches caused by evolving cyber threats, preventable mistakes, and other dangers."[26] "Although there's been a slight increased investment over last year in technology, privacy and security budgets, and personnel with technical expertise, the majority of healthcare organizations still don't have sufficient security budget to curtail or minimize data breach incidents."[27] "The research found that many healthcare organizations and their business associates are negligent in the handling of patient information."[28] These findings bolster the conclusion that organizations have a long way to go before they can achieve compliance.

---

21. *See id.* at 157–59.
22. Ponemon Inst. LLC, Sixth Annual Benchmark Study on Privacy & Security of Healthcare Data (May 2016), http://www.hhs.gov/hipaa/for-professionals/compliance-enforcement/audit/protocol/index.html.
23. *Id.* at 1.
24. *Id.*
25. *See id.* at 19.
26. *Id.* at 1.
27. *Id.*
28. *Id.* at 2.

Small healthcare provider and billing organizations are particularly vulnerable, according to a recent survey of these organizations conducted by vendor NueMD, a cloud-based medical practice management application company.[29] While 70 percent of respondents claim to have a HIPAA compliance plan, other metrics suggest that many respondents are not actually complying:

- Only 58 percent of respondents provide annual staff training (implying over 40 percent are not conducting training).
- Only a little over 50 percent of respondents have appointed a security or privacy officer, despite administrative requirements of security management (implying almost half have not).
- Only 68 percent of respondents knew of the requirement to have BAAs with vendors, and 26 percent completely neglected to review and update their BAAs.
- Only a third or less of respondents were confident that their mobile, e-mail, text, and social media devices were HIPAA-compliant.[30]

Despite these findings, 83 percent of respondents stated they were very or somewhat confident that their organizations are compliant.[31] Most of the respondents have admitted facts that preclude compliance and yet over 80 percent believe that they are complying. Accordingly, not only are many respondents apparently out of compliance, even worse, they may be unaware that they have a problem.

In sum, all the sources of information about compliance lead to the conclusion that a significant percentage of organizations are not complying with security requirements. While organizations may not have felt the consequences of noncompliance, the enforcement infrastructure is in place to impose penalties. With increasing regulatory oversight we are recently seeing, coupled with increasing knowledge and interest among lawyers representing plaintiffs harmed by data breaches, the inevitable conclusion is that a large segment of organizations is facing a considerable and ever-increasing legal risk of potential penalties and liabilities due to organizations' inability or unwillingness to comply fully with HIPAA's security requirements.

---

29. NueMD, 2016 HIPAA Survey Update (2016), http://www.nuemd.com/hipaa/survey/2016/.

30. *See id.*

31. *See id.*

B. STATUTES REGARDING CIVIL AND CRIMINAL PENALTIES FOR HIPAA VIOLATIONS

HIPAA's statutory provisions, as amended by the HITECH Act, provide for civil money penalties[32] and criminal penalties[33] on those who violate HIPAA. The Secretary of HHS can impose certain amounts of civil money penalties on those violating HIPAA depending on the level of culpability of the violator. (References to the "Secretary" in the remainder of this chapter refer to the Secretary of HHS.) 42 U.S.C. § 1320d-5 creates four levels of culpability:

- The first and lowest level of culpability is one in which "the person did not know (and by exercising reasonable diligence would not have known) that" the person violated HIPAA.[34]
- The second level of culpability is one in which "the violation was due to reasonable cause and not to willful neglect."[35]
- The highest levels of culpability are for "willful neglect."[36] Where the violation was due to willful neglect, the applicable civil money penalty depends on whether or not the violator corrected the violation within the statutory time period. That time period is within thirty days "beginning on the first date the person liable for the penalty or damages knew, or by exercising reasonable diligence would have known, that the failure to comply occurred."[37] The Secretary of HHS may extend this thirty-day time period "based on the nature and extent of the failure to comply"[38] or provide assistance as determined to be appropriate by HHS.[39]
  - o The third level of culpability is one in which the violation was due to "willful neglect" but was corrected within the above time period.[40]

---

32. 42 U.S.C. § 1320d-5.
33. *Id.* § 1320d-6.
34. *Id.* § 1320d-5(a)(1)(A).
35. *Id.* § 1320d-5(a)(1)(B).
36. *Id.* § 1320d-5(a)(1)(C).
37. *Id.* § 1320d-5(b)(2)(A). (The reference in subsection (a)(1)(C) to subsection (b)(3)(A) appears to be an error.)
38. *Id.* § 1320d-5(b)(2)(B)(i).
39. *Id.* § 1320d-5(b)(2)(B)(ii).
40. *Id.* § 1320d-5(a)(1)(C)(i).

o The fourth and highest level of culpability is one in which the violation was due to "willful neglect" but was not corrected within the above time period.[41]

Section 7.C.3 below lists the amounts of civil money penalties[42] corresponding to these four tiers. HHS must initiate a formal investigation if a preliminary investigation indicates "willful neglect."[43]

These penalties apply to "any person who violates a provision of this part."[44] Section 1320d-5 appears in part C of Subchapter XI of Chapter 7 of Title 42. Part C includes all administrative simplification provisions. Therefore, section 1320d-5 applies to the HIPAA Security, Privacy, and Breach Notification Rules.

Also, section 1320d-5(a)(2) imports procedures from 42 U.S.C. § 1320a-7a, including:

- A six-year statute of limitations.[45]
- Review by a U.S. court of appeals of any determination by HHS; the proper circuit is the one in which the person resides.[46]
- The authority for HHS to compromise and collect civil money penalties and assessments.[47]
- In the case of HHS determinations to impose penalties, notification of medical or professional organizations, state supervisory agencies, utilization and quality control peer review organizations, and licensing agencies or organizations.[48]
- Procedures for seeking injunctive relief in federal court.[49]

Finally, HHS has the authority to waive penalties not due to willful neglect.[50]

42 U.S.C. § 1320d-6 imposes criminal penalties for violations of "this part," which again refers to any of the administrative simplification

---

41. *Id.* § 1320d-5(a)(1)(C)(ii).
42. *Id.* § 1320d-5(a)(3).
43. *Id.* § 1320d-5(c)(2).
44. *Id.* § 1320d-5(a)(1).
45. *Id.* § 1320a-7a(c).
46. *Id.* § 1320a-7a(e).
47. *Id.* § 1320a-7a(f).
48. *Id.* § 1320a-7a(h).
49. *Id.* § 1320a-7a(k).
50. *Id.* § 1320d-5(b)(3).

provisions of HIPAA.[51] Specifically, a criminal violation occurs if a person knowingly and in violation of HIPAA "obtains individually identifiable health information relating to an individual."[52] Likewise, a criminal violation occurs if a person knowingly and in violation of HIPAA "discloses individually identifiable health information to another person."[53] For a violation to occur, the individually identifiable health information must be maintained by a covered entity and the person obtained or disclosed such information without authorization.[54]

Criminal penalties fall into three tiers. The default punishment for a criminal violation is a fine not more than $50,000, imprisonment of up to one year, or both.[55] If the violator committed the offense under false pretenses, the maximum fine goes up to $100,000, the maximum prison sentence goes up to five years, and a court can impose both as a sentence.[56] "[I]f the offense is committed with intent to sell, transfer, or use individually identifiable health information for commercial advantage, personal gain, or malicious harm," the maximum fine is $250,000, the maximum prison sentence is ten years, and both can be imposed.[57] Once a criminal penalty is imposed on the alleged violator, no further penalty can be sought by HHS for a civil money penalty or by a state attorney general for statutory penalties.[58]

C. THE FINAL ENFORCEMENT RULE

HHS delegated enforcement responsibility for violations of the Security Rule to the OCR in July 2009. OCR enforces HIPAA and performs education and outreach for HIPAA compliance, with role-based training. OCR also offers a training program for state attorneys general who believe that residents of their states have been injured by violations of the HIPAA Security Rule and desire to enforce the Security Rule themselves.

The Final Enforcement Rule[59] is the current set of HHS regulations promulgated for the compliance with and the enforcement of

---

51. *Id.* § 1320d-6(a).
52. *Id.* § 1320d-6(a)(2).
53. *Id.* § 1320d-6(a)(3).
54. *Id.* § 1320d-6(a).
55. *Id.* § 1320d-6(b)(1).
56. *Id.* § 1320d-6(b)(2).
57. *Id.* § 1320d-6(b)(3).
58. *Id.* § 1320d-5(b)(1).
59. HIPAA Administration simplification: Enforcement; Final Enforcement Rule, 71 Fed. Reg. 8390 (2006).

HIPAA Rules. The Final Enforcement Rule applies to the Security, Privacy, and Breach Notification Rules. The rule's provisions appear in 45 C.F.R. part 160, subparts C, D, and E. The Final Enforcement Rule took effect on March 16, 2006 and was amended in 2009 and as part of the Omnibus Final Rule in 2013 to implement changes required by the HITECH Act.[60]

Subpart C covers the complaints to the Secretary, compliance reviews, and investigative procedures. Subpart D establishes the bases and amount for civil money penalties, and procedures surrounding notices of proposed determination imposing civil money penalties. Subpart E describes procedures for hearings to challenge the imposition of civil money penalties.

1. Compliance Reviews and Complaint Investigations

HHS has authority to initiate HIPAA compliance reviews of covered entities and their business associates.[61] The Secretary will initiate a compliance review is "to determine whether a covered entity or business associate is complying with the applicable administrative simplification provisions when a preliminary review of the facts indicates a possible violation due to willful neglect."[62] Compliance reviews are usually the result of reported breaches. The Secretary, however, may also initiate a compliance review in any other circumstance it deems appropriate.[63]

Any person who believes an organization is not complying with the Security Rule may file a complaint with the Secretary of HHS.[64] HHS will investigate complaints of possible HIPAA violations due to willful neglect.[65] Before the HITECH Act, the process of collecting complaints and investigating them was HHS's primary means of enforcing the Security Rule. Nonetheless, as noted above in section 7.A, this process was perceived as inadequate to enforce HIPAA. Consequently, the Congress enacted some provisions of the HITECH Act later supported

---

60. Modifications to the HIPAA Privacy, Security, Enforcement, and Breach Notification Rules under the Health Information Technology for Economic and Clinical Health Act and the Genetic Information Nondiscrimination Act; Other Modifications to the HIPAA Rules; Final Rule, 78 Fed. Reg. 5566 (2013) [hereinafter Omnibus Final Rule].

61. 45 C.F.R. § 160.308.

62. *Id.* § 160.308(a).

63. *See id.* § 160.308(b).

64. *Id.* § 160.306(a).

65. 42 U.S.C. § 1320d-5(c)(2).

by the Final Omnibus Rule to increase the effectiveness of HIPAA enforcement.[66]

While investigating a complaint, HHS may issue subpoenas to compel testimony or the production of evidence.[67] Organizations must cooperate with any compliance review or investigation.[68] They must also allow HHS to access their records to determine compliance.[69] It may be possible that HHS will ask one organization to permit access to records to determine compliance by a different organization. For instance, a business associate's records may bear on whether or not a covered entity is properly complying.

2. HHS Actions Following a Compliance Review or Investigation

Following completion of a compliance review or an investigation of a complaint, the Secretary may take a number of actions. It may close the compliance review or investigation, it may informally resolve it, or it may take further steps to impose a civil money penalty. The subsections below describe these options in more detail.

a. Informal Resolutions

Following the completion of a compliance review or investigation, if the Secretary finds no potential violations, it will inform the organization that had been the subject of the review or investigation.[70] Presumably, at that point, the Secretary will close the matter without further action. If, however, the Secretary finds that a violation occurred, it has two options. First, it may attempt to resolve the matter informally. It may ask the organization to demonstrate that it is complying, complete a corrective action plan, or perform some other kind of agreement; following such corrective measures, the Secretary will notify the organization of the informal resolution of the matter.[71]

Nonetheless, the matter may not settle, either because of the seriousness of the violations or the lack of cooperation by the organization. If the matter is not resolved informally, the Secretary will notify the alleged violator and give it an opportunity to submit evidence of

---

66. HITECH Act §§ 13410 (investigation of willful neglect, increased penalties, and enforcement actions by state attorneys general), 13411 (audit program).

67. 45 C.F.R. § 160.314(a).

68. *Id.* § 160.310(b).

69. *Id.* § 160.310(c).

70. 45 C.F.R. § 160.312(b).

71. *Id.* § 160.312(a)(1), (a)(2).

any mitigating factors or affirmative defenses. The alleged violator has thirty days to submit such evidence.[72] After considering any mitigating evidence, the Secretary will either find no violation and close the matter, resolve it informally at that point, or take additional actions against the alleged violator.

b. Notice of Proposed Determination

If, following a compliance review or investigation that is not either closed for lack of a violation or resolved informally, the Secretary has the authority to propose that a civil money penalty be imposed against the organization. Specifically, if the Secretary finds that a civil money penalty is appropriate, it will inform the alleged violator in a notice of proposed determination.[73] A notice of proposed determination will include:

- The statutory basis for a penalty.
- The Secretary's findings of fact on which it bases the proposed penalty.
- The reasons why the violations warrant a penalty.
- The amount of the proposed penalty and how it was calculated.
- Any circumstances that the Secretary considered in determining the amount of the proposed penalty.
- Instructions on how to respond to the notice.[74]

c. Challenging a Notice of Proposed Determination

An organization that receives a notice of proposed determination that proposes a civil money penalty can challenge the notice. Specifically, it can request a hearing to dispute the basis or amount of the proposed civil money penalty.[75] The alleged violator has ninety days to submit a request for hearing.[76] If it fails to challenge the notice of proposed determination within the time limit, the alleged violator has waived

---

72. *Id.* § 160.312(a)(3)(i). If the Secretary serves the notification by mail, it has an extra five days to respond. *Id.* § 160.526(c).

73. *Id.* § 160.312(a)(3)(ii).

74. *See id.* § 160.420(a).

75. *See Id.* § 160.420(b).

76. *Id.* § 160.420(a)(6). Although section 160.420 does not say so, if the Secretary serves the notice of proposed determination by mail, presumably it has an extra five days to respond. *Id.* § 160.526(c). Nonetheless, given the lack of an express reference to section 160.526, it may be prudent to assume that no such extension applies.

further review and the Secretary will impose the penalty or any lesser penalty as appropriate.[77]

Once the alleged violator has requested a hearing, an entire set of prehearing and hearing procedures apply, including:

- Limited discovery in the form of document production requests and requests for electronically stored information.[78]
- Subpoenas compelling testimony at the hearing and/or production of documents at or before the hearing.[79]
- Motion practice.[80]
- Sanctions, including discovery sanctions.[81]
- A hearing on the record, in which the Secretary generally has the burden of proof except for affirmative defenses and mitigating factors.[82]

Affirmative defenses include the lack of willful neglect and a claim that the alleged violator corrected the issue within the relevant time period.[83] Also, if the alleged violator has already received criminal penalties, the prior penalties preclude further civil money penalties.[84]

An administrative law judge (ALJ) presides at the hearing and issues a decision based on findings of fact and conclusions of law.[85] The ALJ may affirm the Secretary's proposed penalty, increase it, or reduce it.[86] If the organization is unsuccessful in challenging the penalty at the hearing, it can appeal the ALJ's decision to the HHS Departmental Appeals Board. The deadline to appeal is thirty days from the service of the ALJ's decision.[87] The board hears the appeal based on briefs and there is no right to appear personally before the board.[88]

---

77. *Id.* § 160.422.
78. *Id.* § 160.516(a), (b). No other forms of discovery, such as requests for admissions, interrogatories, or depositions are authorized. *Id.* § 160.516(c).
79. *Id.* § 160.520.
80. *Id.* § 160.528.
81. *Id.* § 160.530.
82. *Id.* § 160.534.
83. *Id.* § 160.410(c).
84. *Id.* § 160.410(a)(2).
85. *Id.* §§ 160.534(a), 160.546(a).
86. *Id.* § 160.546(b).
87. *Id.* § 160.548(a).
88. *Id.* § 160.548(c), (d).

The board's ruling becomes the final decision of the Secretary sixty days after service.[89] If the alleged violator is dissatisfied with the board's ruling, it can file a motion with the board to reconsider its decision. The decision of the board on the motion becomes the final decision of the Secretary immediately upon service.[90]

If the alleged violator is dissatisfied with the final decision of the Secretary, it can seek judicial review of the Secretary's decision in the US court of appeals for the circuit in which it resides.[91] The deadline to seek judicial review is 60 days from the date the Secretary's decision became final.[92] If the alleged violator is not satisfied with the results of judicial review in the court of appeals, presumably its last resort is seeking review by the U.S. Supreme Court.

3. Basis and Amount of Civil Money Penalties

"[T]he Secretary will impose a civil money penalty upon a covered entity or business associate if the Secretary determines that the covered entity or business associate has violated an administrative simplification provision."[93] Thus, any violation of the Security Rule, Breach Notification Rule, or Privacy Rule could warrant a civil money penalty. If more than one covered entity or business associate was responsible for a violation, the Secretary will impose a civil money penalty on each responsible organization.[94] Members of an affiliated covered entity (ACE)[95] are jointly and severally responsible for the violations based on the acts or omissions of the ACE, unless it can establish that another member was responsible for the violation.[96]

Covered entities are liable for violations based on the acts or omissions of their agents,[97] including their workforce members and business associates, acting within the scope of their agency.[98] Because subcontractors of business associates are themselves "business

---

89. *Id.* § 160.548(j)(1).

90. *Id.* § 160.548(j).

91. 42 U.S.C. § 1320a-7a(e).

92. 45 C.F.R. § 160.548(k)(1). Time is extended five days if the decision is served by mail. *Id.* § 160.548(j)(5).

93. 45 C.F.R. § 160.402(a).

94. *Id.* § 160.402(b)(1).

95. For a discussion of affiliated covered entities, see section 4.A.5 *supra*.

96. 45 C.F.R. § 160.402(b)(2).

97. The regulation refers the federal common law of agency for purposes of determining who is an "agent" of the covered entity. *Id.* § 160.402(c)(1).

98. *Id.*

associates,"[99] subcontractors of a covered entity's business associates constituting subagents may also trigger liability for the covered entity. Likewise, business associates are liable for violations based on the acts or omissions of their agents, including their workforce members and subcontractors, acting within the scope of their agency.[100]

The Final Enforcement Rule also establishes criteria for the proper amount of a civil money penalty the Secretary will impose.[101] The rule describes four levels of culpability, each with its own range of civil money penalties. These are the same four tiers as the ones described in section 7.B above based on 42 U.S.C. § 1320d-5(a)(1).

- The first and lowest level of culpability is one in which "the covered entity or business associate did not know and, by exercising reasonable diligence, would not have known that" the organization violated HIPAA.[102]
- The second level of culpability is one in which "the violation was due to reasonable cause and not to willful neglect."[103]
- The third level of culpability is one in which the violation was "due to willful neglect and was corrected" within thirty days of the violation.[104]
- The fourth and highest level of culpability is one in which the violation "was due to willful neglect and was not corrected during the 30-day period."[105]

Table 7.1 shows the range for civil money penalties associated with each of these four tiers. The far left column describes each of the above four tiers. The next column shows the minimum civil money penalty to be imposed for each violation. The column after that shows the maximum civil money penalty for each violation. The far right column shows the maximum penalties that the Secretary can impose for all vio-

---

99. *Id.* § 160.103(3)(iii) (definition of "business associate").

100. *Id.* § 160.402(c)(2).

101. *Id.* § 160.404.

102. *Id.* § 160.404(b)(2)(i).

103. *Id.* § 160.404(b)(2)(ii).

104. *Id.* § 160.404(b)(2)(iii). The 30 days begin to run "on the first date the covered entity or business associate liable for the penalty knew, or, by exercising reasonable diligence, would have known that the violation occurred." *Id.*

105. *Id.* § 160.404(b)(2)(iv). Again, the 30 days begins to run "on the first date the covered entity or business associate liable for the penalty knew, or, by exercising reasonable diligence, would have known that the violation occurred." *Id.*

Table 7.1. Amount of Civil Money Penalties

Level of Culpability	Minimum Penalty per Violation	Maximum Penalty per Violation	Maximum Penalties for All Violations of an Identical Provision in a Calendar Year
Did not know and, by exercising reasonable diligence, would not have known	$100	$50,000	$1.5 million
Due to reasonable cause and not to willful neglect	$1000	$50,000	$1.5 million
Due to willful neglect and was corrected within 30 days	$10,000	$50,000	$1.5 million
Due to willful neglect and was not corrected within 30 days	$50,000	None	$1.5 million

lations of an identical administrative simplification provision in a single calendar year.[106]

Note that a single incident or breach could involve a number of violations. HHS stated, "[A] covered entity or business associate may be liable for multiple violations of multiple requirements, and a violation of each requirement may be counted separately."[107] Thus, the Secretary could impose per violation penalties for each provision violated. For instance, if a covered entity hired an untrustworthy workforce member that gained unauthorized access to PHI, the Secretary could impose a civil money penalty for violating the requirement to screen workforce members during hiring,[108] as well as one for violating the requirement to manage access to PHI.[109] HHS, however, will not double-count violations. If the Secretary cites a violation of a provision with a specific requirement, and a more general provision encompasses the same

---

106. The amounts in the table apply to violations on or after February 18, 2009. *Id.* § 160.404(b)(2). Lower amounts apply to violations before that date: no more than $100 per violation or $25,000 for identical violations during a calendar year. *Id.* § 160.404(b)(1). The HITECH Act increased the penalties associated with violations. Accordingly, later violations trigger higher amounts of civil money penalties.

107. Omnibus Final Rule, *supra* note 60, at 5584.

108. *See* 45 C.F.R. § 164.308(a)(3)(ii)(B).

109. *See id.* § 164.308(a)(4)(i).

requirement, the Secretary can impose a civil money penalty for only one of these provisions.[110]

The maximum penalty works the same way. For example, if the covered entity hired multiple untrustworthy workforce members, it would have multiple violations of the workforce screening requirement. All such violations in a single calendar year could not trigger more than $1.5 million in civil money penalties.

Nonetheless, "one covered entity or business associate may be subject to multiple violations up to a $1.5 million cap for each violation, which would result in a total penalty above $1.5 million."[111] Thus, if all of those untrustworthy workforce members gained unauthorized access to PHI, the covered entity may not only pay up to $1.5 million for not adequately screening those workers during a calendar year, it could also pay up to another $1.5 million for not properly managing access to PHI during the same year. If there are multiple types of violations underlying a single data breach, the civil money penalties could add up to a significant amount.

When determining the appropriate amount of a civil money penalty to assess, the Secretary can consider various factors. These factors may act as mitigating or aggravating factors depending on the circumstances. For instance, the Secretary can take into account the nature and extent of the violation, including the number of affected individuals and the time period in which the violation occurred.[112] The Secretary can also consider the nature and extent of the harm from a violation. Harm may include physical, financial, or reputational harm, or hindering access to healthcare.[113] Moreover, the Secretary can consider past conduct, such as a history of noncompliance, correcting previous violations, responding to technical assistance from the Secretary, and responses to prior complaints.[114] The Secretary may consider the financial condition of the organization, including considerations of financial difficulties that may explain noncompliance, the possibility that a penalty could harm the ability to provide or pay for care, and the size of the organization.[115] Finally, the Secretary can take into account any other matters that justice may require that the Secretary consider.[116]

---

110. *See id.* § 160.404(b)(3).
111. Omnibus Final Rule, *supra* note 60, at 5584.
112. 45 C.F.R. § 160.408(a).
113. *Id.* § 160.408(b).
114. *Id.* § 160.408(c).
115. *Id.* § 160.408(d).
116. *Id.* § 160.408(e).

D. THE COMPLIANCE AUDIT PROGRAM

In order to strengthen HHS's ability to enforce HIPAA's security and privacy requirements, the HITECH Act required HHS to begin a program of compliance auditing. "The Secretary shall provide for periodic audits to ensure that covered entities and business associates that are subject to the requirements of this subchapter and subparts C and E of part 164 of title 45, Code of Federal Regulations, as such provisions are in effect as of February 17, 2009, comply with such requirements."[117] Subpart C of 45 C.F.R. part 164 contains provisions of the Security Rule and subpart E contains the Privacy Rule. The reference to "this subchapter" would include the privacy provisions of the HITECH Act, which include the requirements imposed on business associates and the breach notification requirements of the act. The Secretary of HHS delegated the auditing function to the OCR.

HHS announced that the goal of its audit program is to assess the state of HIPAA compliance.

> The audit program is an important part of OCR's overall health information privacy, security, and breach notification compliance activities. OCR uses the audit program to assess the HIPAA compliance efforts of a range of entities covered by HIPAA regulations. The audits present an opportunity to examine mechanisms for compliance, identify best practices, discover risks and vulnerabilities that may not have come to light through OCR's ongoing complaint investigations and compliance reviews, and enable us to get out in front of problems before they result in breaches. OCR will broadly identify best practices gleaned through the audit process and will provide guidance targeted to identified compliance challenges.[118]

Nonetheless, the implication of "get[ting] out in front of problems" is that there may be references from the audit program to the audit program for organizations found to have deficient practices. Indeed, HHS later states, "Should an audit report indicate a serious compliance issue, OCR may initiate a compliance review to further investigate."[119]

---

117. 42 U.S.C. § 17940.

118. HHS, HIPAA Privacy, Security, and Breach Notification Audit Program, http://www.hhs.gov/hipaa/for-professionals/compliance-enforcement/audit/index.html (last visited Apr. 9, 2016) [hereinafter Audit Program Website].

119. *Id.*

OCR has already completed Phase 1 of its Privacy, Security, and Breach Notification Audit Program. "In 2011 and 2012, OCR implemented a pilot audit program to assess the controls and processes implemented by 115 covered entities to comply with HIPAA's requirements. OCR also conducted an extensive evaluation of the effectiveness of the pilot program."[120] The pilot program found two-thirds of the entities audited had no complete and accurate risk assessment and 58 of 59 providers had at least one security finding or observation issue.[121] Thus, the issues uncovered seem to corroborate the lack of compliance observed in section 7.A above.

Having completed Phase 1, HHS is now undertaking Phase 2 of its audit program.

> Drawing on that experience and the results of the evaluation, OCR is implementing phase two of the program, which will audit both covered entities and business associates. As part of this program, OCR is developing enhanced protocols (sets of instructions) to be used in the next round of audits and pursuing a new strategy to test the efficacy of desk audits in evaluating the compliance efforts of the HIPAA regulated industry.[122]

Any organization of any size is subject to auditing. HHS will create a pool of potential auditees based on different sampling criteria based on type of entity, size of entity, geographical location, and other factors.[123] OCR will then contact pool members and ask them to complete a questionnaire.[124] A copy of the questionnaire is available on the HHS website.[125] "OCR will choose auditees through random sampling of the audit pool. Selected auditees will then be notified of their participation."[126] OCR will communicate with potential auditees by e-mail.[127]

---

120. *Id.*

121. Linda Sanches, Office for Civil Rights, HIPAA Privacy, Security and Breach Notification Audits 27 (Apr. 23, 2013), http://www.hcca-info.org/Portals/0/PDFs/Resources/Conference_Handouts/Compliance_Institute/2013/Tuesday/500/504print2.pdf (slide 27 is on page 14 of the pdf).

122. Audit Program Website, *supra* note 118.

123. *See id.*

124. *See id.* If a potential auditee does not respond to HHS's requests for information, it is still subject to auditing in the future. *See id.*

125. HHS, Audit Pre-Screening Questionnaire, http://www.hhs.gov/hipaa/for-professionals/compliance-enforcement/audit/questionnaire/index.html (last visited Apr. 9, 2016).

126. Audit Program Website, *supra* note 118.

127. *See id.*

1. How Audits Will Work

Phase 2 will involve both what HHS calls "desk audits" as well as on-site audits. "Desk audits" involve HHS auditors reviewing the auditee's policies, procedures, and other documentation. "Entities selected for an audit will be sent an email notification of their selection and will be asked to provide documents and other data in response to a document request letter. Audited entities will submit documents on-line via a new secure audit portal on OCR's website."[128] After the auditee submits its documentation, "[a]uditors will review documentation and then develop and share draft findings with the entity."[129] "Auditees will have the opportunity to respond to these draft findings; their written responses will be included in the final audit report. Audit reports generally describe how the audit was conducted, discuss any findings, and contain entity responses to the draft findings."[130] Auditees will have ten business days to review and return written comments, if any, to the auditor. The auditor will complete a final audit report for each entity within thirty business days after the auditee's response. OCR will share a copy of the final report with the audited entity.[131] Presumably, the purpose of the documentation review is to determine if the auditee has sufficient policies, procedures, and subordinate documentation to address all requirements of the Security Rule, Breach Notification Rule, and Privacy Rule.

In addition to "desk audits," HHS will conduct some on-site visits. "[A]uditees should be prepared for a site visit when OCR deems it appropriate."[132] An on-site audit would give the auditors the ability to check what the auditee says in its documentation. For instance, if a medical clinic auditee's documentation states that the auditee has an on-premises virtual private network server located within a secure locked room, auditors could come on-site to view the physical surroundings of the server and determine if, in fact, its physical settings match what the auditee says in its documentation. Auditors might look at the door and check its lock. They may determine if the server room is completely separated by walls and the door from the rest of the clinic.

HHS described the way an on-site visit would work.

> The auditors will schedule an entrance conference and provide more
> information about the onsite audit process and expectations for the

---

128. Audit Program Website, *supra* note 118.
129. *Id.*
130. *Id.*
131. *Id.*
132. *Id.*

audit. Each onsite audit will be conducted over three to five days onsite, depending on the size of the entity. Onsite audits will be more comprehensive than desk audits and cover a wider range of requirements from the HIPAA Rules. Like the desk audit, entities will have 10 business days to review the draft findings and provide written comments to the auditor. The auditor will complete a final audit report for each entity within 30 business days after the auditee's response. OCR will share a copy of the final report with the audited entity.[133]

Phase 2 is starting with desk audits to be followed later by on-site audits.

OCR plans to conduct desk and onsite audits for both covered entities and their business associates. The first set of audits will be desk audits of covered entities followed by a second round of desk audits of business associates. These audits will examine compliance with specific requirements of the Privacy, Security, or Breach Notification Rules and auditees will be notified of the subject(s) of their audit in a document request letter. All desk audits in this phase will be completed by the end of December 2016.

The third set of audits will be onsite and will examine a broader scope of requirements from the HIPAA Rules than desk audits. Some desk auditees may be subject to a subsequent onsite audit.[134]

Audits are at HHS's expense. Auditees are not responsible for paying the auditors.[135]

As mentioned above, if the auditors find a "serious compliance issue," OCR may undertake a compliance review to further investigate the facts and circumstances surrounding the issue.[136] A compliance review could then lead to a notice of proposed determination and the imposition of civil money penalties. HHS noted that although OCR does not post findings of the results of individual audits, communications and information about the results of audits may be subject to Freedom of Information Act requests.[137]

Ultimately, OCR will review aggregated audit results based on all the audits it will perform. It can then report on the state of compliance efforts and determine possible avenues of assistance and corrective actions to facilitate compliance. The outcome of that effort may be tools and

---

133. *Id.*
134. *Id.*
135. *See id.*
136. *Id.*
137. *See id.*

guidance to help organizations help themselves to improve compliance and prevent breaches.[138]

2. Achieving Readiness for an Audit

The key for an organization to achieve readiness for a security audit is to be prepared to present and defend its policies, procedures, documentation, and underlying practices. The other parts of this book provide guidance on creating a security and breach notification program and documenting the program with appropriate policies, procedures, and other documents. Thus, for any organization that has read this book and implemented its guidance, it will already have developed the policies, procedures, and subordinate documentation that can satisfy a desk audit.

On-site audits will pose a greater challenge. In an on-site audit, auditors may ask for artifacts (evidence) that the organization is actually implementing the controls depicted in its documentation. Again, if any organization implementing the guidance in other parts of this book will have developed its documentation based on practices that satisfy all applicable aspects of the Security Rule and Breach Notification Rule. For instance, it will have undertaken its own periodic assessments[139] to make sure that its documentation complies with the Security Rule and Breach Notification and that it is in compliance with its own security documentation. Moreover, it will base its documentation not only on what the Security Rule and Breach Notification Rule say, but also on the practices it is actually maintaining. It will not have simply copied practices from forms or other organizations' documentation that may bear no relationship with its business. Finally, an organization following the guidance in this book will update its documentation to account for changes in technology, changes in threats, its evolving business context, and changes in requirements. Its documentation is not simply "shelfware" that it writes once and then puts on the shelf never to review again.

In sum, the best way to prepare for an audit is to implement the guidance in the other parts of this book. Nonetheless, an organization can take additional audit-specific steps to increase its readiness for an OCR audit. First, it is worth reviewing OCR's current audit protocol to take note of what questions auditors will ask. A current copy of the

---

138. *See id.*
139. *See* 45 C.F.R. § 164.308(a)(8).

audit protocol is on the HHS website.[140] An organization can prepare itself to answer all of the applicable questions in the protocol. Not every line item on the protocol will apply. For instance, a covered entity is not going to have policies and procedures to satisfy the requirement that business associates notify covered entities of breaches unless it otherwise acts as a business associate for other covered entities. Accordingly, the organization should review the protocol to determine which of the line items apply to it and be prepared to address those.

Second, the organization should conduct its own "tabletop exercise." It should set aside time to undertake a test of its program by pretending that it has been selected for an audit. It can then review the documentation that an auditor would request and assess in a desktop audit. The exercise can pose questions such as:

- Do the policies and procedures of the organization cover all requirements of the Security and Breach Notification Rules?
- Is the organization's risk assessment still current?
- When was the last time the organization updated its documentation? Is it time for new versions of the documentation?
- Has the organization checked to make sure its documentation matches its current technology, the threats it faces, and its evolving business?
- Is the organization doing what it says it is doing in its documentation?
- Have any recent incidents or breaches made it apparent that some aspects of the security program should change to reduce risks to the organization?

After answering these questions, it can conduct a mock on-site audit of itself by reviewing its administrative, physical, and technical safeguards. Are these safeguards fully implemented? Are they operating as documented? Does the organization have the evidence to support its security practices? For instance, if the organization purports to run background checks on all of its new hires, does it have ready access to a current copy of the blank questionnaire each new hire fills out to give to the service provider performing the background check? Also, if the organization says that it uses two-factor authentication to access certain databases, does it have a workforce member that can demonstrate how

---

140. HHS, Audit Protocol—Current, http://www.hhs.gov/hipaa/for-professionals /compliance-enforcement/audit/protocol-current/index.html (last visited Apr. 9, 2016).

it works and the devices needed to show both factors of authentication? If the mock on-site audit reveals any deficiencies, the organization can address them before it receives a real notification that OCR has selected it for an on-site audit.

Third, the organization should develop resources to help it prepare for an audit. Besides this book, there are many sources for information on improving its HIPAA-HITECH security program through professional associations. They include the American Bar Association Section of Science & Technology Law and the ABA's Health Law Section. These professional associations provide content and programming on preparing for OCR audits. Moreover, the Internet contains an enormous amount of information about preparing for audits and HIPAA compliance generally. For instance, the National Institute of Standards and Technology Special Publication 800-66 provides a good introduction to implementing the Security Rule.[141] Staying abreast of enforcement trends and compliance challenges through news services will help the organization understand and address what are potentially OCR's greatest concerns.

Fourth, the organization may want to obtain outside help to prepare for audits. It may find it helpful to retain security consultants, auditors, and outside counsel to review documentation and its security practices. Having an outside firm run a mock audit may make it easier for the organization to devote the time and attention needed to conduct a thorough review of documentation and practices, as well as the perspective of seeing many clients and industry trends that can provide useful feedback for improving the organization's security program.

E. CIVIL ACTIONS BY STATE ATTORNEYS GENERAL

As another method of strengthening HIPAA enforcement, the HITECH Act authorized state attorneys general to file civil enforcement actions in federal district court to redress HIPAA violations.[142]

> [I]n any case in which the attorney general of a State has reason to believe that an interest of one or more of the residents of that State

---

141. Matthew Scholl et al., Nat'l Inst. of Standards & Tech., Special Publ'n 800-66, An Introductory Resource Guide for Implementing the Health Insurance Portability and Accountability Act (HIPAA) Security Rule (rev. 1, Oct. 2008), http://csrc.nist.gov/publications/nistpubs/800-66-Rev1/SP-800-66-Revision1.pdf.

142. 42 U.S.C. § 1320d-5(d).

has been or is threatened or adversely affected by any person who violates a provision of this part, the attorney general of the State, as parens patriae, may bring a civil action on behalf of such residents of the State in a district court of the United States of appropriate jurisdiction . . . .[143]

The attorney general can seek an injunction to enjoin further violations or obtain statutory damages.[144] The amount recoverable in statutory damages cannot exceed $100 per violation or a total of $25,000 for all violations of an identical requirement.[145] A court can use the factors that bear on determining the amount of civil money penalties to help it determine the appropriate amount of statutory damages.[146] The court may also award costs and attorney's fees to the attorney general if the attorney general prevails in a successful action.[147]

This procedure supplements but does not supplant other enforcement activity. It does not prevent an attorney general from using the powers otherwise available under state law to address privacy or security breaches or violations.[148] Also, if the Secretary of HHS has instituted proceedings to seek civil money penalties with respect to a violation, a state attorney general may not file a civil action based on the same violation.[149]

The attorney general must serve prior notice on the Secretary of HHS of an intention to file an action. The Secretary may intervene in the attorney general's action and have the right to file petitions for any appeal.[150] The applicable statute of limitations is six years.[151] The general federal venue provisions of 28 U.S.C. § 1391 apply to any attorney general action.[152] The attorney general can serve a defendant in any district in which the defendant is an inhabitant or it maintains a physical place of business.[153] Accordingly, before filing a civil enforcement action, the attorney general's office should check to make sure that it

---

143. *Id.* § 1320d-5(d)(1).
144. *See id.* 1320d-5(d)(1)(A), (d)(1)(B).
145. *Id.* § 1320d-5(d)(2)(A), (d)(2)(B).
146. *See id.* § 1320d-5(d)(2)(C).
147. *See id.* § 1320d-5(d)(3).
148. *See id.* § 1320d-5(d)(5).
149. *See id.* § 1320d-5(d)(7).
150. *See id.* § 1320d-5(d)(4).
151. *See id.* § 1320d-5(d)(8) (referring to the limitation in 42 U.S.C. § 1320a-7a(c)(1)).
152. *See id.* § 1320d-5(d)(6)(A).
153. *See id.* § 1320d-5(d)(6)(B).

is the action in a federal district in which venue is appropriate and in which it can obtain service on the defendant. For instance, if suburban New Jersey residents are affected by lax security practices in a hospital in Manhattan, the attorney general of New Jersey may, depending on the facts, need to file suit against the hospital in the Southern District of New York because that is where the defendant resides, that is where the events giving rise to the claim occurred, and the hospital's physical place of business is there.

The statute, however, creates carve-outs from the ability of an attorney general to maintain an enforcement action. For instance, a prior criminal conviction for a HIPAA action bars further action for civil money penalties or statutory damages in an attorney general action.[154] Also, an attorney general may not recover statutory damages if the organization has already corrected the failure to comply within thirty days.[155] In addition, the Secretary has the authority to waive payment of statutory damages.[156] Moreover, an enforcement action does not bar OCR from using informal means to seek corrective actions without penalties.[157] Presumably, if such efforts to obtain corrective action are successful, the Secretary may want to waive some or all of any statutory penalties being sought by an attorney general.

Research reveals only a few publicized attorney general enforcement actions. Accordingly, it does not appear to be a popular procedure. A 2014 article stated that only two attorneys general have filed suits and that limited budgets may have deterred some attorneys general from pursuing enforcement actions.[158] Attorneys general have announced a few more actions, but they remain few in number. Research reveals the following announced cases:

- The Connecticut attorney general's action against Health Net, which lost an unencrypted hard drive containing PHI about 500,000 Connecticut citizens and 1.5 million consumers nationwide, was settled in 2010 for a $250,000 payment of statutory

---

154. *See id.* § 1320d-5(b)(1).

155. *See id.* § 1320d-5(b)(2)(A). The time runs from when the organization knew of the violation or, by exercising reasonable diligence, would have known. *See id.*

156. *See id.* § 1320d-5(b)(3).

157. *See id.* § 1320d-5(e).

158. Kimberly Leonard, *State Attorneys General Not Leaping to Embrace HIPAA Enforcement*, CTR. FOR PUB. INTEGRITY (Sept. 20, 2011; updated May 19, 2014), https://www.publicintegrity.org/2011/09/20/6666/state-attorneys-general-not-leaping-embrace-hipaa-enforcement.

damages, a promise to pay an additional $500,000 if misuse of the data occurred, and undergoing a corrective action plan.[159]

- The Vermont attorney general's action against the Health Net over the same incident was settled in 2011. "The settlement requires the defendants to pay $55,000 to the State, submit to a data-security audit, and file reports with the State regarding the company's information security programs for the next two years."[160]

- The Massachusetts attorney general filed a state court[161] suit against South Shore Hospital after its shipping services failed to deliver unencrypted backup tapes containing PHI failed to reach its data sanitization vendor. The attorney general asserted claims under the Massachusetts Consumer Protection Act and HIPAA, which were settled in 2012 for $750,000.[162]

- The Minnesota attorney general filed a state court action against Accretive Health, one of the nation's largest medical debt collectors. The $2.5 million settlement in 2012 covered allegations based on the theft of a laptop with unencrypted PHI, but also claims based on embedding debt collectors in a hospital's emergency room.[163]

- The Massachusetts attorney general filed a state court suit against former owners of a medical billing practice and four pathology groups after they improperly disposed of paper

---

159. Press Release, Office of the Conn. Att'y Gen., Attorney General Announces Health Net Settlement Involving Massive Security Breach Compromising Private Medical and Financial Info (Jul. 6, 2010), http://www.ct.gov/ag/cwp/view.asp?A=2341&Q=462754.

160. Press Release, Office of the Vt. Att'y Gen., Attorney General Settles Security Breach Allegations against Health Insurer (Jan. 18, 2011, http://ago.vermont.gov/focus/news/attorney -general-settles-security-breach-allegations-against-health-insurer.php).

161. The attorney general filed the case in state court citing the HITECH Act despite its provisions permitting suits in federal court and mentioning nothing about state court.

162. Press Release, Mass. Att'y Gen.'s Office, South Shore Hospital to Pay $750,000 to Settle Data Breach Allegations (May 24, 2012), http://www.mass.gov/ago/news-and-updates /press-releases/2012/2012-05-24-south-shore-hospital-data-breach-settlement.html. $275,000 of the settlement amount reflected the attorney general's credit for amounts South Shore Hospital spent on security measures after the breach. *Id.*

163. Jessica Silver-Greenberg, *Medical Debt Collector to Settle Suit for $2.5 Million*, N.Y. TIMES (Jul. 30, 2012), http://www.nytimes.com/2012/07/31/business/medical-debt-collector -to-pay-2-5-million-settlement.html. In fact, Attorney General Swanson lists this case as the first example in her list of accomplishments on her personal web page. Lori Swanson, Attorney General Lori Swanson, http://loriswanson.com (list visited Apr. 9, 2016) ("Lori Swanson is the only state official in the country who kicked collection agencies out of hospital emergency rooms.").

records with sensitive PHI in a public dump, which were found by a *Boston Globe* photographer. To settle the claims, in 2013 the former owners paid $140,000.[164]

- The Massachusetts attorney general filed a state court suit against Women & Infants Hospital of Rhode Island after it lost track of 19 backup tapes containing unencrypted sensitive PHI about 12,127 Massachusetts residents. The claim was settled in 2014 for $150,000.[165]

- The Massachusetts attorney general filed a state court action against Beth Israel Deaconess Medical Center of Boston based on claims surrounding the theft of a personal laptop from a doctor's office. The doctor also used the laptop for business purposes; it contained unencrypted sensitive data on over 4,000 patients and employees. In 2014, the center paid $100,000 to settle the claims.[166]

- The Indiana attorney general filed a state court action against Joseph Beck, doing business as Beck Family Dentistry. In 2011, the Indiana Board of Dentistry revoked Beck's license to practice for fraudulent billing and negligence. He hired a company to dispose of his paper records. Sixty boxes of the records containing sensitive information about 5,600 patients were later found in an Indianapolis dumpster, triggering the enforcement action.[167] Beck settled the attorney general's claims in 2015 by paying $12,000.[168]

- Connecticut's attorney general settled claims in 2015 without filing suit in a matter involving EMC Corporation, Hartford

---

164. Press Release, Mass. Att'y Gen.'s Office, Former Owners of Medical Billing Practice, Pathology Groups Agree to Pay $140,000 to Settle Claims that Patients' Health Information was Disposed of at Georgetown Dump (Jan. 7, 2013), http://www.mass.gov/ago/news-and -updates/press-releases/2013/140k-settlement-over-medical-info-disposed-of-at-dump.html.

165. Press Release, Mass. Att'y Gen.'s Office, Women & Infants Hospital to Pay $150,000 to Settle Data Breach Allegations Involving Massachusetts Patients (Jul. 23, 2014), http://www .mass.gov/ago/news-and-updates/press-releases/2014/2014-07-23-women-infants-hospital.html.

166. Press Release, Mass. Att'y Gen.'s Office, Beth Israel Deaconess Medical Center to Pay $100,000 over Data Breach Allegations (Nov. 21, 2014), http://www.mass.gov/ago/news-and -updates/press-releases/2014/2014-11-21-beth-israel-data-breach.html.

167. Kelly Soderlund, *Indiana Dentist Is First Sued by State for Violating HIPAA*, ADA News (Mar. 2, 2015), http://www.ada.org/en/publications/ada-news/2015-archive/march /indiana-dentist-is-first-sued-by-state-for-violating-hipaa.

168. State of Indiana v. Beck, No. 49D10-1412-PL-041613 (Consent Judgment Jan. 5, 2015), *reprinted at* http://content.govdelivery.com/attachments/INSTATE/2015/01/08/file _attachments/354358/Beck%2BConsent%2BJudgment.pdf.

Hospital, and VNA HealthCare that arose from the theft of a laptop containing unencrypted PHI about 8,883 Connecticut residents from an EMC employee's home. The parties resolved the potential claim by agreeing to pay the state $90,000.[169]

- Without filing suit, the attorney general of New York resolved potential claims against the University of Rochester Medical Center stemming from a nurse who provided a list of 3,403 patients (which included diagnoses) to her future employer without authorization for purposes of announcing her new position. The 2015 settlement included a payment of $15,000 and a commitment to training.[170]

In reviewing this record of enforcement activity, some conclusions are possible, although they are based on only a small group of cases. Of the ten cases, all but one concerned the loss or theft of a device or disposal of records. The loss or theft of a device containing unencrypted PHI is still a common reason for a breach. The frequency of breaches due to the loss or theft of devices containing unencrypted PHI underscores how encrypting data can make a big difference in reducing risk. Also, organizations may spend a great deal of time and energy in securing networks, but these cases show simple encryption and secure disposal practices are also crucial. People also may not consider the necessity of securing paper records. Finally, I note that these actions are not yet covering the breaches from hacking, phishing, and ransomware that are common today. Perhaps we may see more enforcement activities in upcoming years as attorneys general become more familiar with these threats and possibly see instances of patient harm.

F. SECURITY ISSUES IDENTIFIED IN ENFORCEMENT ACTIVITY

Examples of HHS enforcement activities are more numerous than state attorney general actions. Like the state attorney general actions, an examination of different cases shows the kinds of issues that are

---

169. Marianne Kolbasuk McGee, *State Fines Hospital, EMC after Breach*, BANK INFO SECURITY, Nov. 9, 2015, http://www.bankinfosecurity.com/state-fines-hospital-emc-after-breach-a-8669/op-1.

170. Press Release, N.Y. State Office of the Att'y Gen., A.G. Schneiderman Announces Settlement with University of Rochester to Prevent Future Patient Privacy Breaches (Dec. 2, 2015), http://www.ag.ny.gov/press-release/ag-schneiderman-announces-settlement-university-rochester-prevent-future-patient.

likely at this time to create legal risk for organizations. HHS posted a list of case examples with various types of violations involving different types of organizations.[171] The cases most applicable to security practices appear below.

- A pharmacy kept pseudoephedrine log books in a location at the pharmacy counter that made the PHI in the books visible to the public. OCR required the national pharmacy chain to change its procedures and train pharmacies' workforce.
- A municipal social service agency sent PHI to computer vendors that were not business associates. OCR required the agency to adopt new procedures and train its workforce.
- A computer system flaw caused a national health maintenance organization to send an explanation of benefits to a complainant's unauthorized family member.[172]

The remaining issues identified in the OCR list relate to privacy practices.

In addition to the list of case examples, HHS posts announcements about resolution agreements and ALJ proceedings. There has only been one case in which a respondent challenged a notice of proposed determination: *Director of the Office for Civil Rights v. Lincare, Inc.*[173] *Lincare* was only the second time that OCR instituted formal proceedings to seek civil money penalties. It was the first security-related case, and did not even involve a Security Rule violation. In *Lincare*, a home healthcare company's manager kept paper PHI in her car, which she shared with her husband. Her husband was not entitled to access the PHI. When she moved out of her house, she abandoned the paper PHI, and her husband notified OCR that he had the PHI. The ALJ entered summary judgment in favor of HHS, stating that Lincare failed to safeguard the paper PHI as required by the Privacy Rule. Apparently, only paper PHI was involved. Therefore, OCR had to proceed under the Privacy Rule's safeguards requirement,[174] rather than the Security Rule, which covers only electronic PHI.

---

171. HHS, All Case Examples, http://www.hhs.gov/hipaa/for-professionals/compliance-enforcement/examples/all-cases/index.html (last visited Apr. 9, 2016).

172. *See id.*

173. No. C-14-1056, Decision No. CR4505 (Jan. 13, 2016), *reprinted at* http://www.hhs.gov/sites/default/files/lincare_decision_remediated.pdf.

174. 45 C.F.R. § 164.530(c).

Table 7.2. Resolution Agreements Concerning Security Violations

Date of Announcement of Resolution Agreement	Name of Settling Party or Parties	Type of Organization(s)	Conduct Triggering Enforcement	Amount Paid by Settling Party	Other Key Obligations of the Settling Party
7/16/2008	Providence Health & Services	Covered entity	Loss of backup media and laptops containing unencrypted ePHI	$100,000	Implement a corrective action plan, including encryption and three years of compliance reports
1/16/2009	CVS Pharmacy, Inc.	Covered entity	Disposing of paper PHI (old prescriptions and bottles) without shredding or destroying it	$2.25 million	Implement a corrective action plan, including revised policies, training workers, and three years of compliance reports
6/7/2010	Rite Aid Corp.	Covered entity	Disposing of paper PHI (old prescriptions and bottles) without shredding or destroying it	$1 million	Implement a corrective action plan, including revised policies, training workers, and three years of compliance reports
12/13/2010	Management Services Organization Washington, Inc.	Covered entity	Allowing a marketing affiliate to access PHI; failing to manage access to PHI	$35,000	Implement a corrective action plan, including revised policies, training workers, and two years of HHS monitoring
2/24/2011	General Hospital Corporation and Massachusetts General Physicians Organization Inc.	Covered entities	Paper PHI left on subway	$1 million	Implement a corrective action plan, including revised policies, training workers, and three years of compliance reports

(Continued)

Table 7.2. Resolution Agreements Concerning Security Violations (Continued)

Date of Announcement of Resolution Agreement	Name of Settling Party or Parties	Type of Organization(S)	Conduct Triggering Enforcement	Amount Paid by Settling Party	Other Key Obligations of the Settling Party
7/7/2011	UCLA Health System	Covered entity	Snooping (unauthorized access to ePHI)	$865,000	Implement a corrective action plan, including revised policies, training workers, and three years of compliance reports
3/9/2012	Blue Cross Blue Shield of Tennessee	Covered entity	Theft of 57 hard drives containing unencrypted ePHI	$1.5 million	Implement a corrective action plan, including revised policies, training workers, and two biannual compliance reports
4/17/2012	Phoenix Cardiac Surgery, P.C.	Covered entity	The physician practice was posting clinical and surgical appointments for its patients on an Internet-based calendar that was publicly accessible	$100,000	Implement a corrective action plan, including revised policies, training workers, and a compliance report
6/26/2012	Alaska Department of Health and Social Services	Covered entity	Theft of USB drive containing unencrypted ePHI from a car	$1.7 million	Implement a corrective action plan, including revised policies, training workers, and three years of compliance reports

Date of Announcement of Resolution Agreement	Name of Settling Party or Parties	Type of Organization(S)	Conduct Triggering Enforcement	Amount Paid by Settling Party	Other Key Obligations of the Settling Party
9/17/2012	Massachusetts Eye and Ear Infirmary and Massachusetts Eye and Ear Associates Inc.	Covered entity	Theft of laptop containing unencrypted ePHI (lack of risk analysis, access management, and incident response policies)	$1.5 million	Implement a corrective action plan, including revised policies, training workers, and three years of compliance reports
1/2/2013	Hospice of North Idaho	Covered entity	Theft of laptop containing unencrypted ePHI (lack of risk analysis and mobile device policies)	$50,000	Implement a corrective action plan, including reporting security incidents to HHS for two years
7/11/2013	Wellpoint Inc.	Covered entity	Security weaknesses in online application database exposed ePHI to unauthorized access	$1.7 million	None
8/14/2013	Affinity Health Plan, Inc.	Covered entity	Returned multiple photocopiers to a leasing agent without removing ePHI from their hard drives (did not include the erasure issue in a risk analysis)	$1,215,780	Implement a corrective action plan, including retrieving the old hard drives, conduct a risk analysis, and revise policies and procedures

(Continued)

Table 7.2. Resolution Agreements Concerning Security Violations (Continued)

Date of Announcement of Resolution Agreement	Name of Settling Party or Parties	Type of Organization(s)	Conduct Triggering Enforcement	Amount Paid by Settling Party	Other Key Obligations of the Settling Party
12/24/2013	Adult & Pediatric Dermatology, P.C.	Covered entity	Theft of USB drive containing unencrypted ePHI from a car	$150,000	Implement a corrective action plan that includes a risk analysis and reporting of security incidents and implementation status
3/7/2014	Skagit County, Washington	Covered entity	ePHI had been inadvertently moved to a publicly accessible server	$215,000	Implement a corrective action plan that includes a risk analysis, revised policies, training workers, and three years of compliance reports
4/22/2014	Concentra Health Services	Covered entity	Theft of laptop containing unencrypted ePHI (despite risk analysis identifying lack of encryption as a risk)	$1,725,220	Implement a corrective action plan that includes a risk analysis, reporting on implementing encryption, and training
4/22/2014	QCA Health Plan, Inc.	Covered entity	Theft of laptop containing unencrypted ePHI from car	$250,000	Implement a corrective action plan that includes a risk analysis, training, and three years of compliance reports
5/7/2014	New York and Presbyterian Hospital (NYP) and Columbia University (CU)	Covered entities	Deactivation of server controls resulted in ePHI being accessible on Internet search engines	$4.8 million (NYP has paid OCR a monetary settlement of $3,300,000 and CU $1,500,000)	Implement a corrective action plan that includes a risk analysis, revised policies, training workers, and three years of compliance reports

Date of Announcement of Resolution Agreement	Name of Settling Party or Parties	Type of Organization(S)	Conduct Triggering Enforcement	Amount Paid by Settling Party	Other Key Obligations of the Settling Party
6/23/2014	Parkview Health System, Inc.	Covered entity	Workers left boxes of paper PHI on retiring physician's driveway while he was away and no one was supervising it	$80,000	Implement a corrective action plan that includes revised policies, training workers, and a compliance report
12/2/2014	Anchorage Community Mental Health Services, Inc.	Covered entity	Malware attack causing a breach of ePHI	$150,000	Implement a corrective action plan that includes a risk analysis, revised policies, training workers, and two years of compliance reports
4/22/2015	Cornell Prescription Pharmacy	Covered entity	Improper disposal of paper records containing PHI on premises	$125,000	Implement a corrective action plan that includes revised policies, training workers, and two years of compliance reports
6/10/2015	St. Elizabeth's Medical Center	Covered entity	• Use of online file sharing service without conducting a risk analysis • Inadequate incident response • Separate incident of compromise of unsecured ePHI on a laptop and USB drive	$218,400	Implement a corrective action plan that includes a self-assignment, revised policies, training worker, and a report

(Continued)

Table 7.2. Resolution Agreements Concerning Security Violations (Continued)

Date of Announcement of Resolution Agreement	Name of Settling Party or Parties	Type of Organization(S)	Conduct Triggering Enforcement	Amount Paid by Settling Party	Other Key Obligations of the Settling Party
9/2/2015	Cancer Care Group, P.C.	Covered entity	Theft of laptop and USB drive containing unencrypted ePHI from car	$750,000	Implement a corrective action plan that includes a risk analysis, revised policies, training workers, and three years of compliance reports
11/25/2015	Lahey Hospital and Medical Center	Covered entity	Theft of laptop containing unencrypted ePHI, plus failure to conduct risk analysis, physically protect a workstation, track use by a single account, log workstation activity, and prevent unauthorized disclosure of PHI	$850,000	Implement a corrective action plan that includes a risk analysis, revised policies, training workers, and a compliance report

Date of Announcement of Resolution Agreement	Name of Settling Party or Parties	Type of Organization(S)	Conduct Triggering Enforcement	Amount Paid by Settling Party	Other Key Obligations of the Settling Party
11/30/2015	Triple-S Management Corporation, on behalf of its wholly owned subsidiaries, Triple-S Salud Inc., Triple-C Inc. and Triple-S Advantage Inc., formerly known as American Health Medicare Inc.	Covered entity	Multiple breach notifications led OCR to investigate, and the investigation uncovered multiple violations, including failing to implement safeguards, disclosure of PHI to a vendor without a BAA, and failure to conduct a risk analysis	$3.5 million	Implement a corrective action plan that includes a risk analysis, revised policies, training workers, and a compliance report
12/14/2015	The Board of Regents of the University of Washington, on behalf of University of Washington–University of Washington Medicine	Affiliated covered entity	ePHI accessed after malware attack	$750,000	Implement a corrective action plan that includes a risk analysis and submitting a risk management plan

(Continued)

Table 7.2. Resolution Agreements Concerning Security Violations (Continued)

Date of Announcement of Resolution Agreement	Name of Settling Party or Parties	Type of Organization(S)	Conduct Triggering Enforcement	Amount Paid by Settling Party	Other Key Obligations of the Settling Party
3/16/2016	North Memorial Health Care of Minnesota	Covered entity	Theft of business associate's laptop containing unencrypted ePHI, plus failure to conduct a risk analysis and to use a BAA	$1.55 million	Implement a corrective action plan that includes a risk analysis and submitting a risk management plan, revised policies, training workers, and two years of compliance reports
3/17/2016	Feinstein Institute for Medical Research	Covered entity	Theft of laptop containing unencrypted ePHI from car	$3.9 million	Implement a corrective action plan that includes a risk analysis, revised policies, training workers, and three years of compliance reports

Source: Dep't of Health & Human Servs., Health Information Privacy, Resolution Agreements, http://www.hhs.gov/hipaa/for-professionals /compliance-enforcement/agreements/index.html.

A review of OCR's case against Lincare and the twenty-eight resolution agreements shown in table 7.2 reveals a number of trends. First, as with the state attorney general actions discussion above in section 7.E, the loss or theft of devices or media containing unencrypted PHI was the top trigger for enforcement actions. These cases accounted for thirteen of the twenty-eight resolution agreements. As with the attorney general actions, improper disposal of PHI was the next most common scenario with five resolution agreements. Malware accounted for only two resolution agreements. Nonetheless, with increasing cases of phishing, spear phishing, and ransomware attacks, we may see more enforcement activity addressing malware and social engineering. Organizations could reduce their risk of enforcement greatly simply by implementing encryption and ensuring proper disposal of PHI.

OCR has more recently focused on the lack of a risk assessment. Conducting a risk assessment is a fundamental step in securing PHI. Accordingly, organizations should prioritize conducting or updating a risk assessment of their businesses.

The cases involving ePHI accessible through the Internet are interesting because OCR may have had no evidence of the misuse of the ePHI. Placing ePHI in Internet-accessible locations *could have* caused misuse, but without logs or other evidence, OCR and the covered entities involved may have had no knowledge one way or the other whether the conduct *actually did* cause misuse. The lesson learned from these cases is that OCR is serious about pursuing organizations in situations where "access" to PHI through the public Internet occurred even in the absence of proof of actual harm or compromise. This position is consistent with the discussion of the Breach Notification Rule, which requires a breach notification in the absence of evidence to prove or disprove the occurrence of compromise or where there is evidence of equal weight confirming and disconfirming a compromise.[175]

Also of note are the targets of HHS enforcement activities. HHS has entered into no resolution agreements with business associates. The *Lincare* case and the twenty-eight resolution agreements involved covered entities. Moreover, almost all of the resolution agreements involved security breaches or both security and privacy breaches, as opposed to pure privacy breaches.

---

175. See *supra* section 6.D.2.

The amounts of the resolution payments vary greatly. Nonetheless, more recent resolution agreements have involved larger payments. Accordingly, OCR may be seeking more money as time goes on.

Finally, all of the resolution agreements seem to have included a corrective action plan. More recent resolution agreements call for the covered entity to undertake a risk assessment to redress the issue of absent risk assessments discussed above. Most frequently, they include requirements to update policies and procedures, train workforce members about these policies, and report compliance efforts to HHS over time, most frequently three years.

CHAPTER 8

Litigation and Risk Management

Chapter 7 covers the authority for the Department of Health and Human Services (HHS) and the states to enforce HIPAA security requirements, as well as case examples and the lessons learned from those cases. This chapter turns to the topic of litigation instituted by private plaintiffs, as well as managing the risk of liability, enforcement actions, and first-party risks. Section 8.A discusses civil actions by private plaintiffs relating to HIPAA violations. HIPAA has no private right of action, but plaintiffs can, in some cases, use common law and statutory claims to seek compensation from organizations that violate HIPAA. Section 8.B explains risk management principles and the use of cyber risk insurance as a risk management tool. Managing information security risks will help covered entities and business associates (referred to in this chapter by the shorthand term "organizations") prevent data breaches and thereby minimize their legal risks stemming from breaches.

A. LITIGATION TO REDRESS ALLEGED HIPAA VIOLATIONS

1. No Private Right of Action

HIPAA, the HITECH Act, and the regulations contain no provisions that would permit individuals harmed in some way by a violation to sue the violating organization. Rather, Congress authorized the Secretary of HHS to investigate complaints from individuals and to conduct compliance reviews. Under HIPAA and the Final Enforcement Rule, HHS, rather than private plaintiffs, would enforce HIPAA and its regulations and seek civil money penalties and injunctive relief to redress violations.

As noted in section 7.A, however, HIPAA enforcement was perceived as insufficient. Congress therefore enacted the HITECH Act's provisions to strengthen enforcement capabilities, such as allowing state attorneys general to file civil actions in federal court to seek statutory damages for HIPAA violations. In addition, private plaintiffs began filing civil actions based on violations of HIPAA. Courts have uniformly confirmed that HIPAA has no private right of action.[1] Accordingly, plaintiffs seeking relief for alleged HIPAA violations have had to rely upon other causes of action to assert claims for HIPAA violations.

2. In re Anthem Data Breach Litigation

a. Background Concerning the Anthem Litigation

The case that may prove to be the ultimate archetype lawsuit seeking remedies for allegedly insufficient healthcare security practices is *In re Anthem Data Breach Litigation*.[2] Anthem, Inc. is one of the largest health insurance companies in the United States, providing coverage through Blue Cross Blue Shield affiliates in various states and additional affiliates. In February 2015, the company announced that attackers had compromised its member database and accessed almost 80 million records without authorization. The Anthem breach is by far the largest healthcare data breach to date.[3]

Attackers compromised Anthem's database of members and former members. Apparently, they later used personal information taken from members to commit acts of identity theft. Accordingly, the plaintiffs in this case have claimed actual damages, not just the possibility of future damages.

> So why target Anthem? If Anthem were a bank, the quote attributed to Willie Sutton would be a perfect fit. Allegedly, when asked why he robbed banks, Sutton said "because that's where the money is . . ."
>
> Thus, Anthem was targeted because the attacker(s) wanted information, and Anthem has millions of records at their disposal; they

---

1. *E.g.*, Dodd v. Jones, 623 F.3d 563, 569 (8th Cir. 2010); Wilkerson v. Shinseki, 606 F.3d 1256, 1267 n.4 (10th Cir. 2010); Miller v. Nichols, 586 F.3d 53, 59–60 (1st Cir. 2009), *cert. denied*, 599 U.S. 1008 (2010); Webb v. Smart Document Solutions, LLC, 499 F.3d 1078, 1081 (9th Cir. 2007); Acara v. Banks, 470 F.3d 569, 570–72 (5th Cir. 2006) (per curiam).

2. No. 15-MD-02617-LHK (MDL transfer order filed N.D. Cal. June 12, 2015).

3. Nia Williams, *Big Healthcare Breaches Affected Millions before Anthem's Hack*, MODERN HEALTHCARE VITALSIGNS BLOG, Feb. 10, 2015, http://www.modernhealthcare.com /article/20150210/blog/302109995.

went where the data was. Perhaps there's more to it than that, but if not, the fact the data was there is all the reason the attacker(s) needed.[4]

Based on public statements, it appears that Anthem database administrators fell victim to a phishing attack; attackers tricked them into giving up their log-in credentials to gain access to the member database.[5] Once attackers had access to the database, they could steal information from it and use it for identity theft. Anthem members affected by the breach contend they sustained various forms of damage as a result of the breach, including losses from the identify theft incidents.

The resulting massive data breach triggered numerous suits. Following various actions filed around the country, the Judicial Panel on Multidistrict Litigation (MDL) issued an order on June 12, 2015, transferring the actions to the U.S. District Court for the Northern District of California for consolidated proceedings. With the magnitude of the breach and the nationwide nature of the actions and claims based on numerous states, this lawsuit may prove to be the most significant medical data breach case to date.

The plaintiffs filed a consolidated amended class action complaint in the MDL action. The main defendants, the Anthem affiliates and a group of non-Anthem Blue Cross Blue Shield entities, filed two separate motions to dismiss. On February 14, 2016, the court granted these motions in part and denied them in part. On March 11, 2016, the plaintiffs filed a second consolidated amended class action complaint, which is the operative complaint at the time of this writing.

Anthem is the most important case discussed in this book. Besides the sheer size of the case in terms of the number of potential members in the various classes, the case will test the ability of plaintiffs to plead and prove a wide variety of key types of state law claims that expressly identify violations of the HIPAA Security Rule as their basis. As discussed above, HIPAA has no private right of action. Consequently, the plaintiffs must rely on a number of alternative types of claims. *Anthem* will likely prove to be an important test case for many of these alternative causes of action.

Moreover, the case implicates a large number of states' laws. The Northern District of California is the transferee court under MDL

---

4. Steve Ragan, *Anthem. How Does a Breach Like This Happen?*, CSO, Feb. 9, 2015, *reprinted at* http://www.csoonline.com/article/2881532/business-continuity/anthem-how-does-a-breach-like-this-happen.html.

5. *See id.*

rules, and "the MDL transferee court is generally bound by the same substantive legal standards, if not always the same interpretation of them, as would have applied in the transferor court."[6] Thus, the Northern District "must apply the law of the transferor forum, that is, the law of the state in which the action was filed."[7] Therefore, the case will not only test different kinds of state law claims, it will also test claims from many states in a single case.

Finally, since the plaintiffs had a security report from Anthem's security consultant Mandiant showing what went wrong with Anthem's security practices, the plaintiffs have been able to be very specific about the types of vulnerabilities that led to the breach, and that they believe are actionable, at an early stage of the case. It appears the Mandiant report provided a useful roadmap for plaintiffs to build a case that Anthem failed to use reasonable and appropriate security practices.

b. The Alleged Causes of the Anthem Breach

The plaintiffs in *Anthem* identified five ways in which Anthem and its affiliates allegedly failed to secure members' protected health information (PHI):

- First, the plaintiffs contend that Anthem failed to protect the member database that hackers compromised by allegedly:
  - Failing to implement two-factor authentication to access the database.
  - Failing to require users to rotate passwords, claiming that some users kept the same password for years.
  - Failing to limit access to those employees who have a need for access for job-related purposes.[8]
- Second, the plaintiffs allege Anthem and its affiliates failed to train employees to identify, report, and delete phishing e-mails.[9]
- Third, the plaintiffs claim Anthem and its affiliates failed to implement monitoring and alerting systems to alert them that

---

6. Anthem, ___ F. Supp. 3d ___, No. 15-MD-02617-LHK, 2016 WL 589760, at *4 (N.D. Cal. Feb. 14, 2016) (quoting *In re* Korean Air Lines, Co., 642 F.3d 685, 699 (9th Cir. 2011)).

7. *Id.* at *10 (quoting *In re* Vioxx Prods. Liab. Litig., 478 F. Supp. 2d 897, 903 (E.D. La. 2007)).

8. Second Consolidated Amended Class Action Complaint, ¶ 343, at 104, *In re* Anthem, Inc. Data Breach Litig., No. 15-MD-02617-LHK (N.D. Cal. Mar. 11, 2016).

9. *Id.* ¶ 344, at 104.

a cyberattack was underway, which, the plaintiffs say, could have prevented exfiltration of data.[10]
- Fourth, to the extent Anthem and its affiliates had monitoring and alerting systems, the plaintiffs say Anthem ignored the alerts.[11]
- Fifth, Anthem points to the lack of database encryption as a cause of the breach; according to plaintiffs, if the database had been encrypted, the attackers would have been unable to use the information in it.[12]

In sum, the *Anthem* plaintiffs argue that these five vulnerabilities discussed in the Mandiant report evidence Anthem's failure to secure their personal information as required by HIPAA and other applicable law. The second vulnerability, failing to train employees about phishing, suggests that the plaintiffs agree that phishing e-mails were at least a partial cause of the breach. Moreover, if database administrators at Anthem fell victim to phishing attacks, and if multifactor authentication had been required for access to the member database, attackers could not have accessed the database without having the other authenticator(s). For instance, if a physical hardware token were required to access the database in addition to a password, an attacker would have had to steal the token as well as use a phishing social engineering attack to steal the password, which would have greatly reduced the risk of compromise.[13]

Encryption in this particular instance, however, might not have prevented the breach. Database administrators with legitimate access to the database are able to decrypt information in it when they use it. If an attacker were able to compromise an administrator account, even if the database were encrypted, the attacker could step in the shoes of the administrator and decrypt the information in the database. Encryption can stop an intruder in the network able to see files from viewing information in the files; the attacker would only see encrypted information in the files. If an attacker compromises a database administrator's account,

---

10. *Id.* ¶ 345, at 105.
11. *Id.* ¶ 346, at 105.
12. *Id.* ¶ 347, at 105. After describing these five alleged vulnerabilities, the plaintiffs redacted some of the additional details concerning the defendants' alleged failures to protect the member database. *Id.* ¶¶ 348-64, at 105-08. Accordingly, the only public information about plaintiffs' claims relates to these five vulnerabilities.
13. *See* Ragan, *supra* note 4, at 2.

however, the attacker can use the account to decrypt information in the database.[14]

In any case, the plaintiffs' listing of security vulnerabilities in the *Anthem* complaint provides helpful information to organizations. By avoiding what plaintiffs allege were the key vulnerabilities, organizations can learn from the Anthem experience. They can avoid these vulnerabilities and thereby reduce their risk of liability in the future.

c. The Causes of Action Asserted in Anthem

Since HIPAA has no private right of action, plaintiffs seeking redress for alleged HIPAA violations must find causes of action outside of HIPAA to assert. For the most part, medical data breach cases assert causes of action based entirely on state law. *Anthem* is no exception. The second consolidated amended class action complaint contains thirteen counts, all based on state law. These causes of action are:

- Negligence: Plaintiffs claim that the defendants owed them a duty to secure their PHI, the defendants breached that duty by failing to secure the PHI, and the breach caused damage to plaintiffs.
- Negligence per se: Plaintiffs allege that the defendants had a duty to secure PHI under HIPAA, as well as the Federal Trade Commission Act, the Gramm-Leach-Bliley Act, and state information security laws; the defendants breached that duty by failing to secure the PHI, and the breach caused damage to plaintiffs. Using negligence per se arguments, plaintiffs contend that these laws set a standard of care, and they point to alleged violations of these laws as evidence that defendants' conduct fell below the standard.
- Breach of contract: Plaintiffs contend that defendants entered into binding contracts with them to provide health insurance coverage, or that plaintiffs were third-party beneficiaries of certain group contracts; that these contracts incorporated statements of privacy practices promising privacy and confidentiality; that defendants' security practices materially

---

14. "The problem is, while HIPAA requires that identifying information be encrypted, that protection goes by the wayside once an attacker compromises an administrator's credentials. So even if the data was encrypted, it didn't matter once the attacker(s) had total control over the database." *Id.* at 1 (emphasis omitted).

breached these promises; and that plaintiffs sustained damages as a result.

- Breach of the implied covenant of good faith and fair dealing: Plaintiffs say there is an implied covenant in agreements with defendants in which they would act in good faith and not impair the rights of other parties to receive their benefits under the relevant agreements, which defendants allegedly breached by not adequately protecting plaintiffs' PHI.
- Negligent misrepresentation: Plaintiffs argue that the defendants made negligent misrepresentations about their security practices, on which plaintiffs relied to their detriment; given the alleged failures to maintain security, plaintiffs claim they sustained damages.
- Unjust enrichment: Plaintiffs contend they conferred a benefit on defendants by paying them based on receiving reasonable security practices to protect PHI, but received services worth less because of inadequate security; plaintiffs claim defendants should disgorge the difference.
- Claims based on state consumer protection laws: Under the laws of various states, plaintiff state that they have been harmed by defendants' alleged unfair and deceptive trade practices. Plaintiffs identify violations of the laws of thirty-one states.
- Claims based on eighteen state data breach laws: Plaintiffs seek to recover damages for violations of state laws requiring defendants to secure certain categories of personal information and failing to notify plaintiffs in a timely fashion under their breach notification laws.
- Claims based on six state unfair insurance practice statutes: Plaintiffs say that defendants operating in particular jurisdictions engaged in unfair trade practices in the insurance business in violation of the specified laws.
- Causes of action for violations of twelve state insurance privacy laws: Plaintiffs allege that defendants operating in specific jurisdictions violated laws against disclosing personal insurance information without authorization.
- Claims asserting violations of seven states' medical and health information privacy laws: Plaintiffs say that defendants in each particular jurisdiction violated laws prohibiting the disclosure of medical records without authorization.

The case is still in the early stage of proceedings. The court, however, has issued one substantive published opinion in the case.[15] The court dismissed with leave to amend the California and New Jersey contract claims, the New York unjust enrichment claim, and the Georgia Information and Privacy Protection Act claims. The court also dismissed plaintiffs' fraud claim under the California Unfair Competition Law with leave to amend. The court dismissed with prejudice the plaintiffs' Indiana negligence claim, claims under Kentucky's Consumer Protection Act and Data Breach Act, and a plaintiff's California breach of contract claim based on a group contract whose governing law is federal law. Otherwise, the court denied the motions to dismiss.[16] Because the case is so important for the reasons listed above, these rulings from the *Anthem* case are likely to influence healthcare data breach cases in the future.

3. Claims Asserted by Alleged Victims of Data Breaches

Individuals affected by data breaches alleging violations of HIPAA security requirements have filed class actions against organizations that purportedly failed to protect their PHI. As mentioned in section 8.A.1 above, they cannot sue under HIPAA itself. Rather, they have asserted a wide variety of state law claims, both common law and statutory claims. This section discusses the key reported decisions in cases of this kind.[17]

Perhaps the most important recent case, aside from *Anthem*, was the decision in *Resnick v. AvMed, Inc.* in the U.S. Court of Appeals for the Eleventh Circuit.[18] *Resnick* involved a Florida corporation, defendant AvMed, which operates private and government health plans. The case arose from a data breach involving the theft of two unencrypted laptops containing PHI, including names, contact information, and Social Security numbers. The breach affected about 1.2 million current or former AvMed members and allegedly resulted in actual identity theft incidents.[19]

---

15. Anthem, ___ F. Supp. 3d ___, 2016 WL 589760.

16. *Id.* at *45.

17. This section focuses on cases asserting security violations, as opposed to privacy violations. HIPAA privacy violation cases may provide useful authority on specific HIPAA-related procedural and substantive issues. *See, e.g.,* Byrne v. Avery Ctr. for Obstetrics & Gynecology, P.C., 102 A.3d 32 (Conn. 2014) (HIPAA does not preempt a patient's negligence /negligence per se and negligent infliction of emotional distress claims based on medical practice's response to former boyfriend's subpoena in his paternity action against the patient without alerting the patient). Nevertheless, they are generally beyond the scope of this book.

18. 693 F.3d 1317 (11th Cir. 2012).

19. *See id.* at 1322.

a. Standing

Standing under Article III of the U.S. Constitution is a jurisdictional requirement to proceed in federal court. Litigants must show that their cases present a "case" or "controversy" within the meaning of Article III. A plaintiff must show "injury in fact" that is "concrete and particularized," "fairly traceable to the challenged action of the defendant," and "is likely, as opposed to merely speculative," to "be redressed by a favorable decision."[20] In *Resnick*, the plaintiffs asserted incidents of actual identity theft that harmed them, which were sufficient to support standing.[21] The monetary damages were sufficient to show an injury in fact. Moreover, the allegations of identity theft following the breach were sufficient to trace the injuries to AvMed's failures. Finally, the plaintiffs alleged that a monetary award would redress their injury. Thus, the plaintiffs satisfied all of requirements for Article III standing in federal court.[22]

States do not have an analog to Article III, which limits the jurisdiction of federal courts. State law does contain various standing requirements for certain kinds of claims. These standing requirements vary by state law.

The court in *In re Anthem Data Breach Litigation*[23] held that plaintiffs adequately alleged injury in fact sufficient for standing to assert their California Unfair Competition Law (UCL) cause of action. The court held that the "benefit of the bargain" losses were sufficient to establish economic injury. Similar to claims of unjust enrichment discussed in section 8.A.3.g below, "benefit of the bargain" damages rest on the argument that plaintiffs overpaid for health insurance since defendants took the money that should have covered adequate data security practices and kept the money.[24] Accordingly, the court declined to dismiss the plaintiffs' UCL claim for lack of standing.

---

20. *Id.* at 1323 (quoting Friends of the Earth, Inc. v. Laidlaw Envtl. Servs. (TOC), Inc., 528 U.S. 167, 180–81 (2000)).

21. *Id.* at 1322, 1323–24.

22. *Id.* at 1323–24. *Accord* Smith v. Triad of Ala., LLC, No. 1:14-CV-324-WKW, 2015 WL 5793318, at *6–11 (M.D. Ala. Sept. 29, 2015) (plaintiffs adequately alleged standing to support a claim under the Fair Credit Reporting Act based on actual identity theft incidents resulting from the compromise of apparently paper personal information at the defendant hospital).

23. ___ F. Supp. 3d ____, No. 15-MD-02617-LHK, 2016 WL 589760 (N.D. Cal. Feb. 14, 2016).

24. *See id.* at *18–19.

b. Negligence

Plaintiffs have had mixed success with negligence claims. To plead and prove negligence, a plaintiff must typically allege:

- The defendant owes the plaintiff a duty.
- Defendant breached that duty in that the defendant's conduct fell below the applicable standard.
- The defendant's breach injured the plaintiff.
- A compensable injury was proximately caused by the defendant's breach of duty.[25]

In *Resnick*, the court held that the plaintiffs sufficiently alleged a nexus between a laptop theft involving unencrypted data and later identity theft incidents to meet federal pleading standards[26] and to survive a motion a dismiss.[27] Accordingly, the court reversed a decision dismissing the plaintiffs' negligence claim.

Moreover, the court in *Weinberg v. Advanced Data Processing, Inc.*[28] permitted a negligence claim to survive a motion dismiss following a data breach in which a rogue employee of a billing and processing service business stole sensitive personal information from an ambulance service's patients and used it for identity theft purposes.[29] This is one of the few reported decisions relating to the conduct of a business associate, as opposed to a covered entity, although the court did not specifically address its status as a business associate. Although the court did not permit the use of HIPAA violations as the basis of a negligence per se claim,[30] the court held that since the defendants voluntarily agreed to provide billing and payment processing services, they assumed a duty to act carefully and not put patients at an undue risk of harm, for example by neglecting to implement data security policies and procedures.

---

25. *See, e.g.*, Resnick, 693 F.3d at 1325; Anthem, 2016 WL 589760, at *9 (quoting Pisciotta v. Old Nat'l Bancorp, 499 F.3d 629, 635 (7th Cir. 2007)).

26. Under federal pleading standards applied to motions to dismiss under Federal Rule of Civil Procedure 12(b)(6), although the plaintiff's allegations are accepted as true, the court need not accept conclusions of law and the complaint must contain sufficient factual matter to state a claim for relief that is plausible on its face. *See* Ashcroft v. Iqbal, 556 U.S. 662, 678, 681 (2009); Bell Atl. Corp. v. Twombly, 550 U.S. 544, 555, 570 (2007).

27. Resnick, 693 F.3d at 1326–28.

28. ___ F. Supp. 3d ___, No. 15-CIV-61598-BLOOM/Valle, 2015 WL 8098555 (S.D. Fla. Nov. 17, 2015).

29. *See id.* at *1.

30. *Id.* at *4.

Therefore, the plaintiffs sufficiently alleged a duty that could support a negligence claim.[31]

The court in *In re Anthem Data Breach Litigation*,[32] however, dismissed the negligence claim based on a type of preemption argument. Indiana has a data breach notification law. Citing *Pisciotta v. Old National Bancorp* from the Seventh Circuit,[33] the court held that the breach notification's law exclusive delegation of enforcement rights to the Indiana attorney general evinced a legislative intent not to allow private plaintiff actions for negligence.[34] Otherwise, though, plaintiffs have been able to assert negligence claims without limitation by data breach notification laws.

Also, in *Paul v. Providence Health System—Oregon*,[35] the court rejected a negligence claim arising from a data breach in which disks and tapes containing patient records for approximately 365,000 patients were stolen from the car of an employee of the defendant healthcare provider. The media contained patient names, contact information, Social Security numbers, and patient care information.[36] To allege purely economic loss under Oregon law, as opposed to physical injury, the plaintiffs had to allege a duty beyond simply the duty of reasonable care.[37] The plaintiffs failed to allege any such duty by a medical provider to protect patient information beyond the duty to protect against foreseeable harm.[38] Accordingly, the court affirmed dismissal of the plaintiffs' negligence claim for economic damages.[39]

c. Negligence Per Se

Negligence per se is a type of negligence in which a violation of a law intended to protect the public acts as the basis for the claim. A plaintiff must plead and prove a violation of a statute establishing a duty to take precautions to protect a particular class of persons from a particular type of injury. Moreover, the violation must be the proximate cause of the plaintiffs' injury.[40]

---

31. *See id.* at *4–5.
32. ___ F. Supp. 3d ___, No. 15-MD-02617-LHK, 2016 WL 589760 (N.D. Cal. Feb. 14, 2016).
33. 499 F.3d 629 (7th Cir. 2007).
34. Anthem, No. 15-MD-0267-LHK, at *9–11.
35. 240 P.3d 1110 (Or. Ct. App. 2010).
36. *Id.* at 1112.
37. *Id.* at 1115.
38. *See id.* at 1119.
39. *Id.* at 1119–20.
40. *See* Resnick v. AvMed, Inc., 693 F.3d 1317, 1325 (11th Cir. 2012) (quoting Florida state court cases).

In *Smith v. Triad of Alabama, LLC*,[41] the court held that plaintiff victims of a data breach plausibly alleged a negligence per se claim based on HIPAA violations. An insider at the defendant hospital stole what were apparently paper lab reports and files containing personally identifiable information/PHI, which were used for actual identity theft purposes.[42] The court relied on an Alabama Supreme Court case holding that even where a statute provides no private right of action, a violation can still serve as the basis for a negligence per se claim.[43] In light of that case, and the lack of precedent for disallowing a claim based on a HIPAA violation, the court declined to dismiss the plaintiffs' negligence per se claim.[44]

By contrast, the court in *Weinberg v. Advanced Data Processing, Inc.*[45] did not permit plaintiffs to pursue a negligence per se claim based on a HIPAA violation. The case concerned a data breach in which an employee of a billing and processing service business associate stole sensitive personal information from an ambulance service's patients and used it for identity theft purposes.[46] The court reasoned that HIPAA did not create a private right of action. Therefore, under what is essentially a preemption argument, the court did not permit the HIPAA violations to serve as the basis of a negligence per se claim.[47]

A negligence per se argument failed for different reasons in *Resnick*.[48] *Resnick* held that the plaintiffs sufficiently showed a nexus between a laptop theft of unencrypted data and resulting identity theft incidents sufficient to meet federal pleading standards. The plaintiffs, however, did not allege violations of HIPAA as the basis for their negligence per se claim. Instead, they alleged a violation of a Florida law barring disclosures of patient records without patient consent.[49] The court held that the law applies only to hospitals, ambulatory surgical centers, and mobile surgical facilities. AvMed, however, was an integrated managed-care organization. As a result, the court held that the Florida law did not

---

41. No. 1:14-CV-324-WKW, 2015 WL 5793318 (M.D. Ala. Sept. 29, 2015).

42. *Id.* at *3.

43. *Id.* at *11 (citing Allen v. Delchamps, Inc., 624 So. 2d 1065, 1067–68 (Ala. 1993)).

44. *Id.* at *11–13.

45. ___ F. Supp. 3d ___, No. 15-CIV 61598-BLOOM/Valle, 2015 WL 8098555 (S.D. Fla. Nov. 17, 2015).

46. *See id.* at *1.

47. *Id.* at *4.

48. 693 F.3d 1317, 1326–28 (11th Cir. 2012).

49. Fla. Stat. § 395.3025(4).

apply to AvMed. Thus, it could not serve as the basis for a negligence per se claim against AvMed.[50] Accordingly, the court affirmed dismissal of the plaintiffs' negligence per se claim.

d. Breach of Contract

A plaintiff victim of a data breach alleging a breach of contract claim will rely on express statements in a binding contract in which the defendant promised to protect PHI. A plaintiff alleging a breach of implied contract claim will allege an implied obligation under a binding contract with the defendant to protect PHI. In either case, the plaintiff will claim that the defendant's conduct breached its obligation to protect PHI and, as a result, the plaintiff sustained damages.

In *Resnick*, the court held that the plaintiffs adequately pleaded claims for breach of contract and breach of implied contract sufficient to meet federal pleading standards.[51] The plaintiffs' complaint included sufficient facts to show a nexus between a laptop theft of unencrypted data and identity theft incidents that occurred after the theft.[52] Consequently, the court reversed the district court's dismissal of the contract and implied contract claims.

Likewise, in *Smith v. Triad of Alabama, LLC*,[53] the court held that the plaintiffs adequately alleged an express contract claim, based on language in the defendant's notice of privacy practices.[54] An insider at the defendant hospital had presumably compromised paper lab reports and files from an unsecured room and used the personally identifiable information in them for actual identity theft purposes.[55] The court held that these allegations, while slight, were sufficient to allege a claim that the parties entered into a contract that Triad breached.[56] Based on the same reasoning, the court declined to dismiss the plaintiffs' implied contract claim.[57]

In re Anthem Data Breach Litigation,[58] however, rejected a California breach of contract claim. The court reviewed the contract claim and

---

50. Resnick, 693 F.3d at 1328–29.
51. *See id.* at 1326–28.
52. *Id.*
53. No. 1:14-CV-324-WKW, 2015 WL 5793318 (M.D. Ala. Sept. 29, 2015).
54. *See id.* at *14–15.
55. *See id.* at *3.
56. *See id.* at *15.
57. *See id.*
58. ___ F. Supp. 3d ___, No. 15-MD-02617-LHK, 2016 WL 589760 (N.D. Cal. Feb. 14, 2016).

held that plaintiffs failed to allege specific contractual provisions promising data security protection that the defendants allegedly breached. The court looked to the allegations in the complaint, public websites and privacy notices, exhibits to the complaint, and applicable law incorporated into the defendants' documentation and found insufficient identification of allegedly breached contract provisions.[59] The court also rejected the implied contract claims for lack of specifics about the nature and scope of the alleged implied contract.[60] The court dismissed the California contract claim, but allowed leave to amend.

e. Breach of the Implied Covenant of Good Faith and Fair Dealing

A claim for breach of the implied covenant of good faith and fair dealing rests on the legal doctrine that implied in every contract is an obligation for each party to act in good faith and deal with the other party fairly.[61] Courts will analyze a breach of that duty using a breach of contract analysis.[62] The plaintiff must allege a conscious and deliberate act that unfairly frustrates the parties' common purpose and disappoints the other party's expectation.[63]

In *Resnick*, the court addressed a claim for breach of the implied covenant of good faith and fair dealing. According to the court, the plaintiffs alleged sufficient facts to show a nexus between a laptop theft of unencrypted data and identity theft incidents that occurred after the theft.[64] The court, however, held that the plaintiffs failed to state a claim because they did not allege that AvMed's failure to secure their data resulted from conscious and deliberate acts to frustrate the common purpose of the agreement.[65]

f. Breach of Fiduciary Duty

Some plaintiff victims of data breaches have asserted breach of fiduciary duty claims against the organizations that allowed a compromise of PHI to occur. To assert a breach of fiduciary duty claim, the plaintiff

---

59. *See id.* at *12–15. The court reached the same result regarding the New Jersey contract claim, *see id.* at *16, and the New York unjust enrichment claim, which the court treated as a contract claim, *see id.* at *17.

60. *Id.* at *15.

61. *See* Resnick v. AvMed, Inc., 693 F.3d 1317, 1329 (11th Cir. 2012).

62. *See id.* at 1325.

63. *Id.* at 1329.

64. *Id.* at 1326–28.

65. *Id.* at 1329.

must allege a fiduciary relationship with the defendant by which the defendant had an obligation to protect the plaintiff's PHI. The plaintiff must also allege a breach of that duty. Finally, the plaintiff must show that damages resulted from the breach.[66]

In *Resnick*, the court held that the plaintiffs adequately alleged a claim for breach of fiduciary duty pursuant to federal pleading standards. The court held that the allegations were sufficient factual material to show a nexus between a laptop theft of unencrypted data and identity theft incidents that occurred after the theft.[67] Therefore, the court reversed the trial court's order dismissing the breach of fiduciary duty claim.

In contrast, the breach of fiduciary duty claim in *Weinberg v. Advanced Data Processing, Inc.*[68] failed to survive a motion to dismiss. The *Weinberg* case arose from a data breach in which a billing and processing service business associate's employee stole sensitive personal information from an ambulance service's patients and used it for identity theft.[69] The court held that the allegations of breach of fiduciary duty were insufficient to establish the existence of a fiduciary duty. The plaintiffs admitted the defendants never undertook to counsel them or protect them in any way regarding their sensitive information.[70] Therefore, the court dismissed their breach of fiduciary duty cause of action.

g. Unjust Enrichment/Restitution

Plaintiffs asserting claims for unjust enrichment or restitution point to the money they have paid for services from the defendant. They contend that part of the money was to pay for securing their data. When a defendant allegedly failed to secure that data properly, the defendant had taken the plaintiffs' money without delivering adequate security. The plaintiffs argue that it would be inequitable for the defendant to retain that part of the money that should have paid for adequate security. Accordingly, the plaintiff will seek restitution of a portion of the money that represents what the defendant should have spent on security.

---

66. *See id.* at 1325.
67. *Id.* at 1326–28.
68. ___ F. Supp. 3d ___, No. 15-CIV-61598-BLOOM/Valle, 2015 WL 8098555 (S.D. Fla. Nov. 17, 2015).
69. *See id.* at *1.
70. *Id.* at *5.

A plaintiff asserting an unjust enrichment/restitution claim must typically plead and prove:

- The plaintiff conferred a benefit on the defendant.
- The defendant had knowledge of the benefit.
- The defendant has accepted or retained the benefit conferred.
- The circumstances are such that it would be inequitable for the defendant to retain the benefit without paying fair value for it.[71]

In *Resnick*, the court held that the plaintiffs adequately pleaded an unjust enrichment/restitution claim. They pointed to a monetary benefit to the defendant in the form of monthly premiums, which should have covered the cost of data management and security. The plaintiffs stated that AvMed failed to implement industry-standard security measures. Plaintiffs argued that AvMed should not be permitted to retain the portion of premiums that AvMed should have earmarked for security measures. The court held that the plaintiffs alleged sufficient facts for their unjust enrichment/restitution claim to survive a motion to dismiss.[72]

A similar result occurred in *Weinberg v. Advanced Data Processing, Inc.*,[73] in which the plaintiffs' unjust enrichment claim survived a motion to dismiss. The employee of one of the defendant business associates[74] performing billing and payment processing for an ambulance service stole sensitive personal information and used it for identity theft purposes.[75] The plaintiffs paid for the ambulance service and contended that their payment benefited the ambulance service and the business associate. A portion of their payment should have supported adequate security controls. They were able to maintain an unjust enrichment claim against the defendants. The fact that the ambulance service was a payment intermediary did not preclude a claim against the defendant business associates.[76]

---

71. *See* Resnick, 693 F.3d at 1328.

72. *Id.*

73. ___ F. Supp. 3d ___, No. 15-CIV-61598-BLOOM/Valle, 2015 WL 8098555 (S.D. Fla. Nov. 17, 2015).

74. The employee worked for defendant Intermedix Corp., *id.* at *1, which is the parent of the other defendant, Advanced Data Processing, Inc., *id.* at *1 n.1. The court groups them together in its analysis.

75. *See id.* at *1.

76. *See id.* at *6–7.

h. Invasion of Privacy Claims

Some plaintiffs have attempted to assert common law invasion of privacy claims arising out of events possibly constituting HIPAA security violations. For instance, they could assert that a covered entity allowed a data breach resulting in an intrusion into seclusion by an attacker accessing their PHI. Also, they could claim the covered entity allowed the public disclosure of private facts by permitting the compromise and dissemination of PHI in a data breach.

The courts have rejected such invasion of privacy claims. For instance, in *Sheldon v. Kettering Health Network*,[77] the court affirmed dismissal of an invasion of privacy based on wrongful intrusion into medical records. Under the facts of an administrative director's unauthorized access to medical records, discussed in greater detail in section 8.A.4.a below, the court held that the plaintiffs had no viable privacy claim because they failed to allege the defendant acted intentionally. The claim was based on the defendant's allegedly negligent conduct in detecting or stopping the conduct of the director. Moreover, the court had rejected the respondeat superior liability of the defendant for the conduct of the director. Therefore, the intrusion cause of action failed to state a claim upon which relief could be granted.[78]

Likewise, in *Smith v. Triad of Alabama, LLC*,[79] the court held that plaintiffs could not assert a claim based on public disclosure of private facts. The defendant hospital allegedly permitted an insider to steal (apparently paper) PHI from lab reports and files containing personally identifiable information.[80] Nonetheless, the hospital itself did not disseminate any information about patients to the public. Therefore, the privacy claim failed as a matter of law.[81]

i. Statutory Claims

Plaintiffs asserting HIPAA-related security violations may use claims under various federal and state laws to seek redress. For instance, plaintiffs sometimes allege violations of state laws that bar businesses from engaging in unfair or deceptive trade practices. California's Unfair Competition Law (UCL) is one such law.[82]

---

77. 40 N.E.3d 661 (Ohio Ct. App. 2015), appeal denied, 45 N.E.3d 244 (Ohio 2016).
78. *See id.* at 676–77.
79. No. 1:14-CV-324-WKW, 2015 WL 5793318 (M.D. Ala. Sept. 29, 2015).
80. *Id.* at *3.
81. *Id.* at 13–14.
82. CAL. BUS. & PROF. CODE § 17200 *et seq.*

For instance, the *In re Anthem Data Breach Litigation*,[83] the court permitted statutory claims for unfair and deceptive trade practices to proceed. One of the claims asserted violations of California's UCL. The UCL provides a cause of action for conduct that is unlawful, unfair, or fraudulent.[84] Regarding the unlawful prong of the claim, the plaintiffs identified HIPAA as one of the laws violated. The court held that the complaint adequately alleged violations of law for the UCL unlawfulness claim to survive a motion to dismiss.[85] The court also found the factual issues regarding unfairness precluded dismissal of the unfairness claim under the UCL.[86] The court, however, dismissed the fraud claim under the UCL, because the plaintiffs did not allege when the alleged misrepresentations about data security occurred relative to when plaintiffs allegedly were deceived. The defendants' statements should precede the dates of alleged deception.[87]

The court also analyzed the elements of New York's General Business Law section 349. Section 349 prohibits deceptive acts or practices in business. The court held that the plaintiffs adequately alleged a claim under section 349.[88]

The court, however, held that the plaintiffs could not maintain an action under the Kentucky Consumer Protection Act (KCPA).[89] The court reasoned that the law does not permit a putative class action to maintain a claim under the KCPA.[90] Thus, the court dismissed the plaintiffs' KCPA claim with prejudice.

Finally, the court dismissed without prejudice the plaintiffs' claim under Georgia's Insurance Information and Privacy Protection Act (IIPA). The law precludes "disclosure" of personal information collected by insurance companies without authorization.[91] The court held that the word "disclosure" suggests that the holder of information committed an affirmative voluntary act. The court held that involuntary exposure of information by a hacking attack and data breach does not fall within

---

83. ___ F. Supp. 3d ___, No. 15-MD-02617-LHK, 2016 WL 589760 (N.D. Cal. Feb. 14, 2016).

84. *Id.* at *17.

85. *Id.* at *21.

86. *Id.* at *21–22.

87. *See id.* at *22–23.

88. *Id.* at *23–28. The court also denied without prejudice the defendants' motion to the extent it argued that ERISA preempted the section 349 claim. *See id.* at *29–30.

89. Ky. Rev. Stat. §§ 367.170 *et seq.*

90. Anthem, 2016 WL 589760, at *30–32.

91. *See* Ga. Code Ann. 33-39-14.

the meaning of "disclosure."[92] Consequently, the plaintiffs did not properly allege a claim under the IIPA, although the court granted leave to amend the IIPA claim.

In addition, the plaintiffs adequately alleged violations of federal the Fair Credit Reporting Act (FCRA) in *Smith v. Triad of Alabama, LLC.*[93] The court pointed to obligations under the act for consumer reporting agencies to adopt reasonable procedures for the confidentiality of personal information.[94] The plaintiffs alleged that defendant failed to take protective measures to protect their personal information after an insider stole (presumably paper) lab reports and files from an unsecured room. Following the breach, actual identity theft incidents occurred.[95] Triad did not contest that it is a consumer reporting agency and did not otherwise offer a substantive argument against the claim.[96] Given that the plaintiffs adequately alleged facts to support standing, the court did not dismiss the plaintiffs' FCRA claim.

Plaintiff patients, however, were unsuccessful in asserting a statutory unfair trade practices claim[97] in *Paul v. Providence Health System— Oregon.*[98] The case stemmed from a data breach in which disks and tapes containing patient records for approximately 365,000 patients were stolen from the car of an employee of the defendant healthcare provider. The disks and tapes contained patient names, contact information, Social Security numbers, and patient care information.[99] The plaintiffs did not, unlike *Smith*, allege that actual identity theft incidents occurred. Rather, the plaintiffs alleged that they incurred costs, such as credit monitoring services, postage, long distance charges, and time lost from employment, to prevent possible future harm.[100] The court held that the expenses to prevent potential loss are not recoverable as an "ascertainable loss of money or property" from a violation sufficient to support a claim under the Oregon Unfair Trade Practices

---

92. Anthem, 2016 WL 589760, at *32–33.
93. No. 1:14-CV-324-WKW, 2015 WL 5793318 (M.D. Ala. Sept. 29, 2015).
94. *Id.* at *5 (quoting 15 U.S.C. § 1681(b)).
95. *Id.* at *3.
96. *Id.* at *6.
97. The plaintiffs relied on Or. Rev. Stat. § 646.638(1) as the basis for their claim under the Oregon Unlawful Trade Practices Act. It permits any person suffering an ascertainable loss of money or property based on certain unlawful conduct to recover damages in a civil action.
98. 240 P.3d 1110 (Or. Ct. App. 2010).
99. *Id.* at 1112.
100. *Id.* at 1120.

Act.[101] Accordingly, the court affirmed the lower court's dismissal of the plaintiffs' statutory claim.

Wentworth-Douglass Hospital v. Young & Novis Professional Association[102] is a different kind of case, because it involved a hospital suing physicians and a professional association because the physicians had copied and then deleted PHI after their contract to provide pathology services expired. The hospital believed the physicians had no right to delete the PHI and should have made it available to the hospital. The hospital alleged violations of the Computer Fraud and Abuse Act (CFAA)[103] and New Hampshire state law based on a claim that the physicians should not have deleted the PHI. Unlike a typical data breach case, no patients were parties to the case.

The court declined to grant summary judgment to the defendants on the CFAA claims. The defendants argued that they had a legal obligation to delete PHI securely when it is no longer needed based on media reuse and PHI disposal requirements of 45 C.F.R. § 164.310(d)(1), (d)(2). The court rejected their argument based on genuine issues of material fact concerning the proper procedures for disposal of PHI.[104] The hospital, however, was unable to resist summary judgment on its claim based on an alleged violation of the New Hampshire Consumer Protection Act. The hospital's statutory claim relied on a provision of the act prohibiting unfair and deceptive trade practices,[105] but the court held that the claim was not viable. The court reasoned that the "defendants' conduct, as alleged, does not rise to the level of rascality necessary to support a cause of action" under the act.[106]

4. Special Types of Cases

In the cases about HIPAA security, two special types of cases have emerged. First, some cases concern alleged snooping by employees into medical records. Second, other cases relate to employment claims. This section covers each of these types of cases in turn.

---

101. *See id.* at 1122.

102. No. 10-CV-120-SM, 2012 WL 1081172 (D.N.H. Mar. 30, 2012) *on reconsideration,* No. 10-CV-120-SM, 2012 WL 2522963 (D.N.H. June 29, 2012).

103. 18 U.S.C. § 1030.

104. Wentworth-Douglass Hosp., 2012 WL 1081172, at *3. Upon reconsideration, however, the court granted two of the doctors summary judgment on the hospital's CFAA claim based on unauthorized access. Otherwise, the court upheld the original opinion. 2012 WL 2522963, at *2-5.

105. N.H. REV. STAT. ANN. § 358-A:2.

106. Wentworth-Douglass Hosp., 2012 WL 1081172, at *5.

a. Snooping Cases

"Snooping" cases arise from alleged unauthorized access into medical records by workers at a healthcare provider. Section 7.A.1 *infra* describes news accounts of some of these incidents. Two cases arise from accusations from a patient that a worker was snooping on her medical records. In the unpublished *Ware v. Bronson Methodist Hospital*,[107] the Court of Appeals of Michigan affirmed some of a lower court ruling rejecting the defendant Bronson Methodist Hospital's summary disposition motion in a snooping case filed by plaintiff Angela Ware.

Ware delivered a child at the hospital after completing privacy authorization forms warning the hospital not to allow her ex-husband's then girlfriend (later wife), Patricia Wark, a nurse at the hospital, to have access to her medical records. She recorded her warning in all capital letters with two exclamation points. Nurses assured her that the hospital had policies protecting patient privacy. Nonetheless, on the third day of her admission, a hospital employee told Ware that Wark accessed her medical records. Wark allegedly shared Ware's PHI with Ware's ex-husband for use in custody proceedings against her.[108]

The court held that the hospital was not vicariously liable for Wark's alleged invasion of privacy or intentional infliction of emotional distress, because these acts were beyond the scope of her employment.[109] Also, the court held that the hospital's adoption of confidentiality policies sounded in medical malpractice and was subject to Michigan's malpractice statute of limitations. To the extent Ware asserted the selection of policies was actionable, her claims were time barred.[110] However, the enforcement of the hospital's own policies did not sound in medical malpractice and were not subject to the malpractice statute of limitations. A claim based on allegedly negligent failure to enforce the hospital's existing policies was not time barred.[111] Finally, since contract claims for medical care must be in writing, the statute of frauds bars an implied contract claim based on an alleged duty to protect her records.[112] The court in essence narrowed the case to a negligence claim based on the alleged failure to enforce the hospital's existing

---

107. No. 307886, 2014 WL 5689877 (Mich. Ct. App. Nov. 4, 2014) (per curiam) (unpublished opinion), appeal denied 886 N. W. zd 456 (M. ch. 2015).
108. *See id.* at *1.
109. *See id.* at *2–3.
110. *See id.* at *4–5.
111. *See id.* at *5–6.
112. *See id.* at *6–7.

confidentiality procedures. The negligence claim survived summary disposition proceedings and could go to trial, which for the plaintiff was a successful outcome.

Although the plaintiff could try her negligence claim in *Ware*, a similarly situated Ohio woman lost both a state lawsuit and a federal lawsuit against Kettering Health Network (KHN). Vicki Sheldon, at some point, received healthcare services from KHN. Her now-former husband, Duane Sheldon, served as an administrative director for KHN. In furtherance of an affair with a subordinate, Duane Sheldon and the subordinate gained unauthorized access to Vicki Sheldon's medical records. In response, Vicki Sheldon filed a federal qui tam action against KHN, alleging that KHN falsely certified its compliance with audit controls requirements in the HIPAA Security Rule in connection with its acceptance of "meaningful use" funds[113] to promote the adoption of electronic health record technology.[114] The crux of the plaintiff's position is that KHN's failure to regularly run and monitor so-called "CLARITY" reports using the EPIC electronic health record software violated HIPAA and, if KHN had monitored such reports, it could have detected Duane Sheldon's unauthorized access earlier and put a stop to it.[115]

During the pendency of the qui tam action, plaintiff's counsel also filed a state court action against KHN alleging various state common law causes of action. The trial court dismissed the action and Sheldon appealed.[116] The court of appeals distinguished between Duane Sheldon's intentional accessing of health records and KHN's alleged failure to protect against unauthorized access and detect Duane Sheldon's access.[117] The court held, first, that KHN was not responsible for Duane Sheldon's conduct under the doctrine of respondeat superior, reasoning that his acts were beyond the scope of his employment.[118] Sheldon had dismissed her claims against her ex-husband without prejudice.[119] Thus,

---

113. For an explanation of "meaningful use" incentive payments to support the adoption of electronic health record technology, see *supra* section 3.E.

114. United States *ex rel.* Sheldon v. Kettering Health Network, 816 F.3d 399, 404–06 (6th Cir. 2016).

115. *See* Sheldon v. Kettering Health Network, 40 N.E.3d 661, 670 (Ohio Ct. App. 2015), *appeal denied*, 45 N.E.3d 244 (Ohio 2016).

116. *Id.* at 664–65.

117. *See id.* at 667.

118. *See id.* at 667–69.

119. *See* Sheldon v. Kettering Health Network, No. 2014 CV 03304 (dismissal filed Nov. 4, 2014) (dismissing all claims against Duane Sheldon without prejudice).

Sheldon apparently decided not to pursue her ex-husband and would focus only on recovering from KHN. The court's ruling further focused the case on KHN's own conduct, as opposed to attributing Duane Sheldon's conduct to KHN.[120]

Regarding KHN's conduct, the court noted the lack of a private right of action for HIPAA violations.[121] The court held that HIPAA does not preempt claims based on Ohio law for unauthorized disclosures of medical records,[122] but no such claim was possible here, since KHN did not intentionally disclose anything.[123] Further, the court held that HIPAA violations are not sufficiently positive and definitive to establish a standard of care sufficient to support a negligence per se claim.[124] Moreover, Sheldon could not maintain invasion of privacy or intentional infliction of emotional distress claims against KHN, since she did not allege that KHN acted intentionally.[125] Finally, the court held that the remaining possible claims that could be asserted in an amended complaint were not viable and thus the trial court did not err in denying leave to amend the complaint.[126] Consequently, the court affirmed the trial court's dismissal of claims against KHN.

The federal case fared no better. The United States declined to intervene, the trial court dismissed the complaint against KHN, and Sheldon appealed. The Sixth Circuit held that Sheldon failed to allege a false statement of KHN that could support a False Claims Act. First, KHN did not violate requirements to have policies and procedures to prevent unauthorized access, because, according to plaintiff's own allegations,

---

120. The court declined to follow the HIPAA privacy case Walgreen Co. v. Hinchy, 21 N.E.3d 99 (Ind. Ct. App. 2014), *on reh'g*, 25 N.E.3d 748 (Ind. Ct. App. 2015, *transfer denied*, 29 N.E.3d 1274 (Ind. 2015). In *Walgreen*, the court affirmed a $1.8 million judgment, for which the pharmacy chain and one of its pharmacists were 80 percent responsible after the pharmacist accessed her boyfriend's former girlfriend's records to check for potential sexually transmitted diseases, which the boyfriend used to confront the former girlfriend. *Walgreen* held that, as a matter of Indiana law, the issue of respondeat superior was a jury issue. 21 N.E.3d at 106–09. In *Sheldon*, the Ohio Court of Appeals held that Ohio law is stricter than Indiana law and depends on whether the conduct is actuated by a purpose to serve the master. The court found no facts to support Sheldon's claim because the court saw no part of the activity that had a purpose to serve KHN. 40 N.E.3d at 668–69.

121. 40 N.E.3d at 670.

122. *See id.* at 671–72.

123. *See id.* at 672–73, 675.

124. *See id.* at 674.

125. *See id.* at 676–77.

126. *See id.* at 677–79.

KHN had some policies and procedures in place.[127] Second, neither the HITECH Act nor the HIPAA Security Rule provisions invoked by meaningful use standards require hospitals to use any particular brand of electronic health record software or to generate any particular kind of report.[128] Alternatively, the Sixth Circuit held that the federal claim would be barred by res judicata, given that Sheldon had lost her state court suit by the time the district court issued its opinion, and the nearly identical state suit arose from a common nucleus of operative facts as the federal action.[129]

Finally, a court rejected an employer's claims of snooping against an employee in the unpublished opinion in *University of Virginia Medical Center v. Jordan*.[130] The plaintiff University of Virginia Medical Center wanted to fire defendant Susan Jordan, a nurse at the hospital. The hospital claimed the plaintiff was snooping into the records of her ex-husband. In administrative proceedings, however, Jordan won reinstatement and back pay. Moreover, when the hospital attempted to appeal, the circuit court and later the Court of Appeals of Virginia affirmed the administrative ruling.[131]

The court of appeals held that the hospital failed to prove HIPAA violations. A number of crucial factors led to the court's ruling in Jordan's favor. First, the ex-husband testified that he had completed the hospital's authorization form twice to allow disclosures of his medical records to his ex-wife.[132] The court stated that nothing in federal law (HIPAA) forbids access by a worker at the patient's request.[133] Finally, the court held that it had no authority to second-guess the administrative hearing officer's decision that Jordan did not violate the hospital's policies.[134]

The employee, defendant Jordan, had received a favorable ruling in administrative proceedings, including reinstatement and back pay, which the circuit court and the court of appeals affirmed. The university had sought to fire Jordan for unauthorized access to her ex-husband's medical records, but the administrative proceedings and later the courts

---

127. Sheldon, 816 F. 3d at 409–10.
128. *See id.* at 411.
129. *See id.* at 414–18.
130. No. 0790-15-2, 2016 WL 392005 (Va. Ct. App. Feb. 2, 2016) (unpublished opinion).
131. *See id.* at *1.
132. *See id.* at *3.
133. *Id.* at *4.
134. *See id.* at *5.

determined that her viewing of the records was justified and at her ex-husband's express request.[135]

b. Employment Cases

Some of the reported cases alleging HIPAA violations concern employment claims. Some of the rulings favor employers, while others favor employees. Two of them concern employees that allegedly violated HIPAA security requirements. In the unpublished *Aldrich v. Rural Health Services Consortium*,[136] an assistant to a rural clinic's chief financial officer, plaintiff Sarah Aldrich, began forwarding e-mails from her company e-mail account to her personal Yahoo account, including e-mails containing patient PHI. She forwarded the e-mails to her personal account in the mistaken belief that she should preserve evidence of a former coworker's age discrimination lawsuit against the clinic. After she continued to refuse to delete the e-mails, the clinic fired her. She asserted retaliation claims under the federal Age Discrimination in Employment Act (ADEA) and Tennessee state law, alleging the clinic fired her for refusing to spoliate evidence related to the lawsuit.[137]

The U.S. Court of Appeals for the Sixth Circuit affirmed a summary judgment in favor of the clinic. The court reasoned that since Aldrich sent e-mails indiscriminately to her Yahoo account, and none of them related to the age discrimination case, she was not engaged in activity protected by the ADEA. Her violation of HIPAA made her use of e-mails "patently unreasonable."[138] Thus, a reasonable jury could not find she was engaged in protected activity.[139]

Another plaintiff failed to prove retaliation claims against a university health system in *Fatemi v. Rahn*.[140] The plaintiff, Dr. Nasrin Fatemi, was a neurosurgery resident for the University of Arkansas for Medical Sciences (UAMS). After UAMS terminated her residency, she alleged gender discrimination and other claims against UAMS. Dr. Fatemi

---

135. While not a snooping case, Picco v. Glenn, No. 12-cv-02858-RM-MJW, 2015 WL 2128486 (D. Colo. May 5, 2015), notes that hospitals should maintain a log of access to PHI in accordance with the audit controls requirement in the Security Rule, 45 C.F.R. § 164.312(b). *Picco*, 2015 WL 2128486, ¶ 8, at *8. Access logs will play a vital role in any investigation of alleged snooping and in any later legal proceedings.

136. 579 F. App'x 335 (6th Cir. 2014) (unpublished opinion).

137. *See id.* at 336.

138. *Id.* at 338.

139. *Id.*

140. No. 4:13-cv-742-DPM, 2015 WL 159695 (E.D. Ark. Jan. 12, 2015).

kept certain patients' records without authorization, either for research purposes or to help her discrimination claims. UAMS notified patients of the breach without naming her in the notification. The court held that she failed to provide sufficient evidence of retaliation against her, because UAMS acted in good faith to comply with HIPAA, and she failed to prove any employment-related harm.[141]

The U.S. District Court for the Southern District of Indiana rejected another claim based on alleged retaliation in *Farr v. St. Francis Hospital & Health Centers*.[142] The plaintiff, respiratory therapist David Farr, brought suit after the defendant hospital fired him based on pornography found on his work computer. Farr claimed that a virus had caused the pornography to be retrieved and saved on his computer without his knowledge.[143] The court held as a matter of Indiana law that the hospital had no duty of care to protect employees against harm caused by viruses.[144] Moreover, the court held that Indiana law recognizes no wrongful discharge cause of action based on an employer's attempt to cover up a HIPAA violation. The court reasoned that the generalized public policy underlying HIPAA does not support a new exception to the employment at will doctrine.[145] Accordingly, the court dismissed the plaintiff's negligence and wrongful discharge causes of action.

Despite these rulings in favor of employers, the courts have also ruled in favor of whistleblowers wrongfully terminated after calling HIPAA violations to the attention of their employers in two unpublished opinions. In *Cutler v. Dike*,[146] David Cutler, a product manager/privacy officer of an electronic medical records software company, complained to management after he thought the company's patient records were not properly protected after a move. He apparently performed work for a number of related businesses connected to the medical practice of his employer's CEO defendant Anthony Dike. Cutler claimed he told Dike there was no working firewall and that the records of the medical practice were at risk. Cutler thought it was his duty to bring the risk to the attention of Dike, but Dike fired him.[147]

---

141. *See id.* at *1–2.
142. No. 1:06-cv-779-SEB-JMS, 2007 WL 2793396 (S.D. Ind. Sept. 26, 2007), aff'd on other grounds, 570 F. 3d 829 (7th Cir. 2008).
143. *See id.* at *1.
144. *See id.* at *3.
145. *See id.* at *4–5.
146. No. B210624, 2010 WL 3341663 (Cal. Ct. App. Aug. 26, 2010) (unpublished opinion).
147. *See id.* at *1–2, 3–4.

The California Court of Appeal affirmed a superior court judgment in favor of Cutler against his employers.[148] Among other things, the court affirmed Cutler's wrongful termination claim in violation of public policy.[149] Contrary to the Indiana decision in *Farr*, the court noted a strong public policy in favor of protecting confidential patient information. The court cited the evidence of the lack of firewall protection and the risk to patient information. As a result, the court found that substantial evidence supported the jury's findings in Cutler's favor.[150]

The court based its rulings in part on general information security duties to secure PHI imposed on covered entities.[151] On appeal, the defendants argued that they were not covered entities. The conduct at issue in the case, which occurred in 2005, predated the HITECH Act's imposition of Security Rule requirements on business associates. Moreover, the defendants appear to be business associates. The court, though, held that that the defendants had waived the argument because they failed to raise it in the trial court.[152] Under current law, because the HIPAA Security Rule now applies to business associates, the defendants' conduct would have created legal risk for themselves.

Likewise, the court declined to dismiss a state law retaliatory discharge claim in violation of public policy in *DePaolo v. Triad Healthcare*.[153] The court did not discuss the nature of the alleged HIPAA violations of the employer, defendant Triad Healthcare. It merely reported that plaintiff Peter DePaolo, a "systems administrator,"[154] reported HIPAA security violations to Triad, and Triad fired him. DePaolo wanted Triad to report a breach to HHS.[155] Triad attempted to argue that it did not force DePaolo to participate in any violations.[156] The court, however, held that DePaolo adequately alleged a retaliatory discharge claim.[157] The court also permitted a state law claim to proceed in the case based on alleged retaliation for protected speech activity.[158]

---

148. The court, however, reversed the judgment against Dike.
149. *See id.* at *9–11 (citing CAL. LAB. CODE § 1102.5(c)).
150. *See id.* at *10.
151. *See id.* (citing 45 C.F.R. § 164.306(a)(1)–(a)(2)).
152. *See id.* at *11.
153. No. UWYCV1360190515, 2013 WL 6671551 (Conn. Super. Ct. Nov. 26, 2013) (unpublished opinion).
154. *Id.* at *1.
155. *See id.*
156. *See id.* at *4.
157. *See id.* at *6.
158. *See id.* at *1–4.

Finally, the employee prevailed in the unpublished *University of Virginia Medical Center v. Jordan* case discussed in the previous section.[159] The employee, defendant Susan Jordan, had received a favorable ruling in administrative proceedings, including reinstatement and back pay, which the circuit court and the court of appeals affirmed.[160] The university had sought to fire Jordan for unauthorized access to her ex-husband's medical records, but the administrative proceedings and later the courts determined that her viewing of the records was justified and at her ex-husband's express request.[161]

B. RISK MANAGEMENT

1. General Risk Management Principles

Risk management is assessing, mitigating, minimizing, accepting, or shifting risk. Risk management defines an overall process. Section 5.B.1 above discusses the risk assessment and risk management process in detail. Risk management is not a one-time event; it requires periodic monitoring to be successful. Risk may be minimized through security and management controls. Insurance and contractual indemnification provisions are mechanisms for shifting risk. Section 8.B.2 below covers cyber risk insurance that may assist covered entities and business associate organizations in managing their HIPAA-HITECH risks.

The organization's first step in risk management is risk analysis. Risk analysis begins with identification of the organization's PHI, both electronic and nonelectronic. An organization conducting a risk analysis under HIPAA will identify all reasonably anticipated threats to the confidentiality, integrity, and availability of the PHI, created, received, maintained, and transmitted by the organization. The organization must consider PHI in its possession and in transit between it and other parties. Risk analysis involves review of the organization's system hardware, software, system activity, and system policies and procedures to identify security vulnerabilities. A thorough and accurate risk analysis should consider likely relevant losses that would be expected if the security measures were not in place, as well as the costs that would result from those losses. Relevant losses include losses caused by various threats, such as unauthorized uses and disclosures and loss

---

159. No. 0790-15-2, 2016 WL 392005 (Va. Ct. App. Feb. 2, 2016) (unpublished opinion).
160. *See id.* at *1–2.
161. *See id.* at *3–5.

of data integrity that could be expected to occur without the security measures.

Organizations should include legal risk analysis as part of their overall risk analysis. They should consider potential liability scenarios and assess their likelihood and impact. Legal risk may stem from alleged failures to comply with HIPAA or the Security Rule. It may also arise from data breaches or security incidents. Frequently, a data breach will trigger scrutiny that then leads to accusations of noncompliance.

Organizations are required to "ensure"[162] the security of PHI. The word "ensure" in isolation suggests an absolute requirement, although the Security Rule expressly provides for a flexible approach to security in which the organization balances identifiable risks to the security of the information with the costs associated with measures to safeguard the information. Drawing the balance will require considering factors such as the size, capability, and complexity of the organization.[163]

The "addressable" security standards[164] provide organizations with a certain amount of flexibility to implement compliant security practices. The covered entity must assess whether the addressable implementation specification is a reasonable and appropriate safeguard in its environment, when analyzed with reference to the likely contribution to protecting the entity's PHI. If a safeguard is determined to be reasonable and appropriate, the specification must be implemented. If not, the covered entity must document why the specification is not reasonable and appropriate. The covered entity must then implement an alternative measure, if reasonable and appropriate.

Accordingly, an organization's risk management process should assure that each identified threat is evaluated with regard to the cost of protecting against it, the likelihood and frequency of its occurrence, and the magnitude of the loss caused by a threat. "Adequate security" means security commensurate with the risk and magnitude of the harm resulting from the loss, misuse, or unauthorized access to or modification of information. This analysis includes assuring that systems and applications operate effectively and provide reasonable and appropriate

---

162. An organization must "[e]nsure the confidentiality, integrity, and availability of all electronic protected health information the covered entity or business associate creates, receives, maintains, or transmits." 45 C.F.R. § 164.306(a)(1).

163. *See id.* § 164.306(b).

164. *Id.* § 164.306(d).

confidentiality, integrity, and availability through use of cost-effective management, personnel, and operational and technical controls.

Technical controls alone cannot create a compliant environment. Security requires controls to address people, process, and technology.[165] Personnel training and implementation of security practices and security procedures are as important as technical controls.[166]

Adequate risk management requires the creation, ongoing review, and regular updates of appropriate policies and procedures for the security of PHI, both during storage and while in transit and for the training of all personnel with access to PHI. In addition to minimizing risk through the effective use of security and operational and technical controls, the risk management process should include awareness of which risks are insurable and the cost of possible insurance. Insurance policies for risks to computer systems and networks are increasingly common. Organizations can shift risk through insurance to protect themselves against catastrophic losses from a security threat. Section 8.B.2 describes cyber risk insurance in more detail. Risk shifting can also occur through contracts. Indemnification provisions in business associate agreements may allocate or shift risks between the parties to establish which party will be responsible for which liabilities.[167]

Following efforts at shifting risks, it may be that some residual level of risk remains for a covered entity, and it will have to accept that risk. For instance, the price of insurance premiums may be excessive in light of the likely risks, or certain kinds of risk may not correspond to existing insurance products. In that case, the organization should monitor the level of accepted risk and determine whether future opportunities for risk management can reduce that level. Larger organizations may want to implement a self-insurance program, such as by setting up a

---

165. Bruce Schneier, *"People, Process, and Technology,"* SCHNEIER ON SECURITY, Jan. 30, 2013, https://www.schneier.com/blog/archives/2013/01/people_process.html.

166. Schneier acknowledges the point that the complexity of the technology and computer-fast timescales make automated tools helpful to cope with security threats. Nonetheless, the human role in information security remains critical. Among other things, "sometimes human intelligence is required to make sense of an attack, and to formulate an appropriate response." *Id.*

167. For additional information concerning risk management, *see* NAT'L INST. OF STANDARDS & TECH. JOINT TASK FORCE TRANSFORMATION INITIATIVE INTERAGENCY WORKING GRP., NIST SPECIAL PUBL'N 800-39, MANAGING INFORMATION SECURITY RISK: ORGANIZATION, MISSION, AND INFORMATION SYSTEM VIEW (Mar. 2011), *reprinted at* http://csrc.nist.gov/publications/nistpubs/800-39/SP800-39-final.pdf.

self-insured retention or captive insurance entity, to pay for losses arising from accepted risks.

2. Cyber Risk Insurance

Businesses are beginning to mitigate the risk of privacy violations and information security threats with cyber risk insurance policies, including in the healthcare field. Covered entities and business associate organizations can obtain cyber risk insurance to obtain both first-party and third-party coverage. For instance, despite the enormous magnitude of the Anthem data breach, the breach may not have harmed the company's financial position in the short run because of its insurance coverage.[168]

Risk managers in the healthcare setting, however, should carefully analyze the coverages of cyber risk policies. These coverages may provide key protections but will have limits and exclusions. Consequently, insurance may not address all of the risks that an organization faces regarding its security practices.

"Cyber risk insurance policies" are policies that cover certain information security and privacy risks. The trigger for coverage in these policies will include some kind of privacy or security breach. A privacy breach may include unauthorized access to personal information, for example after a theft or loss of the information. A privacy breach may also involve a business violating privacy laws or failing to provide fundamental privacy protections, such as offering customers access to their personal information, including for the process of updating, supplementing, or correcting the information held by the business.

Security breaches may occur from unauthorized access or use of personal information or a device it is stored on, stemming from such causes as the theft or loss of a device or the failure of a security control. Policies may also cover losses from malicious software. In addition, coverage may extend to breaches in the form of denial of service attacks against the business's systems. Finally, the policy may cover breaches resulting from the transmission of malicious software to a third party.

Cyber risk policies may provide third-party coverage, by which the insurance carrier defends the insured business against lawsuits, proceedings, and other claims against the business by an allegedly damaged

---

168. *See* Adam Rubenfire, *Anthem Hack Will Shake up Market for Cyber Risk Insurance*, Modern Healthcare, Feb. 5, 2015, http://www.modernhealthcare.com/article/20150205/NEWS/302059939.

third party. The policy may state that the carrier has the right and duty to defend the insured business in any such proceedings. Under third-party coverage, the insurance carrier will pay judgments and settlements up to a certain amount. They may also pay fines, civil money penalties, and amounts to settle government enforcement actions, subject to possible public policy restrictions.

These policies may also provide first-party coverage, which means that the carrier will make the insured business whole for loss or expense it might otherwise incur. For instance, cyber risk policies may say that the carrier may pay for consultants to assist the insured business following a security breach. The coverage may include payment for forensic consultants to investigate possible unauthorized access to personally identifiable information, such as PHI, as a result of a breach. Some policies also include coverage for attorneys to determine whether the insured business has an obligation to make breach notifications and to help draft the notifications to affected individuals. The cost of making the notifications themselves may be covered, including printing, handling, postage, e-mail, and media services to provide the notice. Moreover, the carrier may also provide training and education to the business and its workers to help the business prevent data breaches from occurring in the first place.

Further, some policies include ransomware coverage. They may pay for assistance in trying to recover information following a ransomware attack. Moreover, these policies may include coverage for amounts paid in ransom. Ransomware coverage may be of particular interest given the swift increase in recent ransomware incidents involving covered entities.

Finally, carriers may pay for the cost of credit monitoring services and identity restoration to assist individuals whose personal information was compromised in a breach. Carrier-paid credit monitoring expenses frequently last for twelve months from the time the service becomes available after a breach. Fraud specialists paid by the carrier can help affected individuals detect identity theft involving the misuse of their personal information, stop further identity theft, and restore the information about the individual to the status it had before the breach occurred. For instance, fraud specialists can work with credit agencies to remove adverse information from the individual's credit report caused by identity theft conduct of attackers.

Carriers are beginning to market cyber risk policies in the healthcare market. Carriers marketing cyber risk policies to covered entity or

business associate organizations may not be healthcare-specific policies. Rather, the policies may be forms offered generally to the market
of organizations with privacy or security risks to personal information
of various kinds. Nevertheless, carriers are now marketing their policies
to the healthcare market, noting the risks that are specific to it, such as
the effect of HIPAA-HITECH requirements, the large volume of PHI
processed, and the need to share PHI with a broad range of service providers and vendors.[169]

A cyber risk policy may cover privacy or security liability from a
breach, along with the costs of incident response and breach notification in connection with the compromise of sensitive personal information of customers of an organization. Policies commonly sold today do
not cover the compromise of phones, though. They may cover tablets,
nonphone personal digital assistants, or certain USB media, but not
phones. Distinctions may blur between smartphones and tablets in light
of today's newer "phablet" combination devices, which are large enough
to offer tablet functionality but can make phone calls as a smartphone
might. The compromise of a phablet may lead to a coverage dispute
with the insurance carrier if the carrier denies coverage after a security breach based on an argument that the phablet is a phone and not a
computer.

The way in which a security breach occurs may also lead to coverage disputes. For instance, cyber risk policies commonly cover the
device of an employee when the employee is on a business trip. Thus,
if an employee uses a convention center network and his or her device
becomes infected by malicious software, the policy may cover any compromise of the data.

If that same employee uses a home network and his or her device
becomes infected by malicious software, however, an organization's
cyber risk carrier might deny coverage. Any loss happening within
the user's home would be considered a risk covered by the employee's
homeowner's insurance policy. Consequently, the organization's cyber
risk carrier might point to the homeowner's insurance carrier to say
that it is responsible. Nonetheless, the homeowner's insurance carrier
might say that it has no coverage for such a risk. The result may be the

---

169. *See, e.g.,* Aon Risk Solutions, *Healthcare Cyber Risk and Solutions* 1–2, http://www
.aon.com/attachments/risk-services/cyber/Aon-Cyber-Risk-Solutions-Healthcare.pdf   (last
visited May 1, 2016).

loss of information and a possible requirement to undertake a costly breach notification without insurance coverage.

Given the possibility of these gaps in coverage, an organization's risk managers should work with counsel and management when analyzing possible cyber risk coverage. They should determine if the contemplated policy is adequate to cover the risks the organization will face. The organization's risk assessment should inform the analysis of whether a potential policy's coverages are adequate in light of their limitations and policy exclusions. The organization will need to look at policies it may purchase and weigh the scope of what they cover against their costs. The organization will want to purchase a cost-effective policy that addresses the key risks it faces and does not include critical gaps in coverage caused by the carrier's exclusions. Cost-effective policies can help organizations manage the risk of liability and large first-party losses from a data breach.

Even if an organization purchases cyber risk insurance, the policy may cover risks only if the organization uses certain business and technology practices. Risk managers should determine if the organization should, by policy, prevent employees from using their devices in certain ways or in certain places. Thus, if the organization has a policy that does not cover network risk arising from the use of home networks, and if the organization wants to minimize its risk of noncoverage, it may tell workers to use their mobile devices outside the work environment only during business travel or in public places. Alternatively, the organization may decide that home productivity is so important that it cannot prohibit home use. In that case, it may want to determine the security environment in the home and provide training and support to workers working from home to mitigate the risk of information security threats. In the end, the organization may decide to accept any residual risk given the importance of productivity for some workers in their home settings.

In any event, organizations should explore cyber risk insurance coverage as one element of their risk management programs. Traditional insurance coverage may not include protection for cyber risks. In fact, their traditional policies may specifically exclude cyber risks. Organizations without cyber risk coverage may face liabilities that threaten their very existence and not even know it. Organizations with existing coverage should regularly reappraise their limits of liability to make sure the level of coverage is reasonable in light of the level of their legal risks.

"The cost of insurance coverage and breach response is minimal compared to the legal and regulatory costs associated with a massive attack that can wreck a company's coffers if the response isn't adequate. . . ."[170] Accordingly, robust cyber risk coverage is becoming a critical component of healthcare organizations' risk management efforts.

---

170. Rubenfire, *supra* note 168.

CHAPTER 9

Emerging Technologies

The previous chapters in this book cover HIPAA as law and the Security Rule's specific requirements. The Security Rule, however, predates many of the newer technologies that have posed special problems for HIPAA compliance. This chapter discusses some of the newer technologies, why they pose special security challenges, and policies and procedures a covered entity or business associate can use to address these problems. In addition, this chapter discusses emerging technologies—technologies that the healthcare industry, as of the date of this publication, is just starting to adopt. The latter sections of this chapter cover their security issues and policies and procedures to mitigate their risk.

A full explanation of each of these technologies would take an entire book. Accordingly, a thorough description of each technology is beyond the scope of this chapter. Nonetheless, this chapter provides a brief introduction to these technologies and some high-level information about managing security risks.

Covered entities and business associates must comply with the Security Rule. I refer in this chapter to "the organization" and the security-related factors it will consider. "The organization" is a shorthand term for the covered entity or business associate contemplating or actually using the technology in question.

The first and most general guidance for any of these technologies is integrating considerations of the technology in the organization's risk analysis and risk management process. It should consider the potential threats and vulnerabilities arising from use of the technology; determine the likelihood and frequency of the threat or vulnerability causing harm, the magnitude of the harm that could occur, and the cost of controls needed to mitigate the risk of the harms; and determine whether adoption of the technology is worth it in light of the expected benefits of the technology, the harm from threats or vulnerabilities, and the cost of controls needed to mitigate the risk. This analysis applies to each of the technologies below and is not repeated below. The sections below discuss risk management considerations that are specific for each technology.

Another general consideration concerns the use of individual accounts on personal information technology services to store, share, or process protected health information (PHI). For instance, patients may take photos of injuries or other medical conditions and send them by text message to their doctors personal cell phone.

In addition, workers may be collecting, storing, processing, and sharing PHI using personal accounts on popular file-sharing services such as Dropbox, Box, Google Drive, and Microsoft OneDrive. Their employers may or may not be aware their workers are using these services. The use of personal information technology services to perform work tasks is sometimes referred to as "Shadow IT."

Organizations should address the use of personal IT services in several ways. First, they should analyze the use of personal IT services as part of the risk analysis and management functions. Workers are generally seeking the most efficient way to perform work tasks. In some cases, healthcare practitioners may feel that using personal services in an urgent case, with its attendant risks, is better than taking a risk with a patient, delaying care, sustaining the resulting harm, or other emergency or urgent circumstances.

The organization's management must make an informed risk decision about different ways workers can communicate and share information. It may help the organization to find easy-to-use and secure alternatives to popular services to mitigate the risk. For some organizations, after a risk analysis, the organization may accept the risks of personal communications systems to handle a patient emergency or urgent situation. They may, however, want to adopt countervailing controls, such as immediate transfer of the information to normal systems when the emergency is over, deletion of any PHI in personal systems, logging and preserving the communication, and reporting the event to management.

In any event, the organization should train its workforce on the policies and procedures it adopts, refresh the training periodically, and assess compliance with the organization's policies and procedures. Assessment would help management know whether workers are circumventing a ban on the use of personal IT services. If the organization permits some limited use of personal IT services in urgent situations, the organization can assess whether workers are following procedures for the use of countervailing controls. The results of these assessments can inform future risk decisions and updates to policies and procedures.

A. CLOUD COMPUTING

Cloud computing refers to the use of Internet resources to deliver applications and information technology infrastructure without the need for users to maintain software, hardware, and other local resources. "Cloud computing is a model for enabling ubiquitous, convenient, on-demand network access to a shared pool of configurable computing resources (e.g., networks, servers, storage, applications, and services) that can be rapidly provisioned and released with minimal management effort or service provider interaction."[1] For instance, an individual user may use a "software as a service" application such as web-based mail via a web browser, as opposed to using e-mail client software on the user's local machine.

Businesses can use "platform as a service" infrastructure to deploy applications. The business can use the platform to offer applications (either its own or others') on the infrastructure for others (e.g., customers) to access via a web browser or special application. The cloud service provider manages the networks, servers, storage, and application hosting, while the business can focus on the application. Also, a business can use a cloud service provider's "infrastructure as a service." The business can establish metered server, storage, and networking services on demand and as needed. It can run an entire virtual data center, but is responsible for managing its own data, operating systems, and middleware.

In healthcare, cloud computing conveys a number of advantages. Individual users may have access to more work information from more than just their workstations in their work setting. They may be able to access information from mobile devices. Cloud computing can make healthcare delivery faster and more efficient. Moreover, the organization can outsource some of the time, effort, resources, and institutional knowledge required to manage information technologies, while focusing on the core operations, applications, and data management

---

1. Peter Mell & Timothy Grance, Nat'l Inst. of Standards & Tech., Special Publ'n 800-145, The NIST Definition of Cloud Computing (Sept. 2011).

functions relating to healthcare. The organization can focus on healthcare rather than information technology management.

Cloud computing raises a number of security issues. First, the organization loses some control over some of its infrastructure. Since it is not managing the devices, people, and procedures for managing the application it uses and the data being hosted in the cloud service, it does not have direct oversight over these aspects of its infrastructure. The lack of direct control is a risk. Second, when users have access to data at locations beyond the workspace, devices and data with access to information via the cloud could be compromised. Third, cloud systems can be vulnerable to a cloud tenant (one user of the infrastructure) gaining unauthorized access to the resources of another tenant.

To mitigate these risks, besides including cloud computing in its risk management process, the organization should consider the following risk mitigation steps (besides those discussed elsewhere in this book):

- After undertaking a risk assessment, the organization may decide that the risks of cloud computing outweigh the benefits. In that case, the organization may be better off with on-premises solutions.

- The organization's risk assessment may militate in favor of having a service provider set up a private cloud infrastructure, or a hybrid infrastructure based on private and public components, rather than using a public (shared cloud). While likely more expensive than a public cloud service, having a private cloud or cloud components dedicated to only its own use would give the organization more control and reduce the risk of unauthorized access by other businesses sharing the infrastructure.

- The organization should undertake due diligence of any cloud service provider to understand its security services and posture. This due diligence should occur before obtaining the services and signing an agreement.

- In some cases, an organization may be able to obtain and exercise the right to conduct a security assessment of the service provider. In most cases, a vendor will not want or be able to permit its customers to conduct individual security assessments. Accordingly, the organization may satisfy itself that the cloud service provider is secure by checking for security certifications, such as the completion of a certification under ISO 27001[2] or a SOC 2 report.[3]

- The organization should carefully manage access to its cloud tenancy and accounts. Based on its risk assessment, it will likely want to require multifactor authentication, such as the use of a one-time code sent to a cell phone via SMS in addition to a password.
- Some of the most prominent examples of Shadow IT are cloud file-sharing services. Organizations should have policies and procedures about the use of cloud file-sharing services, implement and train their workforce members on them, assess compliance with them, and hold workforce members accountable for any violations.

B. SOCIAL MEDIA

By now, people in the United States are well familiar with different social media services. Examples include Facebook, Twitter, and LinkedIn. People use social media to share life's events with family and friends. They can share videos and images. They can tell friends where they have been.

In the healthcare field, social media raise the risk of privacy and perhaps security violations. A hospital worker, for instance, could report to friends or the public about meeting a celebrity at work. The worker might even disclose the reason for the celebrity's visit or treatment.

---

2. Int'l Org. for Standardization, Information technology—Security techniques—Information security management systems—Requirements, ISO/IEC 27001 (2d ed. Oct. 1, 2013).

3. A "SOC report" is a "Service Organization Controls" report. A SOC 2 report is a report on controls at a service organization (such as a cloud service provider) relevant to security, availability, processing integrity, confidentiality, or privacy. In the United States, the American Institute of CPAs (AICPA) has developed and maintains the criteria under which an auditing firm can issue a SOC 2 report. The AICPA states that a SOC 2 report given to a customer can help the customer "gain confidence and place trust in a service organization's systems." AICPA Service Organization Controls (SOC) Reports for Service Organizations, http://www.aicpa .org/InterestAreas/FRC/AssuranceAdvisoryServices/Pages/ServiceOrganization'sManagement .aspx (last visited Apr. 11, 2016). A customer may or may not be able to access the results of a SOC 2 report, but would want to know that it has been done. A cloud service provider may want to provide a SOC 3 report to customers in order to provide the results of an assessment to customers as a marketing tool. SOC 3 reports are intended to be freely distributed. *See id.*

On the face of it, such a disclosure would constitute a violation of the Privacy Rule. If a worker gained unauthorized access to a celebrity's PHI and posted it on social media, that conduct would almost certainly constitute a Security Rule violation. In addition, workers may be using social media messaging services to communicate PHI as a form of Shadow IT discussed above.

In order to mitigate the risks associated with social media, the organization should have policies and procedures addressing social media. It should prohibit posting text, photos, or videos of patients without authorization. The organization should train workers on what the policies and procedures require and prohibit. It should also assess compliance to determine if workers are complying with the organization's policies and procedures. It should be aware of and comply with state social media privacy laws. Finally, assessments can provide useful feedback for updating the organization's risk assessment, as well as its policies and procedures.

C. MOBILE COMPUTING

At the time the Department of Health and Human Services (HHS) issued the Security Rule, healthcare information technology focused largely on the use of traditional computing devices: desktop computers, laptops, servers, minicomputers, and mainframes. Since then, the world has undergone a "mobile transformation" in which consumer devices such as smartphones, tablets, smart watches, and other new mobile computing devices have created new computing platforms that did not exist before.

Laptops provided a bridge from in-office information technology to mobile computing. Phones and tablets have continued this trend. Part of the motivation for the increasing use of mobile devices is the "consumerization" of information technology: workers see new popular consumer devices for personal use and want to use these same devices for business use.[4]

Some businesses allow users to "bring your own device" (BYOD) to work under a BYOD policy. Users own their own BYOD devices. Other companies allow users to "choose your own device" (CYOD) where users must purchase one of a limited set of devices, which the business is

---

4. For a discussion of the "mobile transformation" and consumerization, see STEPHEN WU, A LEGAL GUIDE TO ENTERPRISE MOBILE MANAGEMENT 1–2, 9–13 (2013).

willing to support. Finally, some businesses own user devices, but allow workers to use them for limited personal purposes in a model known as COPE: corporate-owned, personally enabled. COPE gives the organization maximum control, but it can save money through BYOD or CYOD.

The security and privacy issues associated with these newer computing devices pose security challenges not seen with traditional computing devices. The easy portability of mobile devices means that theft and loss are much larger threats than with servers, desktops, and mainframe computers. Operating systems, security functions, and computer forensics tools for phones and tablets are different from those used in desktop, laptop, and server computers. Methods of securing mobile devices and their applications are different as well.

HHS offers web content in a portal that provides useful guidance in securing PHI stored or accessible using mobile devices.[5] Also, the American Bar Association Section of Science & Technology Law published my previous book on this topic: *An Enterprise Guide to Mobile Device Management.* The book has a chapter on securing data processed and stored on mobile devices.[6] The National Institute of Standards and Technology has also published guidance on securing mobile devices.[7]

These resources provide a large number of guidelines on securing mobile devices and the data they process. They are too numerous to mention here. Nonetheless, given that stolen and lost laptops are the top trigger for HHS enforcement activity, the organization should train its workforce to prevent the theft or loss of mobile devices as a top priority. In addition, the organization should ensure that mobile devices storing or processing PHI are using encryption to protect data.

It might have been possible to argue in 2003, when HHS issued the Security Rule, that using encryption in some environments was not reasonable and appropriate. It was harder to encrypt data on devices then, given the need for special, less common applications or hardware. Now, however, encryption is much easier with common and relatively inexpensive (or free) encryption applications, self-encrypting drives,

---

5. HHS, Privacy & Security, Your Mobile Device and Health Information Privacy and Security, https://www.healthit.gov/providers-professionals/your-mobile-device-and-health-information-privacy-and-security (last visited Apr. 11, 2016).

6. Wu, *supra* note 4, at 39–73.

7. Murugiah Souppaya & Karen Scarfone, Nat'l Inst. of Standards & Tech., NIST Special Publ'n 800-124, Guidelines for Managing the Security of Mobile Devices in the Enterprise (Rev. 1, June 2013), *reprinted at* http://nvlpubs.nist.gov/nistpubs/SpecialPublications/NIST.SP.800-124r1.pdf.

and encryption built into some operating systems and devices. Many security experts contend that using encryption is the number one thing an organization can do to reduce its data breach risk. By extension, encryption is the top tool to reduce legal risk of enforcement activity or private plaintiff claims. Today, there is simply no excuse for storing PHI on media or computing devices without encryption.

Moreover, the organization should determine which users it should permit to use mobile devices for work purposes. It should have policies and procedures concerning the use of mobile devices and segregating personal and work data and applications. These policies and procedures should account for the ways mobile devices may facilitate the use of Shadow IT.

Additionally, special mobile device management (MDM) software can improve the security of the data on the device. MDM software can separate work data from personal data on personal devices used for work functions. Mobile application management can control which kinds of applications can be used on mobile devices. Finally, mobile information management can allow users to access and share data securely using different devices.

A multitiered approach may help to secure an enterprise supporting mobile devices. The enterprise secures networks used by mobile devices and its internal networks (such as limiting access to applications and data when being accessed by a mobile device). It can use MDM software to secure the device. Finally, it can use software to secure the data themselves. For instance, some digital rights management applications allow an organization to put expiration dates on files used, after which they cannot be accessed.

D. PUBLIC KEY INFRASTRUCTURE

Public key infrastructure (PKI) technology allows an organization to provide assurances of integrity and confidentiality of data. Although PKI dates to the late 1970s, no other security technology is able to provide equivalent assurances of integrity and confidentiality today. The Transport Layer Security (TLS) protocol and its predecessor Secure Sockets Layer (SSL) protocol have served as the most widely deployed standards for securing electronic communications and commerce over the web.

TLS and SSL are examples of PKI technology. People using a browser to shop on a secure site see a padlock on the screen and sometimes a green bar on the browser, which indicate that TLS or SSL is protecting communications between the browser and the site's server. TLS or SSL provide assurances that a user is communicating with an authenticated site and that communications between the browser and server are encrypted to protect the confidentiality of the communicated information, such as payment card information used in a web transaction.

Another example of PKI technology is the digital signature. A digital signature can be used to secure an e-mail, a pdf, or any other file. A digital signature uses a certain kind of cryptography to provide assurances that an e-mail or file came from a certain person (or organization) and has not been altered since it was signed. A remote device with a cryptographic key can authenticate itself to a server to provide assurances that the server is communicating with an authorized device to receive communications. This functionality is particularly helpful for communication with smart/networked and Internet of Things devices. Communicating machines can authenticate each other before trusting their communications.

PKI is a fundamental technology with many potential applications in healthcare. While PKI is a technology to promote security, PKIs may be vulnerable to attack. For instance, authentication procedures should be robust enough to detect and prevent impersonation by attackers seeking to obtain credentials without authorization. An organization must manage its keys to prevent their compromise; compromised keys can be used to impersonate those persons or machines to whom the keys belong. In addition, a PKI will need to upgrade the strength of cryptographic keys, algorithms, and other aspects of cryptographic management over time. Newer, more powerful computers today can compromise cryptographic keys that yesterday's computing systems could not. Future computers will be able to compromise keys in use today. Accordingly, managing a PKI means constant transitioning to stronger technology over time.

The American Bar Association Section of Science & Technology Law published a key business, legal, and technical guide to operating a PKI in 2003.[8] The National Institute of Standards and Technology has also published a number of guides on PKI.[9] A healthcare organization

---

8. INFO. SEC. COMM., ABA SEC. OF SCI. & TECH. LAW, PUBLIC KEY INFRASTRUCTURE ASSESSMENT GUIDELINES (2003).

9. A list of all NIST special publications appears here: http://csrc.nist.gov/publications /PubsSPs.html.

may wish to outsource its PKI functions to a service provider in order to focus on its core competencies, while obtaining the benefit of PKI technology.

E. TELEMEDICINE

Telemedicine systems permit the delivery of healthcare remotely using communications technology. For instance, a rural patient needing to consult a dermatologist, but unable to travel hours to see the dermatologist in person, could use telemedicine technology to allow the dermatologist to view the patient's skin condition remotely. The patient could visit a local clinic that has a video conferencing link to the dermatologist. A nurse could use a handheld high-resolution camera to allow the remote doctor to see a close-up image of the condition. Communications can be synchronous—a live consultation—or asynchronous, where video or images are collected, stored, and later forwarded to another provider for evaluation. It is even possible for a surgeon to remotely control a surgical robot being used to perform an operation.[10]

From a security perspective, an organization using telemedicine systems should be concerned about protecting the confidentiality of the data transmission. Telemedicine systems should use encryption to provide assurances of confidentiality. Moreover, the organization using them should require robust authentication as a condition to accessing the system to ensure that only authenticated and authorized users have access to live or stored communications. Finally, the system should use systems intended to check the integrity of any data used to control remote devices, such as a surgical instrument, to ensure that an attacker or error does not cause the remote device to malfunction.

F. AUGMENTED AND VIRTUAL REALITY SYSTEMS

Augmented and virtual reality systems permit an organization to create virtual images or simulated environments. For instance, some systems could create a training environment for surgeons in which they wear goggles to view a simulated operating room and conduct a virtual surgery. If a doctor is using telesurgery to conduct a remote operation, virtual reality technology can show the doctor locally a virtual

---

10. For a discussion of telemedicine, its effectiveness, and legal issues, see Mary Maiberger, *Telemedicine, in* HEALTH CARE IT 63–73 (Arthur E. Peabody Jr. ed., 2013).

representation of what is going on remotely. Devices may even provide haptic feedback to give the surgeon the cues needed to know how much pressure to use with the device. In the future, healthcare providers may use holography to transmit and display 3D images of a patient or remote environment.

Augmented reality allows people to see virtual images within a real physical environment. Users see both the normal physical surroundings and the virtual images or components. For instance, some surgeons have used Google Glass displays and other headsets allowing the user to see virtual images via the device that appear to be in real space. Augmented reality systems provide some of the same benefits as virtual reality systems. In other applications, augmented reality may be more effective. For example, a remote instructor or mentor can cause a local surgeon using an augmented reality display to see guides or pointers to places to look or cut. To the local surgeon, it would appear that the guides are on top of the patient's skin or organs. At the same time, the surgeon would be seeing all of the real detail of the patient through his or her own vision.

As with telemedicine, securing communications with remote users through encryption is important. Protecting the confidentiality of the communications is important to prevent the interception of communications and gaining unauthorized access to the images or video. Only authenticated and authorized users should have access to the systems supporting the device and any stored video or images. Authentication helps to prevent impersonation for purposes of unauthorized viewing or tampering. Finally, the organization should control physical access to the device to prevent tampering, loss, or destruction.

G. BIG DATA

"Big Data" is a jargon term that refers to the collection, analysis, and use of very large volumes of data. Sometimes, because of the huge volume, analysis of the data may yield surprising conclusions. Advertisers use Big Data to determine which advertisements work best with which viewers of media. Analysis of the data allows advertisers to target their advertisements more effectively and save money. The government is collecting Big Data about terrorism to track potential activity more effectively. In the health field, possible sources of Big Data include wearable fitness devices and preexisting databases of medical records and information that can be used to help with differential diagnoses.

The data may feed into artificial intelligence (AI) systems, such as IBM's Watson system, which can observe patterns and draw conclusions from the huge amounts of data being processed.[11]

A security professional would be concerned about the confidentiality of data when it is being collected and transmitted to the platform where the organization can analyze it. Using TLS, Internet Protocol Security (IPsec), or other protocols for encrypting data would provide assurances of confidentiality for data in transit. Moreover, if the data are sensitive, managing access to the databases containing the data is important. If the PHI contains sensitive information about medical conditions or financial information, snoopers or hackers may attempt to gain unauthorized access to the data being collected. Encryption of the data at rest and carefully managing access, such as through multifactor authentication, will mitigate these risks. If third-party vendors are collecting and hosting the data, supervising and assessing the security of those vendors will be important. Providing assurances of the data is important to maintain its reliability. Accidental corruption and tampering are risks. Finally, the organization should provide assurances of the continued availability of data and data sources. They may need dedicated communications facilities if always-on access to data is needed.

H. 3D PRINTING

Using 3D printing technology, it is possible to make custom-made parts with various materials. 3D printing involves additive manufacturing: material is laid down layer by layer. 3D printers can create parts from materials such as plastic, metal, ceramic, food, and even tissues. Scientists are examining whether 3D printing can help to synthesize organs for transplantation purposes. Presently, surgeons can use images to make surgical models or customized guides for use in surgical procedures, such as orthognathic surgery to expand the jaws of patients with sleep apnea to open their airways.

An organization may outsource the manufacturing of 3D printed parts and materials. Accordingly, the organization may need to send PHI to the vendor providing the printed products. Consequently, securing the communications of the PHI to the vendor is important.

---

11. For a discussion of the use of Big Data in healthcare, see Bernard Marr, *How Big Data is Changing Healthcare*, Forbes (Apr. 21, 2015), *reprinted at* http://onforb.es/1bfRQ0b.

Requiring encryption of the communications and the data on the vendor's systems should be a top priority.

Supervising and overseeing the security of the vendor's systems is important as well. The oversight should begin with due diligence on the vendor. It should continue with periodic security reviews. The vendor may want to provide a security certification to the organization to promote a relationship of trust with the organization.

Security reviews should include obtaining assurances of integrity. Because precision in the models and printed products is important, preventing corruption or tampering with the data used to manufacture the printed products is important. Likewise, the vendor should limit physical and network access to its 3D printers. Vendors should manage the risks involved with malicious insiders and hackers seeking to disrupt the vendor's operations.

I. HEALTHTECH—WEARABLES, INGESTIBLES, EMBEDDABLES, AND MORE

Healthtech devices are increasingly common. People are wearing sensor devices that monitor fitness metrics. They can count steps and distance walked or run, calories burned, elevation changes, and heart rate. In the future, people may swallow sensor devices that can monitor or transmit video of the digestive system, may have sensor devices in their bloodstream monitoring the level of a medication, or may ingest smart pills that detect diseases. An organization can also embed devices in a patient, such as a catheter for an insulin pump, a pacemaker, or microchips placed under the skin.

With all of these devices, various security vulnerabilities may be present. Hackers can exploit vulnerabilities to take control of them or otherwise tamper with them. Devices that communicate with systems outside the body entail the risk of interception or interruption. Moreover, once systems collect data from devices on or in the body, the systems are potential targets for attack.

To mitigate these risks, the device manufacturers should design their products with security features in mind. They should thoroughly test the device during the design phase to determine if vulnerabilities pose risks to users. They may want to have an independent third party test the device to check for vulnerabilities and seek any available security certifications for the device. Finally, the vendor hosting the applications and data needs to secure the data and the systems collecting the data. It should use transmission security procedures and technology to secure the communications with the device, encrypt the collected data, and manage access to the infrastructure supporting the devices.

J. THE INTERNET OF THINGS (IOT) AND SMART MEDICAL DEVICES

With the mobile revolution, computing has extended beyond traditional computers to new platforms, such as mobile phones and tablets. The Internet of Things (IoT) takes computing one step further. It extends connectivity to devices that never used to be attached to a computer network. For instance, the IoT now allows building owners to control heating, ventilation, and cooling systems remotely through an Internet connection. Warehouses can track inventory in their facilities. Manufacturers can monitor their equipment via a network connection. With the IoT, machines will be communicating with other machines, making use of data collected by sensors, and transmitting data back to central systems, and control software can monitor and make adjustments via communications with remote devices.

In a related trend, manufacturers are creating medical devices and equipment that can be monitored and controlled through a computer network. That network may or may not be the public Internet; instead, the devices may be intended for control by internal networks. Even if they are not network connected, smarter pieces of hospital equipment are or include what are, in essence, specialized computers. Healthcare is turning increasingly to smart medical devices. These devices may be used for any number of diagnostic, imaging, or treatment purposes. They may make use of sensors that work together with off-the-shelf mobile devices. Examples include sensors that allow an iPhone to take an EKG, check blood glucose levels, or check blood pressure.

All of these systems are subject to attack. For instance, security researcher Billy Rios has received publicity for testing and successfully hacking into a number of network-connected devices. He first received publicity for hacking into a Phillips X-ray management device.[12] He mentioned, at a meeting of the Information Security Committee of the American Bar Association Section of Science & Technology Law, that

---

12. John Leyden, *Paging Dr Evil: Philips Medical Device Control Kit 'Easily Hacked,'* REGISTER, Jan. 18, 2013, http://www.theregister.co.uk/2013/01/18/medical_device_control_kit_security/.

if he had compromised such a device while in service, he could have caused it to deliver excess radiation to a patient.

More recently, Rios found fundamental flaws in a Hospira LifeCare PCA Infusion System, which, if he had compromised one in service, he could have shut off remotely or caused to deliver excess medication. Rios's notification motivated the US Department of Homeland Security (DHS) to issue advisories to notify users of the system vulnerabilities he found.[13] The vulnerabilities uncovered were not obscure ones that only the brightest academics could find. Instead, they were basic errors, such as allowing a buffer overflow error, using hardcoded accounts, and giving unauthenticated users root privileges. DHS wrote, "An attacker with low skill would be able to exploit all but two of these vulnerabilities."[14]

As with healthtech devices, preventing hacking risks involves taking steps during a manufacturer's design process. The device manufacturers should use "security by design" principles to integrate security into the early phases of the design process. Thorough security testing is critical. It can determine if vulnerabilities pose risks to users. An independent third-party test adds credibility to the security design process. The third-party tester can check for vulnerabilities. The organization should carefully cantrol physical access to these systems. Finally, the organization should ensure that the vendor hosting associated applications and data is securing the data and the systems collecting the data. The vendor should use transmission security procedures and technology to secure the communications with the device, protect the collected data with encryption, and use access management to limit access to the infrastructure supporting the devices.

K. ROBOTS

Healthcare organizations are beginning to deploy robots. The use of surgical robots is increasingly common for certain procedures. Service robots now perform tasks in a hospital setting that used to require manual labor, such as wheeling stacks of linens through the facility. Finally, doctors are now starting to use telepresence robots to conduct rounds. For instance, a doctor on call in the middle of the night could remotely control a robot in a medical facility and move it around hallways and

---

13. *E.g.*, ICS-CERT, Hospira LifeCare PCA Infusion System Vulnerabilities (Update B), Advisory (ICSA-15-125-01B) (June 10, 2015).

14. *Id.* at 2.

into rooms, interacting with patients and other workers via the screen, speakers, and microphone on the robot in a similar fashion to video conferencing. Since the system is mobile, the doctor may feel a stronger sense of immersion in the environment and freedom and capability to perform tasks that would normally require physical presence. Using a telepresence robot to interact with patients may also be helpful for patients with highly communicable diseases such as Ebola virus disease.

Again, concerns about hacking are paramount. An attacker could tamper with a surgical robot to injure patients. Some telepresence robots can record images, audio, and video. Someone snooping on a patient could gain unauthorized access to its recordings. Controlling physical access to robots is crucial. Finally, a hacker could intercept or interfere with communications with a robot for malicious or snooping purposes.

The "security by design" principles discussed in section 9.J above apply here as well. Moreover, software and firmware updates will be important to close off any vulnerabilities that may appear. Finally, the vendor hosting associated applications and data needs to be secure. It should secure the data and the systems collecting the data. Transmission security procedures and technology can secure the communications with the device. The vendor should protect the collected data with encryption. Moreover, the organization should limit access to the infrastructure supporting the devices.

L. ARTIFICIAL INTELLIGENCE SYSTEMS

AI is coming to healthcare. We have become familiar with AI systems in our daily lives when we use virtual personal assistant applications such as Apple's Siri, Microsoft's Cortana, Amazon's Alexa, and Google Now. IBM's Watson,[15] combined with Big Data, is helping to support doctors by guiding their decisions when making diagnoses. Other applications making use of AI include systems guiding patients to comply with instructions to take medications and systems to guide caregivers to support patients.[16]

---

15. For information about Watson, see IBM, Meet Watson, http://www.ibm.com/smarterplanet/us/en/ibmwatson/.

16. *See generally* Stephanie Baum, *4 Ways Healthcare Is Putting Artificial Intelligence, Machine Learning to Use*, MEDCITY NEWS, Feb. 14, 2015.

As with robots, the "security by design" principles discussed in section 9.J above apply, too. Designing systems to prevent unauthorized access to user information, maintaining the integrity and reliability of the system, and providing assurances of its availability is important. An organization may want to see results of testing or certifications to make sure the AI system works as advertised. Finally, a vendor may be providing the AI application remotely. Supervising the vendor and overseeing its security becomes important, as is maintaining the security of the communications link with the AI system. Finally, some AI systems may require a persistent Internet connection in order to communicate with the user. Preserving connectivity, with backup capabilities if needed, becomes important to maintain availability.

M. RESULTING PERVASIVE COMPUTING AND COMMUNICATIONS

The newer and emerging technologies described above work together in a synergistic fashion. For instance, AI systems may be able to provide diagnostic guidance if they have the support of Big Data. In addition, PKI can help to secure machine-to-machine communications among IoT devices. When viewed from a larger perspective, these technologies work together and augment each other to permit pervasive computing. Consider figure 9.1.

One device may make use of many, and perhaps someday all, of these technologies. For instance, a portable telesurgery field robot is not only a robot: it is a mobile device, it may receive and transmit Big Data, it may be part of the IoT connected to the cloud, and it may make use of public key infrastructure technology (PKI) to secure communications to and from the device.

Consider also a future in which we have autonomous vehicles serving as ambulances. Such autonomous vehicles would be robots. They would receive Big Data in the form of maps, and generate Big Data in the form of speed and location information that people can monitor to determine traffic patterns or help them avoid areas of congestion. They would be connected to the IoT, supported by cloud computing infrastructure. They may have an augmented reality windshield to show extra information about features of the physical world. They may have a 3D printer on board to manufacture items to help deliver care to patients. They would likely also use PKI to secure communications

Figure 9.1. Pervasive Computing

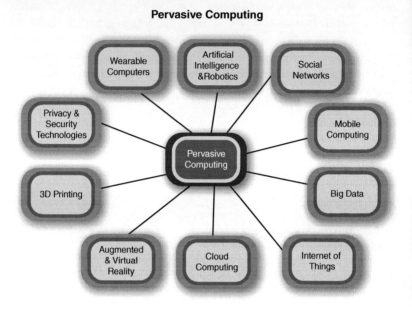

with supporting infrastructure. Finally, they may interact with wearable computing devices to monitor the health of the patient. Other onboard medical devices may involve functionality depicted on all the boxes shown in the diagram.

Coupled by increasing network connectivity via broadband, WiFi, and cellular connectivity, our devices increasingly allow us to experience and use computing in an increasing percentage of our daily functions, and access data and computing resources to perform work from any device, anywhere, and anytime.

These trends will also impact healthcare. Imagine a world of pervasive computing and connectivity used for the delivery and support of healthcare services. Patients could obtain telemedicine services as long as they have a mobile device connected to one or another mode of using the mobile Internet. Remote doctors could consult with patients and colleagues anywhere and anytime without being limited to an office or clinical setting.

Moreover, machines will increasingly add intelligence to the infra-structure. AI systems can monitor patients in or out of a hospital and provide alerts if something goes wrong. Robots will become pervasive in hospitals and clinics, performing tasks impossible or too dull for humans, or making life easier for professionals. The world of healthcare will increasingly manage itself, reducing the need for human oversight and reducing costs.

Profound changes in healthcare will occur in upcoming decades. With emerging technologies, we will encounter security threats we can-not even imagine today. Nonetheless, healthcare organizations will, at all times, face a regulatory and risk management imperative to pro-tect their information technology systems from reasonably anticipated security threats. Accordingly, the best that healthcare organizations can do is to be prepared for future threats and risks by regularly reapprais-ing their technology environments and implementing cost-effective security controls to manage their risks.

CHAPTER 10

Conclusion

The news media will continue to report a steady stream of high-profile information security breaches. The healthcare industry is not immune to this phenomenon. It has had, and will continue to have, its own breaches affecting high-profile celebrities and the public alike. These breaches will continue to trigger governmental enforcement activities and private plaintiff actions.

Nevertheless, the HIPAA Security Rule provides an effective roadmap for implementing standard information technology security practices to prevent security breaches in the healthcare field. Organizations willing to implement the Security Rule can greatly reduce their legal risk. Furthermore, the healthcare field now includes requirements for notifying patients about breaches of their health information, just as companies must report breaches in payment card information and certain other categories of sensitive information. The stakes are high. Health records are extremely sensitive and a significant breach could lead to embarrassing disclosures about large numbers of people and could lead to identity theft. Moreover, as we have seen with Anthem, breaches causing identity theft and affecting large numbers of individuals almost inevitably result in litigation.

Unfortunately, covered entities and business associates have been slow to comply. Even though the compliance deadlines for the HIPAA Security Rule and the HIPAA Final Omnibus Rule passed, many providers, payers, and business associates have not reached full compliance. These organizations have failed to comply even as a significant number of them have experienced security breaches. As seen with the loss of laptops containing unencrypted protected health information, many of these breaches are entirely and easily avoidable. They risk enforcement actions, civil actions by private plaintiffs, and the loss of reputation. Moreover, emerging healthcare technologies, such as the Internet of Things, Big Data, artificial intelligence, and robotics, will only increase the information security challenges faced by covered entities and business associates in coming years and decades.

The good news is that the HIPAA Security Rule gives covered entities a great deal of flexibility in how to implement the regulations. The Security Rule is not a "one size fits all" set of requirements. Thus, compliance is a realistic goal. Moreover, covered entities and many business associates have a basic understanding of what they need to do to comply after years of education about HIPAA. Finally, the principles in this book can be helpful to manage the risks involved with emerging healthcare technologies.

The purpose of this publication is to provide covered entities and business associates with even more information in significant detail about the Security Rule and its background. The thorough coverage of the Security Rule's provisions should provide an information security professional's perspective about what the regulations mean and how covered entities and business associates can comply. Hopefully, it will help more organizations meet the goal of full compliance and, more importantly, defensible security.

HIPAA Administrative Simplification Provisions

This Appendix contains the administrative simplification provisions in Title II, Subtitle F of HIPAA, as codified in Part C of Subchapter XI of Chapter 7 in Title 42 of the United States Code as additions to the Social Security Act. The sections below are numbered as they appear in Title 42 of the United States Code. This Appendix contains the latest version of these provisions as amended, including footnotes that appear in the official pages of the United States Code. The HITECH Act amended some of these provisions.

§1320d. Definitions

For purposes of this part:

(1) Code set

The term "code set" means any set of codes used for encoding data elements, such as tables of terms, medical concepts, medical diagnostic codes, or medical procedure codes.

(2) Health care clearinghouse

The term "health care clearinghouse" means a public or private entity that processes or facilitates the processing of nonstandard data elements of health information into standard data elements.

(3) Health care provider

The term "health care provider" includes a provider of services (as defined in section 1395x(u) of this title), a provider of medical or other health services (as defined in section 1395x(s) of this title), and any other person furnishing health care services or supplies.

(4) Health information

The term "health information" means any information, whether oral or recorded in any form or medium, that—

(A) is created or received by a health care provider, health plan, public health authority, employer, life insurer, school or university, or health care clearinghouse; and

(B) relates to the past, present, or future physical or mental health or condition of an individual, the provision of health care to an individual, or the past, present, or future payment for the provision of health care to an individual.

(5) Health plan
The term "health plan" means an individual or group plan that provides, or pays the cost of, medical care (as such term is defined in section 300gg–91 of this title). Such term includes the following, and any combination thereof:

(A) A group health plan (as defined in section 300gg–91(a) of this title), but only if the plan—

(i) has 50 or more participants (as defined in section 1002(7) of title 29); or

(ii) is administered by an entity other than the employer who established and maintains the plan.

(B) A health insurance issuer (as defined in section 300gg–91(b) of this title).

(C) A health maintenance organization (as defined in section 300gg–91(b) of this title).

(D) Parts A, B, C, or D of the Medicare program under subchapter XVIII of this chapter.

(E) The medicaid program under subchapter XIX of this chapter.

(F) A Medicare supplemental policy (as defined in section 1395ss(g)(1) of this title).

(G) A long-term care policy, including a nursing home fixed indemnity policy (unless the Secretary determines that such a policy does not provide sufficiently comprehensive coverage of a benefit so that the policy should be treated as a health plan).

(H) An employee welfare benefit plan or any other arrangement which is established or maintained for the purpose of offering or providing health benefits to the employees of 2 or more employers.

(I)   The health care program for active military personnel under title 10.

(J)   The veterans health care program under chapter 17 of title 38.

(K)   The Civilian Health and Medical Program of the Uniformed Services (CHAMPUS), as defined in section 1072(4) of title 10.

 (L) The Indian health service program under the Indian Health Care Improvement Act (25 U.S.C. 1601 et seq.).

(M) The Federal Employees Health Benefit Plan under chapter 89 of title 5.

(6) Individually identifiable health information

The term "individually identifiable health information" means any information, including demographic information collected from an individual, that—

(A) is created or received by a health care provider, health plan, employer, or health care clearinghouse; and

(B) relates to the past, present, or future physical or mental health or condition of an individual, the provision of health care to an individual, or the past, present, or future payment for the provision of health care to an individual, and—

(i)   identifies the individual; or

(ii)   with respect to which there is a reasonable basis to believe that the information can be used to identify the individual.

(7) Standard

The term "standard", when used with reference to a data element of health information or a transaction referred to in section 1320d–2(a)(1) of this title, means any such data element or transaction that meets each of the standards and implementation specifications adopted or established by the Secretary with respect to the data element or transaction under sections 1320d–1 through 1320d–3 of this title.

(8) Standard setting organization

The term "standard setting organization" means a standard setting organization accredited by the American National Standards Institute, including the National Council for Prescription Drug Programs, that develops standards for information transactions, data elements, or any other standard that is necessary to, or will facilitate, the implementation of this part.

(9) Operating rules

The term "operating rules" means the necessary business rules and guidelines for the electronic exchange of information that are not defined by a standard or its implementation specifications as adopted for purposes of this part.

§1320d–1. General requirements for adoption of standards

(a) Applicability

Any standard adopted under this part shall apply, in whole or in part, to the following persons:

(1) A health plan.

(2) A health care clearinghouse.

(3) A health care provider who transmits any health information in electronic form in connection with a transaction referred to in section 1320d–2(a)(1) of this title.

(b) Reduction of costs

Any standard adopted under this part shall be consistent with the objective of reducing the administrative costs of providing and paying for health care.

(c) Role of standard setting organizations

(1) In general

Except as provided in paragraph (2), any standard adopted under this part shall be a standard that has been developed, adopted, or modified by a standard setting organization.

(2) Special rules

(A) Different standards

The Secretary may adopt a standard that is different from any standard developed, adopted, or modified by a standard setting organization, if—

(i) the different standard will substantially reduce administrative costs to health care providers and health plans compared to the alternatives; and

(ii) the standard is promulgated in accordance with the rulemaking procedures of subchapter III of chapter 5 of title 5.

(B) No standard by standard setting organization
If no standard setting organization has developed, adopted, or modified any standard relating to a standard that the Secretary is authorized or required to adopt under this part—

(i) paragraph (1) shall not apply; and

(ii) subsection (f) of this section shall apply.

(3) Consultation requirement

(A) In general
A standard may not be adopted under this part unless—

(i) in the case of a standard that has been developed, adopted, or modified by a standard setting organization, the organization consulted with each of the organizations described in subparagraph (B) in the course of such development, adoption, or modification; and

(ii) in the case of any other standard, the Secretary, in complying with the requirements of subsection (f) of this section, consulted with each of the organizations described in subparagraph (B) before adopting the standard.

(B) Organizations described
The organizations referred to in subparagraph (A) are the following:

(i) The National Uniform Billing Committee.

(ii) The National Uniform Claim Committee.

(iii) The Workgroup for Electronic Data Interchange.

(iv) The American Dental Association.

(d) Implementation specifications
The Secretary shall establish specifications for implementing each of the standards adopted under this part.

(e) Protection of trade secrets

Except as otherwise required by law, a standard adopted under this part shall not require disclosure of trade secrets or confidential commercial information by a person required to comply with this part.

(f) Assistance to Secretary

In complying with the requirements of this part, the Secretary shall rely on the recommendations of the National Committee on Vital and Health Statistics established under section 242k(k) of this title, and shall consult with appropriate Federal and State agencies and private organizations. The Secretary shall publish in the Federal Register any recommendation of the National Committee on Vital and Health Statistics regarding the adoption of a standard under this part.

(g) Application to modifications of standards

This section shall apply to a modification to a standard (including an addition to a standard) adopted under section 1320d–3(b) of this title in the same manner as it applies to an initial standard adopted under section 1320d–3(a) of this title.

§1320d–2. Standards for information transactions and data elements

(a) Standards to enable electronic exchange

(1) In general

The Secretary shall adopt standards for transactions, and data elements for such transactions, to enable health information to be exchanged electronically, that are appropriate for—

(A) the financial and administrative transactions described in paragraph (2); and

(B) other financial and administrative transactions determined appropriate by the Secretary, consistent with the goals of improving the operation of the health care system and reducing administrative costs, and subject to the requirements under paragraph (5).

(2) Transactions

The transactions referred to in paragraph (1)(A) are transactions with respect to the following:

(A) Health claims or equivalent encounter information.

(B) Health claims attachments.

(C) Enrollment and disenrollment in a health plan.

(D) Eligibility for a health plan.

(E) Health care payment and remittance advice.

(F) Health plan premium payments.

(G) First report of injury.

(H) Health claim status.

(I) Referral certification and authorization.

(J) Electronic funds transfers.

(3) Accommodation of specific providers
The standards adopted by the Secretary under paragraph (1) shall accommodate the needs of different types of health care providers.

(4) Requirements for financial and administrative transactions

(A) In general
The standards and associated operating rules adopted by the Secretary shall—

(i) to the extent feasible and appropriate, enable determination of an individual's eligibility and financial responsibility for specific services prior to or at the point of care;

(ii) be comprehensive, requiring minimal augmentation by paper or other communications;

(iii) provide for timely acknowledgment, response, and status reporting that supports a transparent claims and denial management process (including adjudication and appeals); and

(iv) describe all data elements (including reason and remark codes) in unambiguous terms, require that such data elements be required or conditioned upon set values in other fields, and prohibit additional conditions (except where necessary to implement State or Federal law, or to protect against fraud and abuse).

(B) Reduction of clerical burden
In adopting standards and operating rules for the transactions referred to under paragraph (1), the Secretary shall seek to reduce the number and complexity of forms (including paper and electronic forms) and data entry required by patients and providers.

(5) **Consideration of standardization of activities and items**

(A) In general
For purposes of carrying out paragraph (1)(B), the Secretary shall solicit, not later than January 1, 2012, and not less than every 3 years thereafter, input from entities described in subparagraph (B) on—

(i) whether there could be greater uniformity in financial and administrative activities and items, as determined appropriate by the Secretary; and

(ii) whether such activities should be considered financial and administrative transactions (as described in paragraph (1)(B)) for which the adoption of standards and operating rules would improve the operation of the health care system and reduce administrative costs.

(B) Solicitation of input
For purposes of subparagraph (A), the Secretary shall seek input from—

(i) the National Committee on Vital and Health Statistics, the Health Information Technology Policy Committee, and the Health Information Technology Standards Committee; and

(ii) standard setting organizations and stakeholders, as determined appropriate by the Secretary.

(b) Unique health identifiers

(1) In general
The Secretary shall adopt standards providing for a standard unique health identifier for each individual, employer, health plan,

and health care provider for use in the health care system. In carrying out the preceding sentence for each health plan and health care provider, the Secretary shall take into account multiple uses for identifiers and multiple locations and specialty classifications for health care providers.

(2) Use of identifiers

The standards adopted under paragraph (1) shall specify the purposes for which a unique health identifier may be used.

(c) Code sets

(1) In general

The Secretary shall adopt standards that—

> (A) select code sets for appropriate data elements for the transactions referred to in subsection (a)(1) of this section from among the code sets that have been developed by private and public entities; or
>
> (B) establish code sets for such data elements if no code sets for the data elements have been developed.

(2) Distribution

The Secretary shall establish efficient and low-cost procedures for distribution (including electronic distribution) of code sets and modifications made to such code sets under section 1320d–3(b) of this title.

(d) Security standards for health information

(1) Security standards

The Secretary shall adopt security standards that—

> (A) take into account—
>
>> (i)   the technical capabilities of record systems used to maintain health information;
>>
>> (ii) the costs of security measures;
>>
>> (iii) the need for training persons who have access to health information;
>>
>> (iv) the value of audit trails in computerized record systems; and

(v) the needs and capabilities of small health care providers and rural health care providers (as such providers are defined by the Secretary); and

(B) ensure that a health care clearinghouse, if it is part of a larger organization, has policies and security procedures which isolate the activities of the health care clearinghouse with respect to processing information in a manner that prevents unauthorized access to such information by such larger organization.

(2) Safeguards

Each person described in section 1320d–1(a) of this title who maintains or transmits health information shall maintain reasonable and appropriate administrative, technical, and physical safeguards—

(A) to ensure the integrity and confidentiality of the information;

(B) to protect against any reasonably anticipated—

(i) threats or hazards to the security or integrity of the information; and

(ii) unauthorized uses or disclosures of the information; and

(C) otherwise to ensure compliance with this part by the officers and employees of such person.

(e) Electronic signature

(1) Standards

The Secretary, in coordination with the Secretary of Commerce, shall adopt standards specifying procedures for the electronic transmission and authentication of signatures with respect to the transactions referred to in subsection (a)(1) of this section.

(2) Effect of compliance

Compliance with the standards adopted under paragraph (1) shall be deemed to satisfy Federal and State statutory requirements for written signatures with respect to the transactions referred to in subsection (a)(1) of this section.

(f) Transfer of information among health plans

The Secretary shall adopt standards for transferring among health plans appropriate standard data elements needed for the coordination of benefits, the sequential processing of claims, and other data elements for individuals who have more than one health plan.

(g) Operating rules

(1) In general

The Secretary shall adopt a single set of operating rules for each transaction referred to under subsection (a)(1) with the goal of creating as much uniformity in the implementation of the electronic standards as possible. Such operating rules shall be consensus-based and reflect the necessary business rules affecting health plans and health care providers and the manner in which they operate pursuant to standards issued under Health Insurance Portability and Accountability Act of 1996.

(2) Operating rules development

In adopting operating rules under this subsection, the Secretary shall consider recommendations for operating rules developed by a qualified nonprofit entity that meets the following requirements:

(A) The entity focuses its mission on administrative simplification.

(B) The entity demonstrates a multi-stakeholder and consensus-based process for development of operating rules, including representation by or participation from health plans, health care providers, vendors, relevant Federal agencies, and other standard development organizations.

(C) The entity has a public set of guiding principles that ensure the operating rules and process are open and transparent, and supports nondiscrimination and conflict of interest policies that demonstrate a commitment to open, fair, and nondiscriminatory practices.

(D) The entity builds on the transaction standards issued under Health Insurance Portability and Accountability Act of 1996.

(E) The entity allows for public review and updates of the operating rules.

(3) Review and recommendations

The National Committee on Vital and Health Statistics shall—

(A) advise the Secretary as to whether a nonprofit entity meets the requirements under paragraph (2);

(B) review the operating rules developed and recommended by such nonprofit entity;

(C) determine whether such operating rules represent a consensus view of the health care stakeholders and are consistent with and do not conflict with other existing standards;

(D) evaluate whether such operating rules are consistent with electronic standards adopted for health information technology; and

(E) submit to the Secretary a recommendation as to whether the Secretary should adopt such operating rules.

(4) Implementation

(A) In general

The Secretary shall adopt operating rules under this subsection, by regulation in accordance with subparagraph (C), following consideration of the operating rules developed by the non-profit entity described in paragraph (2) and the recommendation submitted by the National Committee on Vital and Health Statistics under paragraph (3)(E) and having ensured consultation with providers.

(B) Adoption requirements; effective dates

(i) Eligibility for a health plan and health claim status

The set of operating rules for eligibility for a health plan and health claim status transactions shall be adopted not later than July 1, 2011, in a manner ensuring that such operating rules are effective not later than January 1, 2013, and may allow for the use of a machine readable identification card.

(ii) Electronic funds transfers and health care payment and remittance advice

The set of operating rules for electronic funds transfers and health care payment and remittance advice transactions shall—

(I) allow for automated reconciliation of the electronic payment with the remittance advice; and

(II) be adopted not later than July 1, 2012, in a manner ensuring that such operating rules are effective not later than January 1, 2014.

(iii) Health claims or equivalent encounter information, enrollment and disenrollment in a health plan, health plan premium payments, referral certification and authorization

The set of operating rules for health claims or equivalent encounter information, enrollment and disenrollment in a health plan, health plan premium payments, and referral certification and authorization transactions shall be adopted not later than July 1, 2014, in a manner ensuring that such operating rules are effective not later than January 1, 2016.

(C) Expedited rulemaking

The Secretary shall promulgate an interim final rule applying any standard or operating rule recommended by the National Committee on Vital and Health Statistics pursuant to paragraph (3). The Secretary shall accept and consider public comments on any interim final rule published under this subparagraph for 60 days after the date of such publication.

(h) Compliance

(1) Health plan certification

(A) Eligibility for a health plan, health claim status, electronic funds transfers, health care payment and remittance advice

Not later than December 31, 2013, a health plan shall file a statement with the Secretary, in such form as the Secretary may require, certifying that the data and information systems for such plan are in compliance with any applicable standards (as described under paragraph (7) of section 1320d of this title) and associated operating rules (as described under paragraph (9) of such section) for electronic funds transfers, eligibility for a health plan, health claim status, and health care payment and remittance advice, respectively.

(B) Health claims or equivalent encounter information, enrollment and disenrollment in a health plan, health plan premium payments, health claims attachments, referral certification and authorization

Not later than December 31, 2015, a health plan shall file a statement with the Secretary, in such form as the Secretary may require, certifying that the data and information systems for such plan are in compliance with any applicable standards and associated operating rules for health claims or equivalent encounter information, enrollment and disenrollment in a health plan, health plan premium payments, health claims attachments, and referral certification and authorization, respectively. A health plan shall provide the same level of documentation to certify compliance with such transactions as is required to certify compliance with the transactions specified in subparagraph (A).

(2)   Documentation of compliance
A health plan shall provide the Secretary, in such form as the Secretary may require, with adequate documentation of compliance with the standards and operating rules described under paragraph (1). A health plan shall not be considered to have provided adequate documentation and shall not be certified as being in compliance with such standards, unless the health plan—

(A)   demonstrates to the Secretary that the plan conducts the electronic transactions specified in paragraph (1) in a manner that fully complies with the regulations of the Secretary; and

(B)   provides documentation showing that the plan has completed end-to-end testing for such transactions with their partners, such as hospitals and physicians.

(3)   Service contracts
A health plan shall be required to ensure that any entities that provide services pursuant to a contract with such health plan shall comply with any applicable certification and compliance

requirements (and provide the Secretary with adequate documentation of such compliance) under this subsection.

(4) Certification by outside entity

The Secretary may designate independent, outside entities to certify that a health plan has complied with the requirements under this subsection, provided that the certification standards employed by such entities are in accordance with any standards or operating rules issued by the Secretary.

(5) Compliance with revised standards and operating rules

(A) In general

A health plan (including entities described under paragraph (3)) shall file a statement with the Secretary, in such form as the Secretary may require, certifying that the data and information systems for such plan are in compliance with any applicable revised standards and associated operating rules under this subsection for any interim final rule promulgated by the Secretary under subsection (i) that—

(i) amends any standard or operating rule described under paragraph (1) of this subsection; or

(ii) establishes a standard (as described under subsection (a)(1)(B)) or associated operating rules (as described under subsection (i)(5)) for any other financial and administrative transactions.

(B) Date of compliance

A health plan shall comply with such requirements not later than the effective date of the applicable standard or operating rule.

(6) Audits of health plans

The Secretary shall conduct periodic audits to ensure that health plans (including entities described under paragraph (3)) are in compliance with any standards and operating rules that are described under paragraph (1) or subsection (i)(5).

(i) Review and amendment of standards and operating rules

(1) Establishment

Not later than January 1, 2014, the Secretary shall establish a review committee (as described under paragraph (4)).

(2) **Evaluations and reports**

(A) **Hearings**

Not later than April 1, 2014, and not less than biennially thereafter, the Secretary, acting through the review committee, shall conduct hearings to evaluate and review the adopted standards and operating rules established under this section.

(B) **Report**

Not later than July 1, 2014, and not less than biennially thereafter, the review committee shall provide recommendations for updating and improving such standards and operating rules. The review committee shall recommend a single set of operating rules per transaction standard and maintain the goal of creating as much uniformity as possible in the implementation of the electronic standards.

(3) **Interim final rulemaking**

(A) **In general**

Any recommendations to amend adopted standards and operating rules that have been approved by the review committee and reported to the Secretary under paragraph (2)(B) shall be adopted by the Secretary through promulgation of an interim final rule not later than 90 days after receipt of the committee's report.

(B) **Public comment**

(i) **Public comment period**

The Secretary shall accept and consider public comments on any interim final rule published under this paragraph for 60 days after the date of such publication.

(ii) **Effective date**

The effective date of any amendment to existing standards or operating rules that is adopted through an interim final rule published under this paragraph shall be 25 months following the close of such public comment period.

(4) **Review committee**

(A) **Definition**

For the purposes of this subsection, the term "review committee" means a committee chartered by or within the Department of

Health and Human services that has been designated by the Secretary to carry out this subsection, including—

(i)   the National Committee on Vital and Health Statistics; or

(ii) any appropriate committee as determined by the Secretary.

(B) Coordination of HIT standards
In developing recommendations under this subsection, the review committee shall ensure coordination, as appropriate, with the standards that support the certified electronic health record technology approved by the Office of the National Coordinator for Health Information Technology.

(5) Operating rules for other standards adopted by the Secretary
The Secretary shall adopt a single set of operating rules (pursuant to the process described under subsection (g)) for any transaction for which a standard had been adopted pursuant to subsection (a)(1)(B).

(j) Penalties

(1) Penalty fee

(A) In general
Not later than April 1, 2014, and annually thereafter, the Secretary shall assess a penalty fee (as determined under subparagraph (B)) against a health plan that has failed to meet the requirements under subsection (h) with respect to certification and documentation of compliance with—

(i)   the standards and associated operating rules described under paragraph (1) of such subsection; and

(ii) a standard (as described under subsection (a)(1)(B)) and associated operating rules (as described under subsection (i)(5)) for any other financial and administrative transactions.

(B) Fee amount
Subject to subparagraphs (C), (D), and (E), the Secretary shall assess a penalty fee against a health plan in the amount of $1 per covered life until certification is complete. The penalty

shall be assessed per person covered by the plan for which its data systems for major medical policies are not in compliance and shall be imposed against the health plan for each day that the plan is not in compliance with the requirements under subsection (h).

(C) Additional penalty for misrepresentation
A health plan that knowingly provides inaccurate or incomplete information in a statement of certification or documentation of compliance under subsection (h) shall be subject to a penalty fee that is double the amount that would otherwise be imposed under this subsection.

(D) Annual fee increase
The amount of the penalty fee imposed under this subsection shall be increased on an annual basis by the annual percentage increase in total national health care expenditures, as determined by the Secretary.

(E) Penalty limit
A penalty fee assessed against a health plan under this subsection shall not exceed, on an annual basis—

> (i) an amount equal to $20 per covered life under such plan; or

> (ii) an amount equal to $40 per covered life under the plan if such plan has knowingly provided inaccurate or incomplete information (as described under subparagraph (C)).

(F) Determination of covered individuals
The Secretary shall determine the number of covered lives under a health plan based upon the most recent statements and filings that have been submitted by such plan to the Securities and Exchange Commission.

(2) Notice and dispute procedure
The Secretary shall establish a procedure for assessment of penalty fees under this subsection that provides a health plan with reasonable notice and a dispute resolution procedure prior to provision of a notice of assessment by the Secretary of the Treasury (as described under paragraph (4)(B)).

(3) Penalty fee report

Not later than May 1, 2014, and annually thereafter, the Secretary shall provide the Secretary of the Treasury with a report identifying those health plans that have been assessed a penalty fee under this subsection.

(4) Collection of penalty fee

(A) In general

The Secretary of the Treasury, acting through the Financial Management Service, shall administer the collection of penalty fees from health plans that have been identified by the Secretary in the penalty fee report provided under paragraph (3).

(B) Notice

Not later than August 1, 2014, and annually thereafter, the Secretary of the Treasury shall provide notice to each health plan that has been assessed a penalty fee by the Secretary under this subsection. Such notice shall include the amount of the penalty fee assessed by the Secretary and the due date for payment of such fee to the Secretary of the Treasury (as described in subparagraph (C)).

(C) Payment due date

Payment by a health plan for a penalty fee assessed under this subsection shall be made to the Secretary of the Treasury not later than November 1, 2014, and annually thereafter.

(D) Unpaid penalty fees

Any amount of a penalty fee assessed against a health plan under this subsection for which payment has not been made by the due date provided under subparagraph (C) shall be—

(i) increased by the interest accrued on such amount, as determined pursuant to the underpayment rate established under section 6621 of the Internal Revenue Code of 1986; and

(ii) treated as a past-due, legally enforceable debt owed to a Federal agency for purposes of section 6402(d) of the Internal Revenue Code of 1986.

(E) Administrative fees
Any fee charged or allocated for collection activities conducted by the Financial Management Service will be passed on to a health plan on a pro-rata basis and added to any penalty fee collected from the plan.

§1320d–3. Timetables for adoption of standards

(a) Initial standards
The Secretary shall carry out section 1320d–2 of this title not later than 18 months after August 21, 1996, except that standards relating to claims attachments shall be adopted not later than 30 months after August 21, 1996.

(b) Additions and modifications to standards

(1) In general
Except as provided in paragraph (2), the Secretary shall review the standards adopted under section 1320d–2 of this title, and shall adopt modifications to the standards (including additions to the standards), as determined appropriate, but not more frequently than once every 12 months. Any addition or modification to a standard shall be completed in a manner which minimizes the disruption and cost of compliance.

(2) Special rules

(A) First 12-month period
Except with respect to additions and modifications to code sets under subparagraph (B), the Secretary may not adopt any modification to a standard adopted under this part during the 12-month period beginning on the date the standard is initially adopted, unless the Secretary determines that the modification is necessary in order to permit compliance with the standard.

(B) Additions and modifications to code sets

(i) In general
The Secretary shall ensure that procedures exist for the routine maintenance, testing, enhancement, and expansion of code sets.

(ii) Additional rules
If a code set is modified under this subsection, the modified code set shall include instructions on how data

elements of health information that were encoded prior to the modification may be converted or translated so as to preserve the informational value of the data elements that existed before the modification. Any modification to a code set under this subsection shall be implemented in a manner that minimizes the disruption and cost of complying with such modification.

§1320d–4. Requirements

(a) Conduct of transactions by plans

(1) In general

If a person desires to conduct a transaction referred to in section 1320d–2(a)(1) of this title with a health plan as a standard transaction—

(A) the health plan may not refuse to conduct such transaction as a standard transaction;

(B) the insurance plan may not delay such transaction, or otherwise adversely affect, or attempt to adversely affect, the person or the transaction on the ground that the transaction is a standard transaction; and

(C) the information transmitted and received in connection with the transaction shall be in the form of standard data elements of health information.

(2) Satisfaction of requirements

A health plan may satisfy the requirements under paragraph (1) by—

(A) directly transmitting and receiving standard data elements of health information; or

(B) submitting nonstandard data elements to a health care clearinghouse for processing into standard data elements and transmission by the health care clearinghouse, and receiving standard data elements through the health care clearinghouse.

(3) Timetable for compliance

Paragraph (1) shall not be construed to require a health plan to comply with any standard, implementation specification, or modification to a standard or specification adopted or established by the Secretary under sections 1320d–1 through 1320d–3 of this title at any time prior to the date on which the plan is required to comply with the standard or specification under subsection (b) of this section.

(b) Compliance with standards

(1) Initial compliance

(A) In general
Not later than 24 months after the date on which an initial standard or implementation specification is adopted or established under sections 1320d–1 and 1320d–2 of this title, each person to whom the standard or implementation specification applies shall comply with the standard or specification.

(B) Special rule for small health plans
In the case of a small health plan, paragraph (1) shall be applied by substituting "36 months" for "24 months". For purposes of this subsection, the Secretary shall determine the plans that qualify as small health plans.

(2) Compliance with modified standards
If the Secretary adopts a modification to a standard or implementation specification under this part, each person to whom the standard or implementation specification applies shall comply with the modified standard or implementation specification at such time as the Secretary determines appropriate, taking into account the time needed to comply due to the nature and extent of the modification. The time determined appropriate under the preceding sentence may not be earlier than the last day of the 180-day period beginning on the date such modification is adopted. The Secretary may extend the time for compliance for small health plans, if the Secretary determines that such extension is appropriate.

(3) Construction
Nothing in this subsection shall be construed to prohibit any person from complying with a standard or specification by—

(A) submitting nonstandard data elements to a health care clearinghouse for processing into standard data elements and transmission by the health care clearinghouse; or

(B) receiving standard data elements through a health care clearinghouse.

§1320d–5. General penalty for failure to comply with requirements and standards

(a) General penalty

(1) In general

Except as provided in subsection (b) of this section, the Secretary shall impose on any person who violates a provision of this part—

> (A) in the case of a violation of such provision in which it is established that the person did not know (and by exercising reasonable diligence would not have known) that such person violated such provision, a penalty for each such violation of an amount that is at least the amount described in paragraph (3)(A) but not to exceed the amount described in paragraph (3)(D);

> (B) in the case of a violation of such provision in which it is established that the violation was due to reasonable cause and not to willful neglect, a penalty for each such violation of an amount that is at least the amount described in paragraph (3)(B) but not to exceed the amount described in paragraph (3)(D); and

> (C) in the case of a violation of such provision in which it is established that the violation was due to willful neglect—

>> (i)   if the violation is corrected as described in subsection (b)(3)(A),[1] a penalty in an amount that is at least the amount described in paragraph (3)(C) but not to exceed the amount described in paragraph (3)(D); and

>> (ii) if the violation is not corrected as described in such subsection, a penalty in an amount that is at least the amount described in paragraph (3)(D).

In determining the amount of a penalty under this section for a violation, the Secretary shall base such determination on the nature and extent of the violation and the nature and extent of the harm resulting from such violation.

---

1. So in original. Probably should be "(b)(2)(A)".

(2) Procedures

The provisions of section 1320a–7a of this title (other than subsections (a) and (b) and the second sentence of subsection (f)) shall apply to the imposition of a civil money penalty under this subsection in the same manner as such provisions apply to the imposition of a penalty under such section 1320a–7a of this title.

(3) Tiers of penalties described

For purposes of paragraph (1), with respect to a violation by a person of a provision of this part—

> (A) the amount described in this subparagraph is $100 for each such violation, except that the total amount imposed on the person for all such violations of an identical requirement or prohibition during a calendar year may not exceed $25,000;
>
> (B) the amount described in this subparagraph is $1,000 for each such violation, except that the total amount imposed on the person for all such violations of an identical requirement or prohibition during a calendar year may not exceed $100,000;
>
> (C) the amount described in this subparagraph is $10,000 for each such violation, except that the total amount imposed on the person for all such violations of an identical requirement or prohibition during a calendar year may not exceed $250,000; and
>
> (D) the amount described in this subparagraph is $50,000 for each such violation, except that the total amount imposed on the person for all such violations of an identical requirement or prohibition during a calendar year may not exceed $1,500,000.

(b) Limitations

(1) Offenses otherwise punishable

No penalty may be imposed under subsection (a) and no damages obtained under subsection (d) with respect to an act if a penalty has been imposed under section 1320d–6 of this title with respect to such act.

(2) Failures due to reasonable cause

(A) In general

Except as provided in subparagraph (B) or subsection (a)(1)(C), no penalty may be imposed under subsection (a) and no damages obtained under subsection (d) if the failure to comply is corrected during the 30-day period beginning on the first date the person liable for the penalty or damages knew, or by exercising reasonable diligence would have known, that the failure to comply occurred.

(B) Extension of period

(i) No penalty

With respect to the imposition of a penalty by the Secretary under subsection (a), the period referred to in subparagraph (A) may be extended as determined appropriate by the Secretary based on the nature and extent of the failure to comply.

(ii) Assistance

If the Secretary determines that a person failed to comply because the person was unable to comply, the Secretary may provide technical assistance to the person during the period described in subparagraph (A). Such assistance shall be provided in any manner determined appropriate by the Secretary.

(3) Reduction

In the case of a failure to comply which is due to reasonable cause and not to willful neglect, any penalty under subsection (a) and any damages under subsection (d) that is[2] not entirely waived under paragraph (3)[3] may be waived to the extent that the payment of such penalty[4] would be excessive relative to the compliance failure involved.

(c) Noncompliance due to willful neglect

(1) In general

A violation of a provision of this part due to willful neglect is a violation for which the Secretary is required to impose a penalty under subsection (a)(1).

(2) Required investigation

For purposes of paragraph (1), the Secretary shall formally investigate any complaint of a violation of a provision of this part if a

---

2. So in original. Probably should be "are".
3. So in original. Probably should be "(2)".
4. So in original. The words "or damages" probably should appear after "penalty".

preliminary investigation of the facts of the complaint indicate such a possible violation due to willful neglect.

(d) Enforcement by State attorneys general

(1) Civil action

Except as provided in subsection (b), in any case in which the attorney general of a State has reason to believe that an interest of one or more of the residents of that State has been or is threatened or adversely affected by any person who violates a provision of this part, the attorney general of the State, as parens patriae, may bring a civil action on behalf of such residents of the State in a district court of the United States of appropriate jurisdiction—

(A) to enjoin further such violation by the defendant; or

(B) to obtain damages on behalf of such residents of the State, in an amount equal to the amount determined under paragraph (2).

(2) Statutory damages

(A) In general

For purposes of paragraph (1)(B), the amount determined under this paragraph is the amount calculated by multiplying the number of violations by up to $100. For purposes of the preceding sentence, in the case of a continuing violation, the number of violations shall be determined consistent with the HIPAA privacy regulations (as defined in section 1320d–9(b)(3) of this title) for violations of subsection (a).

(B) Limitation

The total amount of damages imposed on the person for all violations of an identical requirement or prohibition during a calendar year may not exceed $25,000.

(C) Reduction of damages

In assessing damages under subparagraph (A), the court may consider the factors the Secretary may consider in determining the amount of a civil money penalty under subsection (a) under the HIPAA privacy regulations.

(3) Attorney fees

In the case of any successful action under paragraph (1), the court, in its discretion, may award the costs of the action and reasonable attorney fees to the State.

(4) Notice to Secretary

The State shall serve prior written notice of any action under paragraph (1) upon the Secretary and provide the Secretary with a copy of its complaint, except in any case in which such prior notice is not feasible, in which case the State shall serve such notice immediately upon instituting such action. The Secretary shall have the right—

(A) to intervene in the action;

(B) upon so intervening, to be heard on all matters arising therein; and

(C) to file petitions for appeal.

(5) Construction

For purposes of bringing any civil action under paragraph (1), nothing in this section shall be construed to prevent an attorney general of a State from exercising the powers conferred on the attorney general by the laws of that State.

(6) Venue; service of process

(A) Venue

Any action brought under paragraph (1) may be brought in the district court of the United States that meets applicable requirements relating to venue under section 1391 of title 28.

(B) Service of process

In an action brought under paragraph (1), process may be served in any district in which the defendant—

(i) is an inhabitant; or

(ii) maintains a physical place of business.

(7) Limitation on State action while Federal action is pending

If the Secretary has instituted an action against a person under subsection (a) with respect to a specific violation of this part, no State attorney general may bring an action under this subsection against the person with respect to such violation during the pendency of that action.

(8) Application of CMP statute of limitation

A civil action may not be instituted with respect to a violation of this part unless an action to impose a civil money penalty may be instituted under subsection (a) with respect to such violation consistent with the second sentence of section 1320a–7a(c)(1) of this title.

(e) Allowing continued use of corrective action
Nothing in this section shall be construed as preventing the Office for Civil Rights of the Department of Health and Human Services from continuing, in its discretion, to use corrective action without a penalty in cases where the person did not know (and by exercising reasonable diligence would not have known) of the violation involved.

§1320d–6. Wrongful disclosure of individually identifiable health information

(a) Offense
A person who knowingly and in violation of this part—

(1) uses or causes to be used a unique health identifier;

(2) obtains individually identifiable health information relating to an individual; or

(3) discloses individually identifiable health information to another person, shall be punished as provided in subsection (b) of this section. For purposes of the previous sentence, a person (including an employee or other individual) shall be considered to have obtained or disclosed individually identifiable health information in violation of this part if the information is maintained by a covered entity (as defined in the HIPAA privacy regulation described in section 1320d–9(b)(3) of this title) and the individual obtained or disclosed such information without authorization.

(b) Penalties
A person described in subsection (a) of this section shall—

(1) be fined not more than $50,000, imprisoned not more than 1 year, or both;

(2) if the offense is committed under false pretenses, be fined not more than $100,000, imprisoned not more than 5 years, or both; and

(3) if the offense is committed with intent to sell, transfer, or use individually identifiable health information for commercial advantage, personal gain, or malicious harm, be fined not more than $250,000, imprisoned not more than 10 years, or both.

§1320d–7. Effect on State law

(a) General effect

(1) General rule

Except as provided in paragraph (2), a provision or requirement under this part, or a standard or implementation specification adopted or established under sections 1320d–1 through 1320d–3 of this title, shall supersede any contrary provision of State law, including a provision of State law that requires medical or health plan records (including billing information) to be maintained or transmitted in written rather than electronic form.

(2) Exceptions

A provision or requirement under this part, or a standard or implementation specification adopted or established under sections 1320d–1 through 1320d–3 of this title, shall not supersede a contrary provision of State law, if the provision of State law—

 (A) is a provision the Secretary determines—

  (i) is necessary—

   (I) to prevent fraud and abuse;

   (II) to ensure appropriate State regulation of insurance and health plans;

   (III) for State reporting on health care delivery or costs; or

   (IV) for other purposes; or

  (ii) addresses controlled substances; or

 (B) subject to section 264(c)(2) of the Health Insurance Portability and Accountability Act of 1996, relates to the privacy of individually identifiable health information.

(b) Public health

Nothing in this part shall be construed to invalidate or limit the authority, power, or procedures established under any law providing for the reporting of disease or injury, child abuse, birth, or death, public health surveillance, or public health investigation or intervention.

(c) State regulatory reporting

Nothing in this part shall limit the ability of a State to require a health plan to report, or to provide access to, information for management audits, financial audits, program monitoring and evaluation, facility licensure or certification, or individual licensure or certification.

§1320d–8. Processing payment transactions by financial institutions

To the extent that an entity is engaged in activities of a financial institution (as defined in section 3401 of title 12), or is engaged in authorizing, processing, clearing, settling, billing, transferring, reconciling, or collecting payments, for a financial institution, this part, and any standard adopted under this part, shall not apply to the entity with respect to such activities, including the following:

(1) The use or disclosure of information by the entity for authorizing, processing, clearing, settling, billing, transferring, reconciling or collecting, a payment for, or related to, health plan premiums or health care, where such payment is made by any means, including a credit, debit, or other payment card, an account, check, or electronic funds transfer.

(2) The request for, or the use or disclosure of, information by the entity with respect to a payment described in paragraph (1)-

    (A) for transferring receivables;

    (B) for auditing;

    (C) in connection with—

        (i) a customer dispute; or

        (ii) an inquiry from, or to, a customer;

    (D) in a communication to a customer of the entity regarding the customer's transactions, payment card, account, check, or electronic funds transfer;

    (E) for reporting to consumer reporting agencies; or

    (F) for complying with—

        (i) a civil or criminal subpoena; or

        (ii) a Federal or State law regulating the entity.

§1320d–9. Application of HIPAA regulations to genetic information

(a) In general

The Secretary shall revise the HIPAA privacy regulation (as defined in subsection (b)) so it is consistent with the following:

(1) Genetic information shall be treated as health information described in section 1320d(4)(B) of this title.

(2) The use or disclosure by a covered entity that is a group health plan, health insurance issuer that issues health insurance coverage, or issuer of a medicare supplemental policy of protected health information that is genetic information about an individual for underwriting purposes under the group health plan, health insurance coverage, or medicare supplemental policy shall not be a permitted use or disclosure.

(b) Definitions

For purposes of this section:

(1) Genetic information; genetic test; family member

The terms "genetic information", "genetic test", and "family member" have the meanings given such terms in section 300gg–91 of this title, as amended by the Genetic Information Nondiscrimination Act of 2007.

(2) Group health plan; health insurance coverage; medicare supplemental policy

The terms "group health plan" and "health insurance coverage" have the meanings given such terms under section 300gg–91 of this title, and the term "medicare supplemental policy" has the meaning given such term in section 1395ss(g) of this title.

(3) HIPAA privacy regulation

The term "HIPAA privacy regulation" means the regulations promulgated by the Secretary under this part and section 264 of the Health Insurance Portability and Accountability Act of 1996 (42 U.S.C. 1320d–2 note).

(4) Underwriting purposes

The term "underwriting purposes" means, with respect to a group health plan, health insurance coverage, or a medicare supplemental policy—

(A) rules for, or determination of, eligibility (including enrollment and continued eligibility) for, or determination of, benefits under the plan, coverage, or policy;

(B) the computation of premium or contribution amounts under the plan, coverage, or policy;

(C) the application of any pre-existing condition exclusion under the plan, coverage, or policy; and

(D) other activities related to the creation, renewal, or replacement of a contract of health insurance or health benefits.

(c) Procedure

The revisions under subsection (a) shall be made by notice in the Federal Register published not later than 60 days after May 21, 2008, and shall be effective upon publication, without opportunity for any prior public comment, but may be revised, consistent with this section, after opportunity for public comment.

(d) Enforcement

In addition to any other sanctions or remedies that may be available under law, a covered entity that is a group health plan, health insurance issuer, or issuer of a medicare supplemental policy and that violates the HIPAA privacy regulation (as revised under subsection (a) or otherwise) with respect to the use or disclosure of genetic information shall be subject to the penalties described in sections 1320d–5 and 1320d–6 of this title in the same manner and to the same extent that such penalties apply to violations of this part.

HITECH Act Privacy Provisions

This section contains the privacy provisions in Title XIII, Subtitle D of the Health Information Technology for Economic and Clinical Health Act (HITECH Act) portion of the American Recovery and Reinvestment Act of 2009, as codified in Title 42 of the United States Code. The sections below are numbered as they appear in Subchapter III of Chapter 156 in Title 42 of the United States Code. This Appendix contains the latest version of these provisions as amended.

FROM TITLE 42—THE PUBLIC HEALTH AND WELFARE
CHAPTER 156—HEALTH INFORMATION TECHNOLOGY
SUBCHAPTER III—PRIVACY

§17921. Definitions

In this subchapter, except as specified otherwise:

(1) Breach

(A) In general

The term "breach" means the unauthorized acquisition, access, use, or disclosure of protected health information which compromises the security or privacy of such information, except where an unauthorized person to whom such information is disclosed would not reasonably have been able to retain such information.

(B) Exceptions

The term "breach" does not include—

(i) any unintentional acquisition, access, or use of protected health information by an employee or individual acting under the authority of a covered entity or business associate if—

(I)   such acquisition, access, or use was made in good faith and within the course and scope of the employment or other professional relationship of such employee or individual, respectively, with the covered entity or business associate; and

(II)   such information is not further acquired, accessed, used, or disclosed by any person; or

(ii)   any inadvertent disclosure from an individual who is otherwise authorized to access protected health information at a facility operated by a covered entity or business associate to another similarly situated individual at same facility; and

(iii)   any such information received as a result of such disclosure is not further acquired, accessed, used, or disclosed without authorization by any person.

(2) Business associate
The term "business associate" has the meaning given such term in section 160.103 of title 45, Code of Federal Regulations.

(3) Covered entity
The term "covered entity" has the meaning given such term in section 160.103 of title 45, Code of Federal Regulations.

(4) Disclose
The terms "disclose" and "disclosure" have the meaning given the term "disclosure" in section 160.103 of title 45, Code of Federal Regulations.

(5) Electronic health record
The term "electronic health record" means an electronic record of health-related information on an individual that is created, gathered, managed, and consulted by authorized health care clinicians and staff.

(6) Health care operations
The term "health care operation" has the meaning given such term in section 164.501 of title 45, Code of Federal Regulations.

(7) Health care provider
The term "health care provider" has the meaning given such term in section 160.103 of title 45, Code of Federal Regulations.

(8) Health plan

The term "health plan" has the meaning given such term in section 160.103 of title 45, Code of Federal Regulations.

(9) National Coordinator

The term "National Coordinator" means the head of the Office of the National Coordinator for Health Information Technology established under section 300jj–11(a) of this title, as added by section 13101.

(10) Payment

The term "payment" has the meaning given such term in section 164.501 of title 45, Code of Federal Regulations.

(11) Personal health record

The term "personal health record" means an electronic record of PHR identifiable health information (as defined in section 17937(f)(2) of this title) on an individual that can be drawn from multiple sources and that is managed, shared, and controlled by or primarily for the individual.

(12) Protected health information

The term "protected health information" has the meaning given such term in section 160.103 of title 45, Code of Federal Regulations.

(13) Secretary

The term "Secretary" means the Secretary of Health and Human Services.

(14) Security

The term "security" has the meaning given such term in section 164.304 of title 45, Code of Federal Regulations.

(15) State

The term "State" means each of the several States, the District of Columbia, Puerto Rico, the Virgin Islands, Guam, American Samoa, and the Northern Mariana Islands.

(16) Treatment

The term "treatment" has the meaning given such term in section 164.501 of title 45, Code of Federal Regulations.

(17) Use

The term "use" has the meaning given such term in section 160.103 of title 45, Code of Federal Regulations.

(18) Vendor of personal health records

The term "vendor of personal health records" means an entity, other than a covered entity (as defined in paragraph (3)), that offers or maintains a personal health record.

PART A—IMPROVED PRIVACY PROVISIONS AND SECURITY PROVISIONS

§17931. Application of security provisions and penalties to business associates of covered entities; annual guidance on security provisions

(a) Application of security provisions

Sections 164.308, 164.310, 164.312, and 164.316 of title 45, Code of Federal Regulations, shall apply to a business associate of a covered entity in the same manner that such sections apply to the covered entity. The additional requirements of this title that relate to security and that are made applicable with respect to covered entities shall also be applicable to such a business associate and shall be incorporated into the business associate agreement between the business associate and the covered entity.

(b) Application of civil and criminal penalties

In the case of a business associate that violates any security provision specified in subsection (a), sections 1320d–5 and 1320d–6 of this title shall apply to the business associate with respect to such violation in the same manner such sections apply to a covered entity that violates such security provision.

(c) Annual guidance

For the first year beginning after February 17, 2009, and annually thereafter, the Secretary of Health and Human Services shall, after consultation with stakeholders, annually issue guidance on the most effective and appropriate technical safeguards for use in carrying out the sections referred to in subsection (a) and the security standards in subpart C of part 164 of title 45, Code of Federal Regulations, including the use of standards developed under section 300jj–12(b)(2)(B)(vi) of this title, as added by section 13101 of this Act, as such provisions are in effect as of the date before February 17, 2009.

§17932. Notification in the case of breach

(a) In general

A covered entity that accesses, maintains, retains, modifies, records, stores, destroys, or otherwise holds, uses, or discloses unsecured protected health information (as defined in subsection (h)(1)) shall, in the case of a breach of such information that is discovered by the covered entity, notify each individual whose unsecured protected health information has been, or is reasonably believed by the covered entity to have been, accessed, acquired, or disclosed as a result of such breach.

(b) Notification of covered entity by business associate

A business associate of a covered entity that accesses, maintains, retains, modifies, records, stores, destroys, or otherwise holds, uses, or discloses unsecured protected health information shall, following the discovery of a breach of such information, notify the covered entity of such breach. Such notice shall include the identification of each individual whose unsecured protected health information has been, or is reasonably believed by the business associate to have been, accessed, acquired, or disclosed during such breach.

(c) Breaches treated as discovered

For purposes of this section, a breach shall be treated as discovered by a covered entity or by a business associate as of the first day on which such breach is known to such entity or associate, respectively, (including any person, other than the individual committing the breach, that is an employee, officer, or other agent of such entity or associate, respectively) or should reasonably have been known to such entity or associate (or person) to have occurred.

(d) Timeliness of notification

(1) In general

Subject to subsection (g), all notifications required under this section shall be made without unreasonable delay and in no case later than 60 calendar days after the discovery of a breach by the covered entity involved (or business associate involved in the case of a notification required under subsection (b)).

(2) Burden of proof

The covered entity involved (or business associate involved in the case of a notification required under subsection (b)), shall have the burden of demonstrating that all notifications were made as required under this part, including evidence demonstrating the necessity of any delay.

(e) Methods of notice

(1) Individual notice

Notice required under this section to be provided to an individual, with respect to a breach, shall be provided promptly and in the following form:

(A) Written notification by first-class mail to the individual (or the next of kin of the individual if the individual is deceased) at the last known address of the individual or the next of kin, respectively, or, if specified as a preference by the individual, by electronic mail. The notification may be provided in one or more mailings as information is available.

(B) In the case in which there is insufficient, or out-of-date contact information (including a phone number, email address, or any other form of appropriate communication) that precludes direct written (or, if specified by the individual under subparagraph (A), electronic) notification to the individual, a substitute form of notice shall be provided, including, in the case that there are 10 or more individuals for which there is insufficient or out-of-date contact information, a conspicuous posting for a period determined by the Secretary on the home page of the Web site of the covered entity involved or notice in major print or broadcast media, including major media in geographic areas where the individuals affected by the breach likely reside. Such a notice in media or web posting will include a toll-free phone number where an individual can learn whether or not the individual's unsecured protected health information is possibly included in the breach.

(C) In any case deemed by the covered entity involved to require urgency because of possible imminent misuse of unsecured protected health information, the covered entity, in addition to notice provided under subparagraph (A), may provide information to individuals by telephone or other means, as appropriate.

(2) Media notice

Notice shall be provided to prominent media outlets serving a State or jurisdiction, following the discovery of a breach described in subsection (a), if the unsecured protected health information of more than 500 residents of such State or jurisdiction is, or is reasonably believed to have been, accessed, acquired, or disclosed during such breach.

(3) Notice to Secretary

Notice shall be provided to the Secretary by covered entities of unsecured protected health information that has been acquired or disclosed in a breach. If the breach was with respect to 500 or more individuals than such notice must be provided immediately. If the breach was with respect to less than 500 individuals, the covered entity may maintain a log of any such breach occurring and annually submit such a log to the Secretary documenting such breaches occurring during the year involved.

(4) Posting on HHS public website

The Secretary shall make available to the public on the Internet website of the Department of Health and Human Services a list that identifies each covered entity involved in a breach described in subsection (a) in which the unsecured protected health information of more than 500 individuals is acquired or disclosed.

(f) Content of notification

Regardless of the method by which notice is provided to individuals under this section, notice of a breach shall include, to the extent possible, the following:

(1) A brief description of what happened, including the date of the breach and the date of the discovery of the breach, if known.

(2) A description of the types of unsecured protected health information that were involved in the breach (such as full name, Social Security number, date of birth, home address, account number, or disability code).

(3) The steps individuals should take to protect themselves from potential harm resulting from the breach.

(4) A brief description of what the covered entity involved is doing to investigate the breach, to mitigate losses, and to protect against any further breaches.

(5) Contact procedures for individuals to ask questions or learn additional information, which shall include a toll-free telephone number, an e-mail address, Web site, or postal address.

(g) Delay of notification authorized for law enforcement purposes
If a law enforcement official determines that a notification, notice, or posting required under this section would impede a criminal investigation or cause damage to national security, such notification, notice, or posting shall be delayed in the same manner as provided under section 164.528(a)(2) of title 45, Code of Federal Regulations, in the case of a disclosure covered under such section.

(h) Unsecured protected health information

(1) Definition

(A) In general
Subject to subparagraph (B), for purposes of this section, the term "unsecured protected health information" means protected health information that is not secured through the use of a technology or methodology specified by the Secretary in the guidance issued under paragraph (2).

(B) Exception in case timely guidance not issued
In the case that the Secretary does not issue guidance under paragraph (2) by the date specified in such paragraph, for purposes of this section, the term "unsecured protected health information" shall mean protected health information that is not secured by a technology standard that renders protected health information unusable, unreadable, or indecipherable to unauthorized individuals and is developed or endorsed by a standards developing organization that is accredited by the American National Standards Institute.

(2) Guidance
For purposes of paragraph (1) and section 17937(f)(3) of this title, not later than the date that is 60 days after February 17, 2009, the Secretary shall, after consultation with stakeholders, issue (and annually update) guidance specifying the technologies and methodologies that render protected health information unusable, unreadable, or indecipherable to unauthorized individuals, including the use of standards developed under section 300jj–12(b)(2)(B)(vi) of this title, as added by section 13101 of this Act.

(i) Report to Congress on breaches

(1) In general

Not later than 12 months after February 17, 2009, and annually thereafter, the Secretary shall prepare and submit to the Committee on Finance and the Committee on Health, Education, Labor, and Pensions of the Senate and the Committee on Ways and Means and the Committee on Energy and Commerce of the House of Representatives a report containing the information described in paragraph (2) regarding breaches for which notice was provided to the Secretary under subsection (e)(3).

(2) Information

The information described in this paragraph regarding breaches specified in paragraph (1) shall include—

(A) the number and nature of such breaches; and

(B) actions taken in response to such breaches.

(j) Regulations; effective date

To carry out this section, the Secretary of Health and Human Services shall promulgate interim final regulations by not later than the date that is 180 days after February 17, 2009. The provisions of this section shall apply to breaches that are discovered on or after the date that is 30 days after the date of publication of such interim final regulations.

§17933. Education on health information privacy

(a) Regional office privacy advisors

Not later than 6 months after February 17, 2009, the Secretary shall designate an individual in each regional office of the Department of Health and Human Services to offer guidance and education to covered entities, business associates, and individuals on their rights and responsibilities related to Federal privacy and security requirements for protected health information.

(b) Education initiative on uses of health information

Not later than 12 months after February 17, 2009, the Office for Civil Rights within the Department of Health and Human Services shall develop and maintain a multi-faceted national education initiative to enhance public transparency regarding the uses of protected health information, including programs to educate individuals about the potential uses of their protected health information, the effects of such uses, and the rights of individuals with respect to such uses. Such programs shall be conducted in a variety of languages and present information in a clear and understandable manner.

§17934. Application of privacy provisions and penalties to business associates of covered entities

(a) Application of contract requirements

In the case of a business associate of a covered entity that obtains or creates protected health information pursuant to a written contract (or other written arrangement) described in section 164.502(e)(2) of title 45, Code of Federal Regulations, with such covered entity, the business associate may use and disclose such protected health information only if such use or disclosure, respectively, is in compliance with each applicable requirement of section 164.504(e) of such title. The additional requirements of this subchapter that relate to privacy and that are made applicable with respect to covered entities shall also be applicable to such a business associate and shall be incorporated into the business associate agreement between the business associate and the covered entity.

(b) Application of knowledge elements associated with contracts

Section 164.504(e)(1)(ii) of title 45, Code of Federal Regulations, shall apply to a business associate described in subsection (a), with respect to compliance with such subsection, in the same manner that such section applies to a covered entity, with respect to compliance with the standards in sections 164.502(e) and 164.504(e) of such title, except that in applying such section 164.504(e)(1)(ii) each reference to the business associate, with respect to a contract, shall be treated as a reference to the covered entity involved in such contract.

(c) Application of civil and criminal penalties

In the case of a business associate that violates any provision of subsection (a) or (b), the provisions of sections 1176 and 1177 of the Social Security Act (42 U.S.C. 1320d–5, 1320d–6) shall apply to the business associate with respect to such violation in the same manner as such provisions apply to a person who violates a provision of part C of title XI of such Act [42 U.S.C. 1320d et seq.].

§17935. Restrictions on certain disclosures and sales of health information; accounting of certain protected health information disclosures; access to certain information in electronic format

(a) Requested restrictions on certain disclosures of health information

In the case that an individual requests under paragraph (a)(1)(i)(A) of section 164.522 of title 45, Code of Federal Regulations, that a covered entity restrict the disclosure of the protected health information of the individual, notwithstanding paragraph (a)(1)(ii) of such section, the covered entity must comply with the requested restriction if—

(1) except as otherwise required by law, the disclosure is to a health plan for purposes of carrying out payment or health care operations (and is not for purposes of carrying out treatment); and

(2) the protected health information pertains solely to a health care item or service for which the health care provider involved has been paid out of pocket in full.

(b) Disclosures required to be limited to the limited data set or the minimum necessary

(1) In general

(A) In general

Subject to subparagraph (B), a covered entity shall be treated as being in compliance with section 164.502(b)(1) of title 45, Code of Federal Regulations, with respect to the use, disclosure, or request of protected health information described in such section, only if the covered entity limits such protected health information, to the extent practicable, to the limited data set (as defined in section 164.514(e)(2) of such title) or, if needed by such entity, to the minimum necessary to accomplish the intended purpose of such use, disclosure, or request, respectively.

(B) Guidance

Not later than 18 months after February 17, 2009, the Secretary shall issue guidance on what constitutes "minimum necessary" for purposes of subpart E of part 164 of title 45, Code of Federal Regulation. In issuing such guidance the Secretary shall take into consideration the guidance under section 17953(c) of this title and the information necessary to improve patient outcomes and to detect, prevent, and manage chronic disease.

(C) Sunset

Subparagraph (A) shall not apply on and after the effective date on which the Secretary issues the guidance under subparagraph (B).

(2) Determination of minimum necessary

For purposes of paragraph (1), in the case of the disclosure of protected health information, the covered entity or business associate disclosing such information shall determine what constitutes the minimum necessary to accomplish the intended purpose of such disclosure.

(3) Application of exceptions

The exceptions described in section 164.502(b)(2) of title 45, Code of Federal Regulations, shall apply to the requirement under paragraph (1) as of the effective date described in section 13423 in the same manner that such exceptions apply to section 164.502(b)(1) of such title before such date.

(4) Rule of construction

Nothing in this subsection shall be construed as affecting the use, disclosure, or request of protected health information that has been de-identified.

(c) Accounting of certain protected health information disclosures required if covered entity uses electronic health record

(1) In general

In applying section 164.528 of title 45, Code of Federal Regulations, in the case that a covered entity uses or maintains an electronic health record with respect to protected health information—

(A) the exception under paragraph (a)(1)(i) of such section shall not apply to disclosures through an electronic health record made by such entity of such information; and

(B) an individual shall have a right to receive an accounting of disclosures described in such paragraph of such information made by such covered entity during only the three years prior to the date on which the accounting is requested.

(2) Regulations

The Secretary shall promulgate regulations on what information shall be collected about each disclosure referred to in paragraph (1), not later than 6 months after the date on which the Secretary adopts standards on accounting for disclosure described in the section 300jj–12(b)(2)(B)(iv) of this title, as added by section 13101. Such regulations shall only require such information to be collected through an electronic health record in a manner that takes into account the interests of the individuals in learning the circumstances under which their protected health information is being disclosed and takes into account the administrative burden of accounting for such disclosures.

(3) Process

In response to an request from an individual for an accounting, a covered entity shall elect to provide either an—

(A) accounting, as specified under paragraph (1), for disclosures of protected health information that are made by such covered entity and by a business associate acting on behalf of the covered entity; or

(B) accounting, as specified under paragraph (1), for disclosures that are made by such covered entity and provide a list of all business associates acting on behalf of the covered entity, including contact information for such associates (such as mailing address, phone, and email address).

A business associate included on a list under subparagraph (B) shall provide an accounting of disclosures (as required under paragraph (1) for a covered entity) made by the business associate upon a request made by an individual directly to the business associate for such an accounting.

(4) Effective date

(A) Current users of electronic records

In the case of a covered entity insofar as it acquired an electronic health record as of January 1, 2009, paragraph (1) shall apply to disclosures, with respect to protected health information, made by the covered entity from such a record on and after January 1, 2014.

(B) Others

In the case of a covered entity insofar as it acquires an electronic health record after January 1, 2009, paragraph (1) shall apply to disclosures, with respect to protected health information, made by the covered entity from such record on and after the later of the following:

(i)   January 1, 2011; or

(ii) the date that it acquires an electronic health record.

(C) Later date

The Secretary may set an effective date that is later that the date specified under subparagraph (A) or (B) if the Secretary determines that such later date is necessary, but in no case may the date specified under—

(i)   subparagraph (A) be later than 2016; or

(ii) subparagraph (B) be later than 2013.

(d) Prohibition on sale of electronic health records or protected health information

(1) In general

Except as provided in paragraph (2), a covered entity or business associate shall not directly or indirectly receive remuneration in exchange for any protected health information of an individual unless the covered entity obtained from the individual, in accordance with section 164.508 of title 45, Code of Federal Regulations, a valid authorization that includes, in accordance with such section, a specification of whether the protected health information can be further exchanged for remuneration by the entity receiving protected health information of that individual.

(2) Exceptions

Paragraph (1) shall not apply in the following cases:

(A) The purpose of the exchange is for public health activities (as described in section 164.512(b) of title 45, Code of Federal Regulations).

(B) The purpose of the exchange is for research (as described in sections 164.501 and 164.512(i) of title 45, Code of Federal Regulations) and the price charged reflects the costs of preparation and transmittal of the data for such purpose.

(C) The purpose of the exchange is for the treatment of the individual, subject to any regulation that the Secretary may promulgate to prevent protected health information from inappropriate access, use, or disclosure.

(D) The purpose of the exchange is the health care operation specifically described in subparagraph (iv) of paragraph (6) of the definition of healthcare operations in section 164.501 of title 45, Code of Federal Regulations.

(E) The purpose of the exchange is for remuneration that is provided by a covered entity to a business associate for activities involving the exchange of protected health information that the business associate undertakes on behalf of and at the specific request of the covered entity pursuant to a business associate agreement.

(F) The purpose of the exchange is to provide an individual with a copy of the individual's protected health information pursuant to section 164.524 of title 45, Code of Federal Regulations.

(G) The purpose of the exchange is otherwise determined by the Secretary in regulations to be similarly necessary and appropriate as the exceptions provided in subparagraphs (A) through (F).

(3) Regulations
Not later than 18 months after February 17, 2009, the Secretary shall promulgate regulations to carry out this subsection. In promulgating such regulations, the Secretary—

(A) shall evaluate the impact of restricting the exception described in paragraph (2)(A) to require that the price charged for the purposes described in such paragraph reflects the costs of the preparation and transmittal of the data for such purpose, on research or public health activities, including those conducted by or for the use of the Food and Drug Administration; and

(B) may further restrict the exception described in paragraph (2)(A) to require that the price charged for the purposes described in such paragraph reflects the costs of the preparation and transmittal of the data for such purpose, if the Secretary finds that such further restriction will not impede such research or public health activities.

(4) Effective date
Paragraph (1) shall apply to exchanges occurring on or after the date that is 6 months after the date of the promulgation of final regulations implementing this subsection.

(e) Access to certain information in electronic format
In applying section 164.524 of title 45, Code of Federal Regulations, in the case that a covered entity uses or maintains an electronic health record with respect to protected health information of an individual—

(1) the individual shall have a right to obtain from such covered entity a copy of such information in an electronic format and, if the individual chooses, to direct the covered entity to transmit such copy directly to an entity or person designated by the individual, provided that any such choice is clear, conspicuous, and specific; and

(2) notwithstanding paragraph (c)(4) of such section, any fee that the covered entity may impose for providing such individual with a copy of such information (or a summary or explanation of such information) if such copy (or summary or explanation) is in an electronic form shall not be greater than the entity's labor costs in responding to the request for the copy (or summary or explanation).

§17936. Conditions on certain contacts as part of health care operations

(a) Marketing

(1) In general
A communication by a covered entity or business associate that is about a product or service and that encourages recipients of the communication to purchase or use the product or service shall not be considered a health care operation for purposes of subpart E of part 164 of title 45, Code of Federal Regulations, unless the communication is made as described in subparagraph (i), (ii), or (iii) of paragraph (1) of the definition of marketing in section 164.501 of such title.

(2) Payment for certain communications

A communication by a covered entity or business associate that is described in subparagraph (i), (ii), or (iii) of paragraph (1) of the definition of marketing in section 164.501 of title 45, Code of Federal Regulations, shall not be considered a health care operation for purposes of subpart E of part 164 of title 45, Code of Federal Regulations if the covered entity receives or has received direct or indirect payment in exchange for making such communication, except where—

(A)(i)   such communication describes only a drug or biologic that is currently being prescribed for the recipient of the communication; and

(ii) any payment received by such covered entity in exchange for making a communication described in clause (i) is reasonable in amount;

(B)   each of the following conditions apply—

(i)   the communication is made by the covered entity; and

(ii) the covered entity making such communication obtains from the recipient of the communication, in accordance with section 164.508 of title 45, Code of Federal Regulations, a valid authorization (as described in paragraph (b) of such section) with respect to such communication; or

(C)   each of the following conditions apply—

(i)   the communication is made by a business associate on behalf of the covered entity; and

(ii) the communication is consistent with the written contract (or other written arrangement described in section 164.502(e)(2) of such title) between such business associate and covered entity.

(3) Reasonable in amount defined

For purposes of paragraph (2), the term "reasonable in amount" shall have the meaning given such term by the Secretary by regulation.

(4) Direct or indirect payment

For purposes of paragraph (2), the term "direct or indirect payment" shall not include any payment for treatment (as defined in section 164.501 of title 45, Code of Federal Regulations) of an individual.

(b) Opportunity to opt out of fundraising

The Secretary shall by rule provide that any written fundraising communication that is a healthcare operation as defined under section 164.501 of title 45, Code of Federal Regulations, shall, in a clear and conspicuous manner, provide an opportunity for the recipient of the communications to elect not to receive any further such communication. When an individual elects not to receive any further such communication, such election shall be treated as a revocation of authorization under section 164.508 of title 45, Code of Federal Regulations.

(c) Effective date

This section shall apply to written communications occurring on or after the effective date specified under section 13423.

§17937. Temporary breach notification requirement for vendors of personal health records and other non-HIPAA covered entities

(a) In general

In accordance with subsection (c), each vendor of personal health records, following the discovery of a breach of security of unsecured PHR identifiable health information that is in a personal health record maintained or offered by such vendor, and each entity described in clause (ii), (iii), or (iv) of section 17953(b)(1)(A) of this title, following the discovery of a breach of security of such information that is obtained through a product or service provided by such entity, shall—

(1) notify each individual who is a citizen or resident of the United States whose unsecured PHR identifiable health information was acquired by an unauthorized person as a result of such a breach of security; and

(2) notify the Federal Trade Commission.

(b) Notification by third party service providers

A third party service provider that provides services to a vendor of personal health records or to an entity described in clause (ii), (iii), or (iv) of section 17953(b)(1)(A) of this title in connection with the offering or maintenance of a personal health record or a related product or service and that accesses, maintains, retains, modifies, records, stores, destroys, or otherwise holds, uses, or discloses unsecured PHR identifiable health information in such a record as a result of such services shall, following the discovery of a breach of security of such information, notify such vendor or entity, respectively, of such breach. Such notice shall include the identification of each individual whose unsecured PHR identifiable health information has been, or is reasonably believed to have been, accessed, acquired, or disclosed during such breach.

(c) Application of requirements for timeliness, method, and content of notifications
Subsections (c), (d), (e), and (f) of section 17932 of this title shall apply to a notification required under subsection (a) and a vendor of personal health records, an entity described in subsection (a) and a third party service provider described in subsection (b), with respect to a breach of security under subsection (a) of unsecured PHR identifiable health information in such records maintained or offered by such vendor, in a manner specified by the Federal Trade Commission.

(d) Notification of the Secretary
Upon receipt of a notification of a breach of security under subsection (a)(2), the Federal Trade Commission shall notify the Secretary of such breach.

(e) Enforcement
A violation of subsection (a) or (b) shall be treated as an unfair and deceptive act or practice in violation of a regulation under section 57a(a)(1)(B) of title 15 regarding unfair or deceptive acts or practices.

(f) Definitions
For purposes of this section:

(1) Breach of security
The term "breach of security" means, with respect to unsecured PHR identifiable health information of an individual in a personal health record, acquisition of such information without the authorization of the individual.

(2) PHR identifiable health information
The term "PHR identifiable health information" means individually identifiable health information, as defined in section 1320d(6)

of this title, and includes, with respect to an individual, information—

(A) that is provided by or on behalf of the individual; and

(B) that identifies the individual or with respect to which there is a reasonable basis to believe that the information can be used to identify the individual.

(3) Unsecured PHR identifiable health information

(A) In general
Subject to subparagraph (B), the term "unsecured PHR identifiable health information" means PHR identifiable health information that is not protected through the use of a technology or methodology specified by the Secretary in the guidance issued under section 17932(h)(2) of this title.

(B) Exception in case timely guidance not issued
In the case that the Secretary does not issue guidance under section 17932(h)(2) of this title by the date specified in such section, for purposes of this section, the term "unsecured PHR identifiable health information" shall mean PHR identifiable health information that is not secured by a technology standard that renders protected health information unusable, unreadable, or indecipherable to unauthorized individuals and that is developed or endorsed by a standards developing organization that is accredited by the American National Standards Institute.

(g) Regulations; effective date; sunset

(1) Regulations; effective date
To carry out this section, the Federal Trade Commission shall promulgate interim final regulations by not later than the date that is 180 days after February 17, 2009. The provisions of this section shall apply to breaches of security that are discovered on or after the date that is 30 days after the date of publication of such interim final regulations.

(2) Sunset
If Congress enacts new legislation establishing requirements for notification in the case of a breach of security, that apply to entities that are not covered entities or business associates, the provisions of this section shall not apply to breaches of security discovered on or after the effective date of regulations implementing such legislation.

§17938. Business associate contracts required for certain entities

Each organization, with respect to a covered entity, that provides data transmission of protected health information to such entity (or its business associate) and that requires access on a routine basis to such protected health information, such as a Health Information Exchange Organization, Regional Health Information Organization, E-prescribing Gateway, or each vendor that contracts with a covered entity to allow that covered entity to offer a personal health record to patients as part of its electronic health record, is required to enter into a written contract (or other written arrangement) described in section 164.502(e)(2) of title 45, Code of Federal Regulations and a written contract (or other arrangement) described in section 164.308(b) of such title, with such entity and shall be treated as a business associate of the covered entity for purposes of the provisions of this subchapter and subparts C and E of part 164 of title 45, Code of Federal Regulations, as such provisions are in effect as of February 17, 2009.

§17939. Improved enforcement

(a) **In general**

   (1) **Omitted**

   (2) **Enforcement under Social Security Act**
   Any violation by a covered entity under thus subchapter is subject to enforcement and penalties under section 1176 and 1177 of the Social Security Act [42 U.S.C. 1320d–5, 1320d–6].

(b) **Effective date; regulations**

   (1) The amendments made by subsection (a) shall apply to penalties imposed on or after the date that is 24 months after February 17, 2009.

   (2) Not later than 18 months after February 17, 2009, the Secretary of Health and Human Services shall promulgate regulations to implement such amendments.

(c) **Distribution of certain civil monetary penalties collected**

   (1) **In general**
   Subject to the regulation promulgated pursuant to paragraph (3), any civil monetary penalty or monetary settlement collected with respect

to an offense punishable under this subchapter or section 1176 of the Social Security Act (42 U.S.C. 1320d–5) insofar as such section relates to privacy or security shall be transferred to the Office for Civil Rights of the Department of Health and Human Services to be used for purposes of enforcing the provisions of this subchapter and subparts C and E of part 164 of title 45, Code of Federal Regulations, as such provisions are in effect as of February 17, 2009.

(2) GAO report
Not later than 18 months after February 17, 2009, the Comptroller General shall submit to the Secretary a report including recommendations for a methodology under which an individual who is harmed by an act that constitutes an offense referred to in paragraph (1) may receive a percentage of any civil monetary penalty or monetary settlement collected with respect to such offense.

(3) Establishment of methodology to distribute percentage of CMPS collected to harmed individuals
Not later than 3 years after February 17, 2009, the Secretary shall establish by regulation and based on the recommendations submitted under paragraph (2), a methodology under which an individual who is harmed by an act that constitutes an offense referred to in paragraph (1) may receive a percentage of any civil monetary penalty or monetary settlement collected with respect to such offense.

(4) Application of methodology
The methodology under paragraph (3) shall be applied with respect to civil monetary penalties or monetary settlements imposed on or after the effective date of the regulation.

(d) Tiered increase in amount of civil monetary penalties

(1) to (3) Omitted

(4) Effective date
The amendments made by this subsection shall apply to violations occurring after February 17, 2009.

(e) Enforcement through State attorneys general

(1), (2) Omitted

(3) Effective date
The amendments made by this subsection shall apply to violations occurring after February 17, 2009.

§17940. Audits

The Secretary shall provide for periodic audits to ensure that covered entities and business associates that are subject to the requirements of this subchapter and subparts C and E of part 164 of title 45, Code of Federal Regulations, as such provisions are in effect as of February 17, 2009, comply with such requirements.

PART B—RELATIONSHIP TO OTHER LAWS; REGULATORY REFERENCES; EFFECTIVE DATE; REPORTS

§17951. Relationship to other laws

(a) Application of HIPAA State preemption

Section 1178 of the Social Security Act (42 U.S.C. 1320d–7) shall apply to a provision or requirement under this subchapter in the same manner that such section applies to a provision or requirement under part C of title XI of such Act [42 U.S.C. 1320d et seq.] or a standard or implementation specification adopted or established under sections 1172 through 1174 of such Act [42 U.S.C. 1320d–1 to 1320d–3].

(b) Health Insurance Portability and Accountability Act of 1996

The standards governing the privacy and security of individually identifiable health information promulgated by the Secretary under sections 262(a) and 264 of the Health Insurance Portability and Accountability Act of 1996 shall remain in effect to the extent that they are consistent with this subchapter. The Secretary shall by rule amend such Federal regulations as required to make such regulations consistent with this subchapter.

(c) Construction

Nothing in this subchapter shall constitute a waiver of any privilege otherwise applicable to an individual with respect to the protected health information of such individual.

§17952. Regulatory references

Each reference in this subchapter to a provision of the Code of Federal Regulations refers to such provision as in effect on February 17, 2009 (or to the most recent update of such provision).

§17953. Studies, reports, guidance

(a) Report on compliance

(1) In general

For the first year beginning after February 17, 2009, and annually thereafter, the Secretary shall prepare and submit to the Committee on Health, Education, Labor, and Pensions of the Senate and the Committee on Ways and Means and the Committee on Energy and Commerce of the House of Representatives a report concerning complaints of alleged violations of law, including the provisions of this subchapter as well as the provisions of subparts C and E of part 164 of title 45, Code of Federal Regulations, (as such provisions are in effect as of February 17, 2009) relating to privacy and security of health information that are received by the Secretary during the year for which the report is being prepared. Each such report shall include, with respect to such complaints received during the year—

(A) the number of such complaints;

(B) the number of such complaints resolved informally, a summary of the types of such complaints so resolved, and the number of covered entities that received technical assistance from the Secretary during such year in order to achieve compliance with such provisions and the types of such technical assistance provided;

(C) the number of such complaints that have resulted in the imposition of civil monetary penalties or have been resolved through monetary settlements, including the nature of the complaints involved and the amount paid in each penalty or settlement;

(D) the number of compliance reviews conducted and the outcome of each such review;

(E) the number of subpoenas or inquiries issued;

(F) the Secretary's plan for improving compliance with and enforcement of such provisions for the following year; and

(G) the number of audits performed and a summary of audit findings pursuant to section 17940 of this title.

(2) Availability to public

Each report under paragraph (1) shall be made available to the public on the Internet website of the Department of Health and Human Services.

(b) Study and report on application of privacy and security requirements to non-HIPAA covered entities

(1) Study

Not later than one year after February 17, 2009, the Secretary, in consultation with the Federal Trade Commission, shall conduct a study, and submit a report under paragraph (2), on privacy and security requirements for entities that are not covered entities or business associates as of February 17, 2009, including—

> (A) requirements relating to security, privacy, and notification in the case of a breach of security or privacy (including the applicability of an exemption to notification in the case of individually identifiable health information that has been rendered unusable, unreadable, or indecipherable through technologies or methodologies recognized by appropriate professional organization or standard setting bodies to provide effective security for the information) that should be applied to—
>
> > (i) vendors of personal health records;
> >
> > (ii) entities that offer products or services through the website of a vendor of personal health records;
> >
> > (iii) entities that are not covered entities and that offer products or services through the websites of covered entities that offer individuals personal health records;
> >
> > (iv) entities that are not covered entities and that access information in a personal health record or send information to a personal health record; and
> >
> > (v) third party service providers used by a vendor or entity described in clause (i), (ii), (iii), or (iv) to assist in providing personal health record products or services;
>
> (B) a determination of which Federal government agency is best equipped to enforce such requirements recommended to be applied to such vendors, entities, and service providers under subparagraph (A); and

(C) a timeframe for implementing regulations based on such findings.

(2) Report
The Secretary shall submit to the Committee on Finance, the Committee on Health, Education, Labor, and Pensions, and the Committee on Commerce of the Senate and the Committee on Ways and Means and the Committee on Energy and Commerce of the House of Representatives a report on the findings of the study under paragraph (1) and shall include in such report recommendations on the privacy and security requirements described in such paragraph.

(c) Guidance on implementation specification to de-identify protected health information
Not later than 12 months after February 17, 2009, the Secretary shall, in consultation with stakeholders, issue guidance on how best to implement the requirements for the de-identification of protected health information under section 164.514(b) of title 45, Code of Federal Regulations.

(d) GAO report on treatment disclosures
Not later than one year after February 17, 2009, the Comptroller General of the United States shall submit to the Committee on Health, Education, Labor, and Pensions of the Senate and the Committee on Ways and Means and the Committee on Energy and Commerce of the House of Representatives a report on the best practices related to the disclosure among health care providers of protected health information of an individual for purposes of treatment of such individual. Such report shall include an examination of the best practices implemented by States and by other entities, such as health information exchanges and regional health information organizations, an examination of the extent to which such best practices are successful with respect to the quality of the resulting health care provided to the individual and with respect to the ability of the health care provider to manage such best practices, and an examination of the use of electronic informed consent for disclosing protected health information for treatment, payment, and health care operations.

(e) Report required
Not later than 5 years after February 17, 2009, the Government Accountability Office shall submit to Congress and the Secretary of

Health and Human Services a report on the impact of any of the provisions of this Act on health insurance premiums, overall health care costs, adoption of electronic health records by providers, and reduction in medical errors and other quality improvements.

(f) Study

The Secretary shall study the definition of "psychotherapy notes" in section 164.501 of title 45, Code of Federal Regulations, with regard to including test data that is related to direct responses, scores, items, forms, protocols, manuals, or other materials that are part of a mental health evaluation, as determined by the mental health professional providing treatment or evaluation in such definitions and may, based on such study, issue regulations to revise such definition.

Regulations Establishing General Administrative Requirements

45 C.F.R. PART 160

This Appendix contains the provisions of 45 C.F.R. Part 160, which are the General Administrative Requirements of Subchapter C of Subtitle A of Title 45 of the Code of Federal Regulations. Part 160 covers the general provisions of the administrative data standards and related requirements of Subchapter C. Its general provisions in Subpart A cover the scope and applicability of Subchapter C, definitions that apply to the entire Subchapter, and compliance dates. Subpart B discusses the preemptive effect of regulations in Subchapter C.

The remainder of Subchapter C concerns enforcement. Subpart C establishes procedures by which HHS promotes compliance with the administrative simplification provisions, including those covering security and privacy. It also covers complaints, HHS compliance reviews, and HHS investigations. Subpart D describes the basis and amount of civil money penalties HHS can impose for HIPAA violations. Subpart E concerns procedures for conducting hearings by which a party can challenge a Notice of Proposed Determination in which HHS states its intention to penalize it. It also governs procedures for appeal to the HHS Departmental Appeals Board and judicial review in a U.S. Court of Appeals.

SUBPART A—GENERAL PROVISIONS

§160.101 Statutory basis and purpose.

The requirements of this subchapter implement sections 1171–1180 of the Social Security Act (the Act), sections 262 and 264 of Public

Law 104-191, section 105 of Public Law 110-233, sections 13400–13424 of Public Law 111-5, and section 1104 of Public Law 111-148.

[78 FR 5687, Jan. 25, 2013]

§160.102 Applicability.

(a) Except as otherwise provided, the standards, requirements, and implementation specifications adopted under this subchapter apply to the following entities:

(1) A health plan.

(2) A health care clearinghouse.

(3) A health care provider who transmits any health information in electronic form in connection with a transaction covered by this subchapter.

(b) Where provided, the standards, requirements, and implementation specifications adopted under this subchapter apply to a business associate.

(c) To the extent required under the Social Security Act, 42 U.S.C. 1320a-7c(a)(5), nothing in this subchapter shall be construed to diminish the authority of any Inspector General, including such authority as provided in the Inspector General Act of 1978, as amended (5 U.S.C. App.).

[65 FR 82798, Dec. 28, 2000, as amended at 67 FR 53266, Aug. 14, 2002; 78 FR 5687, Jan. 25, 2013]

§160.103 Definitions.

Except as otherwise provided, the following definitions apply to this subchapter:

Act means the Social Security Act.

Administrative simplification provision means any requirement or prohibition established by:

(1) 42 U.S.C. 1320d-1320d-4, 1320d-7, 1320d-8, and 1320d-9;

(2) Section 264 of Pub. L. 104-191;

(3) Sections 13400–13424 of Public Law 111-5; or

(4) This subchapter.

ALJ means Administrative Law Judge.

ANSI stands for the American National Standards Institute.

Business associate: (1) Except as provided in paragraph (4) of this definition, business associate means, with respect to a covered entity, a person who:

(i)   On behalf of such covered entity or of an organized health care arrangement (as defined in this section) in which the covered entity participates, but other than in the capacity of a member of the workforce of such covered entity or arrangement, creates, receives, maintains, or transmits protected health information for a function or activity regulated by this subchapter, including claims processing or administration, data analysis, processing or administration, utilization review, quality assurance, patient safety activities listed at 42 CFR 3.20, billing, benefit management, practice management, and repricing; or

(ii)   Provides, other than in the capacity of a member of the workforce of such covered entity, legal, actuarial, accounting, consulting, data aggregation (as defined in §164.501 of this subchapter), management, administrative, accreditation, or financial services to or for such covered entity, or to or for an organized health care arrangement in which the covered entity participates, where the provision of the service involves the disclosure of protected health information from such covered entity or arrangement, or from another business associate of such covered entity or arrangement, to the person.

(2)   A covered entity may be a business associate of another covered entity.

(3)   Business associate includes:

(i)   A Health Information Organization, E-prescribing Gateway, or other person that provides data transmission services with respect to protected health information to a covered entity and that requires access on a routine basis to such protected health information.

(ii)   A person that offers a personal health record to one or more individuals on behalf of a covered entity.

(iii) A subcontractor that creates, receives, maintains, or transmits protected health information on behalf of the business associate.

(4) *Business associate* does not include:

(i) A health care provider, with respect to disclosures by a covered entity to the health care provider concerning the treatment of the individual.

(ii) A plan sponsor, with respect to disclosures by a group health plan (or by a health insurance issuer or HMO with respect to a group health plan) to the plan sponsor, to the extent that the requirements of §164.504(f) of this subchapter apply and are met.

(iii) A government agency, with respect to determining eligibility for, or enrollment in, a government health plan that provides public benefits and is administered by another government agency, or collecting protected health information for such purposes, to the extent such activities are authorized by law.

(iv) A covered entity participating in an organized health care arrangement that performs a function or activity as described by paragraph (1)(i) of this definition for or on behalf of such organized health care arrangement, or that provides a service as described in paragraph (1)(ii) of this definition to or for such organized health care arrangement by virtue of such activities or services.

Civil money penalty or *penalty* means the amount determined under §160.404 of this part and includes the plural of these terms.

CMS stands for Centers for Medicare & Medicaid Services within the Department of Health and Human Services.

Compliance date means the date by which a covered entity or business associate must comply with a standard, implementation specification, requirement, or modification adopted under this subchapter.

Covered entity means:

(1) A health plan.

(2) A health care clearinghouse.

(3) A health care provider who transmits any health information in electronic form in connection with a transaction covered by this subchapter.

Disclosure means the release, transfer, provision of access to, or divulging in any manner of information outside the entity holding the information.

EIN stands for the employer identification number assigned by the Internal Revenue Service, U.S. Department of the Treasury. The EIN is the taxpayer identifying number of an individual or other entity (whether or not an employer) assigned under one of the following:

(1) 26 U.S.C. 6011(b), which is the portion of the Internal Revenue Code dealing with identifying the taxpayer in tax returns and statements, or corresponding provisions of prior law.

(2) 26 U.S.C. 6109, which is the portion of the Internal Revenue Code dealing with identifying numbers in tax returns, statements, and other required documents.

Electronic media means:

(1) Electronic storage material on which data is or may be recorded electronically, including, for example, devices in computers (hard drives) and any removable/transportable digital memory medium, such as magnetic tape or disk, optical disk, or digital memory card;

(2) Transmission media used to exchange information already in electronic storage media. Transmission media include, for example, the Internet, extranet or intranet, leased lines, dial-up lines, private networks, and the physical movement of removable/transportable electronic storage media. Certain transmissions, including of paper, via facsimile, and of voice, via telephone, are not considered to be transmissions via electronic media if the information being exchanged did not exist in electronic form immediately before the transmission.

Electronic protected health information means information that comes within paragraphs (1)(i) or (1)(ii) of the definition of *protected health information* as specified in this section.

Employer is defined as it is in 26 U.S.C. 3401(d).

Family member means, with respect to an individual:

(1) A dependent (as such term is defined in 45 CFR 144.103), of the individual; or

(2) Any other person who is a first-degree, second-degree, third-degree, or fourth-degree relative of the individual or of a dependent

of the individual. Relatives by affinity (such as by marriage or adoption) are treated the same as relatives by consanguinity (that is, relatives who share a common biological ancestor). In determining the degree of the relationship, relatives by less than full consanguinity (such as half-siblings, who share only one parent) are treated the same as relatives by full consanguinity (such as siblings who share both parents).

(i) First-degree relatives include parents, spouses, siblings, and children.

(ii) Second-degree relatives include grandparents, grandchildren, aunts, uncles, nephews, and nieces.

(iii) Third-degree relatives include great-grandparents, great-grandchildren, great aunts, great uncles, and first cousins.

(iv) Fourth-degree relatives include great-great grandparents, great-great grandchildren, and children of first cousins.

Genetic information means:

(1) Subject to paragraphs (2) and (3) of this definition, with respect to an individual, information about:

(i) The individual's genetic tests;

(ii) The genetic tests of family members of the individual;

(iii) The manifestation of a disease or disorder in family members of such individual; or

(iv) Any request for, or receipt of, genetic services, or participation in clinical research which includes genetic services, by the individual or any family member of the individual.

(2) Any reference in this subchapter to genetic information concerning an individual or family member of an individual shall include the genetic information of:

(i) A fetus carried by the individual or family member who is a pregnant woman; and

(ii) Any embryo legally held by an individual or family member utilizing an assisted reproductive technology.

(3) Genetic information excludes information about the sex or age of any individual.

Genetic services means:

(1) A genetic test;

(2) Genetic counseling (including obtaining, interpreting, or assessing genetic information); or

(3) Genetic education.

Genetic test means an analysis of human DNA, RNA, chromosomes, proteins, or metabolites, if the analysis detects genotypes, mutations, or chromosomal changes. Genetic test does not include an analysis of proteins or metabolites that is directly related to a manifested disease, disorder, or pathological condition.

Group health plan (also see definition of *health plan* in this section) means an employee welfare benefit plan (as defined in section 3(1) of the Employee Retirement Income and Security Act of 1974 (ERISA), 29 U.S.C. 1002(1)), including insured and self-insured plans, to the extent that the plan provides medical care (as defined in section 2791(a)(2) of the Public Health Service Act (PHS Act), 42 U.S.C. 300gg-91(a)(2)), including items and services paid for as medical care, to employees or their dependents directly or through insurance, reimbursement, or otherwise, that:

(1) Has 50 or more participants (as defined in section 3(7) of ERISA, 29 U.S.C. 1002(7)); or

(2) Is administered by an entity other than the employer that established and maintains the plan.

HHS stands for the Department of Health and Human Services.

Health care means care, services, or supplies related to the health of an individual. *Health care* includes, but is not limited to, the following:

(1) Preventive, diagnostic, therapeutic, rehabilitative, maintenance, or palliative care, and counseling, service, assessment, or procedure with respect to the physical or mental condition, or functional status, of an individual or that affects the structure or function of the body; and

(2) Sale or dispensing of a drug, device, equipment, or other item in accordance with a prescription.

Health care clearinghouse means a public or private entity, including a billing service, repricing company, community health management information system or community health information system, and "value-added" networks and switches, that does either of the following functions:

(1) Processes or facilitates the processing of health information received from another entity in a nonstandard format or containing nonstandard data content into standard data elements or a standard transaction.

(2) Receives a standard transaction from another entity and processes or facilitates the processing of health information into nonstandard format or nonstandard data content for the receiving entity.

Health care provider means a provider of services (as defined in section 1861(u) of the Act, 42 U.S.C. 1395x(u)), a provider of medical or health services (as defined in section 1861(s) of the Act, 42 U.S.C. 1395x(s)), and any other person or organization who furnishes, bills, or is paid for health care in the normal course of business.

Health information means any information, including genetic information, whether oral or recorded in any form or medium, that:

(1) Is created or received by a health care provider, health plan, public health authority, employer, life insurer, school or university, or health care clearinghouse; and

(2) Relates to the past, present, or future physical or mental health or condition of an individual; the provision of health care to an individual; or the past, present, or future payment for the provision of health care to an individual.

Health insurance issuer (as defined in section 2791(b)(2) of the PHS Act, 42 U.S.C. 300gg-91(b)(2) and used in the definition of *health plan* in this section) means an insurance company, insurance service, or insurance organization (including an HMO) that is licensed to engage in the business of insurance in a State and is subject to State law that regulates insurance. Such term does not include a group health plan.

Health maintenance organization (HMO) (as defined in section 2791(b) (3) of the PHS Act, 42 U.S.C. 300gg-91(b)(3) and used in the definition of *health plan* in this section) means a federally qualified HMO, an organization recognized as an HMO under State law, or a similar organization regulated for solvency under State law in the same manner and to the same extent as such an HMO.

Health plan means an individual or group plan that provides, or pays the cost of, medical care (as defined in section 2791(a)(2) of the PHS Act, 42 U.S.C. 300gg-91(a)(2)).

(1) *Health plan* includes the following, singly or in combination:

(i) A group health plan, as defined in this section.

(ii) A health insurance issuer, as defined in this section.

(iii) An HMO, as defined in this section.

(iv) Part A or Part B of the Medicare program under title XVIII of the Act.

(v) The Medicaid program under title XIX of the Act, 42 U.S.C. 1396, *et seq.*

(vi) The Voluntary Prescription Drug Benefit Program under Part D of title XVIII of the Act, 42 U.S.C. 1395w-101 through 1395w-152.

(vii) An issuer of a Medicare supplemental policy (as defined in section 1882(g)(1) of the Act, 42 U.S.C. 1395ss(g)(1)).

(viii) An issuer of a long-term care policy, excluding a nursing home fixed indemnity policy.

(ix) An employee welfare benefit plan or any other arrangement that is established or maintained for the purpose of offering or providing health benefits to the employees of two or more employers.

(x) The health care program for uniformed services under title 10 of the United States Code.

(xi) The veterans health care program under 38 U.S.C. chapter 17.

(xii) The Indian Health Service program under the Indian Health Care Improvement Act, 25 U.S.C. 1601, *et seq.*

(xiii) The Federal Employees Health Benefits Program under 5 U.S.C. 8902, *et seq.*

(xiv) An approved State child health plan under title XXI of the Act, providing benefits for child health assistance that meet the requirements of section 2103 of the Act, 42 U.S.C. 1397, *et seq.*

(xv) The Medicare Advantage program under Part C of title XVIII of the Act, 42 U.S.C. 1395w-21 through 1395w-28.

(xvi) A high risk pool that is a mechanism established under State law to provide health insurance coverage or comparable coverage to eligible individuals.

(xvii) Any other individual or group plan, or combination of individual or group plans, that provides or pays for the cost of medical care (as defined in section 2791(a)(2) of the PHS Act, 42 U.S.C. 300gg-91(a)(2)).

(2) *Health plan* excludes:

(i) Any policy, plan, or program to the extent that it provides, or pays for the cost of, excepted benefits that are listed in section 2791(c)(1) of the PHS Act, 42 U.S.C. 300gg-91(c)(1); and

(ii) A government-funded program (other than one listed in paragraph (1)(i)–(xvi) of this definition):

(A) Whose principal purpose is other than providing, or paying the cost of, health care; or

(B) Whose principal activity is:

(1) The direct provision of health care to persons; or

(2) The making of grants to fund the direct provision of health care to persons.

Implementation specification means specific requirements or instructions for implementing a standard.

Individual means the person who is the subject of protected health information.

Individually identifiable health information is information that is a subset of health information, including demographic information collected from an individual, and:

(1) Is created or received by a health care provider, health plan, employer, or health care clearinghouse; and

(2) Relates to the past, present, or future physical or mental health or condition of an individual; the provision of health care to an individual; or the past, present, or future payment for the provision of health care to an individual; and

(i)   That identifies the individual; or

(ii)   With respect to which there is a reasonable basis to believe the information can be used to identify the individual.

Manifestation or *manifested* means, with respect to a disease, disorder, or pathological condition, that an individual has been or could reasonably be diagnosed with the disease, disorder, or pathological condition by a health care professional with appropriate training and expertise in the field of medicine involved. For purposes of this subchapter, a disease, disorder, or pathological condition is not manifested if the diagnosis is based principally on genetic information.

Modify or *modification* refers to a change adopted by the Secretary, through regulation, to a standard or an implementation specification.

Organized health care arrangement means:

(1)   A clinically integrated care setting in which individuals typically receive health care from more than one health care provider;

(2)   An organized system of health care in which more than one covered entity participates and in which the participating covered entities:

(i)   Hold themselves out to the public as participating in a joint arrangement; and

(ii)   Participate in joint activities that include at least one of the following:

(A)   Utilization review, in which health care decisions by participating covered entities are reviewed by other participating covered entities or by a third party on their behalf;

(B)   Quality assessment and improvement activities, in which treatment provided by participating covered entities is assessed by other participating covered entities or by a third party on their behalf; or

(C)   Payment activities, if the financial risk for delivering health care is shared, in part or in whole, by participating covered entities through the joint arrangement and if protected health information created or received by a covered entity is reviewed by other participating covered entities or by a third party on their behalf for the purpose of administering the sharing of financial risk.

(3) A group health plan and a health insurance issuer or HMO with respect to such group health plan, but only with respect to protected health information created or received by such health insurance issuer or HMO that relates to individuals who are or who have been participants or beneficiaries in such group health plan;

(4) A group health plan and one or more other group health plans each of which are maintained by the same plan sponsor; or

(5) The group health plans described in paragraph (4) of this definition and health insurance issuers or HMOs with respect to such group health plans, but only with respect to protected health information created or received by such health insurance issuers or HMOs that relates to individuals who are or have been participants or beneficiaries in any of such group health plans.

Person means a natural person, trust or estate, partnership, corporation, professional association or corporation, or other entity, public or private.

Protected health information means individually identifiable health information:

(1) Except as provided in paragraph (2) of this definition, that is:

    (i)   Transmitted by electronic media;

    (ii) Maintained in electronic media; or

    (iii) Transmitted or maintained in any other form or medium.

(2) Protected health information excludes individually identifiable health information:

    (i)   In education records covered by the Family Educational Rights and Privacy Act, as amended, 20 U.S.C. 1232g;

    (ii) In records described at 20 U.S.C. 1232g(a)(4)(B)(iv);

    (iii) In employment records held by a covered entity in its role as employer; and

    (iv) Regarding a person who has been deceased for more than 50 years.

Respondent means a covered entity or business associate upon which the Secretary has imposed, or proposes to impose, a civil money penalty.

Small health plan means a health plan with annual receipts of $5 million or less.

Standard means a rule, condition, or requirement:

(1) Describing the following information for products, systems, services, or practices:

  (i) Classification of components;

  (ii) Specification of materials, performance, or operations; or

  (iii) Delineation of procedures; or

(2) With respect to the privacy of protected health information.

Standard setting organization (SSO) means an organization accredited by the American National Standards Institute that develops and maintains standards for information transactions or data elements, or any other standard that is necessary for, or will facilitate the implementation of, this part.

State refers to one of the following:

(1) For a health plan established or regulated by Federal law, State has the meaning set forth in the applicable section of the United States Code for such health plan.

(2) For all other purposes, *State* means any of the several States, the District of Columbia, the Commonwealth of Puerto Rico, the Virgin Islands, Guam, American Samoa, and the Commonwealth of the Northern Mariana Islands.

Subcontractor means a person to whom a business associate delegates a function, activity, or service, other than in the capacity of a member of the workforce of such business associate.

Trading partner agreement means an agreement related to the exchange of information in electronic transactions, whether the agreement is distinct or part of a larger agreement, between each party to the agreement. (For example, a trading partner agreement may specify, among other things, the duties and responsibilities of each party to the agreement in conducting a standard transaction.)

Transaction means the transmission of information between two parties to carry out financial or administrative activities related to health care. It includes the following types of information transmissions:

(1) Health care claims or equivalent encounter information.

(2) Health care payment and remittance advice.

(3) Coordination of benefits.

(4) Health care claim status.

(5) Enrollment and disenrollment in a health plan.

(6) Eligibility for a health plan.

(7) Health plan premium payments.

(8) Referral certification and authorization.

(9) First report of injury.

(10) Health claims attachments.

(11) Health care electronic funds transfers (EFT) and remittance advice.

(12) Other transactions that the Secretary may prescribe by regulation.

Use means, with respect to individually identifiable health information, the sharing, employment, application, utilization, examination, or analysis of such information within an entity that maintains such information.

Violation or *violate* means, as the context may require, failure to comply with an administrative simplification provision.

Workforce means employees, volunteers, trainees, and other persons whose conduct, in the performance of work for a covered entity or business associate, is under the direct control of such covered entity or business associate, whether or not they are paid by the covered entity or business associate.

[65 FR 82798, Dec. 28, 2000, as amended at 67 FR 38019, May 31, 2002; 67 FR 53266, Aug. 14, 2002; 68 FR 8374, Feb. 20, 2003; 71 FR 8424, Feb. 16, 2006; 76 FR 40495, July 8, 2011; 77 FR 1589, Jan. 10, 2012; 78 FR 5687, Jan. 25, 2013]

§160.104 Modifications.

(a) Except as provided in paragraph (b) of this section, the Secretary may adopt a modification to a standard or implementation specification adopted under this subchapter no more frequently than once every 12 months.

(b) The Secretary may adopt a modification at any time during the first year after the standard or implementation specification is initially adopted, if the Secretary determines that the modification is necessary to permit compliance with the standard or implementation specification.

(c) The Secretary will establish the compliance date for any standard or implementation specification modified under this section.

(1) The compliance date for a modification is no earlier than 180 days after the effective date of the final rule in which the Secretary adopts the modification.

(2) The Secretary may consider the extent of the modification and the time needed to comply with the modification in determining the compliance date for the modification.

(3) The Secretary may extend the compliance date for small health plans, as the Secretary determines is appropriate.

[65 FR 82798, Dec. 28, 2000, as amended at 67 FR 38019, May 31, 2002]

§160.105 Compliance dates for implementation of new or modified standards and implementation specifications.

Except as otherwise provided, with respect to rules that adopt new standards and implementation specifications or modifications to standards and implementation specifications in this subchapter in accordance with §160.104 that become effective after January 25, 2013, covered entities and business associates must comply with the applicable new standards and implementation specifications, or modifications to standards and implementation specifications, no later than 180 days from the effective date of any such standards or implementation specifications.

[78 FR 5689, Jan. 25, 2013]

SUBPART B—PREEMPTION OF STATE LAW

§160.201 Statutory basis.

The provisions of this subpart implement section 1178 of the Act, section 262 of Public Law 104-191, section 264(c) of Public Law 104-191, and section 13421(a) of Public Law 111-5.

[78 FR 5689, Jan. 25, 2013]

§160.202 Definitions.

For purposes of this subpart, the following terms have the following meanings:

Contrary, when used to compare a provision of State law to a standard, requirement, or implementation specification adopted under this subchapter, means:

(1) A covered entity or business associate would find it impossible to comply with both the State and Federal requirements; or

(2) The provision of State law stands as an obstacle to the accomplishment and execution of the full purposes and objectives of part C of title XI of the Act, section 264 of Public Law 104-191, or sections 13400–13424 of Public Law 111-5, as applicable.

More stringent means, in the context of a comparison of a provision of State law and a standard, requirement, or implementation specification adopted under subpart E of part 164 of this subchapter, a State law that meets one or more of the following criteria:

(1) With respect to a use or disclosure, the law prohibits or restricts a use or disclosure in circumstances under which such use or disclosure otherwise would be permitted under this subchapter, except if the disclosure is:

(i) Required by the Secretary in connection with determining whether a covered entity or business associate is in compliance with this subchapter; or

(ii) To the individual who is the subject of the individually identifiable health information.

(2) With respect to the rights of an individual, who is the subject of the individually identifiable health information, regarding access to or amendment of individually identifiable health information, permits greater rights of access or amendment, as applicable.

(3) With respect to information to be provided to an individual who is the subject of the individually identifiable health information about a use, a disclosure, rights, and remedies, provides the greater amount of information.

(4) With respect to the form, substance, or the need for express legal permission from an individual, who is the subject of the individually

identifiable health information, for use or disclosure of individually identifiable health information, provides requirements that narrow the scope or duration, increase the privacy protections afforded (such as by expanding the criteria for), or reduce the coercive effect of the circumstances surrounding the express legal permission, as applicable.

(5) With respect to recordkeeping or requirements relating to accounting of disclosures, provides for the retention or reporting of more detailed information or for a longer duration.

(6) With respect to any other matter, provides greater privacy protection for the individual who is the subject of the individually identifiable health information.

Relates to the privacy of individually identifiable health information means, with respect to a State law, that the State law has the specific purpose of protecting the privacy of health information or affects the privacy of health information in a direct, clear, and substantial way.

State law means a constitution, statute, regulation, rule, common law, or other State action having the force and effect of law.

[65 FR 82798, Dec. 28, 2000, as amended at 67 FR 53266, Aug. 14, 2002; 74 FR 42767, Aug. 24, 2009; 78 FR 5689, Jan. 25, 2013]

§160.203 General rule and exceptions.

A standard, requirement, or implementation specification adopted under this subchapter that is contrary to a provision of State law preempts the provision of State law. This general rule applies, except if one or more of the following conditions is met:

(a) A determination is made by the Secretary under §160.204 that the provision of State law:

    (1) Is necessary:

        (i) To prevent fraud and abuse related to the provision of or payment for health care;

        (ii) To ensure appropriate State regulation of insurance and health plans to the extent expressly authorized by statute or regulation;

        (iii) For State reporting on health care delivery or costs; or

(iv) For purposes of serving a compelling need related to public health, safety, or welfare, and, if a standard, requirement, or implementation specification under part 164 of this subchapter is at issue, if the Secretary determines that the intrusion into privacy is warranted when balanced against the need to be served; or

(2) Has as its principal purpose the regulation of the manufacture, registration, distribution, dispensing, or other control of any controlled substances (as defined in 21 U.S.C. 802), or that is deemed a controlled substance by State law.

(b) The provision of State law relates to the privacy of individually identifiable health information and is more stringent than a standard, requirement, or implementation specification adopted under subpart E of part 164 of this subchapter.

(c) The provision of State law, including State procedures established under such law, as applicable, provides for the reporting of disease or injury, child abuse, birth, or death, or for the conduct of public health surveillance, investigation, or intervention.

(d) The provision of State law requires a health plan to report, or to provide access to, information for the purpose of management audits, financial audits, program monitoring and evaluation, or the licensure or certification of facilities or individuals.

[65 FR 82798, Dec. 28, 2000, as amended at 67 FR 53266, Aug. 14, 2002]

§160.204 Process for requesting exception determinations.

(a) A request to except a provision of State law from preemption under §160.203(a) may be submitted to the Secretary. A request by a State must be submitted through its chief elected official, or his or her designee. The request must be in writing and include the following information:

(1) The State law for which the exception is requested;

(2) The particular standard, requirement, or implementation specification for which the exception is requested;

(3) The part of the standard or other provision that will not be implemented based on the exception or the additional data to be collected based on the exception, as appropriate;

(4) How health care providers, health plans, and other entities would be affected by the exception;

(5) The reasons why the State law should not be preempted by the federal standard, requirement, or implementation specification, including how the State law meets one or more of the criteria at §160.203(a); and

(6) Any other information the Secretary may request in order to make the determination.

(b) Requests for exception under this section must be submitted to the Secretary at an address that will be published in the Federal Register. Until the Secretary's determination is made, the standard, requirement, or implementation specification under this subchapter remains in effect.

(c) The Secretary's determination under this section will be made on the basis of the extent to which the information provided and other factors demonstrate that one or more of the criteria at §160.203(a) has been met.

§160.205 Duration of effectiveness of exception determinations.

An exception granted under this subpart remains in effect until:

(a) Either the State law or the federal standard, requirement, or implementation specification that provided the basis for the exception is materially changed such that the ground for the exception no longer exists; or

(b) The Secretary revokes the exception, based on a determination that the ground supporting the need for the exception no longer exists.

SUBPART C—COMPLIANCE AND INVESTIGATIONS

Source: 71 FR 8424, Feb. 16, 2006, unless otherwise noted.

§160.300 Applicability.

This subpart applies to actions by the Secretary, covered entities, business associates, and others with respect to ascertaining the compliance by covered entities and business associates with, and the enforcement of, the applicable provisions of this part 160 and parts 162 and 164 of this subchapter.

[78 FR 5690, Jan. 25, 2013]

§160.302 [Reserved]

§160.304 Principles for achieving compliance.

(a) *Cooperation.* The Secretary will, to the extent practicable and consistent with the provisions of this subpart, seek the cooperation of covered entities and business associates in obtaining compliance with the applicable administrative simplification provisions.

(b) *Assistance.* The Secretary may provide technical assistance to covered entities and business associates to help them comply voluntarily with the applicable administrative simplification provisions.

[78 FR 5690, Jan. 25, 2013]

§160.306 Complaints to the Secretary.

(a) *Right to file a complaint.* A person who believes a covered entity or business associate is not complying with the administrative simplification provisions may file a complaint with the Secretary.

(b) *Requirements for filing complaints.* Complaints under this section must meet the following requirements:

(1) A complaint must be filed in writing, either on paper or electronically.

(2) A complaint must name the person that is the subject of the complaint and describe the acts or omissions believed to be in violation of the applicable administrative simplification provision(s).

(3) A complaint must be filed within 180 days of when the complainant knew or should have known that the act or omission complained of occurred, unless this time limit is waived by the Secretary for good cause shown.

(4) The Secretary may prescribe additional procedures for the filing of complaints, as well as the place and manner of filing, by notice in the Federal Register.

(c) *Investigation.* (1) The Secretary will investigate any complaint filed under this section when a preliminary review of the facts indicates a possible violation due to willful neglect.

(2) The Secretary may investigate any other complaint filed under this section.

(3) An investigation under this section may include a review of the pertinent policies, procedures, or practices of the covered entity or business associate and of the circumstances regarding any alleged violation.

(4) At the time of the initial written communication with the covered entity or business associate about the complaint, the Secretary will describe the acts and/or omissions that are the basis of the complaint.

[71 FR 8424, Feb. 16, 2006, as amended at 78 FR 5690, Jan. 25, 2013]

§160.308 Compliance reviews.

(a) The Secretary will conduct a compliance review to determine whether a covered entity or business associate is complying with the applicable administrative simplification provisions when a preliminary review of the facts indicates a possible violation due to willful neglect.

(b) The Secretary may conduct a compliance review to determine whether a covered entity or business associate is complying with the applicable administrative simplification provisions in any other circumstance.

[78 FR 5690, Jan. 25, 2013]

§160.310 Responsibilities of covered entities and business associates.

(a) *Provide records and compliance reports.* A covered entity or business associate must keep such records and submit such compliance reports, in such time and manner and containing such information, as the Secretary may determine to be necessary to enable the Secretary to ascertain whether the covered entity or business associate has complied or is complying with the applicable administrative simplification provisions.

(b) *Cooperate with complaint investigations and compliance reviews.* A covered entity or business associate must cooperate with the Secretary, if the Secretary undertakes an investigation or compliance review of the policies, procedures, or practices of the covered entity or business associate to determine whether it is complying with the applicable administrative simplification provisions.

(c) *Permit access to information.* (1) A covered entity or business associate must permit access by the Secretary during normal business hours to its facilities, books, records, accounts, and other sources of information, including protected health information, that are pertinent to ascertaining compliance with the applicable administrative simplification provisions. If the Secretary determines that exigent circumstances exist, such as when documents may be hidden or destroyed, a covered entity or business associate must permit access by the Secretary at any time and without notice.

(2) If any information required of a covered entity or business associate under this section is in the exclusive possession of any other agency, institution, or person and the other agency, institution, or person fails or refuses to furnish the information, the covered entity or business associate must so certify and set forth what efforts it has made to obtain the information.

(3) Protected health information obtained by the Secretary in connection with an investigation or compliance review under this subpart will not be disclosed by the Secretary, except if necessary for ascertaining or enforcing compliance with the applicable administrative simplification provisions, if otherwise required by law, or if permitted under 5 U.S.C. 552a(b)(7).

[78 FR 5690, Jan. 25, 2013]

§160.312 Secretarial action regarding complaints and compliance reviews.

(a) *Resolution when noncompliance is indicated.* (1) If an investigation of a complaint pursuant to §160.306 or a compliance review pursuant to §160.308 indicates noncompliance, the Secretary may attempt to reach a resolution of the matter satisfactory to the Secretary by informal means. Informal means may include demonstrated compliance or a completed corrective action plan or other agreement.

(2) If the matter is resolved by informal means, the Secretary will so inform the covered entity or business associate and, if the matter arose from a complaint, the complainant, in writing.

(3) If the matter is not resolved by informal means, the Secretary will—

(i)   So inform the covered entity or business associate and provide the covered entity or business associate an opportunity to submit written evidence of any mitigating factors or affirmative defenses for consideration under §§160.408 and 160.410 of this part. The covered entity or business associate must submit any such evidence to the Secretary within 30 days (computed in the same manner as prescribed under §160.526 of this part) of receipt of such notification; and

(ii)   If, following action pursuant to paragraph (a)(3)(i) of this section, the Secretary finds that a civil money penalty should be imposed, inform the covered entity or business associate of such finding in a notice of proposed determination in accordance with §160.420 of this part.

(b) *Resolution when no violation is found.* If, after an investigation pursuant to §160.306 or a compliance review pursuant to §160.308, the Secretary determines that further action is not warranted, the Secretary will so inform the covered entity or business associate and, if the matter arose from a complaint, the complainant, in writing.

[78 FR 5690, Jan. 25, 2013]

§160.314 Investigational subpoenas and inquiries.

(a) The Secretary may issue subpoenas in accordance with 42 U.S.C. 405(d) and (e), 1320a-7a(j), and 1320d-5 to require the attendance and testimony of witnesses and the production of any other evidence during an investigation or compliance review pursuant to this part. For purposes of this paragraph, a person other than a natural person is termed an "entity."

(1)   A subpoena issued under this paragraph must—

(i)   State the name of the person (including the entity, if applicable) to whom the subpoena is addressed;

(ii)   State the statutory authority for the subpoena;

(iii)   Indicate the date, time, and place that the testimony will take place;

(iv)   Include a reasonably specific description of any documents or items required to be produced; and

(v) If the subpoena is addressed to an entity, describe with reasonable particularity the subject matter on which testimony is required. In that event, the entity must designate one or more natural persons who will testify on its behalf, and must state as to each such person that person's name and address and the matters on which he or she will testify. The designated person must testify as to matters known or reasonably available to the entity.

(2) A subpoena under this section must be served by—

(i) Delivering a copy to the natural person named in the subpoena or to the entity named in the subpoena at its last principal place of business; or

(ii) Registered or certified mail addressed to the natural person at his or her last known dwelling place or to the entity at its last known principal place of business.

(3) A verified return by the natural person serving the subpoena setting forth the manner of service or, in the case of service by registered or certified mail, the signed return post office receipt, constitutes proof of service.

(4) Witnesses are entitled to the same fees and mileage as witnesses in the district courts of the United States (28 U.S.C. 1821 and 1825). Fees need not be paid at the time the subpoena is served.

(5) A subpoena under this section is enforceable through the district court of the United States for the district where the subpoenaed natural person resides or is found or where the entity transacts business.

(b) Investigational inquiries are non-public investigational proceedings conducted by the Secretary.

(1) Testimony at investigational inquiries will be taken under oath or affirmation.

(2) Attendance of non-witnesses is discretionary with the Secretary, except that a witness is entitled to be accompanied, represented, and advised by an attorney.

(3) Representatives of the Secretary are entitled to attend and ask questions.

(4) A witness will have the opportunity to clarify his or her answers on the record following questioning by the Secretary.

(5) Any claim of privilege must be asserted by the witness on the record.

(6) Objections must be asserted on the record. Errors of any kind that might be corrected if promptly presented will be deemed to be waived unless reasonable objection is made at the investigational inquiry. Except where the objection is on the grounds of privilege, the question will be answered on the record, subject to objection.

(7) If a witness refuses to answer any question not privileged or to produce requested documents or items, or engages in conduct likely to delay or obstruct the investigational inquiry, the Secretary may seek enforcement of the subpoena under paragraph (a)(5) of this section.

(8) The proceedings will be recorded and transcribed. The witness is entitled to a copy of the transcript, upon payment of prescribed costs, except that, for good cause, the witness may be limited to inspection of the official transcript of his or her testimony.

(9)(i) The transcript will be submitted to the witness for signature.

> (A) Where the witness will be provided a copy of the transcript, the transcript will be submitted to the witness for signature. The witness may submit to the Secretary written proposed corrections to the transcript, with such corrections attached to the transcript. If the witness does not return a signed copy of the transcript or proposed corrections within 30 days (computed in the same manner as prescribed under §160.526 of this part) of its being submitted to him or her for signature, the witness will be deemed to have agreed that the transcript is true and accurate.

> (B) Where, as provided in paragraph (b)(8) of this section, the witness is limited to inspecting the transcript, the witness will have the opportunity at the time of inspection to propose corrections to the transcript, with

corrections attached to the transcript. The witness will also have the opportunity to sign the transcript. If the witness does not sign the transcript or offer corrections within 30 days (computed in the same manner as prescribed under §160.526 of this part) of receipt of notice of the opportunity to inspect the transcript, the witness will be deemed to have agreed that the transcript is true and accurate.

(ii) The Secretary's proposed corrections to the record of transcript will be attached to the transcript.

(c) Consistent with §160.310(c)(3), testimony and other evidence obtained in an investigational inquiry may be used by HHS in any of its activities and may be used or offered into evidence in any administrative or judicial proceeding.

§160.316 Refraining from intimidation or retaliation.

A covered entity or business associate may not threaten, intimidate, coerce, harass, discriminate against, or take any other retaliatory action against any individual or other person for—

(a) Filing of a complaint under §160.306;

(b) Testifying, assisting, or participating in an investigation, compliance review, proceeding, or hearing under this part; or

(c) Opposing any act or practice made unlawful by this subchapter, provided the individual or person has a good faith belief that the practice opposed is unlawful, and the manner of opposition is reasonable and does not involve a disclosure of protected health information in violation of subpart E of part 164 of this subchapter.

[71 FR 8424, Feb. 16, 2006, as amended at 78 FR 5691, Jan. 25, 2013]

SUBPART D—IMPOSITION OF CIVIL MONEY PENALTIES

Source: 71 FR 8426, Feb. 16, 2006, unless otherwise noted.

§160.400 Applicability.

This subpart applies to the imposition of a civil money penalty by the Secretary under 42 U.S.C. 1320d-5.

§160.401 Definitions.

As used in this subpart, the following terms have the following meanings:

Reasonable cause means an act or omission in which a covered entity or business associate knew, or by exercising reasonable diligence would have known, that the act or omission violated an administrative simplification provision, but in which the covered entity or business associate did not act with willful neglect.

Reasonable diligence means the business care and prudence expected from a person seeking to satisfy a legal requirement under similar circumstances.

Willful neglect means conscious, intentional failure or reckless indifference to the obligation to comply with the administrative simplification provision violated.

[74 FR 56130, Oct. 30, 2009, as amended at 78 FR 5691, Jan. 25, 2013]

§160.402 Basis for a civil money penalty.

(a) *General rule.* Subject to §160.410, the Secretary will impose a civil money penalty upon a covered entity or business associate if the Secretary determines that the covered entity or business associate has violated an administrative simplification provision.

(b) *Violation by more than one covered entity or business associate.* (1) Except as provided in paragraph (b)(2) of this section, if the Secretary determines that more than one covered entity or business associate was responsible for a violation, the Secretary will impose a civil money penalty against each such covered entity or business associate.

(2) A covered entity that is a member of an affiliated covered entity, in accordance with §164.105(b) of this subchapter, is jointly and severally liable for a civil money penalty for a violation of part 164 of this subchapter based on an act or omission of the affiliated covered entity, unless it is established that another member of the affiliated covered entity was responsible for the violation.

(c) *Violation attributed to a covered entity or business associate.* (1) A covered entity is liable, in accordance with the Federal common law of agency, for a civil money penalty for a violation based on the act or omission of any agent of the covered entity, including a workforce member or business associate, acting within the scope of the agency.

(2) A business associate is liable, in accordance with the Federal common law of agency, for a civil money penalty for a violation based on the act or omission of any agent of the business associate, including a workforce member or subcontractor, acting within the scope of the agency.

[78 FR 5691, Jan. 25, 2013]

§160.404 Amount of a civil money penalty.

(a) The amount of a civil money penalty will be determined in accordance with paragraph (b) of this section and §§160.406, 160.408, and 160.412.

(b) The amount of a civil money penalty that may be imposed is subject to the following limitations:

(1) For violations occurring prior to February 18, 2009, the Secretary may not impose a civil money penalty—

(i) In the amount of more than $100 for each violation; or

(ii) In excess of $25,000 for identical violations during a calendar year (January 1 through the following December 31);

(2) For violations occurring on or after February 18, 2009, the Secretary may not impose a civil money penalty—

(i) For a violation in which it is established that the covered entity or business associate did not know and, by exercising reasonable diligence, would not have known that the covered entity or business associate violated such provision,

(A) In the amount of less than $100 or more than $50,000 for each violation; or

(B) In excess of $1,500,000 for identical violations during a calendar year (January 1 through the following December 31);

(ii) For a violation in which it is established that the violation was due to reasonable cause and not to willful neglect,

(A) In the amount of less than $1,000 or more than $50,000 for each violation; or

(B) In excess of $1,500,000 for identical violations during a calendar year (January 1 through the following December 31);

(iii) For a violation in which it is established that the violation was due to willful neglect and was corrected during the 30-day period beginning on the first date the covered entity or business associate liable for the penalty knew, or, by exercising reasonable diligence, would have known that the violation occurred,

(A) In the amount of less than $10,000 or more than $50,000 for each violation; or

(B) In excess of $1,500,000 for identical violations during a calendar year (January 1 through the following December 31);

(iv) For a violation in which it is established that the violation was due to willful neglect and was not corrected during the 30-day period beginning on the first date the covered entity or business associate liable for the penalty knew, or, by exercising reasonable diligence, would have known that the violation occurred,

(A) In the amount of less than $50,000 for each violation; or

(B) In excess of $1,500,000 for identical violations during a calendar year (January 1 through the following December 31).

(3) If a requirement or prohibition in one administrative simplification provision is repeated in a more general form in another administrative simplification provision in the same subpart, a civil money penalty may be imposed for a violation of only one of these administrative simplification provisions.

[71 FR 8426, Feb. 16, 2006, as amended at 74 FR 56130, Oct. 30, 2009; 78 FR 5691, Jan. 25, 2013]

§160.406 Violations of an identical requirement or prohibition.

The Secretary will determine the number of violations of an administrative simplification provision based on the nature of the covered entity's or business associate's obligation to act or not act under the provision that is violated, such as its obligation to act in a certain manner, or within a certain time, or to act or not act with respect to certain persons. In the case of continuing violation of a provision, a separate violation occurs each day the covered entity or business associate is in violation of the provision.

[78 FR 5691, Jan. 25, 2013]

§160.408 Factors considered in determining the amount of a civil money penalty.

In determining the amount of any civil money penalty, the Secretary will consider the following factors, which may be mitigating or aggravating as appropriate:

(a) The nature and extent of the violation, consideration of which may include but is not limited to:

> (1) The number of individuals affected; and

> (2) The time period during which the violation occurred;

(b) The nature and extent of the harm resulting from the violation, consideration of which may include but is not limited to:

> (1) Whether the violation caused physical harm;

> (2) Whether the violation resulted in financial harm;

> (3) Whether the violation resulted in harm to an individual's reputation; and

> (4) Whether the violation hindered an individual's ability to obtain health care;

(c) The history of prior compliance with the administrative simplification provisions, including violations, by the covered entity or business associate, consideration of which may include but is not limited to:

> (1) Whether the current violation is the same or similar to previous indications of noncompliance;

> (2) Whether and to what extent the covered entity or business associate has attempted to correct previous indications of noncompliance;

(3)   How the covered entity or business associate has responded to technical assistance from the Secretary provided in the context of a compliance effort; and

(4)   How the covered entity or business associate has responded to prior complaints;

(d) The financial condition of the covered entity or business associate, consideration of which may include but is not limited to:

(1)   Whether the covered entity or business associate had financial difficulties that affected its ability to comply;

(2)   Whether the imposition of a civil money penalty would jeopardize the ability of the covered entity or business associate to continue to provide, or to pay for, health care; and

(3)   The size of the covered entity or business associate; and

(e) Such other matters as justice may require.

[78 FR 5691, Jan. 25, 2013]

§160.410 Affirmative defenses.

(a) The Secretary may not:

(1)   Prior to February 18, 2011, impose a civil money penalty on a covered entity or business associate for an act that violates an administrative simplification provision if the covered entity or business associate establishes that the violation is punishable under 42 U.S.C. 1320d-6.

(2)   On or after February 18, 2011, impose a civil money penalty on a covered entity or business associate for an act that violates an administrative simplification provision if the covered entity or business associate establishes that a penalty has been imposed under 42 U.S.C. 1320d-6 with respect to such act.

(b) For violations occurring prior to February 18, 2009, the Secretary may not impose a civil money penalty on a covered entity for a violation if the covered entity establishes that an affirmative defense exists with respect to the violation, including the following:

(1)   The covered entity establishes, to the satisfaction of the Secretary, that it did not have knowledge of the violation, determined in accordance with the Federal common law of agency, and by

exercising reasonable diligence, would not have known that the violation occurred; or

(2) The violation is—

(i) Due to circumstances that would make it unreasonable for the covered entity, despite the exercise of ordinary business care and prudence, to comply with the administrative simplification provision violated and is not due to willful neglect; and

(ii) Corrected during either:

(A) The 30-day period beginning on the first date the covered entity liable for the penalty knew, or by exercising reasonable diligence would have known, that the violation occurred; or

(B) Such additional period as the Secretary determines to be appropriate based on the nature and extent of the failure to comply.

(c) For violations occurring on or after February 18, 2009, the Secretary may not impose a civil money penalty on a covered entity or business associate for a violation if the covered entity or business associate establishes to the satisfaction of the Secretary that the violation is—

(1) Not due to willful neglect; and

(2) Corrected during either:

(i) The 30-day period beginning on the first date the covered entity or business associate liable for the penalty knew, or, by exercising reasonable diligence, would have known that the violation occurred; or

(ii) Such additional period as the Secretary determines to be appropriate based on the nature and extent of the failure to comply.

[78 FR 5692, Jan. 25, 2013]

§160.412 Waiver.

For violations described in §160.410(b)(2) or (c) that are not corrected within the period specified under such paragraphs, the

Secretary may waive the civil money penalty, in whole or in part, to the extent that the payment of the penalty would be excessive relative to the violation.

[8 FR 5692, Jan. 25, 2013]

§160.414 Limitations.

No action under this subpart may be entertained unless commenced by the Secretary, in accordance with §160.420, within 6 years from the date of the occurrence of the violation.

§160.416 Authority to settle.

Nothing in this subpart limits the authority of the Secretary to settle any issue or case or to compromise any penalty.

§160.418 Penalty not exclusive.

Except as otherwise provided by 42 U.S.C. 1320d-5(b)(1) and 42 U.S.C. 299b-22(f)(3), a penalty imposed under this part is in addition to any other penalty prescribed by law.

[78 FR 5692, Jan. 25, 2013]

§160.420 Notice of proposed determination.

(a) If a penalty is proposed in accordance with this part, the Secretary must deliver, or send by certified mail with return receipt requested, to the respondent, written notice of the Secretary's intent to impose a penalty. This notice of proposed determination must include—

(1) Reference to the statutory basis for the penalty;

(2) A description of the findings of fact regarding the violations with respect to which the penalty is proposed (except that, in any case where the Secretary is relying upon a statistical sampling study in accordance with §160.536 of this part, the notice must provide a copy of the study relied upon by the Secretary);

(3) The reason(s) why the violation(s) subject(s) the respondent to a penalty;

(4) The amount of the proposed penalty and a reference to the subparagraph of §160.404 upon which it is based.

(5) Any circumstances described in §160.408 that were considered in determining the amount of the proposed penalty; and

(6) Instructions for responding to the notice, including a statement of the respondent's right to a hearing, a statement that failure to request a hearing within 90 days permits the imposition of the proposed penalty without the right to a hearing under §160.504 or a right of appeal under §160.548 of this part, and the address to which the hearing request must be sent.

(b) The respondent may request a hearing before an ALJ on the proposed penalty by filing a request in accordance with §160.504 of this part.

[71 FR 8426, Feb. 16, 2006, as amended at 74 FR 56131, Oct. 30, 2009]

§160.422 Failure to request a hearing.

If the respondent does not request a hearing within the time prescribed by §160.504 of this part and the matter is not settled pursuant to §160.416, the Secretary will impose the proposed penalty or any lesser penalty permitted by 42 U.S.C. 1320d-5. The Secretary will notify the respondent by certified mail, return receipt requested, of any penalty that has been imposed and of the means by which the respondent may satisfy the penalty, and the penalty is final on receipt of the notice. The respondent has no right to appeal a penalty under §160.548 of this part with respect to which the respondent has not timely requested a hearing.

§160.424 Collection of penalty.

(a) Once a determination of the Secretary to impose a penalty has become final, the penalty will be collected by the Secretary, subject to the first sentence of 42 U.S.C. 1320a-7a(f).

(b) The penalty may be recovered in a civil action brought in the United States district court for the district where the respondent resides, is found, or is located.

(c) The amount of a penalty, when finally determined, or the amount agreed upon in compromise, may be deducted from any sum then or later owing by the United States, or by a State agency, to the respondent.

(d) Matters that were raised or that could have been raised in a hearing before an ALJ, or in an appeal under 42 U.S.C. 1320a-7a(e), may not be raised as a defense in a civil action by the United States to collect a penalty under this part.

§160.426 Notification of the public and other agencies.

Whenever a proposed penalty becomes final, the Secretary will notify, in such manner as the Secretary deems appropriate, the public and the following organizations and entities thereof and the reason it was imposed: the appropriate State or local medical or professional organization, the appropriate State agency or agencies administering or supervising the administration of State health care programs (as defined in 42 U.S.C. 1320a-7(h)), the appropriate utilization and quality control peer review organization, and the appropriate State or local licensing agency or organization (including the agency specified in 42 U.S.C. 1395aa(a), 1396a(a)(33)).

SUBPART E—PROCEDURES FOR HEARINGS

Source: 71 FR 8428, Feb. 16, 2006, unless otherwise noted.

§160.500 Applicability.

This subpart applies to hearings conducted relating to the imposition of a civil money penalty by the Secretary under 42 U.S.C. 1320d-5.

§160.502 Definitions.

As used in this subpart, the following term has the following meaning:

Board means the members of the HHS Departmental Appeals Board, in the Office of the Secretary, who issue decisions in panels of three.

§160.504 Hearing before an ALJ.

(a) A respondent may request a hearing before an ALJ. The parties to the hearing proceeding consist of—

(1) The respondent; and

(2) The officer(s) or employee(s) of HHS to whom the enforcement authority involved has been delegated.

(b) The request for a hearing must be made in writing signed by the respondent or by the respondent's attorney and sent by certified mail, return receipt requested, to the address specified in the notice of proposed determination. The request for a hearing must be mailed within

90 days after notice of the proposed determination is received by the respondent. For purposes of this section, the respondent's date of receipt of the notice of proposed determination is presumed to be 5 days after the date of the notice unless the respondent makes a reasonable showing to the contrary to the ALJ.

(c) The request for a hearing must clearly and directly admit, deny, or explain each of the findings of fact contained in the notice of proposed determination with regard to which the respondent has any knowledge. If the respondent has no knowledge of a particular finding of fact and so states, the finding shall be deemed denied. The request for a hearing must also state the circumstances or arguments that the respondent alleges constitute the grounds for any defense and the factual and legal basis for opposing the penalty, except that a respondent may raise an affirmative defense under §160.410(b)(1) at any time.

(d) The ALJ must dismiss a hearing request where—

(1) On motion of the Secretary, the ALJ determines that the respondent's hearing request is not timely filed as required by paragraphs (b) or does not meet the requirements of paragraph (c) of this section;

(2) The respondent withdraws the request for a hearing;

(3) The respondent abandons the request for a hearing; or

(4) The respondent's hearing request fails to raise any issue that may properly be addressed in a hearing.

§160.506 Rights of the parties.

(a) Except as otherwise limited by this subpart, each party may—

(1) Be accompanied, represented, and advised by an attorney;

(2) Participate in any conference held by the ALJ;

(3) Conduct discovery of documents as permitted by this subpart;

(4) Agree to stipulations of fact or law that will be made part of the record;

(5) Present evidence relevant to the issues at the hearing;

(6) Present and cross-examine witnesses;

(7) Present oral arguments at the hearing as permitted by the ALJ; and

(8) Submit written briefs and proposed findings of fact and conclusions of law after the hearing.

(b) A party may appear in person or by a representative. Natural persons who appear as an attorney or other representative must conform to the standards of conduct and ethics required of practitioners before the courts of the United States.

(c) Fees for any services performed on behalf of a party by an attorney are not subject to the provisions of 42 U.S.C. 406, which authorizes the Secretary to specify or limit their fees.

§160.508 Authority of the ALJ.

(a) The ALJ must conduct a fair and impartial hearing, avoid delay, maintain order, and ensure that a record of the proceeding is made.

(b) The ALJ may—

(1) Set and change the date, time and place of the hearing upon reasonable notice to the parties;

(2) Continue or recess the hearing in whole or in part for a reasonable period of time;

(3) Hold conferences to identify or simplify the issues, or to consider other matters that may aid in the expeditious disposition of the proceeding;

(4) Administer oaths and affirmations;

(5) Issue subpoenas requiring the attendance of witnesses at hearings and the production of documents at or in relation to hearings;

(6) Rule on motions and other procedural matters;

(7) Regulate the scope and timing of documentary discovery as permitted by this subpart;

(8) Regulate the course of the hearing and the conduct of representatives, parties, and witnesses;

(9) Examine witnesses;

(10) Receive, rule on, exclude, or limit evidence;

(11) Upon motion of a party, take official notice of facts;

(12) Conduct any conference, argument or hearing in person or, upon agreement of the parties, by telephone; and

(13) Upon motion of a party, decide cases, in whole or in part, by summary judgment where there is no disputed issue of material fact. A summary judgment decision constitutes a hearing on the record for the purposes of this subpart.

(c) The ALJ—

(1) May not find invalid or refuse to follow Federal statutes, regulations, or Secretarial delegations of authority and must give deference to published guidance to the extent not inconsistent with statute or regulation;

(2) May not enter an order in the nature of a directed verdict;

(3) May not compel settlement negotiations;

(4) May not enjoin any act of the Secretary; or

(5) May not review the exercise of discretion by the Secretary with respect to whether to grant an extension under §160.410(b)(2)(ii)(B) or (c)(2)(ii) of this part or to provide technical assistance under 42 U.S.C. 1320d-5(b)(2)(B).

[71 FR 8428, Feb. 16, 2006, as amended at 78 FR 34266, June 7, 2013]

§160.510 Ex parte contacts.

No party or person (except employees of the ALJ's office) may communicate in any way with the ALJ on any matter at issue in a case, unless on notice and opportunity for both parties to participate. This provision does not prohibit a party or person from inquiring about the status of a case or asking routine questions concerning administrative functions or procedures.

§160.512 Prehearing conferences.

(a) The ALJ must schedule at least one prehearing conference, and may schedule additional prehearing conferences as appropriate, upon reasonable notice, which may not be less than 14 business days, to the parties.

(b) The ALJ may use prehearing conferences to discuss the following—

(1) Simplification of the issues;

(2) The necessity or desirability of amendments to the pleadings, including the need for a more definite statement;

(3) Stipulations and admissions of fact or as to the contents and authenticity of documents;

(4) Whether the parties can agree to submission of the case on a stipulated record;

(5) Whether a party chooses to waive appearance at an oral hearing and to submit only documentary evidence (subject to the objection of the other party) and written argument;

(6) Limitation of the number of witnesses;

(7) Scheduling dates for the exchange of witness lists and of proposed exhibits;

(8) Discovery of documents as permitted by this subpart;

(9) The time and place for the hearing;

(10) The potential for the settlement of the case by the parties; and

(11) Other matters as may tend to encourage the fair, just and expeditious disposition of the proceedings, including the protection of privacy of individually identifiable health information that may be submitted into evidence or otherwise used in the proceeding, if appropriate.

(c) The ALJ must issue an order containing the matters agreed upon by the parties or ordered by the ALJ at a prehearing conference.

§160.514 Authority to settle.

The Secretary has exclusive authority to settle any issue or case without the consent of the ALJ.

§160.516 Discovery.

(a) A party may make a request to another party for production of documents for inspection and copying that are relevant and material to the issues before the ALJ.

(b) For the purpose of this section, the term "documents" includes information, reports, answers, records, accounts, papers and other data and documentary evidence. Nothing contained in this section may be interpreted to require the creation of a document, except that requested data stored in an electronic data storage system must be produced in a form accessible to the requesting party.

(c) Requests for documents, requests for admissions, written interrogatories, depositions and any forms of discovery, other than those permitted under paragraph (a) of this section, are not authorized.

(d) This section may not be construed to require the disclosure of interview reports or statements obtained by any party, or on behalf of any party, of persons who will not be called as witnesses by that party, or analyses and summaries prepared in conjunction with the investigation or litigation of the case, or any otherwise privileged documents.

(e)(1) When a request for production of documents has been received, within 30 days the party receiving that request must either fully respond to the request, or state that the request is being objected to and the reasons for that objection. If objection is made to part of an item or category, the part must be specified. Upon receiving any objections, the party seeking production may then, within 30 days or any other time frame set by the ALJ, file a motion for an order compelling discovery. The party receiving a request for production may also file a motion for protective order any time before the date the production is due.

(2) The ALJ may grant a motion for protective order or deny a motion for an order compelling discovery if the ALJ finds that the discovery sought—

(i) Is irrelevant;

(ii) Is unduly costly or burdensome;

(iii) Will unduly delay the proceeding; or

(iv) Seeks privileged information.

(3) The ALJ may extend any of the time frames set forth in paragraph (e)(1) of this section.

(4) The burden of showing that discovery should be allowed is on the party seeking discovery.

§160.518 Exchange of witness lists, witness statements, and exhibits.

(a) The parties must exchange witness lists, copies of prior written statements of proposed witnesses, and copies of proposed hearing exhibits, including copies of any written statements that the party intends to offer in lieu of live testimony in accordance with §160.538, not more than 60, and not less than 15, days before the scheduled hearing, except that if a respondent intends to introduce the evidence of a statistical expert, the respondent must provide the Secretarial party with a copy of the statistical expert's report not less than 30 days before the scheduled hearing.

(b)(1) If, at any time, a party objects to the proposed admission of evidence not exchanged in accordance with paragraph (a) of this section, the ALJ must determine whether the failure to comply with paragraph (a) of this section should result in the exclusion of that evidence.

(2) Unless the ALJ finds that extraordinary circumstances justified the failure timely to exchange the information listed under paragraph (a) of this section, the ALJ must exclude from the party's case-in-chief—

(i) The testimony of any witness whose name does not appear on the witness list; and

(ii) Any exhibit not provided to the opposing party as specified in paragraph (a) of this section.

(3) If the ALJ finds that extraordinary circumstances existed, the ALJ must then determine whether the admission of that evidence would cause substantial prejudice to the objecting party.

(i) If the ALJ finds that there is no substantial prejudice, the evidence may be admitted.

(ii) If the ALJ finds that there is substantial prejudice, the ALJ may exclude the evidence, or, if he or she does not exclude the evidence, must postpone the hearing for such time as is necessary for the objecting party to prepare and respond to the evidence, unless the objecting party waives postponement.

(c) Unless the other party objects within a reasonable period of time before the hearing, documents exchanged in accordance with paragraph (a) of this section will be deemed to be authentic for the purpose of admissibility at the hearing.

§160.520 Subpoenas for attendance at hearing.

(a) A party wishing to procure the appearance and testimony of any person at the hearing may make a motion requesting the ALJ to issue a subpoena if the appearance and testimony are reasonably necessary for the presentation of a party's case.

(b) A subpoena requiring the attendance of a person in accordance with paragraph (a) of this section may also require the person (whether or not the person is a party) to produce relevant and material evidence at or before the hearing.

(c) When a subpoena is served by a respondent on a particular employee or official or particular office of HHS, the Secretary may comply by designating any knowledgeable HHS representative to appear and testify.

(d) A party seeking a subpoena must file a written motion not less than 30 days before the date fixed for the hearing, unless otherwise allowed by the ALJ for good cause shown. That motion must—

   (1) Specify any evidence to be produced;

   (2) Designate the witnesses; and

   (3) Describe the address and location with sufficient particularity to permit those witnesses to be found.

(e) The subpoena must specify the time and place at which the witness is to appear and any evidence the witness is to produce.

(f) Within 15 days after the written motion requesting issuance of a subpoena is served, any party may file an opposition or other response.

(g) If the motion requesting issuance of a subpoena is granted, the party seeking the subpoena must serve it by delivery to the person named, or by certified mail addressed to that person at the person's last dwelling place or principal place of business.

(h) The person to whom the subpoena is directed may file with the ALJ a motion to quash the subpoena within 10 days after service.

(i) The exclusive remedy for contumacy by, or refusal to obey a subpoena duly served upon, any person is specified in 42 U.S.C. 405(e).

§160.522 Fees.

The party requesting a subpoena must pay the cost of the fees and mileage of any witness subpoenaed in the amounts that would be payable to a witness in a proceeding in United States District Court. A check for witness fees and mileage must accompany the subpoena when served, except that, when a subpoena is issued on behalf of the Secretary, a check for witness fees and mileage need not accompany the subpoena.

§160.524 Form, filing, and service of papers.

(a) *Forms.* (1) Unless the ALJ directs the parties to do otherwise, documents filed with the ALJ must include an original and two copies.

(2) Every pleading and paper filed in the proceeding must contain a caption setting forth the title of the action, the case number, and a designation of the paper, such as motion to quash subpoena.

(3) Every pleading and paper must be signed by and must contain the address and telephone number of the party or the person on whose behalf the paper was filed, or his or her representative.

(4) Papers are considered filed when they are mailed.

(b) *Service.* A party filing a document with the ALJ or the Board must, at the time of filing, serve a copy of the document on the other party. Service upon any party of any document must be made by delivering a copy, or placing a copy of the document in the United States mail, postage prepaid and addressed, or with a private delivery service, to the party's last known address. When a party is represented by an attorney, service must be made upon the attorney in lieu of the party.

(c) *Proof of service.* A certificate of the natural person serving the document by personal delivery or by mail, setting forth the manner of service, constitutes proof of service.

§160.526 Computation of time.

(a) In computing any period of time under this subpart or in an order issued thereunder, the time begins with the day following the act, event or default, and includes the last day of the period unless it is a Saturday, Sunday, or legal holiday observed by the Federal Government, in which event it includes the next business day.

(b) When the period of time allowed is less than 7 days, intermediate Saturdays, Sundays, and legal holidays observed by the Federal Government must be excluded from the computation.

(c) Where a document has been served or issued by placing it in the mail, an additional 5 days must be added to the time permitted for any response. This paragraph does not apply to requests for hearing under §160.504.

§160.528 Motions.

(a) An application to the ALJ for an order or ruling must be by motion. Motions must state the relief sought, the authority relied upon and the facts alleged, and must be filed with the ALJ and served on all other parties.

(b) Except for motions made during a prehearing conference or at the hearing, all motions must be in writing. The ALJ may require that oral motions be reduced to writing.

(c) Within 10 days after a written motion is served, or such other time as may be fixed by the ALJ, any party may file a response to the motion.

(d) The ALJ may not grant a written motion before the time for filing responses has expired, except upon consent of the parties or following a hearing on the motion, but may overrule or deny the motion without awaiting a response.

(e) The ALJ must make a reasonable effort to dispose of all outstanding motions before the beginning of the hearing.

§160.530 Sanctions.

The ALJ may sanction a person, including any party or attorney, for failing to comply with an order or procedure, for failing to defend an action or for other misconduct that interferes with the speedy, orderly or fair conduct of the hearing. The sanctions must reasonably relate to the severity and nature of the failure or misconduct. The sanctions may include—

(a) In the case of refusal to provide or permit discovery under the terms of this part, drawing negative factual inferences or treating the refusal as an admission by deeming the matter, or certain facts, to be established;

(b) Prohibiting a party from introducing certain evidence or otherwise supporting a particular claim or defense;

(c) Striking pleadings, in whole or in part;

(d) Staying the proceedings;

(e) Dismissal of the action;

(f) Entering a decision by default;

(g) Ordering the party or attorney to pay the attorney's fees and other costs caused by the failure or misconduct; and

(h) Refusing to consider any motion or other action that is not filed in a timely manner.

§160.532 Collateral estoppel.

When a final determination that the respondent violated an administrative simplification provision has been rendered in any proceeding in which the respondent was a party and had an opportunity to be heard, the respondent is bound by that determination in any proceeding under this part.

§160.534 The hearing.

(a) The ALJ must conduct a hearing on the record in order to determine whether the respondent should be found liable under this part.

(b) (1) The respondent has the burden of going forward and the burden of persuasion with respect to any:

>   (i)   Affirmative defense pursuant to §160.410 of this part;

>   (ii) Challenge to the amount of a proposed penalty pursuant to §§160.404–160.408 of this part, including any factors raised as mitigating factors; or

>   (iii) Claim that a proposed penalty should be reduced or waived pursuant to §160.412 of this part; and

>   (iv) Compliance with subpart D of part 164, as provided under §164.414(b).

(2) The Secretary has the burden of going forward and the burden of persuasion with respect to all other issues, including issues of liability other than with respect to subpart D of part 164, and the existence of any factors considered aggravating factors in determining the amount of the proposed penalty.

(3) The burden of persuasion will be judged by a preponderance of the evidence.

(c) The hearing must be open to the public unless otherwise ordered by the ALJ for good cause shown.

(d)(1) Subject to the 15-day rule under §160.518(a) and the admissibility of evidence under §160.540, either party may introduce, during its case in chief, items or information that arose or became known after the date of the issuance of the notice of proposed determination or the request for hearing, as applicable. Such items and information may not be admitted into evidence, if introduced—

> (i) By the Secretary, unless they are material and relevant to the acts or omissions with respect to which the penalty is proposed in the notice of proposed determination pursuant to §160.420 of this part, including circumstances that may increase penalties; or

> (ii) By the respondent, unless they are material and relevant to an admission, denial or explanation of a finding of fact in the notice of proposed determination under §160.420 of this part, or to a specific circumstance or argument expressly stated in the request for hearing under §160.504, including circumstances that may reduce penalties.

(2) After both parties have presented their cases, evidence may be admitted in rebuttal even if not previously exchanged in accordance with §160.518.

[71 FR 8428, Feb. 16, 2006, as amended at 74 FR 42767, Aug. 24, 2009; 78 FR 5692, Jan. 25, 2013]

§160.536 Statistical sampling.

(a) In meeting the burden of proof set forth in §160.534, the Secretary may introduce the results of a statistical sampling study as evidence of the number of violations under §160.406 of this part, or the factors considered in determining the amount of the civil money penalty under §160.408 of this part. Such statistical sampling study, if based upon an appropriate sampling and computed by valid statistical methods, constitutes prima facie evidence of the number of violations and the existence of factors material to the proposed civil money penalty as described in §§160.406 and 160.408.

(b) Once the Secretary has made a prima facie case, as described in paragraph (a) of this section, the burden of going forward shifts to the respondent to produce evidence reasonably calculated to rebut the findings of the statistical sampling study. The Secretary will then be given the opportunity to rebut this evidence.

§160.538 Witnesses.

(a) Except as provided in paragraph (b) of this section, testimony at the hearing must be given orally by witnesses under oath or affirmation.

(b) At the discretion of the ALJ, testimony of witnesses other than the testimony of expert witnesses may be admitted in the form of a written statement. The ALJ may, at his or her discretion, admit prior sworn testimony of experts that has been subject to adverse examination, such as a deposition or trial testimony. Any such written statement must be provided to the other party, along with the last known address of the witness, in a manner that allows sufficient time for the other party to subpoena the witness for cross-examination at the hearing. Prior written statements of witnesses proposed to testify at the hearing must be exchanged as provided in §160.518.

(c) The ALJ must exercise reasonable control over the mode and order of interrogating witnesses and presenting evidence so as to:

(1) Make the interrogation and presentation effective for the ascertainment of the truth;

(2) Avoid repetition or needless consumption of time; and

(3) Protect witnesses from harassment or undue embarrassment.

(d) The ALJ must permit the parties to conduct cross-examination of witnesses as may be required for a full and true disclosure of the facts.

(e) The ALJ may order witnesses excluded so that they cannot hear the testimony of other witnesses, except that the ALJ may not order to be excluded—

(1) A party who is a natural person;

(2) In the case of a party that is not a natural person, the officer or employee of the party appearing for the entity pro se or designated as the party's representative; or

(3) A natural person whose presence is shown by a party to be essential to the presentation of its case, including a person engaged in assisting the attorney for the Secretary.

§160.540 Evidence.

(a) The ALJ must determine the admissibility of evidence.

(b) Except as provided in this subpart, the ALJ is not bound by the Federal Rules of Evidence. However, the ALJ may apply the Federal Rules of Evidence where appropriate, for example, to exclude unreliable evidence.

(c) The ALJ must exclude irrelevant or immaterial evidence.

(d) Although relevant, evidence may be excluded if its probative value is substantially outweighed by the danger of unfair prejudice, confusion of the issues, or by considerations of undue delay or needless presentation of cumulative evidence.

(e) Although relevant, evidence must be excluded if it is privileged under Federal law.

(f) Evidence concerning offers of compromise or settlement are inadmissible to the extent provided in Rule 408 of the Federal Rules of Evidence.

(g) Evidence of crimes, wrongs, or acts other than those at issue in the instant case is admissible in order to show motive, opportunity, intent, knowledge, preparation, identity, lack of mistake, or existence of a scheme. This evidence is admissible regardless of whether the crimes, wrongs, or acts occurred during the statute of limitations period applicable to the acts or omissions that constitute the basis for liability in the case and regardless of whether they were referenced in the Secretary's notice of proposed determination under §160.420 of this part.

(h) The ALJ must permit the parties to introduce rebuttal witnesses and evidence.

(i) All documents and other evidence offered or taken for the record must be open to examination by both parties, unless otherwise ordered by the ALJ for good cause shown.

§160.542 The record.

(a) The hearing must be recorded and transcribed. Transcripts may be obtained following the hearing from the ALJ. A party that requests a transcript of hearing proceedings must pay the cost of preparing the transcript unless, for good cause shown by the party, the payment is waived by the ALJ or the Board, as appropriate.

(b) The transcript of the testimony, exhibits, and other evidence admitted at the hearing, and all papers and requests filed in the proceeding constitute the record for decision by the ALJ and the Secretary.

(c) The record may be inspected and copied (upon payment of a reasonable fee) by any person, unless otherwise ordered by the ALJ for good cause shown.

(d) For good cause, the ALJ may order appropriate redactions made to the record.

§160.544 Post hearing briefs.

The ALJ may require the parties to file post-hearing briefs. In any event, any party may file a post-hearing brief. The ALJ must fix the time for filing the briefs. The time for filing may not exceed 60 days from the date the parties receive the transcript of the hearing or, if applicable, the stipulated record. The briefs may be accompanied by proposed findings of fact and conclusions of law. The ALJ may permit the parties to file reply briefs.

§160.546 ALJ's decision.

(a) The ALJ must issue a decision, based only on the record, which must contain findings of fact and conclusions of law.

(b) The ALJ may affirm, increase, or reduce the penalties imposed by the Secretary.

(c) The ALJ must issue the decision to both parties within 60 days after the time for submission of post-hearing briefs and reply briefs, if permitted, has expired. If the ALJ fails to meet the deadline contained in this paragraph, he or she must notify the parties of the reason for the delay and set a new deadline.

(d) Unless the decision of the ALJ is timely appealed as provided for in §160.548, the decision of the ALJ will be final and binding on the parties 60 days from the date of service of the ALJ's decision.

§160.548 Appeal of the ALJ's decision.

(a) Any party may appeal the decision of the ALJ to the Board by filing a notice of appeal with the Board within 30 days of the date of service of the ALJ decision. The Board may extend the initial 30 day period for a period of time not to exceed 30 days if a party files with the Board a request for an extension within the initial 30 day period and shows good cause.

(b) If a party files a timely notice of appeal with the Board, the ALJ must forward the record of the proceeding to the Board.

(c) A notice of appeal must be accompanied by a written brief specifying exceptions to the initial decision and reasons supporting the exceptions. Any party may file a brief in opposition to the exceptions, which may raise any relevant issue not addressed in the exceptions, within 30 days of receiving the notice of appeal and the accompanying brief. The Board may permit the parties to file reply briefs.

(d) There is no right to appear personally before the Board or to appeal to the Board any interlocutory ruling by the ALJ.

(e) Except for an affirmative defense under §160.410(a)(1) or (2) of this part, the Board may not consider any issue not raised in the parties' briefs, nor any issue in the briefs that could have been raised before the ALJ but was not.

(f) If any party demonstrates to the satisfaction of the Board that additional evidence not presented at such hearing is relevant and material and that there were reasonable grounds for the failure to adduce such evidence at the hearing, the Board may remand the matter to the ALJ for consideration of such additional evidence.

(g) The Board may decline to review the case, or may affirm, increase, reduce, reverse or remand any penalty determined by the ALJ.

(h) The standard of review on a disputed issue of fact is whether the initial decision of the ALJ is supported by substantial evidence on the whole record. The standard of review on a disputed issue of law is whether the decision is erroneous.

(i) Within 60 days after the time for submission of briefs and reply briefs, if permitted, has expired, the Board must serve on each party to the appeal a copy of the Board's decision and a statement describing the right of any respondent who is penalized to seek judicial review.

(j)(1) The Board's decision under paragraph (i) of this section, including a decision to decline review of the initial decision, becomes the final decision of the Secretary 60 days after the date of service of the Board's decision, except with respect to a decision to remand to the ALJ or if reconsideration is requested under this paragraph.

(2) The Board will reconsider its decision only if it determines that the decision contains a clear error of fact or error of law. New evidence will not be a basis for reconsideration unless the party demonstrates that the evidence is newly discovered and was not previously available.

(3) A party may file a motion for reconsideration with the Board before the date the decision becomes final under paragraph (j)(1) of this section. A motion for reconsideration must be accompanied by a written brief specifying any alleged error of fact or law and, if the party is relying on additional evidence, explaining why the evidence was not previously available. Any party may file a brief in opposition within 15 days of receiving the motion for reconsideration and the accompanying brief unless this time limit is extended by the Board for good cause shown. Reply briefs are not permitted.

(4) The Board must rule on the motion for reconsideration not later than 30 days from the date the opposition brief is due. If the Board denies the motion, the decision issued under paragraph (i) of this section becomes the final decision of the Secretary on the date of service of the ruling. If the Board grants the motion, the Board will issue a reconsidered decision, after such procedures as the Board determines necessary to address the effect of any error. The Board's decision on reconsideration becomes the final decision of the Secretary on the date of service of the decision, except with respect to a decision to remand to the ALJ.

(5) If service of a ruling or decision issued under this section is by mail, the date of service will be deemed to be 5 days from the date of mailing.

(k)(1) A respondent's petition for judicial review must be filed within 60 days of the date on which the decision of the Board becomes the final decision of the Secretary under paragraph (j) of this section.

(2) In compliance with 28 U.S.C. 2112(a), a copy of any petition for judicial review filed in any U.S. Court of Appeals challenging the final decision of the Secretary must be sent by certified mail, return receipt requested, to the General Counsel of HHS. The petition copy must be a copy showing that it has been time-stamped by the clerk of the court when the original was filed with the court.

(3)   If the General Counsel of HHS received two or more petitions within 10 days after the final decision of the Secretary, the General Counsel will notify the U.S. Judicial Panel on Multidistrict Litigation of any petitions that were received within the 10 day period.

[71 FR 8428, Feb. 16, 2006, as amended at 78 FR 34266, June 7, 2013]

§160.550 Stay of the Secretary's decision.

(a)   Pending judicial review, the respondent may file a request for stay of the effective date of any penalty with the ALJ. The request must be accompanied by a copy of the notice of appeal filed with the Federal court. The filing of the request automatically stays the effective date of the penalty until such time as the ALJ rules upon the request.

(b)   The ALJ may not grant a respondent's request for stay of any penalty unless the respondent posts a bond or provides other adequate security.

(c)   The ALJ must rule upon a respondent's request for stay within 10 days of receipt.

§160.552 Harmless error.

No error in either the admission or the exclusion of evidence, and no error or defect in any ruling or order or in any act done or omitted by the ALJ or by any of the parties is ground for vacating, modifying or otherwise disturbing an otherwise appropriate ruling or order or act, unless refusal to take such action appears to the ALJ or the Board inconsistent with substantial justice. The ALJ and the Board at every stage of the proceeding must disregard any error or defect in the proceeding that does not affect the substantial rights of the parties.

Regulations Comprising the Security Rule, Breach Notification Rule, and Privacy Rule 45 C.F.R. Part 164

This Appendix contains the provisions of 45 C.F.R. Part 164, which are the Security and Privacy requirements of Subchapter C of Subtitle A of Title 45 of the Code of Federal Regulations. Part 164 establishes the core security, privacy, and breach notification requirements of HIPAA. Subpart A covers the scope and applicability of part 164, as well as key definitions. Subpart B is a placeholder and reserved for future. Subpart C is the core of the Security Rule. Subpart D establishes breach notification requirements. Finally, Subpart E contains the Privacy Rule.

SUBPART A—GENERAL PROVISIONS

§164.102 Statutory basis.

The provisions of this part are adopted pursuant to the Secretary's authority to prescribe standards, requirements, and implementation specifications under part C of title XI of the Act, section 264 of Public Law 104-191, and sections 13400-13424 of Public Law 111-5.

[78 FR 5692, Jan. 25, 2013]

§164.103 Definitions.

As used in this part, the following terms have the following meanings:

Common control exists if an entity has the power, directly or indirectly, significantly to influence or direct the actions or policies of another entity.

Common ownership exists if an entity or entities possess an ownership or equity interest of 5 percent or more in another entity.

Covered functions means those functions of a covered entity the performance of which makes the entity a health plan, health care provider, or health care clearinghouse.

Health care component means a component or combination of components of a hybrid entity designated by the hybrid entity in accordance with §164.105(a)(2)(iii)(D).

Hybrid entity means a single legal entity:

(1) That is a covered entity;

(2) Whose business activities include both covered and non-covered functions; and

(3) That designates health care components in accordance with paragraph §164.105(a)(2)(iii)(D).

Law enforcement official means an officer or employee of any agency or authority of the United States, a State, a territory, a political subdivision of a State or territory, or an Indian tribe, who is empowered by law to:

(1) Investigate or conduct an official inquiry into a potential violation of law; or

(2) Prosecute or otherwise conduct a criminal, civil, or administrative proceeding arising from an alleged violation of law.

Plan sponsor is defined as defined at section 3(16)(B) of ERISA, 29 U.S.C. 1002(16)(B).

Required by law means a mandate contained in law that compels an entity to make a use or disclosure of protected health information and that is enforceable in a court of law. *Required by law* includes, but is not limited to, court orders and court-ordered warrants; subpoenas or summons issued by a court, grand jury, a governmental or tribal inspector general, or an administrative body authorized to require the production of information; a civil or an authorized investigative demand; Medicare conditions of participation with respect to health care providers participating in the program; and statutes or regulations that require the production of information, including statutes or regulations that require such information if payment is sought under a government program providing public benefits.

[68 FR 8374, Feb. 20, 2003, as amended at 74 FR 42767, Aug. 24, 2009; 78 FR 34266, June 7, 2013]

§164.104 Applicability.

(a) Except as otherwise provided, the standards, requirements, and implementation specifications adopted under this part apply to the following entities:

(1) A health plan.

(2) A health care clearinghouse.

(3) A health care provider who transmits any health information in electronic form in connection with a transaction covered by this subchapter.

(b) Where provided, the standards, requirements, and implementation specifications adopted under this part apply to a business associate.

[68 FR 8375, Feb. 20, 2003, as amended at 78 FR 5692, Jan. 25, 2013]

§164.105 Organizational requirements.

(a)(1) *Standard: Health care component.* If a covered entity is a hybrid entity, the requirements of this part, other than the requirements of this section, §§164.314, and 164.504, apply only to the health care component(s) of the entity, as specified in this section.

(2) *Implementation specifications:*

(i) *Application of other provisions.* In applying a provision of this part, other than the requirements of this section, §§164.314, and 164.504, to a hybrid entity:

(A) A reference in such provision to a "covered entity" refers to a health care component of the covered entity;

(B) A reference in such provision to a "health plan," "covered health care provider," or "health care clearinghouse," refers to a health care component of the covered entity if such health care component performs the functions of a health plan, health care provider, or health care clearinghouse, as applicable;

(C) A reference in such provision to "protected health information" refers to protected health information that is created or received by or on behalf of the health care component of the covered entity; and

(D) A reference in such provision to "electronic protected health information" refers to electronic protected health information that is created, received, maintained, or transmitted by or on behalf of the health care component of the covered entity.

(ii) *Safeguard requirements.* The covered entity that is a hybrid entity must ensure that a health care component of the entity complies with the applicable requirements of this part. In particular, and without limiting this requirement, such covered entity must ensure that:

(A) Its health care component does not disclose protected health information to another component of the covered entity in circumstances in which subpart E of this part would prohibit such disclosure if the health care component and the other component were separate and distinct legal entities;

(B) Its health care component protects electronic protected health information with respect to another component of the covered entity to the same extent that it would be required under subpart C of this part to protect such information if the health care component and the other component were separate and distinct legal entities;

(C) If a person performs duties for both the health care component in the capacity of a member of the workforce of such component and for another component of the entity in the same capacity with respect to that component, such workforce member must not use or disclose protected health information created or received in the course of or incident to the member's work for the health care component in a way prohibited by subpart E of this part.

(iii) *Responsibilities of the covered entity.* A covered entity that is a hybrid entity has the following responsibilities:

>(A) For purposes of subpart C of part 160 of this subchapter, pertaining to compliance and enforcement, the covered entity has the responsibility of complying with this part.
>
>(B) The covered entity is responsible for complying with §§164.316(a) and 164.530(i), pertaining to the implementation of policies and procedures to ensure compliance with applicable requirements of this part, including the safeguard requirements in paragraph (a)(2)(ii) of this section.
>
>(C) The covered entity is responsible for complying with §§164.314 and 164.504 regarding business associate arrangements and other organizational requirements.
>
>(D) The covered entity is responsible for designating the components that are part of one or more health care components of the covered entity and documenting the designation in accordance with paragraph (c) of this section, provided that, if the covered entity designates one or more health care components, it must include any component that would meet the definition of a covered entity or business associate if it were a separate legal entity. Health care component(s) also may include a component only to the extent that it performs covered functions.

(b)(1) *Standard: Affiliated covered entities.* Legally separate covered entities that are affiliated may designate themselves as a single covered entity for purposes of this part.

(2) *Implementation specifications—*

(i) *Requirements for designation of an affiliated covered entity—*

>(A) Legally separate covered entities may designate themselves (including any health care component of such covered entity) as a single affiliated covered entity, for purposes of this part, if all of the covered entities designated are under common ownership or control.

(B) The designation of an affiliated covered entity must be documented and the documentation maintained as required by paragraph (c) of this section.

(ii) *Safeguard requirements.* An affiliated covered entity must ensure that it complies with the applicable requirements of this part, including, if the affiliated covered entity combines the functions of a health plan, health care provider, or health care clearinghouse, §§164.308(a)(4)(ii)(A) and 164.504(g), as applicable.

(c)(1) *Standard: Documentation.* A covered entity must maintain a written or electronic record of a designation as required by paragraphs (a) or (b) of this section.

(2) *Implementation specification: Retention period.* A covered entity must retain the documentation as required by paragraph (c)(1) of this section for 6 years from the date of its creation or the date when it last was in effect, whichever is later.

[68 FR 8375, Feb. 20, 2003, as amended at 78 FR 5692, Jan. 25, 2013]

§164.106 Relationship to other parts.

In complying with the requirements of this part, covered entities and, where provided, business associates, are required to comply with the applicable provisions of parts 160 and 162 of this subchapter.

[78 FR 5693, Jan. 25, 2013]

SUBPART B [RESERVED]
SUBPART C—SECURITY STANDARDS FOR THE PROTECTION OF ELECTRONIC PROTECTED HEALTH INFORMATION

Authority: 42 U.S.C. 1320d-2 and 1320d-4; sec. 13401, Pub. L. 111-5, 123 Stat. 260.

Source: 68 FR 8376, Feb. 20, 2003, unless otherwise noted.

§164.302 Applicability.

A covered entity or business associate must comply with the applicable standards, implementation specifications, and requirements of this subpart with respect to electronic protected health information of a covered entity.

[78 FR 5693, Jan. 25, 2013]

§164.304 Definitions.

As used in this subpart, the following terms have the following meanings:

Access means the ability or the means necessary to read, write, modify, or communicate data/information or otherwise use any system resource. (This definition applies to "access" as used in this subpart, not as used in subparts D or E of this part.)

Administrative safeguards are administrative actions, and policies and procedures, to manage the selection, development, implementation, and maintenance of security measures to protect electronic protected health information and to manage the conduct of the covered entity's or business associate's workforce in relation to the protection of that information.

Authentication means the corroboration that a person is the one claimed.

Availability means the property that data or information is accessible and useable upon demand by an authorized person.

Confidentiality means the property that data or information is not made available or disclosed to unauthorized persons or processes.

Encryption means the use of an algorithmic process to transform data into a form in which there is a low probability of assigning meaning without use of a confidential process or key.

Facility means the physical premises and the interior and exterior of a building(s).

Information system means an interconnected set of information resources under the same direct management control that shares common functionality. A system normally includes hardware, software, information, data, applications, communications, and people.

Integrity means the property that data or information have not been altered or destroyed in an unauthorized manner.

Malicious software means software, for example, a virus, designed to damage or disrupt a system.

Password means confidential authentication information composed of a string of characters.

Physical safeguards are physical measures, policies, and procedures to protect a covered entity's or business associate's electronic information systems and related buildings and equipment, from natural and environmental hazards, and unauthorized intrusion.

Security or Security measures encompass all of the administrative, physical, and technical safeguards in an information system.

Security incident means the attempted or successful unauthorized access, use, disclosure, modification, or destruction of information or interference with system operations in an information system.

Technical safeguards means the technology and the policy and procedures for its use that protect electronic protected health information and control access to it.

User means a person or entity with authorized access.

Workstation means an electronic computing device, for example, a laptop or desktop computer, or any other device that performs similar functions, and electronic media stored in its immediate environment.

[68 FR 8376, Feb. 20, 2003, as amended at 74 FR 42767, Aug. 24, 2009; 78 FR 5693, Jan. 25, 2013]

§164.306 Security standards: General rules.

(a) *General requirements.* Covered entities and business associates must do the following:

(1) Ensure the confidentiality, integrity, and availability of all electronic protected health information the covered entity or business associate creates, receives, maintains, or transmits.

(2) Protect against any reasonably anticipated threats or hazards to the security or integrity of such information.

(3) Protect against any reasonably anticipated uses or disclosures of such information that are not permitted or required under subpart E of this part.

(4) Ensure compliance with this subpart by its workforce.

(b) *Flexibility of approach.* (1) Covered entities and business associates may use any security measures that allow the covered entity or business associate to reasonably and appropriately implement the standards and implementation specifications as specified in this subpart.

(2) In deciding which security measures to use, a covered entity or business associate must take into account the following factors:

(i) The size, complexity, and capabilities of the covered entity or business associate.

(ii) The covered entity's or the business associate's technical infrastructure, hardware, and software security capabilities.

(iii) The costs of security measures.

(iv) The probability and criticality of potential risks to electronic protected health information.

(c) *Standards.* A covered entity or business associate must comply with the applicable standards as provided in this section and in §§164.308, 164.310, 164.312, 164.314 and 164.316 with respect to all electronic protected health information.

(d) Implementation specifications. In this subpart:

(1) Implementation specifications are required or addressable. If an implementation specification is required, the word "Required" appears in parentheses after the title of the implementation specification. If an implementation specification is addressable, the word "Addressable" appears in parentheses after the title of the implementation specification.

(2) When a standard adopted in §164.308, §164.310, §164.312, §164.314, or §164.316 includes required implementation specifications, a covered entity or business associate must implement the implementation specifications.

(3) When a standard adopted in §164.308, §164.310, §164.312, §164.314, or §164.316 includes addressable implementation specifications, a covered entity or business associate must—

(i) Assess whether each implementation specification is a reasonable and appropriate safeguard in its environment, when analyzed with reference to the likely contribution to protecting electronic protected health information; and

(ii)   As applicable to the covered entity or business associate—

(A)   Implement the implementation specification if reasonable and appropriate; or

(B)   If implementing the implementation specification is not reasonable and appropriate—

(1)   Document why it would not be reasonable and appropriate to implement the implementation specification; and

(2)   Implement an equivalent alternative measure if reasonable and appropriate.

(e)   *Maintenance.* A covered entity or business associate must review and modify the security measures implemented under this subpart as needed to continue provision of reasonable and appropriate protection of electronic protected health information, and update documentation of such security measures in accordance with §164.316(b)(2)(iii).

[68 FR 8376, Feb. 20, 2003; 68 FR 17153, Apr. 8, 2003; 78 FR 5693, Jan. 25, 2013]

§164.308 Administrative safeguards.

(a)   A covered entity or business associate must, in accordance with §164.306:

(1)(i)   *Standard: Security management process.* Implement policies and procedures to prevent, detect, contain, and correct security violations.

(ii)   *Implementation specifications:*

(A)   *Risk analysis (Required).* Conduct an accurate and thorough assessment of the potential risks and vulnerabilities to the confidentiality, integrity, and availability of electronic protected health information held by the covered entity or business associate.

(B)   *Risk management (Required).* Implement security measures sufficient to reduce risks and vulnerabilities to a reasonable and appropriate level to comply with §164.306(a).

(C)   *Sanction policy (Required).* Apply appropriate sanctions against workforce members who fail to comply with the security policies and procedures of the covered entity or business associate.

(D) *Information system activity review (Required)*. Implement procedures to regularly review records of information system activity, such as audit logs, access reports, and security incident tracking reports.

(2) *Standard: Assigned security responsibility*. Identify the security official who is responsible for the development and implementation of the policies and procedures required by this subpart for the covered entity or business associate.

(3)(i) *Standard: Workforce security*. Implement policies and procedures to ensure that all members of its workforce have appropriate access to electronic protected health information, as provided under paragraph (a)(4) of this section, and to prevent those workforce members who do not have access under paragraph (a)(4) of this section from obtaining access to electronic protected health information.

(ii) *Implementation specifications:*

(A) *Authorization and/or supervision (Addressable)*. Implement procedures for the authorization and/or supervision of workforce members who work with electronic protected health information or in locations where it might be accessed.

(B) *Workforce clearance procedure (Addressable)*. Implement procedures to determine that the access of a workforce member to electronic protected health information is appropriate.

(C) *Termination procedures (Addressable)*. Implement procedures for terminating access to electronic protected health information when the employment of, or other arrangement with, a workforce member ends or as required by determinations made as specified in paragraph (a)(3)(ii)(B) of this section.

(4)(i) *Standard: Information access management*. Implement policies and procedures for authorizing access to electronic protected health information that are consistent with the applicable requirements of subpart E of this part.

(ii) *Implementation specifications:*

(A) *Isolating health care clearinghouse functions (Required).* If a health care clearinghouse is part of a larger organization, the clearinghouse must implement policies and procedures that protect the electronic protected health information of the clearinghouse from unauthorized access by the larger organization.

(B) *Access authorization (Addressable).* Implement policies and procedures for granting access to electronic protected health information, for example, through access to a workstation, transaction, program, process, or other mechanism.

(C) *Access establishment and modification (Addressable).* Implement policies and procedures that, based upon the covered entity's or the business associate's access authorization policies, establish, document, review, and modify a user's right of access to a workstation, transaction, program, or process.

(5)(i) *Standard: Security awareness and training.* Implement a security awareness and training program for all members of its workforce (including management).

(ii) Implementation specifications. Implement:

(A) *Security reminders (Addressable).* Periodic security updates.

(B) *Protection from malicious software (Addressable).* Procedures for guarding against, detecting, and reporting malicious software.

(C) *Log-in monitoring (Addressable).* Procedures for monitoring log-in attempts and reporting discrepancies.

(D) *Password management (Addressable).* Procedures for creating, changing, and safeguarding passwords.

(6)(i) *Standard: Security incident procedures.* Implement policies and procedures to address security incidents.

(ii) *Implementation specification: Response and reporting (Required).* Identify and respond to suspected or known security incidents; mitigate, to the extent practicable, harmful effects of security incidents that are known to the covered entity or business associate; and document security incidents and their outcomes.

(7)(i) *Standard: Contingency plan.* Establish (and implement as needed) policies and procedures for responding to an emergency or other occurrence (for example, fire, vandalism, system failure, and natural disaster) that damages systems that contain electronic protected health information.

  (ii) *Implementation specifications:*

  (A) *Data backup plan (Required).* Establish and implement procedures to create and maintain retrievable exact copies of electronic protected health information.

  (B) *Disaster recovery plan (Required).* Establish (and implement as needed) procedures to restore any loss of data.

  (C) *Emergency mode operation plan (Required).* Establish (and implement as needed) procedures to enable continuation of critical business processes for protection of the security of electronic protected health information while operating in emergency mode.

  (D) *Testing and revision procedures (Addressable).* Implement procedures for periodic testing and revision of contingency plans.

  (E) *Applications and data criticality analysis (Addressable).* Assess the relative criticality of specific applications and data in support of other contingency plan components.

(8) *Standard: Evaluation.* Perform a periodic technical and non-technical evaluation, based initially upon the standards implemented under this rule and, subsequently, in response to environmental or operational changes affecting the security of electronic protected health information, that establishes the extent to which a covered entity's or business associate's security policies and procedures meet the requirements of this subpart.

(b)(1) *Business associate contracts and other arrangements.* A covered entity may permit a business associate to create, receive, maintain, or transmit electronic protected health information on the covered entity's behalf only if the covered entity obtains satisfactory assurances, in accordance with §164.314(a), that the business associate will appropriately safeguard the information. A covered entity is not required to obtain such satisfactory assurances from a business associate that is a subcontractor.

(2) A business associate may permit a business associate that is a subcontractor to create, receive, maintain, or transmit electronic protected health information on its behalf only if the business associate obtains satisfactory assurances, in accordance with §164.314(a), that the subcontractor will appropriately safeguard the information.

(3) *Implementation specifications: Written contract or other arrangement (Required).* Document the satisfactory assurances required by paragraph (b)(1) or (b)(2) of this section through a written contract or other arrangement with the business associate that meets the applicable requirements of §164.314(a).

[68 FR 8376, Feb. 20, 2003, as amended at 78 FR 5694, Jan. 25, 2013]

§164.310 Physical safeguards.

A covered entity or business associate must, in accordance with §164.306:

(a)(1) *Standard: Facility access controls.* Implement policies and procedures to limit physical access to its electronic information systems and the facility or facilities in which they are housed, while ensuring that properly authorized access is allowed.

(2) *Implementation specifications:*

(i) *Contingency operations (Addressable).* Establish (and implement as needed) procedures that allow facility access in support of restoration of lost data under the disaster recovery plan and emergency mode operations plan in the event of an emergency.

(ii) *Facility security plan (Addressable).* Implement policies and procedures to safeguard the facility and the equipment therein from unauthorized physical access, tampering, and theft.

(iii) *Access control and validation procedures (Addressable).* Implement procedures to control and validate a person's access to facilities based on their role or function, including visitor control, and control of access to software programs for testing and revision.

(iv) *Maintenance records (Addressable).* Implement policies and procedures to document repairs and modifications to the physical components of a facility which are related to security (for example, hardware, walls, doors, and locks).

(b) *Standard: Workstation use.* Implement policies and procedures that specify the proper functions to be performed, the manner in which those functions are to be performed, and the physical attributes of the surroundings of a specific workstation or class of workstation that can access electronic protected health information.

(c) *Standard: Workstation security.* Implement physical safeguards for all workstations that access electronic protected health information, to restrict access to authorized users.

(d)(1) *Standard: Device and media controls.* Implement policies and procedures that govern the receipt and removal of hardware and electronic media that contain electronic protected health information into and out of a facility, and the movement of these items within the facility.

(2) *Implementation specifications:*

(i) *Disposal (Required).* Implement policies and procedures to address the final disposition of electronic protected health information, and/or the hardware or electronic media on which it is stored.

(ii) *Media re-use (Required).* Implement procedures for removal of electronic protected health information from electronic media before the media are made available for re-use.

(iii) *Accountability (Addressable).* Maintain a record of the movements of hardware and electronic media and any person responsible therefore.

(iv) *Data backup and storage (Addressable).* Create a retrievable, exact copy of electronic protected health information, when needed, before movement of equipment.

[68 FR 8376, Feb. 20, 2003, as amended at 78 FR 5694, Jan. 25, 2013]

§164.312 Technical safeguards.

A covered entity or business associate must, in accordance with §164.306:

(a)(1) *Standard: Access control.* Implement technical policies and procedures for electronic information systems that maintain electronic protected health information to allow access only to those persons or software programs that have been granted access rights as specified in §164.308(a)(4).

    (2) *Implementation specifications:*

        (i) *Unique user identification (Required).* Assign a unique name and/or number for identifying and tracking user identity.

        (ii) *Emergency access procedure (Required).* Establish (and implement as needed) procedures for obtaining necessary electronic protected health information during an emergency.

        (iii) *Automatic logoff (Addressable).* Implement electronic procedures that terminate an electronic session after a predetermined time of inactivity.

        (iv) *Encryption and decryption (Addressable).* Implement a mechanism to encrypt and decrypt electronic protected health information.

(b) *Standard: Audit controls.* Implement hardware, software, and/or procedural mechanisms that record and examine activity in information systems that contain or use electronic protected health information.

(c)(1) *Standard: Integrity.* Implement policies and procedures to protect electronic protected health information from improper alteration or destruction.

    (2) *Implementation specification: Mechanism to authenticate electronic protected health information (Addressable).* Implement electronic mechanisms to corroborate that electronic protected health information has not been altered or destroyed in an unauthorized manner.

(d) *Standard: Person or entity authentication.* Implement procedures to verify that a person or entity seeking access to electronic protected health information is the one claimed.

(e)(1) *Standard: Transmission security.* Implement technical security measures to guard against unauthorized access to electronic protected health information that is being transmitted over an electronic communications network.

(2) *Implementation specifications:*

(i) *Integrity controls (Addressable).* Implement security measures to ensure that electronically transmitted electronic protected health information is not improperly modified without detection until disposed of.

(ii) *Encryption (Addressable).* Implement a mechanism to encrypt electronic protected health information whenever deemed appropriate.

[68 FR 8376, Feb. 20, 2003, as amended at 78 FR 5694, Jan. 25, 2013]

§164.314 Organizational requirements.

(a)(1) *Standard: Business associate contracts or other arrangements.* The contract or other arrangement required by §164.308(b)(3) must meet the requirements of paragraph (a)(2)(i), (a)(2)(ii), or (a)(2)(iii) of this section, as applicable.

(2) *Implementation specifications (Required).*

(i) *Business associate contracts.* The contract must provide that the business associate will—

(A) Comply with the applicable requirements of this subpart;

(B) In accordance with §164.308(b)(2), ensure that any subcontractors that create, receive, maintain, or transmit electronic protected health information on behalf of the business associate agree to comply with the applicable requirements of this subpart by entering into a contract or other arrangement that complies with this section; and

(C) Report to the covered entity any security incident of which it becomes aware, including breaches of unsecured protected health information as required by §164.410.

(ii) *Other arrangements.* The covered entity is in compliance with paragraph (a)(1) of this section if it has another arrangement in place that meets the requirements of §164.504(e)(3).

(iii) *Business associate contracts with subcontractors.* The requirements of paragraphs (a)(2)(i) and (a)(2)(ii) of this section apply to the contract or other arrangement between a business associate and a subcontractor required by §164.308(b)(4) in the same manner as such requirements apply to contracts or other arrangements between a covered entity and business associate.

(b)(1) *Standard: Requirements for group health plans.* Except when the only electronic protected health information disclosed to a plan sponsor is disclosed pursuant to §164.504(f)(1)(ii) or (iii), or as authorized under §164.508, a group health plan must ensure that its plan documents provide that the plan sponsor will reasonably and appropriately safeguard electronic protected health information created, received, maintained, or transmitted to or by the plan sponsor on behalf of the group health plan.

(2) *Implementation specifications (Required).* The plan documents of the group health plan must be amended to incorporate provisions to require the plan sponsor to—

(i) Implement administrative, physical, and technical safeguards that reasonably and appropriately protect the confidentiality, integrity, and availability of the electronic protected health information that it creates, receives, maintains, or transmits on behalf of the group health plan;

(ii) Ensure that the adequate separation required by §164.504(f)(2)(iii) is supported by reasonable and appropriate security measures;

(iii) Ensure that any agent to whom it provides this information agrees to implement reasonable and appropriate security measures to protect the information; and

(iv) Report to the group health plan any security incident of which it becomes aware.

[68 FR 8376, Feb. 20, 2003, as amended at 78 FR 5694, Jan. 25, 2013; 78 FR 34266, June 7, 2013]

§164.316 Policies and procedures and documentation requirements.

A covered entity or business associate must, in accordance with §164.306:

(a) *Standard: Policies and procedures.* Implement reasonable and appropriate policies and procedures to comply with the standards, implementation specifications, or other requirements of this subpart, taking into account those factors specified in §164.306(b)(2)(i), (ii), (iii), and (iv). This standard is not to be construed to permit or excuse an action that violates any other standard, implementation specification, or other requirements of this subpart. A covered entity or business associate may change its policies and procedures at any time, provided that the changes are documented and are implemented in accordance with this subpart.

(b)(1) *Standard: Documentation.* (i) Maintain the policies and procedures implemented to comply with this subpart in written (which may be electronic) form; and

(ii) If an action, activity or assessment is required by this subpart to be documented, maintain a written (which may be electronic) record of the action, activity, or assessment.

(2) *Implementation specifications:*

(i) *Time limit (Required).* Retain the documentation required by paragraph (b)(1) of this section for 6 years from the date of its creation or the date when it last was in effect, whichever is later.

(ii) *Availability (Required).* Make documentation available to those persons responsible for implementing the procedures to which the documentation pertains.

(iii) *Updates (Required).* Review documentation periodically, and update as needed, in response to environmental or operational changes affecting the security of the electronic protected health information.

[68 FR 8376, Feb. 20, 2003, as amended at 78 FR 5695, Jan. 25, 2013]

§164.318 Compliance dates for the initial implementation of the security standards.

(a) *Health plan.* (1) A health plan that is not a small health plan must comply with the applicable requirements of this subpart no later than April 20, 2005.

(2) A small health plan must comply with the applicable requirements of this subpart no later than April 20, 2006.

(b) *Health care clearinghouse.* A health care clearinghouse must comply with the applicable requirements of this subpart no later than April 20, 2005.

(c) *Health care provider.* A covered health care provider must comply with the applicable requirements of this subpart no later than April 20, 2005.

Appendix A to Subpart C of Part 164—Security Standards: Matrix

Standards	Sections	Implementation Specifications (R) = Required, (A) = Addressable
Administrative Safeguards		
Security Management Process	164.308(a)(1)	Risk Analysis (R)
		Risk Management (R)
		Sanction Policy (R)
		Information System Activity Review (R)
Assigned Security Responsibility	164.308(a)(2)	(R)
Workforce Security	164.308(a)(3)	Authorization and/or Supervision (A)
		Workforce Clearance Procedure
		Termination Procedures (A)
Information Access Management	164.308(a)(4)	Isolating Health care Clearinghouse Function (R)
		Access Authorization (A)
		Access Establishment and Modification (A)
Security Awareness and Training	164.308(a)(5)	Security Reminders (A)
		Protection from Malicious Software (A)
		Log-in Monitoring (A)
		Password Management (A)
Security Incident Procedures	164.308(a)(6)	Response and Reporting (R)
Contingency Plan	164.308(a)(7)	Data Backup Plan (R)
		Disaster Recovery Plan (R)
		Emergency Mode Operation Plan (R)
		Testing and Revision Procedure (A)
		Applications and Data Criticality Analysis (A)
Evaluation	164.308(a)(8)	(R)
Business Associate Contracts and Other Arrangement	164.308(b)(1)	Written Contract or Other Arrangement (R)

Physical Safeguards		
Facility Access Controls	164.310(a)(1)	Contingency Operations (A)
		Facility Security Plan (A)
		Access Control and Validation Procedures (A)
		Maintenance Records (A)
Workstation Use	164.310(b)	(R)
Workstation Security	164.310(c)	(R)
Device and Media Controls	164.310(d)(1)	Disposal (R)
		Media Re-use (R)
		Accountability (A)
		Data Backup and Storage (A)
Technical Safeguards (see §164.312)		
Access Control	164.312(a)(1)	Unique User Identification (R)
		Emergency Access Procedure (R)
		Automatic Logoff (A)
		Encryption and Decryption (A)
Audit Controls	164.312(b)	(R)
Integrity	164.312(c)(1)	Mechanism to Authenticate Electronic Protected Health Information (A)
Person or Entity Authentication	164.312(d)	(R)
Transmission Security	164.312(e)(1)	Integrity Controls (A)
		Encryption (A)

SUBPART D—NOTIFICATION IN THE CASE OF BREACH OF UNSECURED PROTECTED HEALTH INFORMATION

Source: 74 FR 42767, Aug. 24, 2009, unless otherwise noted.

§164.400 Applicability.

The requirements of this subpart shall apply with respect to breaches of protected health information occurring on or after September 23, 2009.

§164.402 Definitions.

As used in this subpart, the following terms have the following meanings:

Breach means the acquisition, access, use, or disclosure of protected health information in a manner not permitted under subpart E of this part which compromises the security or privacy of the protected health information.

(1) Breach excludes:

(i) Any unintentional acquisition, access, or use of protected health information by a workforce member or person acting under the authority of a covered entity or a business associate, if such acquisition, access, or use was made in good faith and within the scope of authority and does not result in further use or disclosure in a manner not permitted under subpart E of this part.

(ii) Any inadvertent disclosure by a person who is authorized to access protected health information at a covered entity or business associate to another person authorized to access protected health information at the same covered entity or business associate, or organized health care arrangement in which the covered entity participates, and the information received as a result of such disclosure is not further used or disclosed in a manner not permitted under subpart E of this part.

(iii) A disclosure of protected health information where a covered entity or business associate has a good faith belief that an unauthorized person to whom the disclosure was made would not reasonably have been able to retain such information.

(2) Except as provided in paragraph (1) of this definition, an acquisition, access, use, or disclosure of protected health information in a manner not permitted under subpart E is presumed to be a breach unless the covered entity or business associate, as applicable, demonstrates that there is a low probability that the protected health information has been compromised based on a risk assessment of at least the following factors:

(i) The nature and extent of the protected health information involved, including the types of identifiers and the likelihood of re-identification;

(ii) The unauthorized person who used the protected health information or to whom the disclosure was made;

(iii) Whether the protected health information was actually acquired or viewed; and

(iv) The extent to which the risk to the protected health information has been mitigated.

Unsecured protected health information means protected health information that is not rendered unusable, unreadable, or indecipherable to unauthorized persons through the use of a technology or methodology specified by the Secretary in the guidance issued under section 13402(h)(2) of Public Law 111-5.

[78 FR 5695, Jan. 25, 2013]

§164.404 Notification to individuals.

(a) *Standard*—(1) *General rule.* A covered entity shall, following the discovery of a breach of unsecured protected health information, notify each individual whose unsecured protected health information has been, or is reasonably believed by the covered entity to have been, accessed, acquired, used, or disclosed as a result of such breach.

(2) *Breaches treated as discovered.* For purposes of paragraph (a)(1) of this section, §§164.406(a), and 164.408(a), a breach shall be treated as discovered by a covered entity as of the first day on which such breach is known to the covered entity, or, by exercising reasonable diligence would have been known to the covered entity. A covered entity shall be deemed to have knowledge of a breach if such breach is known, or by exercising reasonable diligence would have been known, to any person, other than the person committing the breach, who is a workforce member or agent of the covered entity (determined in accordance with the federal common law of agency).

(b) *Implementation specification: Timeliness of notification.* Except as provided in §164.412, a covered entity shall provide the notification required by paragraph (a) of this section without unreasonable delay and in no case later than 60 calendar days after discovery of a breach.

(c) *Implementation specifications: Content of notification*—(1) *Elements.* The notification required by paragraph (a) of this section shall include, to the extent possible:

(A) A brief description of what happened, including the date of the breach and the date of the discovery of the breach, if known;

(B) A description of the types of unsecured protected health information that were involved in the breach (such as whether full name, social security number, date of birth, home address, account number, diagnosis, disability code, or other types of information were involved);

(C) Any steps individuals should take to protect themselves from potential harm resulting from the breach;

(D) A brief description of what the covered entity involved is doing to investigate the breach, to mitigate harm to individuals, and to protect against any further breaches; and

(E) Contact procedures for individuals to ask questions or learn additional information, which shall include a toll-free telephone number, an e-mail address, Web site, or postal address.

(2) *Plain language requirement.* The notification required by paragraph (a) of this section shall be written in plain language.

(d) *Implementation specifications: Methods of individual notification.* The notification required by paragraph (a) of this section shall be provided in the following form:

(1) *Written notice.* (i) Written notification by first-class mail to the individual at the last known address of the individual or, if the individual agrees to electronic notice and such agreement has not been withdrawn, by electronic mail. The notification may be provided in one or more mailings as information is available.

(ii) If the covered entity knows the individual is deceased and has the address of the next of kin or personal representative of the individual (as specified under §164.502(g)(4) of subpart E), written notification by first-class mail to either the next of kin or personal representative of the individual. The notification may be provided in one or more mailings as information is available.

(2) *Substitute notice.* In the case in which there is insufficient or out-of-date contact information that precludes written notification to the individual under paragraph (d)(1)(i) of this section, a substitute form of notice reasonably calculated to reach the individual shall be provided. Substitute notice need not be provided

in the case in which there is insufficient or out-of-date contact information that precludes written notification to the next of kin or personal representative of the individual under paragraph (d)(1)(ii).

(i)   In the case in which there is insufficient or out-of-date contact information for fewer than 10 individuals, then such substitute notice may be provided by an alternative form of written notice, telephone, or other means.

(ii)   In the case in which there is insufficient or out-of-date contact information for 10 or more individuals, then such substitute notice shall:

(A)   Be in the form of either a conspicuous posting for a period of 90 days on the home page of the Web site of the covered entity involved, or conspicuous notice in major print or broadcast media in geographic areas where the individuals affected by the breach likely reside; and

(B)   Include a toll-free phone number that remains active for at least 90 days where an individual can learn whether the individual's unsecured protected health information may be included in the breach.

(3)   *Additional notice in urgent situations.* In any case deemed by the covered entity to require urgency because of possible imminent misuse of unsecured protected health information, the covered entity may provide information to individuals by telephone or other means, as appropriate, in addition to notice provided under paragraph (d)(1) of this section.

§164.406 Notification to the media.

(a)   *Standard.* For a breach of unsecured protected health information involving more than 500 residents of a State or jurisdiction, a covered entity shall, following the discovery of the breach as provided in §164.404(a)(2), notify prominent media outlets serving the State or jurisdiction.

(b)   *Implementation specification: Timeliness of notification.* Except as provided in §164.412, a covered entity shall provide the notification required by paragraph (a) of this section without unreasonable delay and in no case later than 60 calendar days after discovery of a breach.

(c) *Implementation specifications: Content of notification.* The notification required by paragraph (a) of this section shall meet the requirements of §164.404(c).

[74 FR 42767, Aug. 24, 2009, as amended at 78 FR 5695, Jan. 25, 2013]

§164.408 Notification to the Secretary.

(a) *Standard.* A covered entity shall, following the discovery of a breach of unsecured protected health information as provided in §164.404(a)(2), notify the Secretary.

(b) *Implementation specifications: Breaches involving 500 or more individuals.* For breaches of unsecured protected health information involving 500 or more individuals, a covered entity shall, except as provided in §164.412, provide the notification required by paragraph (a) of this section contemporaneously with the notice required by §164.404(a) and in the manner specified on the HHS Web site.

(c) *Implementation specifications: Breaches involving less than 500 individuals.* For breaches of unsecured protected health information involving less than 500 individuals, a covered entity shall maintain a log or other documentation of such breaches and, not later than 60 days after the end of each calendar year, provide the notification required by paragraph (a) of this section for breaches discovered during the preceding calendar year, in the manner specified on the HHS web site.

[74 FR 42767, Aug. 24, 2009, as amended at 78 FR 5695, Jan. 25, 2013]

§164.410 Notification by a business associate.

(a) *Standard*—(1) *General rule.* A business associate shall, following the discovery of a breach of unsecured protected health information, notify the covered entity of such breach.

(2) *Breaches treated as discovered.* For purposes of paragraph (a)(1) of this section, a breach shall be treated as discovered by a business associate as of the first day on which such breach is known to the business associate or, by exercising reasonable diligence, would have been known to the business associate. A business associate shall be deemed to have knowledge of a breach if the breach is known, or by exercising reasonable diligence would have been known, to any person, other than the person committing the breach, who is an

employee, officer, or other agent of the business associate (determined in accordance with the Federal common law of agency).

(b) *Implementation specifications: Timeliness of notification.* Except as provided in §164.412, a business associate shall provide the notification required by paragraph (a) of this section without unreasonable delay and in no case later than 60 calendar days after discovery of a breach.

(c) *Implementation specifications: Content of notification.* (1) The notification required by paragraph (a) of this section shall include, to the extent possible, the identification of each individual whose unsecured protected health information has been, or is reasonably believed by the business associate to have been, accessed, acquired, used, or disclosed during the breach.

(2) A business associate shall provide the covered entity with any other available information that the covered entity is required to include in notification to the individual under §164.404(c) at the time of the notification required by paragraph (a) of this section or promptly thereafter as information becomes available.

[74 FR 42767, Aug. 24, 2009, as amended at 78 FR 5695, Jan. 25, 2013]

§164.412 Law enforcement delay.

If a law enforcement official states to a covered entity or business associate that a notification, notice, or posting required under this subpart would impede a criminal investigation or cause damage to national security, a covered entity or business associate shall:

(a) If the statement is in writing and specifies the time for which a delay is required, delay such notification, notice, or posting for the time period specified by the official; or

(b) If the statement is made orally, document the statement, including the identity of the official making the statement, and delay the notification, notice, or posting temporarily and no longer than 30 days from the date of the oral statement, unless a written statement as described in paragraph (a) of this section is submitted during that time.

§164.414 Administrative requirements and burden of proof.

(a) *Administrative requirements.* A covered entity is required to comply with the administrative requirements of §164.530(b), (d), (e), (g), (h), (i), and (j) with respect to the requirements of this subpart.

(b) *Burden of proof.* In the event of a use or disclosure in violation of subpart E, the covered entity or business associate, as applicable, shall have the burden of demonstrating that all notifications were made as required by this subpart or that the use or disclosure did not constitute a breach, as defined at §164.402.

SUBPART E—PRIVACY OF INDIVIDUALLY IDENTIFIABLE HEALTH INFORMATION

Authority: 42 U.S.C. 1320d-2, 1320d-4, and 1320d-9; sec. 264 of Pub. L. 104-191, 110 Stat. 2033-2034 (42 U.S.C. 1320d-2 (note)); and secs. 13400-13424, Pub. L. 111-5, 123 Stat. 258-279.

§164.500 Applicability.

(a) Except as otherwise provided herein, the standards, requirements, and implementation specifications of this subpart apply to covered entities with respect to protected health information.

(b) Health care clearinghouses must comply with the standards, requirements, and implementation specifications as follows:

(1) When a health care clearinghouse creates or receives protected health information as a business associate of another covered entity, the clearinghouse must comply with:

(i) Section 164.500 relating to applicability;

(ii) Section 164.501 relating to definitions;

(iii) Section 164.502 relating to uses and disclosures of protected health information, except that a clearinghouse is prohibited from using or disclosing protected health information other than as permitted in the business associate contract under which it created or received the protected health information;

(iv) Section 164.504 relating to the organizational requirements for covered entities;

(v) Section 164.512 relating to uses and disclosures for which individual authorization or an opportunity to agree or object is not required, except that a clearinghouse is prohibited from using or disclosing protected health information other than as permitted in the business associate contract under which it created or received the protected health information;

(vi) Section 164.532 relating to transition requirements; and

(vii) Section 164.534 relating to compliance dates for initial implementation of the privacy standards.

(2)   When a health care clearinghouse creates or receives protected health information other than as a business associate of a covered entity, the clearinghouse must comply with all of the standards, requirements, and implementation specifications of this subpart.

(c) Where provided, the standards, requirements, and implementation specifications adopted under this subpart apply to a business associate with respect to the protected health information of a covered entity.

(d) The standards, requirements, and implementation specifications of this subpart do not apply to the Department of Defense or to any other federal agency, or non-governmental organization acting on its behalf, when providing health care to overseas foreign national beneficiaries.

[65 FR 82802, Dec. 28, 2000, as amended at 67 FR 53266, Aug. 14, 2002; 68 FR 8381, Feb. 20, 2003; 78 FR 5695, Jan. 25, 2013]

§164.501 Definitions.

As used in this subpart, the following terms have the following meanings:

Correctional institution means any penal or correctional facility, jail, reformatory, detention center, work farm, halfway house, or residential community program center operated by, or under contract to, the United States, a State, a territory, a political subdivision of a State or territory, or an Indian tribe, for the confinement or rehabilitation of persons charged with or convicted of a criminal offense or other persons held in lawful custody. *Other persons* held in lawful custody includes juvenile offenders adjudicated delinquent, aliens detained awaiting deportation, persons committed to mental institutions through the criminal justice system, witnesses, or others awaiting charges or trial.

Data aggregation means, with respect to protected health information created or received by a business associate in its capacity as the business associate of a covered entity, the combining of such protected health information by the business associate with the protected health information received by the business associate in its capacity as a business associate of another covered entity, to permit data analyses that relate to the health care operations of the respective covered entities.

Designated record set means:

(1) A group of records maintained by or for a covered entity that is:

(i) The medical records and billing records about individuals maintained by or for a covered health care provider;

(ii) The enrollment, payment, claims adjudication, and case or medical management record systems maintained by or for a health plan; or

(iii) Used, in whole or in part, by or for the covered entity to make decisions about individuals.

(2) For purposes of this paragraph, the term record means any item, collection, or grouping of information that includes protected health information and is maintained, collected, used, or disseminated by or for a covered entity.

Direct treatment relationship means a treatment relationship between an individual and a health care provider that is not an indirect treatment relationship.

Health care operations means any of the following activities of the covered entity to the extent that the activities are related to covered functions:

(1) Conducting quality assessment and improvement activities, including outcomes evaluation and development of clinical guidelines, provided that the obtaining of generalizable knowledge is not the primary purpose of any studies resulting from such activities; patient safety activities (as defined in 42 CFR 3.20); population-based activities relating to improving health or reducing health care costs, protocol development, case management and care coordination, contacting of health care providers and patients with information about treatment alternatives; and related functions that do not include treatment;

(2) Reviewing the competence or qualifications of health care professionals, evaluating practitioner and provider performance, health plan performance, conducting training programs in which students, trainees, or practitioners in areas of health care learn under supervision to practice or improve their skills as health care providers, training of non-health care professionals, accreditation, certification, licensing, or credentialing activities;

(3) Except as prohibited under §164.502(a)(5)(i), underwriting, enrollment, premium rating, and other activities related to the creation, renewal, or replacement of a contract of health insurance or health benefits, and ceding, securing, or placing a contract for reinsurance of risk relating to claims for health care (including stop-loss insurance and excess of loss insurance), provided that the requirements of §164.514(g) are met, if applicable;

(4) Conducting or arranging for medical review, legal services, and auditing functions, including fraud and abuse detection and compliance programs;

(5) Business planning and development, such as conducting cost-management and planning-related analyses related to managing and operating the entity, including formulary development and administration, development or improvement of methods of payment or coverage policies; and

(6) Business management and general administrative activities of the entity, including, but not limited to:

   (i)   Management activities relating to implementation of and compliance with the requirements of this subchapter;

   (ii) Customer service, including the provision of data analyses for policy holders, plan sponsors, or other customers, provided that protected health information is not disclosed to such policy holder, plan sponsor, or customer.

   (iii) Resolution of internal grievances;

   (iv) The sale, transfer, merger, or consolidation of all or part of the covered entity with another covered entity, or an entity that following such activity will become a covered entity and due diligence related to such activity; and

   (v)   Consistent with the applicable requirements of §164.514, creating de-identified health information or a limited data set, and fundraising for the benefit of the covered entity.

Health oversight agency means an agency or authority of the United States, a State, a territory, a political subdivision of a State or territory, or an Indian tribe, or a person or entity acting under a grant of authority from or contract with such public agency, including the employees or agents of such public agency or its contractors or persons or entities to whom it has granted authority, that is authorized by law to oversee the health care system (whether public or private) or government programs in which health information is necessary to determine eligibility or compliance, or to enforce civil rights laws for which health information is relevant.

Indirect treatment relationship means a relationship between an individual and a health care provider in which:

(1) The health care provider delivers health care to the individual based on the orders of another health care provider; and

(2) The health care provider typically provides services or products, or reports the diagnosis or results associated with the health care, directly to another health care provider, who provides the services or products or reports to the individual.

Inmate means a person incarcerated in or otherwise confined to a correctional institution.

Marketing:

(1) Except as provided in paragraph (2) of this definition, marketing means to make a communication about a product or service that encourages recipients of the communication to purchase or use the product or service.

(2) Marketing does not include a communication made:

(i) To provide refill reminders or otherwise communicate about a drug or biologic that is currently being prescribed for the individual, only if any financial remuneration received by the covered entity in exchange for making the communication is reasonably related to the covered entity's cost of making the communication.

(ii) For the following treatment and health care operations purposes, except where the covered entity receives financial remuneration in exchange for making the communication:

(A) For treatment of an individual by a health care provider, including case management or care coordination for the individual, or to direct or recommend alternative treatments, therapies, health care providers, or settings of care to the individual;

(B) To describe a health-related product or service (or payment for such product or service) that is provided by, or included in a plan of benefits of, the covered entity making the communication, including communications about: the entities participating in a health care provider network or health plan network; replacement of, or enhancements to, a health plan; and health-related products or services available only to a health plan enrollee that add value to, but are not part of, a plan of benefits; or

(C) For case management or care coordination, contacting of individuals with information about treatment alternatives, and related functions to the extent these activities do not fall within the definition of treatment.

(3) *Financial remuneration* means direct or indirect payment from or on behalf of a third party whose product or service is being described. Direct or indirect payment does not include any payment for treatment of an individual.

Payment means:

(1) The activities undertaken by:

(i) Except as prohibited under §164.502(a)(5)(i), a health plan to obtain premiums or to determine or fulfill its responsibility for coverage and provision of benefits under the health plan; or

(ii) A health care provider or health plan to obtain or provide reimbursement for the provision of health care; and

(2) The activities in paragraph (1) of this definition relate to the individual to whom health care is provided and include, but are not limited to:

(i) Determinations of eligibility or coverage (including coordination of benefits or the determination of cost sharing amounts), and adjudication or subrogation of health benefit claims;

(ii) Risk adjusting amounts due based on enrollee health status and demographic characteristics;

(iii) Billing, claims management, collection activities, obtaining payment under a contract for reinsurance (including stop-loss insurance and excess of loss insurance), and related health care data processing;

(iv) Review of health care services with respect to medical necessity, coverage under a health plan, appropriateness of care, or justification of charges;

(v) Utilization review activities, including precertification and preauthorization of services, concurrent and retrospective review of services; and

(vi) Disclosure to consumer reporting agencies of any of the following protected health information relating to collection of premiums or reimbursement:

    (A) Name and address;

    (B) Date of birth;

    (C) Social security number;

    (D) Payment history;

    (E) Account number; and

    (F) Name and address of the health care provider and/or health plan.

Psychotherapy notes means notes recorded (in any medium) by a health care provider who is a mental health professional documenting or analyzing the contents of conversation during a private counseling session or a group, joint, or family counseling session and that are separated from the rest of the individual's medical record. *Psychotherapy notes* excludes medication prescription and monitoring, counseling session start and stop times, the modalities and frequencies of treatment furnished, results of clinical tests, and any summary of the following items: Diagnosis, functional status, the treatment plan, symptoms, prognosis, and progress to date.

Public health authority means an agency or authority of the United States, a State, a territory, a political subdivision of a State or territory, or an Indian tribe, or a person or entity acting under a grant of authority from or contract with such public agency, including the employees or agents of such public agency or its contractors or persons or entities to whom it has granted authority, that is responsible for public health matters as part of its official mandate.

Research means a systematic investigation, including research development, testing, and evaluation, designed to develop or contribute to generalizable knowledge.

Treatment means the provision, coordination, or management of health care and related services by one or more health care providers, including the coordination or management of health care by a health care provider with a third party; consultation between health care providers relating to a patient; or the referral of a patient for health care from one health care provider to another.

[65 FR 82802, Dec. 28, 2000, as amended at 67 FR 53266, Aug. 14, 2002; 68 FR 8381, Feb. 20, 2003; 74 FR 42769, Aug. 24, 2009; 78 FR 5695, Jan. 25, 2013]

§164.502 Uses and disclosures of protected health information: General rules.

(a) *Standard.* A covered entity or business associate may not use or disclose protected health information, except as permitted or required by this subpart or by subpart C of part 160 of this subchapter.

(1) *Covered entities: Permitted uses and disclosures.* A covered entity is permitted to use or disclose protected health information as follows:

(i)   To the individual;

(ii) For treatment, payment, or health care operations, as permitted by and in compliance with §164.506;

(iii) Incident to a use or disclosure otherwise permitted or required by this subpart, provided that the covered entity has complied with the applicable requirements of §§164.502(b), 164.514(d), and 164.530(c) with respect to such otherwise permitted or required use or disclosure;

(iv) Except for uses and disclosures prohibited under §164.502(a)(5)(i), pursuant to and in compliance with a valid authorization under §164.508;

(v)   Pursuant to an agreement under, or as otherwise permitted by, §164.510; and

(vi) As permitted by and in compliance with this section, §164.512, §164.514(e), (f), or (g).

(2) *Covered entities: Required disclosures.* A covered entity is required to disclose protected health information:

(i)   To an individual, when requested under, and required by §164.524 or §164.528; and

(ii)   When required by the Secretary under subpart C of part 160 of this subchapter to investigate or determine the covered entity's compliance with this subchapter.

(3) *Business associates: Permitted uses and disclosures.* A business associate may use or disclose protected health information only as permitted or required by its business associate contract or other arrangement pursuant to §164.504(e) or as required by law. The business associate may not use or disclose protected health information in a manner that would violate the requirements of this subpart, if done by the covered entity, except for the purposes specified under §164.504(e)(2)(i)(A) or (B) if such uses or disclosures are permitted by its contract or other arrangement.

(4) *Business associates: Required uses and disclosures.* A business associate is required to disclose protected health information:

(i)   When required by the Secretary under subpart C of part 160 of this subchapter to investigate or determine the business associate's compliance with this subchapter.

(ii)   To the covered entity, individual, or individual's designee, as necessary to satisfy a covered entity's obligations under §164.524(c)(2)(ii) and (3)(ii) with respect to an individual's request for an electronic copy of protected health information.

(5)   Prohibited uses and disclosures.

(i)   *Use and disclosure of genetic information for underwriting purposes:* Notwithstanding any other provision of this subpart, a health plan, excluding an issuer of a long-term care policy falling within paragraph (1)(viii) of the definition of *health plan,* shall not use or disclose protected health information that is genetic information for underwriting purposes. For purposes of paragraph (a)(5)(i) of this section, underwriting purposes means, with respect to a health plan:

(A)   Except as provided in paragraph (a)(5)(i)(B) of this section:

(*1*)   Rules for, or determination of, eligibility (including enrollment and continued eligibility) for, or determination of, benefits under the plan, coverage, or policy (including changes in deductibles or other cost-sharing mechanisms in return for activities such as completing a health risk assessment or participating in a wellness program);

(2) The computation of premium or contribution amounts under the plan, coverage, or policy (including discounts, rebates, payments in kind, or other premium differential mechanisms in return for activities such as completing a health risk assessment or participating in a wellness program);

(3) The application of any pre-existing condition exclusion under the plan, coverage, or policy; and

(4) Other activities related to the creation, renewal, or replacement of a contract of health insurance or health benefits.

(B) Underwriting purposes does not include determinations of medical appropriateness where an individual seeks a benefit under the plan, coverage, or policy.

(ii) *Sale of protected health information:*

(A) Except pursuant to and in compliance with §164.508(a)(4), a covered entity or business associate may not sell protected health information.

(B) For purposes of this paragraph, sale of protected health information means:

(1) Except as provided in paragraph (a)(5)(ii)(B)(2) of this section, a disclosure of protected health information by a covered entity or business associate, if applicable, where the covered entity or business associate directly or indirectly receives remuneration from or on behalf of the recipient of the protected health information in exchange for the protected health information.

(2) Sale of protected health information does not include a disclosure of protected health information:

(i) For public health purposes pursuant to §164.512(b) or §164.514(e);

(*ii*) For research purposes pursuant to §164.512(i) or §164.514(e), where the only remuneration received by the covered entity or business associate is a reasonable cost-based fee to cover the cost to prepare and transmit the protected health information for such purposes;

(*iii*) For treatment and payment purposes pursuant to §164.506(a);

(*iv*) For the sale, transfer, merger, or consolidation of all or part of the covered entity and for related due diligence as described in paragraph (6)(iv) of the definition of health care operations and pursuant to §164.506(a);

(*v*) To or by a business associate for activities that the business associate undertakes on behalf of a covered entity, or on behalf of a business associate in the case of a subcontractor, pursuant to §§164.502(e) and 164.504(e), and the only remuneration provided is by the covered entity to the business associate, or by the business associate to the subcontractor, if applicable, for the performance of such activities;

(*vi*) To an individual, when requested under §164.524 or §164.528;

(*vii*) Required by law as permitted under §164.512(a); and

(*viii*) For any other purpose permitted by and in accordance with the applicable requirements of this subpart, where the only remuneration received by the covered entity or business associate is a reasonable, cost-based fee to cover the cost to prepare and transmit the protected health information for such purpose or a fee otherwise expressly permitted by other law.

(b) *Standard: Minimum necessary—Minimum necessary applies.* When using or disclosing protected health information or when requesting protected health information from another covered entity or business associate, a covered entity or business associate must make reasonable efforts to limit protected health information to the minimum necessary to accomplish the intended purpose of the use, disclosure, or request.

(2) *Minimum necessary does not apply.* This requirement does not apply to:

(i) Disclosures to or requests by a health care provider for treatment;

(ii) Uses or disclosures made to the individual, as permitted under paragraph (a)(1)(i) of this section or as required by paragraph (a)(2)(i) of this section;

(iii) Uses or disclosures made pursuant to an authorization under §164.508;

(iv) Disclosures made to the Secretary in accordance with subpart C of part 160 of this subchapter;

(v) Uses or disclosures that are required by law, as described by §164.512(a); and

(vi) Uses or disclosures that are required for compliance with applicable requirements of this subchapter.

(c) *Standard: Uses and disclosures of protected health information subject to an agreed upon restriction.* A covered entity that has agreed to a restriction pursuant to §164.522(a)(1) may not use or disclose the protected health information covered by the restriction in violation of such restriction, except as otherwise provided in §164.522(a).

(d) *Standard: Uses and disclosures of de-identified protected health information*—(1) Uses and disclosures to create de-identified information. A covered entity may use protected health information to create information that is not individually identifiable health information or disclose protected health information only to a business associate for such purpose, whether or not the de-identified information is to be used by the covered entity.

(2) *Uses and disclosures of de-identified information.* Health information that meets the standard and implementation specifications for de-identification under §164.514(a) and (b) is considered not to be individually identifiable health information, *i.e.,* de-identified. The requirements of this subpart do not apply to information that

has been de-identified in accordance with the applicable requirements of §164.514, provided that:

(i) Disclosure of a code or other means of record identification designed to enable coded or otherwise de-identified
information to be re-identified constitutes disclosure of protected health information; and

(ii) If de-identified information is re-identified, a covered
entity may use or disclose such re-identified information only
as permitted or required by this subpart.

(e)(1) *Standard: Disclosures to business associates.* (i) A covered entity
may disclose protected health information to a business associate and
may allow a business associate to create, receive, maintain, or transmit protected health information on its behalf, if the covered entity
obtains satisfactory assurance that the business associate will appropriately safeguard the information. A covered entity is not required to
obtain such satisfactory assurances from a business associate that is a
subcontractor.

(ii) A business associate may disclose protected health information to a business associate that is a subcontractor and may
allow the subcontractor to create, receive, maintain, or transmit protected health information on its behalf, if the business
associate obtains satisfactory assurances, in accordance with
§164.504(e)(1)(i), that the subcontractor will appropriately
safeguard the information.

(2) *Implementation specification: Documentation.* The satisfactory
assurances required by paragraph (e)(1) of this section must be
documented through a written contract or other written agreement
or arrangement with the business associate that meets the applicable requirements of §164.504(e).

(f) *Standard: Deceased individuals.* A covered entity must comply
with the requirements of this subpart with respect to the protected
health information of a deceased individual for a period of 50 years following the death of the individual.

(g)(1) *Standard: Personal representatives.* As specified in this paragraph, a covered entity must, except as provided in paragraphs (g)(3)
and (g)(5) of this section, treat a personal representative as the individual for purposes of this subchapter.

(2) *Implementation specification: Adults and emancipated minors.* If under applicable law a person has authority to act on behalf of an individual who is an adult or an emancipated minor in making decisions related to health care, a covered entity must treat such person as a personal representative under this subchapter, with respect to protected health information relevant to such personal representation.

(3)(i) *Implementation specification: Unemancipated minors.* If under applicable law a parent, guardian, or other person acting *in loco parentis* has authority to act on behalf of an individual who is an unemancipated minor in making decisions related to health care, a covered entity must treat such person as a personal representative under this subchapter, with respect to protected health information relevant to such personal representation, except that such person may not be a personal representative of an unemancipated minor, and the minor has the authority to act as an individual, with respect to protected health information pertaining to a health care service, if:

> (A) The minor consents to such health care service; no other consent to such health care service is required by law, regardless of whether the consent of another person has also been obtained; and the minor has not requested that such person be treated as the personal representative;

> (B) The minor may lawfully obtain such health care service without the consent of a parent, guardian, or other person acting *in loco parentis,* and the minor, a court, or another person authorized by law consents to such health care service; or

> (C) A parent, guardian, or other person acting *in loco parentis* assents to an agreement of confidentiality between a covered health care provider and the minor with respect to such health care service.

(ii) Notwithstanding the provisions of paragraph (g)(3)(i) of this section:

> (A) If, and to the extent, permitted or required by an applicable provision of State or other law, including applicable case law, a covered entity may disclose, or provide access in accordance with §164.524 to, protected

health information about an unemancipated minor to a parent, guardian, or other person acting *in loco parentis*;

(B) If, and to the extent, prohibited by an applicable provision of State or other law, including applicable case law, a covered entity may not disclose, or provide access in accordance with §164.524 to, protected health information about an unemancipated minor to a parent, guardian, or other person acting *in loco parentis*; and

(C) Where the parent, guardian, or other person acting *in loco parentis*, is not the personal representative under paragraphs (g)(3)(i)(A), (B), or (C) of this section and where there is no applicable access provision under State or other law, including case law, a covered entity may provide or deny access under §164.524 to a parent, guardian, or other person acting *in loco parentis*, if such action is consistent with State or other applicable law, provided that such decision must be made by a licensed health care professional, in the exercise of professional judgment.

(4) *Implementation specification: Deceased individuals.* If under applicable law an executor, administrator, or other person has authority to act on behalf of a deceased individual or of the individual's estate, a covered entity must treat such person as a personal representative under this subchapter, with respect to protected health information relevant to such personal representation.

(5) *Implementation specification: Abuse, neglect, endangerment situations.* Notwithstanding a State law or any requirement of this paragraph to the contrary, a covered entity may elect not to treat a person as the personal representative of an individual if:

(i) The covered entity has a reasonable belief that:

(A) The individual has been or may be subjected to domestic violence, abuse, or neglect by such person; or

(B) Treating such person as the personal representative could endanger the individual; and

(ii) The covered entity, in the exercise of professional judgment, decides that it is not in the best interest of the individual to treat the person as the individual's personal representative.

(h) *Standard: Confidential communications.* A covered health care provider or health plan must comply with the applicable requirements of §164.522(b) in communicating protected health information.

(i) *Standard: Uses and disclosures consistent with notice.* A covered entity that is required by §164.520 to have a notice may not use or disclose protected health information in a manner inconsistent with such notice. A covered entity that is required by §164.520(b)(1)(iii) to include a specific statement in its notice if it intends to engage in an activity listed in §164.520(b)(1)(iii)(A)–(C), may not use or disclose protected health information for such activities, unless the required statement is included in the notice.

(j) *Standard: Disclosures by whistleblowers and workforce member crime victims*—(1) *Disclosures by whistleblowers.* A covered entity is not considered to have violated the requirements of this subpart if a member of its workforce or a business associate discloses protected health information, provided that:

> (i) The workforce member or business associate believes in good faith that the covered entity has engaged in conduct that is unlawful or otherwise violates professional or clinical standards, or that the care, services, or conditions provided by the covered entity potentially endangers one or more patients, workers, or the public; and

> (ii) The disclosure is to:

>> (A) A health oversight agency or public health authority authorized by law to investigate or otherwise oversee the relevant conduct or conditions of the covered entity or to an appropriate health care accreditation organization for the purpose of reporting the allegation of failure to meet professional standards or misconduct by the covered entity; or

>> (B) An attorney retained by or on behalf of the workforce member or business associate for the purpose of determining the legal options of the workforce member or business associate with regard to the conduct described in paragraph (j)(1)(i) of this section.

(2) *Disclosures by workforce members who are victims of a crime.* A covered entity is not considered to have violated the requirements

of this subpart if a member of its workforce who is the victim of a criminal act discloses protected health information to a law enforcement official, provided that:

(i) The protected health information disclosed is about the suspected perpetrator of the criminal act; and

(ii) The protected health information disclosed is limited to the information listed in §164.512(f)(2)(i).

[65 FR 82802, Dec. 28, 2000, as amended at 67 FR 53267, Aug. 14, 2002; 78 FR 5696, Jan. 25, 2013]

§164.504 Uses and disclosures: Organizational requirements.

(a) *Definitions.* As used in this section:

Plan administration functions means administration functions performed by the plan sponsor of a group health plan on behalf of the group health plan and excludes functions performed by the plan sponsor in connection with any other benefit or benefit plan of the plan sponsor.

Summary health information means information, that may be individually identifiable health information, and:

(1) That summarizes the claims history, claims expenses, or type of claims experienced by individuals for whom a plan sponsor has provided health benefits under a group health plan; and

(2) From which the information described at §164.514(b)(2)(i) has been deleted, except that the geographic information described in §164.514(b)(2)(i)(B) need only be aggregated to the level of a five digit zip code.

(b)–(d) [Reserved]

(e)(1) *Standard: Business associate contracts.* (i) The contract or other arrangement required by §164.502(e)(2) must meet the requirements of paragraph (e)(2), (e)(3), or (e)(5) of this section, as applicable.

(ii) A covered entity is not in compliance with the standards in §164.502(e) and this paragraph, if the covered entity knew of a pattern of activity or practice of the business associate that constituted a material breach or violation of the business associate's obligation under the contract or other arrangement, unless the covered entity took reasonable steps to cure the breach or end the violation, as applicable, and, if such steps were unsuccessful, terminated the contract or arrangement, if feasible.

(iii) A business associate is not in compliance with the standards in §164.502(e) and this paragraph, if the business associate knew of a pattern of activity or practice of a subcontractor that constituted a material breach or violation of the subcontractor's obligation under the contract or other arrangement, unless the business associate took reasonable steps to cure the breach or end the violation, as applicable, and, if such steps were unsuccessful, terminated the contract or arrangement, if feasible.

(2) *Implementation specifications: Business associate contracts.* A contract between the covered entity and a business associate must:

(i)   Establish the permitted and required uses and disclosures of protected health information by the business associate. The contract may not authorize the business associate to use or further disclose the information in a manner that would violate the requirements of this subpart, if done by the covered entity, except that:

(A) The contract may permit the business associate to use and disclose protected health information for the proper management and administration of the business associate, as provided in paragraph (e)(4) of this section; and

(B) The contract may permit the business associate to provide data aggregation services relating to the health care operations of the covered entity.

(ii)   Provide that the business associate will:

(A) Not use or further disclose the information other than as permitted or required by the contract or as required by law;

(B) Use appropriate safeguards and comply, where applicable, with subpart C of this part with respect to electronic protected health information, to prevent use or disclosure of the information other than as provided for by its contract;

(C) Report to the covered entity any use or disclosure of the information not provided for by its contract of which it becomes aware, including breaches of unsecured protected health information as required by §164.410;

(D) In accordance with §164.502(e)(1)(ii), ensure that any subcontractors that create, receive, maintain, or transmit protected health information on behalf of the business associate agree to the same restrictions and conditions that apply to the business associate with respect to such information;

(E) Make available protected health information in accordance with §164.524;

(F) Make available protected health information for amendment and incorporate any amendments to protected health information in accordance with §164.526;

(G) Make available the information required to provide an accounting of disclosures in accordance with §164.528;

(H) To the extent the business associate is to carry out a covered entity's obligation under this subpart, comply with the requirements of this subpart that apply to the covered entity in the performance of such obligation.

(I) Make its internal practices, books, and records relating to the use and disclosure of protected health information received from, or created or received by the business associate on behalf of, the covered entity available to the Secretary for purposes of determining the covered entity's compliance with this subpart; and

(J) At termination of the contract, if feasible, return or destroy all protected health information received from, or created or received by the business associate on behalf of, the covered entity that the business associate still maintains in any form and retain no copies of such information or, if such return or destruction is not feasible, extend the protections of the contract to the information and limit further uses and disclosures to those purposes that make the return or destruction of the information infeasible.

(iii) Authorize termination of the contract by the covered entity, if the covered entity determines that the business associate has violated a material term of the contract.

(3) *Implementation specifications: Other arrangements.* (i) If a covered entity and its business associate are both governmental entities:

> (A) The covered entity may comply with this paragraph and §164.314(a)(1), if applicable, by entering into a memorandum of understanding with the business associate that contains terms that accomplish the objectives of paragraph (e)(2) of this section and §164.314(a)(2), if applicable.

> (B) The covered entity may comply with this paragraph and §164.314(a)(1), if applicable, if other law (including regulations adopted by the covered entity or its business associate) contains requirements applicable to the business associate that accomplish the objectives of paragraph (e)(2) of this section and §164.314(a)(2), if applicable.

(ii) If a business associate is required by law to perform a function or activity on behalf of a covered entity or to provide a service described in the definition of business associate in §160.103 of this subchapter to a covered entity, such covered entity may disclose protected health information to the business associate to the extent necessary to comply with the legal mandate without meeting the requirements of this paragraph and §164.314(a)(1), if applicable, provided that the covered entity attempts in good faith to obtain satisfactory assurances as required by paragraph (e)(2) of this section and §164.314(a)(1), if applicable, and, if such attempt fails, documents the attempt and the reasons that such assurances cannot be obtained.

(iii) The covered entity may omit from its other arrangements the termination authorization required by paragraph (e)(2) (iii) of this section, if such authorization is inconsistent with the statutory obligations of the covered entity or its business associate.

(iv) A covered entity may comply with this paragraph and §164.314(a)(1) if the covered entity discloses only a limited data set to a business associate for the business associate to carry out a health care operations function and the covered entity has a data use agreement with the business associate that complies with §§164.514(e)(4) and 164.314(a)(1), if applicable.

(4) *Implementation specifications: Other requirements for contracts and other arrangements.* (i) The contract or other arrangement between the covered entity and the business associate may permit the business associate to use the protected health information received by the business associate in its capacity as a business associate to the covered entity, if necessary:

> (A) For the proper management and administration of the business associate; or

> (B) To carry out the legal responsibilities of the business associate.

(ii) The contract or other arrangement between the covered entity and the business associate may permit the business associate to disclose the protected health information received by the business associate in its capacity as a business associate for the purposes described in paragraph (e)(4)(i) of this section, if:

> (A) The disclosure is required by law; or

> (B)(*1*) The business associate obtains reasonable assurances from the person to whom the information is disclosed that it will be held confidentially and used or further disclosed only as required by law or for the purposes for which it was disclosed to the person; and

>> (*2*) The person notifies the business associate of any instances of which it is aware in which the confidentiality of the information has been breached.

(5) *Implementation specifications: Business associate contracts with subcontractors.* The requirements of §164.504(e)(2) through (e)(4) apply to the contract or other arrangement required by §164.502(e)(1)(ii) between a business associate and a business associate that is a subcontractor in the same manner as such requirements apply to contracts or other arrangements between a covered entity and business associate.

(f)(1) *Standard: Requirements for group health plans.* (i) Except as provided under paragraph (f)(1)(ii) or (iii) of this section or as otherwise authorized under §164.508, a group health plan, in order to disclose protected health information to the plan sponsor or to provide for or permit the disclosure of protected health information to the plan sponsor by a health insurance issuer or HMO with respect to the group health plan, must ensure that the plan documents restrict uses and disclosures of such information by the plan sponsor consistent with the requirements of this subpart.

> (ii) Except as prohibited by §164.502(a)(5)(i), the group health plan, or a health insurance issuer or HMO with respect to the group health plan, may disclose summary health information to the plan sponsor, if the plan sponsor requests the summary health information for purposes of:
>
> > (A) Obtaining premium bids from health plans for providing health insurance coverage under the group health plan; or
> >
> > (B) Modifying, amending, or terminating the group health plan.
>
> (iii) The group health plan, or a health insurance issuer or HMO with respect to the group health plan, may disclose to the plan sponsor information on whether the individual is participating in the group health plan, or is enrolled in or has disenrolled from a health insurance issuer or HMO offered by the plan.

(2) *Implementation specifications: Requirements for plan documents.* The plan documents of the group health plan must be amended to incorporate provisions to:

> (i) Establish the permitted and required uses and disclosures of such information by the plan sponsor, provided that such permitted and required uses and disclosures may not be inconsistent with this subpart.

(ii)   Provide that the group health plan will disclose protected health information to the plan sponsor only upon receipt of a certification by the plan sponsor that the plan documents have been amended to incorporate the following provisions and that the plan sponsor agrees to:

(A)   Not use or further disclose the information other than as permitted or required by the plan documents or as required by law;

(B)   Ensure that any agents to whom it provides protected health information received from the group health plan agree to the same restrictions and conditions that apply to the plan sponsor with respect to such information;

(C)   Not use or disclose the information for employment-related actions and decisions or in connection with any other benefit or employee benefit plan of the plan sponsor;

(D)   Report to the group health plan any use or disclosure of the information that is inconsistent with the uses or disclosures provided for of which it becomes aware;

(E)   Make available protected health information in accordance with §164.524;

(F)   Make available protected health information for amendment and incorporate any amendments to protected health information in accordance with §164.526;

(G)   Make available the information required to provide an accounting of disclosures in accordance with §164.528;

(H)   Make its internal practices, books, and records relating to the use and disclosure of protected health information received from the group health plan available to the Secretary for purposes of determining compliance by the group health plan with this subpart;

(I)   If feasible, return or destroy all protected health information received from the group health plan that the sponsor still maintains in any form and retain no copies of such information when no longer needed for the purpose for which disclosure was made, except that, if such return or destruction is not feasible, limit further uses and disclosures to those purposes that make the return or destruction of the information infeasible; and

(J) Ensure that the adequate separation required in paragraph (f)(2)(iii) of this section is established.

(iii) Provide for adequate separation between the group health plan and the plan sponsor. The plan documents must:

(A) Describe those employees or classes of employees or other persons under the control of the plan sponsor to be given access to the protected health information to be disclosed, provided that any employee or person who receives protected health information relating to payment under, health care operations of, or other matters pertaining to the group health plan in the ordinary course of business must be included in such description;

(B) Restrict the access to and use by such employees and other persons described in paragraph (f)(2)(iii)(A) of this section to the plan administration functions that the plan sponsor performs for the group health plan; and

(C) Provide an effective mechanism for resolving any issues of noncompliance by persons described in paragraph (f)(2)(iii)(A) of this section with the plan document provisions required by this paragraph.

(3) *Implementation specifications:* Uses and disclosures. A group health plan may:

(i) Disclose protected health information to a plan sponsor to carry out plan administration functions that the plan sponsor performs only consistent with the provisions of paragraph (f)(2) of this section;

(ii) Not permit a health insurance issuer or HMO with respect to the group health plan to disclose protected health information to the plan sponsor except as permitted by this paragraph;

(iii) Not disclose and may not permit a health insurance issuer or HMO to disclose protected health information to a plan sponsor as otherwise permitted by this paragraph unless a statement required by §164.520(b)(1)(iii)(C) is included in the appropriate notice; and (iv) Not disclose protected health information to the plan sponsor for the purpose of employment-related actions or decisions or in connection with any other benefit or employee benefit plan of the plan sponsor.

(g) *Standard: Requirements for a covered entity with multiple covered functions.* (1) A covered entity that performs multiple covered functions that would make the entity any combination of a health plan, a covered health care provider, and a health care clearinghouse, must comply with the standards, requirements, and implementation specifications of this subpart, as applicable to the health plan, health care provider, or health care clearinghouse covered functions performed.

(2) A covered entity that performs multiple covered functions may use or disclose the protected health information of individuals who receive the covered entity's health plan or health care provider services, but not both, only for purposes related to the appropriate function being performed.

[65 FR 82802, Dec. 28, 2000, as amended at 67 FR 53267, Aug. 14, 2002; 68 FR 8381, Feb. 20, 2003; 78 FR 5697, Jan. 25, 2013]

§164.506 Uses and disclosures to carry out treatment, payment, or health care operations.

(a) *Standard: Permitted uses and disclosures.* Except with respect to uses or disclosures that require an authorization under §164.508(a)(2) through (4) or that are prohibited under §164.502(a)(5)(i), a covered entity may use or disclose protected health information for treatment, payment, or health care operations as set forth in paragraph (c) of this section, provided that such use or disclosure is consistent with other applicable requirements of this subpart.

(b) *Standard: Consent for uses and disclosures permitted.* (1) A covered entity may obtain consent of the individual to use or disclose protected health information to carry out treatment, payment, or health care operations.

(2) Consent, under paragraph (b) of this section, shall not be effective to permit a use or disclosure of protected health

information when an authorization, under §164.508, is required or when another condition must be met for such use or disclosure to be permissible under this subpart.

(c) *Implementation specifications: Treatment, payment, or health care operations.* (1) A covered entity may use or disclose protected health information for its own treatment, payment, or health care operations.

(2) A covered entity may disclose protected health information for treatment activities of a health care provider.

(3) A covered entity may disclose protected health information to another covered entity or a health care provider for the payment activities of the entity that receives the information.

(4) A covered entity may disclose protected health information to another covered entity for health care operations activities of the entity that receives the information, if each entity either has or had a relationship with the individual who is the subject of the protected health information being requested, the protected health information pertains to such relationship, and the disclosure is:

(i) For a purpose listed in paragraph (1) or (2) of the definition of health care operations; or

(ii) For the purpose of health care fraud and abuse detection or compliance.

(5) A covered entity that participates in an organized health care arrangement may disclose protected health information about an individual to other participants in the organized health care arrangement for any health care operations activities of the organized health care arrangement.

[67 FR 53268, Aug. 14, 2002, as amended at 78 FR 5698, Jan. 25, 2013]

§164.508 Uses and disclosures for which an authorization is required.

(a) *Standard: Authorizations for uses and disclosures*—(1) *Authorization required: General rule.* Except as otherwise permitted or required by this subchapter, a covered entity may not use or disclose protected health information without an authorization that is valid under this section. When a covered entity obtains or receives a valid authorization for its use or disclosure of protected health information, such use or disclosure must be consistent with such authorization.

(2) *Authorization required: Psychotherapy notes.* Notwithstanding any provision of this subpart, other than the transition provisions in §164.532, a covered entity must obtain an authorization for any use or disclosure of psychotherapy notes, except:

(i)　To carry out the following treatment, payment, or health care operations:

(A)　Use by the originator of the psychotherapy notes for treatment;

(B)　Use or disclosure by the covered entity for its own training programs in which students, trainees, or practitioners in mental health learn under supervision to practice or improve their skills in group, joint, family, or individual counseling; or

(C)　Use or disclosure by the covered entity to defend itself in a legal action or other proceeding brought by the individual; and

(ii)　A use or disclosure that is required by §164.502(a)(2)(ii) or permitted by §164.512(a); §164.512(d) with respect to the oversight of the originator of the psychotherapy notes; §164.512(g)(1); or §164.512(j)(1)(i).

(3) *Authorization required: Marketing.* (i) Notwithstanding any provision of this subpart, other than the transition provisions in §164.532, a covered entity must obtain an authorization for any use or disclosure of protected health information for marketing, except if the communication is in the form of:

(A)　A face-to-face communication made by a covered entity to an individual; or

(B)　A promotional gift of nominal value provided by the covered entity.

(ii)　If the marketing involves financial remuneration, as defined in paragraph (3) of the definition of marketing at §164.501, to the covered entity from a third party, the authorization must state that such remuneration is involved.

(4) *Authorization required: Sale of protected health information.* (i) Notwithstanding any provision of this subpart, other than the transition provisions in §164.532, a covered entity must obtain an authorization for any disclosure of protected health information which is a sale of protected health information, as defined in §164.501 of this subpart. (ii) Such authorization must state that the disclosure will result in remuneration to the covered entity.

(b) *Implementation specifications: General requirements*—(1) *Valid authorizations.* (i) A valid authorization is a document that meets the requirements in paragraphs (a)(3)(ii), (a)(4)(ii), (c)(1), and (c)(2) of this section, as applicable.

> (ii)   A valid authorization may contain elements or information in addition to the elements required by this section, provided that such additional elements or information are not inconsistent with the elements required by this section.

(2) *Defective authorizations.* An authorization is not valid, if the document submitted has any of the following defects:

> (i)   The expiration date has passed or the expiration event is known by the covered entity to have occurred;

> (ii)   The authorization has not been filled out completely, with respect to an element described by paragraph (c) of this section, if applicable;

> (iii)   The authorization is known by the covered entity to have been revoked;

> (iv)   The authorization violates paragraph (b)(3) or (4) of this section, if applicable;

> (v)   Any material information in the authorization is known by the covered entity to be false.

(3) *Compound authorizations.* An authorization for use or disclosure of protected health information may not be combined with any other document to create a compound authorization, except as follows:

> (i)   An authorization for the use or disclosure of protected health information for a research study may be combined with any other type of written permission for the same or another research study. This exception includes combining

an authorization for the use or disclosure of protected health information for a research study with another authorization for the same research study, with an authorization for the creation or maintenance of a research database or repository, or with a consent to participate in research. Where a covered health care provider has conditioned the provision of research-related treatment on the provision of one of the authorizations, as permitted under paragraph (b)(4)(i) of this section, any compound authorization created under this paragraph must clearly differentiate between the conditioned and unconditioned components and provide the individual with an opportunity to opt in to the research activities described in the unconditioned authorization.

(ii) An authorization for a use or disclosure of psychotherapy notes may only be combined with another authorization for a use or disclosure of psychotherapy notes.

(iii) An authorization under this section, other than an authorization for a use or disclosure of psychotherapy notes, may be combined with any other such authorization under this section, except when a covered entity has conditioned the provision of treatment, payment, enrollment in the health plan, or eligibility for benefits under paragraph (b)(4) of this section on the provision of one of the authorizations. The prohibition in this paragraph on combining authorizations where one authorization conditions the provision of treatment, payment, enrollment in a health plan, or eligibility for benefits under paragraph (b)(4) of this section does not apply to a compound authorization created in accordance with paragraph (b)(3)(i) of this section.

(4) *Prohibition on conditioning of authorizations.* A covered entity may not condition the provision to an individual of treatment, payment, enrollment in the health plan, or eligibility for benefits on the provision of an authorization, except:

(i) A covered health care provider may condition the provision of research-related treatment on provision of an authorization for the use or disclosure of protected health information for such research under this section;

(ii) A health plan may condition enrollment in the health plan or eligibility for benefits on provision of an authorization requested by the health plan prior to an individual's enrollment in the health plan, if:

(A) The authorization sought is for the health plan's eligibility or enrollment determinations relating to the individual or for its underwriting or risk rating determinations; and

(B) The authorization is not for a use or disclosure of psychotherapy notes under paragraph (a)(2) of this section; and

(iii) A covered entity may condition the provision of health care that is solely for the purpose of creating protected health information for disclosure to a third party on provision of an authorization for the disclosure of the protected health information to such third party.

(5) *Revocation of authorizations.* An individual may revoke an authorization provided under this section at any time, provided that the revocation is in writing, except to the extent that:

(i)   The covered entity has taken action in reliance thereon; or

(ii) If the authorization was obtained as a condition of obtaining insurance coverage, other law provides the insurer with the right to contest a claim under the policy or the policy itself.

(6) *Documentation.* A covered entity must document and retain any signed authorization under this section as required by §164.530(j).

(c) *Implementation specifications: Core elements and requirements—*
(1) *Core elements.* A valid authorization under this section must contain at least the following elements:

(i)   A description of the information to be used or disclosed that identifies the information in a specific and meaningful fashion.

(ii) The name or other specific identification of the person(s), or class of persons, authorized to make the requested use or disclosure.

(iii) The name or other specific identification of the person(s), or class of persons, to whom the covered entity may make the requested use or disclosure.

(iv) A description of each purpose of the requested use or disclosure. The statement "at the request of the individual" is a sufficient description of the purpose when an individual initiates the authorization and does not, or elects not to, provide a statement of the purpose.

(v) An expiration date or an expiration event that relates to the individual or the purpose of the use or disclosure. The statement "end of the research study," "none," or similar language is sufficient if the authorization is for a use or disclosure of protected health information for research, including for the creation and maintenance of a research database or research repository.

(vi) Signature of the individual and date. If the authorization is signed by a personal representative of the individual, a description of such representative's authority to act for the individual must also be provided.

(2) *Required statements.* In addition to the core elements, the authorization must contain statements adequate to place the individual on notice of all of the following:

(i) The individual's right to revoke the authorization in writing, and either:

(A) The exceptions to the right to revoke and a description of how the individual may revoke the authorization; or

(B) To the extent that the information in paragraph (c)(2)(i)(A) of this section is included in the notice required by §164.520, a reference to the covered entity's notice.

(ii) The ability or inability to condition treatment, payment, enrollment or eligibility for benefits on the authorization, by stating either:

(A) The covered entity may not condition treatment, payment, enrollment or eligibility for benefits on whether the individual signs the authorization when the prohibition on conditioning of authorizations in paragraph (b)(4) of this section applies; or

(B) The consequences to the individual of a refusal to sign the authorization when, in accordance with paragraph (b)(4) of this section, the covered entity can condition treatment, enrollment in the health plan, or eligibility for benefits on failure to obtain such authorization.

(iii) The potential for information disclosed pursuant to the authorization to be subject to redisclosure by the recipient and no longer be protected by this subpart.

(3) *Plain language requirement.* The authorization must be written in plain language.

(4) *Copy to the individual.* If a covered entity seeks an authorization from an individual for a use or disclosure of protected health information, the covered entity must provide the individual with a copy of the signed authorization.

[67 FR 53268, Aug. 14, 2002, as amended at 78 FR 5699, Jan. 25, 2013]

§164.510 Uses and disclosures requiring an opportunity for the individual to agree or to object.

A covered entity may use or disclose protected health information, provided that the individual is informed in advance of the use or disclosure and has the opportunity to agree to or prohibit or restrict the use or disclosure, in accordance with the applicable requirements of this section. The covered entity may orally inform the individual of and obtain the individual's oral agreement or objection to a use or disclosure permitted by this section.

(a) *Standard: Use and disclosure for facility directories—*(1) *Permitted uses and disclosure.* Except when an objection is expressed in accordance with paragraphs (a)(2) or (3) of this section, a covered health care provider may:

(i)   Use the following protected health information to maintain a directory of individuals in its facility:

(A)   The individual's name;

(B)   The individual's location in the covered health care provider's facility;

(C)   The individual's condition described in general terms that does not communicate specific medical information about the individual; and

(D)   The individual's religious affiliation; and

> (ii) Use or disclose for directory purposes such information:
>
> (A) To members of the clergy; or
>
> (B) Except for religious affiliation, to other persons who ask for the individual by name.

(2) *Opportunity to object.* A covered health care provider must inform an individual of the protected health information that it may include in a directory and the persons to whom it may disclose such information (including disclosures to clergy of information regarding religious affiliation) and provide the individual with the opportunity to restrict or prohibit some or all of the uses or disclosures permitted by paragraph (a)(1) of this section.

(3) *Emergency circumstances.* (i) If the opportunity to object to uses or disclosures required by paragraph (a)(2) of this section cannot practicably be provided because of the individual's incapacity or an emergency treatment circumstance, a covered health care provider may use or disclose some or all of the protected health information permitted by paragraph (a)(1) of this section for the facility's directory, if such disclosure is:

> (A) Consistent with a prior expressed preference of the individual, if any, that is known to the covered health care provider; and
>
> (B) In the individual's best interest as determined by the covered health care provider, in the exercise of professional judgment.
>
> (ii) The covered health care provider must inform the individual and provide an opportunity to object to uses or disclosures for directory purposes as required by paragraph (a)(2) of this section when it becomes practicable to do so.

(b) *Standard: Uses and disclosures for involvement in the individual's care and notification purposes*—(1) Permitted uses and disclosures. (i) A covered entity may, in accordance with paragraphs (b)(2), (b)(3), or (b)(5) of this section, disclose to a family member, other relative, or a close personal friend of the individual, or any other person identified by the individual, the protected health information directly relevant to such person's involvement with the individual's health care or payment related to the individual's health care.

(ii) A covered entity may use or disclose protected health information to notify, or assist in the notification of (including identifying or locating), a family member, a personal representative of the individual, or another person responsible for the care of the individual of the individual's location, general condition, or death. Any such use or disclosure of protected health information for such notification purposes must be in accordance with paragraphs (b)(2), (b)(3), (b)(4), or (b)(5) of this section, as applicable.

(2) *Uses and disclosures with the individual present.* If the individual is present for, or otherwise available prior to, a use or disclosure permitted by paragraph (b)(1) of this section and has the capacity to make health care decisions, the covered entity may use or disclose the protected health information if it:

(i) Obtains the individual's agreement;

(ii) Provides the individual with the opportunity to object to the disclosure, and the individual does not express an objection; or

(iii) Reasonably infers from the circumstances, based on the exercise of professional judgment, that the individual does not object to the disclosure.

(3) *Limited uses and disclosures when the individual is not present.* If the individual is not present, or the opportunity to agree or object to the use or disclosure cannot practicably be provided because of the individual's incapacity or an emergency circumstance, the covered entity may, in the exercise of professional judgment, determine whether the disclosure is in the best interests of the individual and, if so, disclose only the protected health information that is directly relevant to the person's involvement with the individual's care or payment related to the individual's health care or needed for notification purposes. A covered entity may use professional judgment and its experience with common practice to make reasonable inferences of the individual's best interest in allowing a person to act on behalf of the individual to pick up filled prescriptions, medical supplies, X-rays, or other similar forms of protected health information.

(4) *Uses and disclosures for disaster relief purposes.* A covered entity may use or disclose protected health information to a public

or private entity authorized by law or by its charter to assist in disaster relief efforts, for the purpose of coordinating with such entities the uses or disclosures permitted by paragraph (b)(1)(ii) of this section. The requirements in paragraphs (b)(2), (b)(3), or (b)(5) of this section apply to such uses and disclosures to the extent that the covered entity, in the exercise of professional judgment, determines that the requirements do not interfere with the ability to respond to the emergency circumstances.

(5) *Uses and disclosures when the individual is deceased.* If the individual is deceased, a covered entity may disclose to a family member, or other persons identified in paragraph (b)(1) of this section who were involved in the individual's care or payment for health care prior to the individual's death, protected health information of the individual that is relevant to such person's involvement, unless doing so is inconsistent with any prior expressed preference of the individual that is known to the covered entity.

[65 FR 82802, Dec. 28, 2000, as amended at 67 FR 53270, Aug. 14, 2002; 78 FR 5699, Jan. 25, 2013]

§164.512 Uses and disclosures for which an authorization or opportunity to agree or object is not required.

A covered entity may use or disclose protected health information without the written authorization of the individual, as described in §164.508, or the opportunity for the individual to agree or object as described in §164.510, in the situations covered by this section, subject to the applicable requirements of this section. When the covered entity is required by this section to inform the individual of, or when the individual may agree to, a use or disclosure permitted by this section, the covered entity's information and the individual's agreement may be given orally.

(a) *Standard: Uses and disclosures required by law.* (1) A covered entity may use or disclose protected health information to the extent that such use or disclosure is required by law and the use or disclosure complies with and is limited to the relevant requirements of such law.

(2) A covered entity must meet the requirements described in paragraph (c), (e), or (f) of this section for uses or disclosures required by law.

(b) *Standard: Uses and disclosures for public health activities*—(1) *Permitted uses and disclosures.* A covered entity may use or disclose protected health information for the public health activities and purposes described in this paragraph to:

(i)   A public health authority that is authorized by law to collect or receive such information for the purpose of preventing or controlling disease, injury, or disability, including, but not limited to, the reporting of disease, injury, vital events such as birth or death, and the conduct of public health surveillance, public health investigations, and public health interventions; or, at the direction of a public health authority, to an official of a foreign government agency that is acting in collaboration with a public health authority;

(ii)   A public health authority or other appropriate government authority authorized by law to receive reports of child abuse or neglect;

(iii)   A person subject to the jurisdiction of the Food and Drug Administration (FDA) with respect to an FDA-regulated product or activity for which that person has responsibility, for the purpose of activities related to the quality, safety or effectiveness of such FDA-regulated product or activity. Such purposes include:

(A)   To collect or report adverse events (or similar activities with respect to food or dietary supplements), product defects or problems (including problems with the use or labeling of a product), or biological product deviations;

(B)   To track FDA-regulated products;

(C)   To enable product recalls, repairs, or replacement, or lookback (including locating and notifying individuals who have received products that have been recalled, withdrawn, or are the subject of lookback); or

(D)   To conduct post marketing surveillance;

(iv)   A person who may have been exposed to a communicable disease or may otherwise be at risk of contracting or spreading a disease or condition, if the covered entity or public health authority is authorized by law to notify such person as necessary in the conduct of a public health intervention or investigation; or

(v)   An employer, about an individual who is a member of the workforce of the employer, if:

(A) The covered entity is a covered health care provider who provides health care to the individual at the request of the employer:

(1)   To conduct an evaluation relating to medical surveillance of the workplace; or

(2)   To evaluate whether the individual has a work-related illness or injury;

(B) The protected health information that is disclosed consists of findings concerning a work-related illness or injury or a workplace-related medical surveillance;

(C) The employer needs such findings in order to comply with its obligations, under 29 CFR parts 1904 through 1928, 30 CFR parts 50 through 90, or under state law having a similar purpose, to record such illness or injury or to carry out responsibilities for workplace medical surveillance; and

(D) The covered health care provider provides written notice to the individual that protected health information relating to the medical surveillance of the workplace and work-related illnesses and injuries is disclosed to the employer:

(1)   By giving a copy of the notice to the individual at the time the health care is provided; or

(2)   If the health care is provided on the work site of the employer, by posting the notice in a prominent place at the location where the health care is provided.

(vi) A school, about an individual who is a student or prospective student of the school, if:

(A) The protected health information that is disclosed is limited to proof of immunization;

(B) The school is required by State or other law to have such proof of immunization prior to admitting the individual; and

(C) The covered entity obtains and documents the agreement to the disclosure from either:

(*1*) A parent, guardian, or other person acting *in loco parentis* of the individual, if the individual is an unemancipated minor; or

(*2*) The individual, if the individual is an adult or emancipated minor.

(2) *Permitted uses.* If the covered entity also is a public health authority, the covered entity is permitted to use protected health information in all cases in which it is permitted to disclose such information for public health activities under paragraph (b)(1) of this section.

(c) *Standard: Disclosures about victims of abuse, neglect or domestic violence*—(1) *Permitted disclosures.* Except for reports of child abuse or neglect permitted by paragraph (b)(1)(ii) of this section, a covered entity may disclose protected health information about an individual whom the covered entity reasonably believes to be a victim of abuse, neglect, or domestic violence to a government authority, including a social service or protective services agency, authorized by law to receive reports of such abuse, neglect, or domestic violence:

(i) To the extent the disclosure is required by law and the disclosure complies with and is limited to the relevant requirements of such law;

(ii) If the individual agrees to the disclosure; or

(iii) To the extent the disclosure is expressly authorized by statute or regulation and:

(A) The covered entity, in the exercise of professional judgment, believes the disclosure is necessary to prevent serious harm to the individual or other potential victims; or

(B) If the individual is unable to agree because of incapacity, a law enforcement or other public official authorized to receive the report represents that the protected health information for which disclosure is sought is not intended to be used against the individual and that an immediate enforcement activity that depends upon the disclosure would be materially and adversely affected by waiting until the individual is able to agree to the disclosure.

(2) *Informing the individual.* A covered entity that makes a disclosure permitted by paragraph (c)(1) of this section must promptly inform the individual that such a report has been or will be made, except if:

(i) The covered entity, in the exercise of professional judgment, believes informing the individual would place the individual at risk of serious harm; or

(ii) The covered entity would be informing a personal representative, and the covered entity reasonably believes the personal representative is responsible for the abuse, neglect, or other injury, and that informing such person would not be in the best interests of the individual as determined by the covered entity, in the exercise of professional judgment.

(d) *Standard: Uses and disclosures for health oversight activities*—(1) *Permitted disclosures.* A covered entity may disclose protected health information to a health oversight agency for oversight activities authorized by law, including audits; civil, administrative, or criminal investigations; inspections; licensure or disciplinary actions; civil, administrative, or criminal proceedings or actions; or other activities necessary for appropriate oversight of:

(i) The health care system;

(ii) Government benefit programs for which health information is relevant to beneficiary eligibility;

(iii) Entities subject to government regulatory programs for which health information is necessary for determining compliance with program standards; or

(iv) Entities subject to civil rights laws for which health information is necessary for determining compliance.

(2) *Exception to health oversight activities.* For the purpose of the disclosures permitted by paragraph (d)(1) of this section, a health oversight activity does not include an investigation or other activity

in which the individual is the subject of the investigation or activity and such investigation or other activity does not arise out of and is not directly related to:

(i)   The receipt of health care;

(ii)   A claim for public benefits related to health; or

(iii)   Qualification for, or receipt of, public benefits or services when a patient's health is integral to the claim for public benefits or services.

(3) *Joint activities or investigations.* Nothwithstanding paragraph (d)(2) of this section, if a health oversight activity or investigation is conducted in conjunction with an oversight activity or investigation relating to a claim for public benefits not related to health, the joint activity or investigation is considered a health oversight activity for purposes of paragraph (d) of this section.

(4) *Permitted uses.* If a covered entity also is a health oversight agency, the covered entity may use protected health information for health oversight activities as permitted by paragraph (d) of this section.

(e) *Standard: Disclosures for judicial and administrative proceedings—*
(1) *Permitted disclosures.* A covered entity may disclose protected health information in the course of any judicial or administrative proceeding:

(i)   In response to an order of a court or administrative tribunal, provided that the covered entity discloses only the protected health information expressly authorized by such order; or

(ii)   In response to a subpoena, discovery request, or other lawful process, that is not accompanied by an order of a court or administrative tribunal, if:

(A)   The covered entity receives satisfactory assurance, as described in paragraph (e)(1)(iii) of this section, from the party seeking the information that reasonable efforts have been made by such party to ensure that the individual who is the subject of the protected health information that has been requested has been given notice of the request; or

(B)   The covered entity receives satisfactory assurance, as described in paragraph (e)(1)(iv) of this section, from the party seeking the information that reasonable efforts have been made by such party to secure a qualified protective order that meets the requirements of paragraph (e)(1)(v) of this section.

(iii) For the purposes of paragraph (e)(1)(ii)(A) of this section, a covered entity receives satisfactory assurances from a party seeking protected health information if the covered entity receives from such party a written statement and accompanying documentation demonstrating that:

(A) The party requesting such information has made a good faith attempt to provide written notice to the individual (or, if the individual's location is unknown, to mail a notice to the individual's last known address);

(B) The notice included sufficient information about the litigation or proceeding in which the protected health information is requested to permit the individual to raise an objection to the court or administrative tribunal; and

(C) The time for the individual to raise objections to the court or administrative tribunal has elapsed, and:

(1) No objections were filed; or

(2) All objections filed by the individual have been resolved by the court or the administrative tribunal and the disclosures being sought are consistent with such resolution.

(iv) For the purposes of paragraph (e)(1)(ii)(B) of this section, a covered entity receives satisfactory assurances from a party seeking protected health information, if the covered entity receives from such party a written statement and accompanying documentation demonstrating that:

(A) The parties to the dispute giving rise to the request for information have agreed to a qualified protective order and have presented it to the court or administrative tribunal with jurisdiction over the dispute; or

(B) The party seeking the protected health information has requested a qualified protective order from such court or administrative tribunal.

(v)   For purposes of paragraph (e)(1) of this section, a qualified protective order means, with respect to protected health information requested under paragraph (e)(1)(ii) of this section, an order of a court or of an administrative tribunal or a stipulation by the parties to the litigation or administrative proceeding that:

(A) Prohibits the parties from using or disclosing the protected health information for any purpose other than the litigation or proceeding for which such information was requested; and

(B)   Requires the return to the covered entity or destruction of the protected health information (including all copies made) at the end of the litigation or proceeding.

(vi) Notwithstanding paragraph (e)(1)(ii) of this section, a covered entity may disclose protected health information in response to lawful process described in paragraph (e)(1)(ii) of this section without receiving satisfactory assurance under paragraph (e)(1)(ii)(A) or (B) of this section, if the covered entity makes reasonable efforts to provide notice to the individual sufficient to meet the requirements of paragraph (e)(1)(iii) of this section or to seek a qualified protective order sufficient to meet the requirements of paragraph (e)(1)(v) of this section.

(2) *Other uses and disclosures under this section.* The provisions of this paragraph do not supersede other provisions of this section that otherwise permit or restrict uses or disclosures of protected health information.

(f) *Standard: Disclosures for law enforcement purposes.* A covered entity may disclose protected health information for a law enforcement purpose to a law enforcement official if the conditions in paragraphs (f)(1) through (f)(6) of this section are met, as applicable.

(1) Permitted disclosures: Pursuant to process and as otherwise required by law. A covered entity may disclose protected health information:

(i)   As required by law including laws that require the reporting of certain types of wounds or other physical injuries, except for laws subject to paragraph (b)(1)(ii) or (c)(1)(i) of this section; or

(ii) In compliance with and as limited by the relevant requirements of:

(A) A court order or court-ordered warrant, or a subpoena or summons issued by a judicial officer;

(B) A grand jury subpoena; or

(C) An administrative request, including an administrative subpoena or summons, a civil or an authorized investigative demand, or similar process authorized under law, provided that:

(1) The information sought is relevant and material to a legitimate law enforcement inquiry;

(2) The request is specific and limited in scope to the extent reasonably practicable in light of the purpose for which the information is sought; and

(3) De-identified information could not reasonably be used.

(2) *Permitted disclosures: Limited information for identification and location purposes.* Except for disclosures required by law as permitted by paragraph (f)(1) of this section, a covered entity may disclose protected health information in response to a law enforcement official's request for such information for the purpose of identifying or locating a suspect, fugitive, material witness, or missing person, provided that:

(i) The covered entity may disclose only the following information:

(A) Name and address;

(B) Date and place of birth;

(C) Social security number;

(D) ABO blood type and rh factor;

(E) Type of injury;

(F) Date and time of treatment;

(G) Date and time of death, if applicable; and

(H) A description of distinguishing physical characteristics, including height, weight, gender, race, hair and eye color, presence or absence of facial hair (beard or moustache), scars, and tattoos.

(ii)   Except as permitted by paragraph (f)(2)(i) of this section, the covered entity may not disclose for the purposes of identification or location under paragraph (f)(2) of this section any protected health information related to the individual's DNA or DNA analysis, dental records, or typing, samples or analysis of body fluids or tissue.

(3)   *Permitted disclosure: Victims of a crime.* Except for disclosures required by law as permitted by paragraph (f)(1) of this section, a covered entity may disclose protected health information in response to a law enforcement official's request for such information about an individual who is or is suspected to be a victim of a crime, other than disclosures that are subject to paragraph (b) or (c) of this section, if:

(i)   The individual agrees to the disclosure; or

(ii)   The covered entity is unable to obtain the individual's agreement because of incapacity or other emergency circumstance, provided that:

(A)   The law enforcement official represents that such information is needed to determine whether a violation of law by a person other than the victim has occurred, and such information is not intended to be used against the victim;

(B)   The law enforcement official represents that immediate law enforcement activity that depends upon the disclosure would be materially and adversely affected by waiting until the individual is able to agree to the disclosure; and

(C)   The disclosure is in the best interests of the individual as determined by the covered entity, in the exercise of professional judgment.

(4)   *Permitted disclosure: Decedents.* A covered entity may disclose protected health information about an individual who has died to a law enforcement official for the purpose of alerting law enforcement of the death of the individual if the covered entity has a suspicion that such death may have resulted from criminal conduct.

(5) *Permitted disclosure: Crime on premises.* A covered entity may disclose to a law enforcement official protected health information that the covered entity believes in good faith constitutes evidence of criminal conduct that occurred on the premises of the covered entity.

(6) *Permitted disclosure: Reporting crime in emergencies.* (i) A covered health care provider providing emergency health care in response to a medical emergency, other than such emergency on the premises of the covered health care provider, may disclose protected health information to a law enforcement official if such disclosure appears necessary to alert law enforcement to:

(A) The commission and nature of a crime;

(B) The location of such crime or of the victim(s) of such crime; and

(C) The identity, description, and location of the perpetrator of such crime.

(ii) If a covered health care provider believes that the medical emergency described in paragraph (f)(6)(i) of this section is the result of abuse, neglect, or domestic violence of the individual in need of emergency health care, paragraph (f)(6)(i) of this section does not apply and any disclosure to a law enforcement official for law enforcement purposes is subject to paragraph (c) of this section.

(g) *Standard: Uses and disclosures about decedents*—(1) *Coroners and medical examiners.* A covered entity may disclose protected health information to a coroner or medical examiner for the purpose of identifying a deceased person, determining a cause of death, or other duties as authorized by law. A covered entity that also performs the duties of a coroner or medical examiner may use protected health information for the purposes described in this paragraph.

(2) *Funeral directors.* A covered entity may disclose protected health information to funeral directors, consistent with applicable law, as necessary to carry out their duties with respect to the decedent. If necessary for funeral directors to carry out their duties, the covered entity may disclose the protected health information prior to, and in reasonable anticipation of, the individual's death.

(h) *Standard: Uses and disclosures for cadaveric organ, eye or tissue donation purposes.* A covered entity may use or disclose protected health information to organ procurement organizations or other entities engaged in the procurement, banking, or transplantation of cadaveric organs, eyes, or tissue for the purpose of facilitating organ, eye or tissue donation and transplantation.

(i) *Standard: Uses and disclosures for research purposes*—(1) *Permitted uses and disclosures.* A covered entity may use or disclose protected health information for research, regardless of the source of funding of the research, provided that:

> (i) *Board approval of a waiver of authorization.* The covered entity obtains documentation that an alteration to or waiver, in whole or in part, of the individual authorization required by §164.508 for use or disclosure of protected health information has been approved by either:
>
> > (A) An Institutional Review Board (IRB), established in accordance with 7 CFR lc.107, 10 CFR 745.107, 14 CFR 1230.107, 15 CFR 27.107, 16 CFR 1028.107, 21 CFR 56.107, 22 CFR 225.107, 24 CFR 60.107, 28 CFR 46.107, 32 CFR 219.107, 34 CFR 97.107, 38 CFR 16.107, 40 CFR 26.107, 45 CFR 46.107, 45 CFR 690.107, or 49 CFR 11.107; or
> >
> > (B) A privacy board that:
> >
> > > (*1*) Has members with varying backgrounds and appropriate professional competency as necessary to review the effect of the research protocol on the individual's privacy rights and related interests;
> > >
> > > (*2*) Includes at least one member who is not affiliated with the covered entity, not affiliated with any entity conducting or sponsoring the research, and not related to any person who is affiliated with any of such entities; and
> > >
> > > (*3*) Does not have any member participating in a review of any project in which the member has a conflict of interest.
>
> (ii) *Reviews preparatory to research.* The covered entity obtains from the researcher representations that:
>
> > (A) Use or disclosure is sought solely to review protected health information as necessary to prepare a research protocol or for similar purposes preparatory to research;

(B) No protected health information is to be removed from the covered entity by the researcher in the course of the review; and

(C) The protected health information for which use or access is sought is necessary for the research purposes.

(iii) *Research on decedent's information.* The covered entity obtains from the researcher:

(A) Representation that the use or disclosure sought is solely for research on the protected health information of decedents;

(B) Documentation, at the request of the covered entity, of the death of such individuals; and

(C) Representation that the protected health information for which use or disclosure is sought is necessary for the research purposes.

(2) *Documentation of waiver approval.* For a use or disclosure to be permitted based on documentation of approval of an alteration or waiver, under paragraph (i)(1)(i) of this section, the documentation must include all of the following:

(i) *Identification and date of action.* A statement identifying the IRB or privacy board and the date on which the alteration or waiver of authorization was approved;

(ii) *Waiver criteria.* A statement that the IRB or privacy board has determined that the alteration or waiver, in whole or in part, of authorization satisfies the following criteria:

(A) The use or disclosure of protected health information involves no more than a minimal risk to the privacy of individuals, based on, at least, the presence of the following elements;

(1) An adequate plan to protect the identifiers from improper use and disclosure;

(2) An adequate plan to destroy the identifiers at the earliest opportunity consistent with conduct of the research, unless there is a health or research justification for retaining the identifiers or such retention is otherwise required by law; and

(*3*)   Adequate written assurances that the protected health information will not be reused or disclosed to any other person or entity, except as required by law, for authorized oversight of the research study, or for other research for which the use or disclosure of protected health information would be permitted by this subpart;

(B) The research could not practicably be conducted without the waiver or alteration; and

(C) The research could not practicably be conducted without access to and use of the protected health information.

(iii) *Protected health information needed.* A brief description of the protected health information for which use or access has been determined to be necessary by the institutional review board or privacy board, pursuant to paragraph (i)(2)(ii)(C) of this section;

(iv) *Review and approval procedures.* A statement that the alteration or waiver of authorization has been reviewed and approved under either normal or expedited review procedures, as follows:

(A) An IRB must follow the requirements of the Common Rule, including the normal review procedures (7 CFR 1c.108(b), 10 CFR 745.108(b), 14 CFR 1230.108(b), 15 CFR 27.108(b), 16 CFR 1028.108(b), 21 CFR 56.108(b), 22 CFR 225.108(b), 24 CFR 60.108(b), 28 CFR 46.108(b), 32 CFR 219.108(b), 34 CFR 97.108(b), 38 CFR 16.108(b), 40 CFR 26.108(b), 45 CFR 46.108(b), 45 CFR 690.108(b), or 49 CFR 11.108(b)) or the expedited review procedures (7 CFR 1c.110, 10 CFR 745.110, 14 CFR 1230.110, 15 CFR 27.110, 16 CFR 1028.110, 21 CFR 56.110, 22 CFR 225.110, 24 CFR 60.110, 28 CFR 46.110, 32 CFR 219.110, 34 CFR 97.110, 38 CFR 16.110, 40 CFR 26.110, 45 CFR 46.110, 45 CFR 690.110, or 49 CFR 11.110);

(B) A privacy board must review the proposed research at convened meetings at which a majority of the privacy board members are present, including at least one member who satisfies the criterion stated in paragraph (i)(1)(i)(B)(2) of this section, and the alteration or waiver of authorization must be approved by the majority of the privacy board members present at the meeting, unless the privacy board elects to use an expedited review procedure in accordance with paragraph (i)(2)(iv)(C) of this section;

(C) A privacy board may use an expedited review procedure if the research involves no more than minimal risk to the privacy of the individuals who are the subject of the protected health information for which use or disclosure is being sought. If the privacy board elects to use an expedited review procedure, the review and approval of the alteration or waiver of authorization may be carried out by the chair of the privacy board, or by one or more members of the privacy board as designated by the chair; and

(v) *Required signature.* The documentation of the alteration or waiver of authorization must be signed by the chair or other member, as designated by the chair, of the IRB or the privacy board, as applicable.

(j) *Standard: Uses and disclosures to avert a serious threat to health or safety*—(1) *Permitted disclosures.* A covered entity may, consistent with applicable law and standards of ethical conduct, use or disclose protected health information, if the covered entity, in good faith, believes the use or disclosure:

(i)(A) Is necessary to prevent or lessen a serious and imminent threat to the health or safety of a person or the public; and

(B) Is to a person or persons reasonably able to prevent or lessen the threat, including the target of the threat; or

(ii) Is necessary for law enforcement authorities to identify or apprehend an individual:

(A) Because of a statement by an individual admitting participation in a violent crime that the covered entity reasonably believes may have caused serious physical harm to the victim; or

(B) Where it appears from all the circumstances that the individual has escaped from a correctional institution or from lawful custody, as those terms are defined in §164.501.

(2) *Use or disclosure not permitted.* A use or disclosure pursuant to paragraph (j)(1)(ii)(A) of this section may not be made if the information described in paragraph (j)(1)(ii)(A) of this section is learned by the covered entity:

> (i) In the course of treatment to affect the propensity to commit the criminal conduct that is the basis for the disclosure under paragraph (j)(1)(ii)(A) of this section, or counseling or therapy; or

> (ii) Through a request by the individual to initiate or to be referred for the treatment, counseling, or therapy described in paragraph (j)(2)(i) of this section.

(3) *Limit on information that may be disclosed.* A disclosure made pursuant to paragraph (j)(1)(ii)(A) of this section shall contain only the statement described in paragraph (j)(1)(ii)(A) of this section and the protected health information described in paragraph (f)(2)(i) of this section.

(4) *Presumption of good faith belief.* A covered entity that uses or discloses protected health information pursuant to paragraph (j)(1) of this section is presumed to have acted in good faith with regard to a belief described in paragraph (j)(1)(i) or (ii) of this section, if the belief is based upon the covered entity's actual knowledge or in reliance on a credible representation by a person with apparent knowledge or authority.

(k) *Standard: Uses and disclosures for specialized government functions—* (1) *Military and veterans activities—*(i) *Armed Forces personnel.* A covered entity may use and disclose the protected health information of individuals who are Armed Forces personnel for activities deemed necessary by appropriate military command authorities to assure the proper execution of the military mission, if the appropriate military authority has published by notice in the Federal Register the following information:

> (A) Appropriate military command authorities; and

> (B) The purposes for which the protected health information may be used or disclosed.

(ii) *Separation or discharge from military service.* A covered entity that is a component of the Departments of Defense or Homeland Security may disclose to the Department of Veterans Affairs (DVA) the protected health information of an individual who is a member of the Armed Forces upon the separation or discharge of the individual from military service for the purpose of a determination by DVA of the individual's eligibility for or entitlement to benefits under laws administered by the Secretary of Veterans Affairs.

(iii) *Veterans.* A covered entity that is a component of the Department of Veterans Affairs may use and disclose protected health information to components of the Department that determine eligibility for or entitlement to, or that provide, benefits under the laws administered by the Secretary of Veterans Affairs.

(iv) *Foreign military personnel.* A covered entity may use and disclose the protected health information of individuals who are foreign military personnel to their appropriate foreign military authority for the same purposes for which uses and disclosures are permitted for Armed Forces personnel under the notice published in the Federal Register pursuant to paragraph (k)(1)(i) of this section.

(2) *National security and intelligence activities.* A covered entity may disclose protected health information to authorized federal officials for the conduct of lawful intelligence, counter-intelligence, and other national security activities authorized by the National Security Act (50 U.S.C. 401, *et seq.*) and implementing authority (*e.g.*, Executive Order 12333).

(3) *Protective services for the President and others.* A covered entity may disclose protected health information to authorized Federal officials for the provision of protective services to the President or other persons authorized by 18 U.S.C. 3056 or to foreign heads of state or other persons authorized by 22 U.S.C. 2709(a)(3), or for the conduct of investigations authorized by 18 U.S.C. 871 and 879.

(4) *Medical suitability determinations.* A covered entity that is a component of the Department of State may use protected health information to make medical suitability determinations and may disclose whether or not the individual was determined to be

medically suitable to the officials in the Department of State who need access to such information for the following purposes:

(i)   For the purpose of a required security clearance conducted pursuant to Executive Orders 10450 and 12968;

(ii)   As necessary to determine worldwide availability or availability for mandatory service abroad under sections 101(a)(4) and 504 of the Foreign Service Act; or

(iii)   For a family to accompany a Foreign Service member abroad, consistent with section 101(b)(5) and 904 of the Foreign Service Act.

(5)   *Correctional institutions and other law enforcement custodial situations*—(i) *Permitted disclosures.* A covered entity may disclose to a correctional institution or a law enforcement official having lawful custody of an inmate or other individual protected health information about such inmate or individual, if the correctional institution or such law enforcement official represents that such protected health information is necessary for:

(A)   The provision of health care to such individuals;

(B)   The health and safety of such individual or other inmates;

(C)   The health and safety of the officers or employees of or others at the correctional institution;

(D)   The health and safety of such individuals and officers or other persons responsible for the transporting of inmates or their transfer from one institution, facility, or setting to another;

(E)   Law enforcement on the premises of the correctional institution; or

(F)   The administration and maintenance of the safety, security, and good order of the correctional institution.

(ii)   *Permitted uses.* A covered entity that is a correctional institution may use protected health information of individuals who are inmates for any purpose for which such protected health information may be disclosed.

(iii)   *No application after release.* For the purposes of this provision, an individual is no longer an inmate when released on parole, probation, supervised release, or otherwise is no longer in lawful custody.

(6) *Covered entities that are government programs providing public benefits.* (i) A health plan that is a government program providing public benefits may disclose protected health information relating to eligibility for or enrollment in the health plan to another agency administering a government program providing public benefits if the sharing of eligibility or enrollment information among such government agencies or the maintenance of such information in a single or combined data system accessible to all such government agencies is required or expressly authorized by statute or regulation.

(ii) A covered entity that is a government agency administering a government program providing public benefits may disclose protected health information relating to the program to another covered entity that is a government agency administering a government program providing public benefits if the programs serve the same or similar populations and the disclosure of protected health information is necessary to coordinate the covered functions of such programs or to improve administration and management relating to the covered functions of such programs.

(7) *National Instant Criminal Background Check System.* A covered entity may use or disclose protected health information for purposes of reporting to the National Instant Criminal Background Check System the identity of an individual who is prohibited from possessing a firearm under 18 U.S.C. 922(g)(4), provided the covered entity:

(i) Is a State agency or other entity that is, or contains an entity that is:

(A) An entity designated by the State to report, or which collects information for purposes of reporting, on behalf of the State, to the National Instant Criminal Background Check System; or

(B) A court, board, commission, or other lawful authority that makes the commitment or adjudication that causes an individual to become subject to 18 U.S.C. 922(g)(4); and

(ii)   Discloses the information only to:

(A)   The National Instant Criminal Background Check System; or

(B)   An entity designated by the State to report, or which collects information for purposes of reporting, on behalf of the State, to the National Instant Criminal Background Check System; and

(iii)(A) Discloses only the limited demographic and certain other information needed for purposes of reporting to the National Instant Criminal Background Check System; and

(B)   Does not disclose diagnostic or clinical information for such purposes.

(l)   *Standard: Disclosures for workers' compensation.* A covered entity may disclose protected health information as authorized by and to the extent necessary to comply with laws relating to workers' compensation or other similar programs, established by law, that provide benefits for work-related injuries or illness without regard to fault.

[65 FR 82802, Dec. 28, 2000, as amended at 67 FR 53270, Aug. 14, 2002; 78 FR 5699, Jan. 25, 2013; 78 FR 34266, June 7, 2013; 81 FR 395, Jan. 6, 2016]

§164.514 Other requirements relating to uses and disclosures of protected health information.

(a)   *Standard: De-identification of protected health information.* Health information that does not identify an individual and with respect to which there is no reasonable basis to believe that the information can be used to identify an individual is not individually identifiable health information.

(b)   *Implementation specifications: Requirements for de-identification of protected health information.* A covered entity may determine that health information is not individually identifiable health information only if:

(1)   A person with appropriate knowledge of and experience with generally accepted statistical and scientific principles and methods for rendering information not individually identifiable:

(i)   Applying such principles and methods, determines that the risk is very small that the information could be used, alone or in combination with other reasonably available information, by an anticipated recipient to identify an individual who is a subject of the information; and

(ii) Documents the methods and results of the analysis that justify such determination; or

(2)(i) The following identifiers of the individual or of relatives, employers, or household members of the individual, are removed:

(A) Names;

(B) All geographic subdivisions smaller than a State, including street address, city, county, precinct, zip code, and their equivalent geocodes, except for the initial three digits of a zip code if, according to the current publicly available data from the Bureau of the Census:

(1) The geographic unit formed by combining all zip codes with the same three initial digits contains more than 20,000 people; and

(2) The initial three digits of a zip code for all such geographic units containing 20,000 or fewer people is changed to 000.

(C) All elements of dates (except year) for dates directly related to an individual, including birth date, admission date, discharge date, date of death; and all ages over 89 and all elements of dates (including year) indicative of such age, except that such ages and elements may be aggregated into a single category of age 90 or older;

(D) Telephone numbers;

(E) Fax numbers;

(F) Electronic mail addresses;

(G) Social security numbers;

(H) Medical record numbers;

(I) Health plan beneficiary numbers;

(J) Account numbers;

(K) Certificate/license numbers;

(L) Vehicle identifiers and serial numbers, including license plate numbers;

(M) Device identifiers and serial numbers;

(N) Web Universal Resource Locators (URLs);

(O) Internet Protocol (IP) address numbers;

(P) Biometric identifiers, including finger and voice prints;

(Q) Full face photographic images and any comparable images; and

(R) Any other unique identifying number, characteristic, or code, except as permitted by paragraph (c) of this section; and

(ii) The covered entity does not have actual knowledge that the information could be used alone or in combination with other information to identify an individual who is a subject of the information.

(c) *Implementation specifications: Re-identification.* A covered entity may assign a code or other means of record identification to allow information de-identified under this section to be re-identified by the covered entity, provided that:

(1) *Derivation.* The code or other means of record identification is not derived from or related to information about the individual and is not otherwise capable of being translated so as to identify the individual; and

(2) *Security.* The covered entity does not use or disclose the code or other means of record identification for any other purpose, and does not disclose the mechanism for re-identification.

(d)(1) *Standard: minimum necessary requirements.* In order to comply with §164.502(b) and this section, a covered entity must meet the requirements of paragraphs (d)(2) through (d)(5) of this section with respect to a request for, or the use and disclosure of, protected health information.

(2) *Implementation specifications:* Minimum necessary uses of protected health information. (i) A covered entity must identify:

(A) Those persons or classes of persons, as appropriate, in its workforce who need access to protected health information to carry out their duties; and

(B) For each such person or class of persons, the category or categories of protected health information to which access is needed and any conditions appropriate to such access.

(ii) A covered entity must make reasonable efforts to limit the access of such persons or classes identified in paragraph (d)(2)(i)(A) of this section to protected health information consistent with paragraph (d)(2)(i)(B) of this section.

(3) *Implementation specification: Minimum necessary disclosures of protected health information.* (i) For any type of disclosure that it makes on a routine and recurring basis, a covered entity must implement policies and procedures (which may be standard protocols) that limit the protected health information disclosed to the amount reasonably necessary to achieve the purpose of the disclosure.

(ii) For all other disclosures, a covered entity must:

(A) Develop criteria designed to limit the protected health information disclosed to the information reasonably necessary to accomplish the purpose for which disclosure is sought; and

(B) Review requests for disclosure on an individual basis in accordance with such criteria.

(iii) A covered entity may rely, if such reliance is reasonable under the circumstances, on a requested disclosure as the minimum necessary for the stated purpose when:

(A) Making disclosures to public officials that are permitted under §164.512, if the public official represents that the information requested is the minimum necessary for the stated purpose(s);

(B) The information is requested by another covered entity;

(C) The information is requested by a professional who is a member of its workforce or is a business associate of the covered entity for the purpose of providing professional services to the covered entity, if the professional represents that the information requested is the minimum necessary for the stated purpose(s); or

(D) Documentation or representations that comply with the applicable requirements of §164.512(i) have been provided by a person requesting the information for research purposes.

(4) *Implementation specifications: Minimum necessary requests for protected health information.* (i) A covered entity must limit any request for protected health information to that which is reasonably necessary to accomplish the purpose for which the request is made, when requesting such information from other covered entities.

(ii) For a request that is made on a routine and recurring basis, a covered entity must implement policies and procedures (which may be standard protocols) that limit the protected health information requested to the amount reasonably necessary to accomplish the purpose for which the request is made.

(iii) For all other requests, a covered entity must:

(A) Develop criteria designed to limit the request for protected health information to the information reasonably necessary to accomplish the purpose for which the request is made; and

(B) Review requests for disclosure on an individual basis in accordance with such criteria.

(5) *Implementation specification: Other content requirement.* For all uses, disclosures, or requests to which the requirements in paragraph (d) of this section apply, a covered entity may not use, disclose or request an entire medical record, except when the entire medical record is specifically justified as the amount that is reasonably necessary to accomplish the purpose of the use, disclosure, or request.

(e)(1) *Standard: Limited data set.* A covered entity may use or disclose a limited data set that meets the requirements of paragraphs (e)(2) and (e)(3) of this section, if the covered entity enters into a data use agreement with the limited data set recipient, in accordance with paragraph (e)(4) of this section.

(2) *Implementation specification: Limited data set:* A limited data set is protected health information that excludes the following direct identifiers of the individual or of relatives, employers, or household members of the individual:

(i) Names;

(ii) Postal address information, other than town or city, State, and zip code;

(iii) Telephone numbers;

(iv) Fax numbers;

(v) Electronic mail addresses;

(vi) Social security numbers;

(vii) Medical record numbers;

(viii) Health plan beneficiary numbers;

(ix) Account numbers;

(x) Certificate/license numbers;

(xi) Vehicle identifiers and serial numbers, including license plate numbers;

(xii) Device identifiers and serial numbers;

(xiii) Web Universal Resource Locators (URLs);

(xiv) Internet Protocol (IP) address numbers;

(xv) Biometric identifiers, including finger and voice prints; and

(xvi) Full face photographic images and any comparable images.

(3) *Implementation specification: Permitted purposes for uses and disclosures.* (i) A covered entity may use or disclose a limited data set under paragraph (e)(1) of this section only for the purposes of research, public health, or health care operations.

(ii) A covered entity may use protected health information to create a limited data set that meets the requirements of paragraph (e)(2) of this section, or disclose protected health information only to a business associate for such purpose, whether or not the limited data set is to be used by the covered entity.

(4) *Implementation specifications: Data use agreement*—(i) *Agreement required.* A covered entity may use or disclose a limited data set under paragraph (e)(1) of this section only if the covered entity obtains satisfactory assurance, in the form of a data use agreement that meets the requirements of this section, that the limited data set recipient will only use or disclose the protected health information for limited purposes.

(ii) *Contents.* A data use agreement between the covered entity and the limited data set recipient must:

(A) Establish the permitted uses and disclosures of such information by the limited data set recipient, consistent with paragraph (e)(3) of this section. The data use agreement may not authorize the limited data set recipient to use or further disclose the information in a manner that would violate the requirements of this subpart, if done by the covered entity;

(B) Establish who is permitted to use or receive the limited data set; and

(C) Provide that the limited data set recipient will:

(*1*) Not use or further disclose the information other than as permitted by the data use agreement or as otherwise required by law;

(*2*) Use appropriate safeguards to prevent use or disclosure of the information other than as provided for by the data use agreement;

(*3*) Report to the covered entity any use or disclosure of the information not provided for by its data use agreement of which it becomes aware;

(*4*) Ensure that any agents to whom it provides the limited data set agree to the same restrictions and conditions that apply to the limited data set recipient with respect to such information; and

(*5*) Not identify the information or contact the individuals.

(iii) *Compliance.* (A) A covered entity is not in compliance with the standards in paragraph (e) of this section if the covered entity knew of a pattern of activity or practice of the limited data set recipient that constituted a material breach or violation of the data use agreement, unless the covered entity took reasonable steps to cure the breach or end the violation, as applicable, and, if such steps were unsuccessful:

(*1*) Discontinued disclosure of protected health information to the recipient; and

(*2*) Reported the problem to the Secretary.

(B) A covered entity that is a limited data set recipient and violates a data use agreement will be in noncompliance with the standards, implementation specifications, and requirements of paragraph (e) of this section.

(f) *Fundraising communications*—(1) *Standard: Uses and disclosures for fundraising.* Subject to the conditions of paragraph (f)(2) of this section, a covered entity may use, or disclose to a business associate or to an institutionally related foundation, the following protected health information for the purpose of raising funds for its own benefit, without an authorization meeting the requirements of §164.508:

(i) Demographic information relating to an individual, including name, address, other contact information, age, gender, and date of birth;

(ii) Dates of health care provided to an individual;

(iii) Department of service information;

(iv) Treating physician;

(v) Outcome information; and

(vi) Health insurance status.

(2) *Implementation specifications: Fundraising requirements.* (i) A covered entity may not use or disclose protected health information for fundraising purposes as otherwise permitted by paragraph (f)(1) of this section unless a statement required by

§164.520(b)(1)(iii)(A) is included in the covered entity's notice of privacy practices.

(ii) With each fundraising communication made to an individual under this paragraph, a covered entity must provide the individual with a clear and conspicuous opportunity to elect not to receive any further fundraising communications. The method for an individual to elect not to receive further fundraising communications may not cause the individual to incur an undue burden or more than a nominal cost.

(iii) A covered entity may not condition treatment or payment on the individual's choice with respect to the receipt of fundraising communications.

(iv) A covered entity may not make fundraising communications to an individual under this paragraph where the individual has elected not to receive such communications under paragraph (f)(2)(ii) of this section.

(v) A covered entity may provide an individual who has elected not to receive further fundraising communications with a method to opt back in to receive such communications.

(g) *Standard: Uses and disclosures for underwriting and related purposes.* If a health plan receives protected health information for the purpose of underwriting, premium rating, or other activities relating to the creation, renewal, or replacement of a contract of health insurance or health benefits, and if such health insurance or health benefits are not placed with the health plan, such health plan may only use or disclose such protected health information for such purpose or as may be required by law, subject to the prohibition at §164.502(a)(5)(i) with respect to genetic information included in the protected health information.

(h)(1) *Standard: Verification requirements.* Prior to any disclosure permitted by this subpart, a covered entity must:

(i) Except with respect to disclosures under §164.510, verify the identity of a person requesting protected health information and the authority of any such person to have access to protected health information under this subpart, if the identity or any such authority of such person is not known to the covered entity; and

(ii)   Obtain any documentation, statements, or representations, whether oral or written, from the person requesting the protected health information when such documentation, statement, or representation is a condition of the disclosure under this subpart.

(2)   *Implementation specifications: Verification*—(i) *Conditions on disclosures.* If a disclosure is conditioned by this subpart on particular documentation, statements, or representations from the person requesting the protected health information, a covered entity may rely, if such reliance is reasonable under the circumstances, on documentation, statements, or representations that, on their face, meet the applicable requirements.

(A)   The conditions in §164.512(f)(1)(ii)(C) may be satisfied by the administrative subpoena or similar process or by a separate written statement that, on its face, demonstrates that the applicable requirements have been met.

(B)   The documentation required by §164.512(i)(2) may be satisfied by one or more written statements, provided that each is appropriately dated and signed in accordance with §164.512(i)(2)(i) and (v).

(ii)   *Identity of public officials.* A covered entity may rely, if such reliance is reasonable under the circumstances, on any of the following to verify identity when the disclosure of protected health information is to a public official or a person acting on behalf of the public official:

(A)   If the request is made in person, presentation of an agency identification badge, other official credentials, or other proof of government status;

(B)   If the request is in writing, the request is on the appropriate government letterhead; or

(C)   If the disclosure is to a person acting on behalf of a public official, a written statement on appropriate government letterhead that the person is acting under the government's authority or other evidence or documentation of agency, such as a contract for services, memorandum of understanding, or purchase order, that establishes that the person is acting on behalf of the public official.

(iii) *Authority of public officials.* A covered entity may rely, if such reliance is reasonable under the circumstances, on any of the following to verify authority when the disclosure of protected health information is to a public official or a person acting on behalf of the public official:

> (A) A written statement of the legal authority under which the information is requested, or, if a written statement would be impracticable, an oral statement of such legal authority;

> (B) If a request is made pursuant to legal process, warrant, subpoena, order, or other legal process issued by a grand jury or a judicial or administrative tribunal is presumed to constitute legal authority.

(iv) *Exercise of professional judgment.* The verification requirements of this paragraph are met if the covered entity relies on the exercise of professional judgment in making a use or disclosure in accordance with §164.510 or acts on a good faith belief in making a disclosure in accordance with §164.512(j).

[65 FR 82802, Dec. 28, 2000, as amended at 67 FR 53270, Aug. 14, 2002; 78 FR 5700, Jan. 25, 2013; 78 FR 34266, June 7, 2013]

§164.520 Notice of privacy practices for protected health information.

(a) *Standard: Notice of privacy practices—*(1) *Right to notice.* Except as provided by paragraph (a)(2) or (3) of this section, an individual has a right to adequate notice of the uses and disclosures of protected health information that may be made by the covered entity, and of the individual's rights and the covered entity's legal duties with respect to protected health information.

(2) *Exception for group health plans.* (i) An individual enrolled in a group health plan has a right to notice:

> (A) From the group health plan, if, and to the extent that, such an individual does not receive health benefits under the group health plan through an insurance contract with a health insurance issuer or HMO; or

(B) From the health insurance issuer or HMO with respect to the group health plan through which such individuals receive their health benefits under the group health plan.

(ii) A group health plan that provides health benefits solely through an insurance contract with a health insurance issuer or HMO, and that creates or receives protected health information in addition to summary health information as defined in §164.504(a) or information on whether the individual is participating in the group health plan, or is enrolled in or has disenrolled from a health insurance issuer or HMO offered by the plan, must:

(A) Maintain a notice under this section; and

(B) Provide such notice upon request to any person. The provisions of paragraph (c)(1) of this section do not apply to such group health plan.

(iii) A group health plan that provides health benefits solely through an insurance contract with a health insurance issuer or HMO, and does not create or receive protected health information other than summary health information as defined in §164.504(a) or information on whether an individual is participating in the group health plan, or is enrolled in or has disenrolled from a health insurance issuer or HMO offered by the plan, is not required to maintain or provide a notice under this section.

(3) *Exception for inmates.* An inmate does not have a right to notice under this section, and the requirements of this section do not apply to a correctional institution that is a covered entity.

(b) *Implementation specifications: Content of notice*—(1) *Required elements.* The covered entity must provide a notice that is written in plain language and that contains the elements required by this paragraph.

(i) *Header.* The notice must contain the following statement as a header or otherwise prominently displayed:

"THIS NOTICE DESCRIBES HOW MEDICAL INFORMATION ABOUT YOU MAY BE USED AND DISCLOSED

AND HOW YOU CAN GET ACCESS TO THIS INFORMA-
TION. PLEASE REVIEW IT CAREFULLY."

(ii) *Uses and disclosures.* The notice must contain:

(A) A description, including at least one example, of
the types of uses and disclosures that the covered entity
is permitted by this subpart to make for each of the following purposes: treatment, payment, and health care
operations.

(B) A description of each of the other purposes for
which the covered entity is permitted or required by this
subpart to use or disclose protected health information
without the individual's written authorization.

(C) If a use or disclosure for any purpose described in
paragraphs (b)(1)(ii)(A) or (B) of this section is prohibited
or materially limited by other applicable law, the description of such use or disclosure must reflect the more stringent law as defined in §160.202 of this subchapter.

(D) For each purpose described in paragraph (b)(1)(ii)(A)
or (B) of this section, the description must include sufficient detail to place the individual on notice of the uses
and disclosures that are permitted or required by this
subpart and other applicable law.

(E) A description of the types of uses and disclosures that
require an authorization under §164.508(a)(2)–(a)(4),
a statement that other uses and disclosures not described
in the notice will be made only with the individual's
written authorization, and a statement that the individual may revoke an authorization as provided by
§164.508(b)(5).

(iii) *Separate statements for certain uses or disclosures.* If the
covered entity intends to engage in any of the following activities, the description required by paragraph (b)(1)(ii)(A) of this
section must include a separate statement informing the individual of such activities, as applicable:

(A) In accordance with §164.514(f)(1), the covered
entity may contact the individual to raise funds for the

covered entity and the individual has a right to opt out of receiving such communications;

(B) In accordance with §164.504(f), the group health plan, or a health insurance issuer or HMO with respect to a group health plan, may disclose protected health information to the sponsor of the plan; or

(C) If a covered entity that is a health plan, excluding an issuer of a long-term care policy falling within paragraph (1)(viii) of the definition of *health plan*, intends to use or disclose protected health information for underwriting purposes, a statement that the covered entity is prohibited from using or disclosing protected health information that is genetic information of an individual for such purposes.

(iv) *Individual rights.* The notice must contain a statement of the individual's rights with respect to protected health information and a brief description of how the individual may exercise these rights, as follows:

(A) The right to request restrictions on certain uses and disclosures of protected health information as provided by §164.522(a), including a statement that the covered entity is not required to agree to a requested restriction, except in case of a disclosure restricted under §164.522(a)(1)

(B) The right to receive confidential communications of protected health information as provided by §164.522(b), as applicable;

(C) The right to inspect and copy protected health information as provided by §164.524;

(D) The right to amend protected health information as provided by §164.526;

(E) The right to receive an accounting of disclosures of protected health information as provided by §164.528; and

(F) The right of an individual, including an individual who has agreed to receive the notice electronically in accordance with paragraph (c)(3) of this section, to obtain a paper copy of the notice from the covered entity upon request.

(v) *Covered entity's duties.* The notice must contain:

(A) A statement that the covered entity is required by law to maintain the privacy of protected health information, to provide individuals with notice of its legal duties and privacy practices with respect to protected health information, and to notify affected individuals following a breach of unsecured protected health information;

(B) A statement that the covered entity is required to abide by the terms of the notice currently in effect; and

(C) For the covered entity to apply a change in a privacy practice that is described in the notice to protected health information that the covered entity created or received prior to issuing a revised notice, in accordance with §164.530(i)(2)(ii), a statement that it reserves the right to change the terms of its notice and to make the new notice provisions effective for all protected health information that it maintains. The statement must also describe how it will provide individuals with a revised notice.

(vi) *Complaints.* The notice must contain a statement that individuals may complain to the covered entity and to the Secretary if they believe their privacy rights have been violated, a brief description of how the individual may file a complaint with the covered entity, and a statement that the individual will not be retaliated against for filing a complaint.

(vii) *Contact.* The notice must contain the name, or title, and telephone number of a person or office to contact for further information as required by §164.530(a)(1)(ii).

(viii)*Effective date.* The notice must contain the date on which the notice is first in effect, which may not be earlier than the date on which the notice is printed or otherwise published.

(2) *Optional elements.* (i) In addition to the information required by paragraph (b)(1) of this section, if a covered entity elects to limit the uses or disclosures that it is permitted to make under this

subpart, the covered entity may describe its more limited uses or disclosures in its notice, provided that the covered entity may not include in its notice a limitation affecting its right to make a use or disclosure that is required by law or permitted by §164.512(j)(1)(i).

(ii) For the covered entity to apply a change in its more limited uses and disclosures to protected health information created or received prior to issuing a revised notice, in accordance with §164.530(i)(2)(ii), the notice must include the statements required by paragraph (b)(1)(v)(C) of this section.

(3) *Revisions to the notice.* The covered entity must promptly revise and distribute its notice whenever there is a material change to the uses or disclosures, the individual's rights, the covered entity's legal duties, or other privacy practices stated in the notice. Except when required by law, a material change to any term of the notice may not be implemented prior to the effective date of the notice in which such material change is reflected.

(c) *Implementation specifications: Provision of notice.* A covered entity must make the notice required by this section available on request to any person and to individuals as specified in paragraphs (c)(1) through (c)(3) of this section, as applicable.

(1) *Specific requirements for health plans.* (i) A health plan must provide the notice:

(A) No later than the compliance date for the health plan, to individuals then covered by the plan;

(B) Thereafter, at the time of enrollment, to individuals who are new enrollees.

(ii) No less frequently than once every three years, the health plan must notify individuals then covered by the plan of the availability of the notice and how to obtain the notice.

(iii) The health plan satisfies the requirements of paragraph (c)(1) of this section if notice is provided to the named insured of a policy under which coverage is provided to the named insured and one or more dependents.

(iv) If a health plan has more than one notice, it satisfies the requirements of paragraph (c)(1) of this section by providing the notice that is relevant to the individual or other person requesting the notice.

(v)   If there is a material change to the notice:

(A)   A health plan that posts its notice on its web site in accordance with paragraph (c)(3)(i) of this section must prominently post the change or its revised notice on its web site by the effective date of the material change to the notice, and provide the revised notice, or information about the material change and how to obtain the revised notice, in its next annual mailing to individuals then covered by the plan.

(B)   A health plan that does not post its notice on a web site pursuant to paragraph (c)(3)(i) of this section must provide the revised notice, or information about the material change and how to obtain the revised notice, to individuals then covered by the plan within 60 days of the material revision to the notice.

(2)   *Specific requirements for certain covered health care providers.* A covered health care provider that has a direct treatment relationship with an individual must:

(i)   Provide the notice:

(A)   No later than the date of the first service delivery, including service delivered electronically, to such individual after the compliance date for the covered health care provider; or

(B)   In an emergency treatment situation, as soon as reasonably practicable after the emergency treatment situation.

(ii)   Except in an emergency treatment situation, make a good faith effort to obtain a written acknowledgment of receipt of the notice provided in accordance with paragraph (c)(2)(i) of this section, and if not obtained, document its good faith efforts to obtain such acknowledgment and the reason why the acknowledgment was not obtained;

(iii)   If the covered health care provider maintains a physical service delivery site:

(A)   Have the notice available at the service delivery site for individuals to request to take with them; and

(B) Post the notice in a clear and prominent location where it is reasonable to expect individuals seeking service from the covered health care provider to be able to read the notice; and

(iv) Whenever the notice is revised, make the notice available upon request on or after the effective date of the revision and promptly comply with the requirements of paragraph (c)(2)(iii) of this section, if applicable.

(3) *Specific requirements for electronic notice.* (i) A covered entity that maintains a web site that provides information about the covered entity's customer services or benefits must prominently post its notice on the web site and make the notice available electronically through the web site.

(ii) A covered entity may provide the notice required by this section to an individual by e-mail, if the individual agrees to electronic notice and such agreement has not been withdrawn. If the covered entity knows that the e-mail transmission has failed, a paper copy of the notice must be provided to the individual. Provision of electronic notice by the covered entity will satisfy the provision requirements of paragraph (c) of this section when timely made in accordance with paragraph (c)(1) or (2) of this section.

(iii) For purposes of paragraph (c)(2)(i) of this section, if the first service delivery to an individual is delivered electronically, the covered health care provider must provide electronic notice automatically and contemporaneously in response to the individual's first request for service. The requirements in paragraph (c)(2)(ii) of this section apply to electronic notice.

(iv) The individual who is the recipient of electronic notice retains the right to obtain a paper copy of the notice from a covered entity upon request.

(d) *Implementation specifications: Joint notice by separate covered entities.* Covered entities that participate in organized health care arrangements may comply with this section by a joint notice, provided that:

(1)   The covered entities participating in the organized health care arrangement agree to abide by the terms of the notice with respect to protected health information created or received by the covered entity as part of its participation in the organized health care arrangement;

(2)   The joint notice meets the implementation specifications in paragraph (b) of this section, except that the statements required by this section may be altered to reflect the fact that the notice covers more than one covered entity; and

(i)   Describes with reasonable specificity the covered entities, or class of entities, to which the joint notice applies;

(ii)   Describes with reasonable specificity the service delivery sites, or classes of service delivery sites, to which the joint notice applies; and

(iii)   If applicable, states that the covered entities participating in the organized health care arrangement will share protected health information with each other, as necessary to carry out treatment, payment, or health care operations relating to the organized health care arrangement.

(3)   The covered entities included in the joint notice must provide the notice to individuals in accordance with the applicable implementation specifications of paragraph (c) of this section. Provision of the joint notice to an individual by any one of the covered entities included in the joint notice will satisfy the provision requirement of paragraph (c) of this section with respect to all others covered by the joint notice.

(e)   *Implementation specifications: Documentation.* A covered entity must document compliance with the notice requirements, as required by §164.530(j), by retaining copies of the notices issued by the covered entity and, if applicable, any written acknowledgments of receipt of the notice or documentation of good faith efforts to obtain such written acknowledgment, in accordance with paragraph (c)(2)(ii) of this section.

[65 FR 82802, Dec. 28, 2000, as amended at 67 FR 53271, Aug. 14, 2002; 78 FR 5701, Jan. 25, 2013]

§164.522 Rights to request privacy protection for protected health information.

(a)(1) *Standard: Right of an individual to request restriction of uses and disclosures.* (i) A covered entity must permit an individual to request that the covered entity restrict:

> (A) Uses or disclosures of protected health information about the individual to carry out treatment, payment, or health care operations; and

> (B) Disclosures permitted under §164.510(b).

(ii) Except as provided in paragraph (a)(1)(vi) of this section, a covered entity is not required to agree to a restriction.

(iii) A covered entity that agrees to a restriction under paragraph (a)(1)(i) of this section may not use or disclose protected health information in violation of such restriction, except that, if the individual who requested the restriction is in need of emergency treatment and the restricted protected health information is needed to provide the emergency treatment, the covered entity may use the restricted protected health information, or may disclose such information to a health care provider, to provide such treatment to the individual.

(iv) If restricted protected health information is disclosed to a health care provider for emergency treatment under paragraph (a)(1)(iii) of this section, the covered entity must request that such health care provider not further use or disclose the information.

(v) A restriction agreed to by a covered entity under paragraph (a) of this section, is not effective under this subpart to prevent uses or disclosures permitted or required under §164.502(a)(2)(ii), §164.510(a) or §164.512.

(vi) A covered entity must agree to the request of an individual to restrict disclosure of protected health information about the individual to a health plan if:

> (A) The disclosure is for the purpose of carrying out payment or health care operations and is not otherwise required by law; and

(B)   The protected health information pertains solely to a health care item or service for which the individual, or person other than the health plan on behalf of the individual, has paid the covered entity in full.

(2) *Implementation specifications:* Terminating a restriction. A covered entity may terminate a restriction, if:

(i)   The individual agrees to or requests the termination in writing;

(ii)   The individual orally agrees to the termination and the oral agreement is documented; or

(iii)   The covered entity informs the individual that it is terminating its agreement to a restriction, except that such termination is:

(A)   Not effective for protected health information restricted under paragraph (a)(1)(vi) of this section; and

(B)   Only effective with respect to protected health information created or received after it has so informed the individual.

(3) *Implementation specification: Documentation.* A covered entity must document a restriction in accordance with §160.530(j) of this subchapter.

(b)(1) *Standard: Confidential communications requirements.* (i) A covered health care provider must permit individuals to request and must accommodate reasonable requests by individuals to receive communications of protected health information from the covered health care provider by alternative means or at alternative locations.

(ii)   A health plan must permit individuals to request and must accommodate reasonable requests by individuals to receive communications of protected health information from the health plan by alternative means or at alternative locations, if the individual clearly states that the disclosure of all or part of that information could endanger the individual.

(2) *Implementation specifications: Conditions on providing confidential communications.* (i) A covered entity may require the individual to make a request for a confidential communication described in paragraph (b)(1) of this section in writing.

(ii) A covered entity may condition the provision of a reasonable accommodation on:

(A) When appropriate, information as to how payment, if any, will be handled; and

(B) Specification of an alternative address or other method of contact.

(iii) A covered health care provider may not require an explanation from the individual as to the basis for the request as a condition of providing communications on a confidential basis.

(iv) A health plan may require that a request contain a statement that disclosure of all or part of the information to which the request pertains could endanger the individual.

[65 FR 82802, Dec. 28, 2000, as amended at 67 FR 53271, Aug. 14, 2002; 78 FR 5701, Jan. 25, 2013]

§164.524 Access of individuals to protected health information.

(a) *Standard: Access to protected health information*—(1) *Right of access.* Except as otherwise provided in paragraph (a)(2) or (a)(3) of this section, an individual has a right of access to inspect and obtain a copy of protected health information about the individual in a designated record set, for as long as the protected health information is maintained in the designated record set, except for:

(i) Psychotherapy notes; and

(ii) Information compiled in reasonable anticipation of, or for use in, a civil, criminal, or administrative action or proceeding.

(2) *Unreviewable grounds for denial.* A covered entity may deny an individual access without providing the individual an opportunity for review, in the following circumstances.

(i) The protected health information is excepted from the right of access by paragraph (a)(1) of this section.

(ii) A covered entity that is a correctional institution or a covered health care provider acting under the direction of the correctional institution may deny, in whole or in part, an inmate's request to obtain a copy of protected health information, if obtaining such copy would jeopardize the health, safety, security, custody, or rehabilitation of the individual or of other inmates, or the safety of any officer, employee, or other person at the correctional institution or responsible for the transporting of the inmate.

(iii) An individual's access to protected health information created or obtained by a covered health care provider in the course of research that includes treatment may be temporarily suspended for as long as the research is in progress, provided that the individual has agreed to the denial of access when consenting to participate in the research that includes treatment, and the covered health care provider has informed the individual that the right of access will be reinstated upon completion of the research.

(iv) An individual's access to protected health information that is contained in records that are subject to the Privacy Act, 5 U.S.C. 552a, may be denied, if the denial of access under the Privacy Act would meet the requirements of that law.

(v) An individual's access may be denied if the protected health information was obtained from someone other than a health care provider under a promise of confidentiality and the access requested would be reasonably likely to reveal the source of the information.

(3) *Reviewable grounds for denial.* A covered entity may deny an individual access, provided that the individual is given a right to have such denials reviewed, as required by paragraph (a)(4) of this section, in the following circumstances:

(i) A licensed health care professional has determined, in the exercise of professional judgment, that the access requested is reasonably likely to endanger the life or physical safety of the individual or another person;

(ii) The protected health information makes reference to another person (unless such other person is a health care provider) and a licensed health care professional has determined, in the exercise of professional judgment, that the access requested is reasonably likely to cause substantial harm to such other person; or

(iii) The request for access is made by the individual's personal representative and a licensed health care professional has determined, in the exercise of professional judgment, that the provision of access to such personal representative is reasonably likely to cause substantial harm to the individual or another person.

(4) *Review of a denial of access.* If access is denied on a ground permitted under paragraph (a)(3) of this section, the individual has the right to have the denial reviewed by a licensed health care professional who is designated by the covered entity to act as a reviewing official and who did not participate in the original decision to deny. The covered entity must provide or deny access in accordance with the determination of the reviewing official under paragraph (d)(4) of this section.

(b) *Implementation specifications: Requests for access and timely action*—(1) *Individual's request for access.* The covered entity must permit an individual to request access to inspect or to obtain a copy of the protected health information about the individual that is maintained in a designated record set. The covered entity may require individuals to make requests for access in writing, provided that it informs individuals of such a requirement.

(2) *Timely action by the covered entity.* (i) Except as provided in paragraph (b)(2)(ii) of this section, the covered entity must act on a request for access no later than 30 days after receipt of the request as follows.

(A) If the covered entity grants the request, in whole or in part, it must inform the individual of the acceptance of the request and provide the access requested, in accordance with paragraph (c) of this section.

(B) If the covered entity denies the request, in whole or in part, it must provide the individual with a written denial, in accordance with paragraph (d) of this section.

(ii) If the covered entity is unable to take an action required by paragraph (b)(2)(i)(A) or (B) of this section within the time required by paragraph (b)(2)(i) of this section, as applicable, the covered entity may extend the time for such actions by no more than 30 days, provided that:

(A) The covered entity, within the time limit set by paragraph (b)(2)(i) of this section, as applicable, provides the individual with a written statement of the reasons for the delay and the date by which the covered entity will complete its action on the request; and

(B) The covered entity may have only one such extension of time for action on a request for access.

(c) *Implementation specifications: Provision of access.* If the covered entity provides an individual with access, in whole or in part, to protected health information, the covered entity must comply with the following requirements.

(1) *Providing the access requested.* The covered entity must provide the access requested by individuals, including inspection or obtaining a copy, or both, of the protected health information about them in designated record sets. If the same protected health information that is the subject of a request for access is maintained in more than one designated record set or at more than one location, the covered entity need only produce the protected health information once in response to a request for access.

(2) *Form of access requested.* (i) The covered entity must provide the individual with access to the protected health information in the form and format requested by the individual, if it is readily producible in such form and format; or, if not, in a readable hard copy form or such other form and format as agreed to by the covered entity and the individual.

(ii) Notwithstanding paragraph (c)(2)(i) of this section, if the protected health information that is the subject of a request for access is maintained in one or more designated record sets electronically and if the individual requests an electronic copy of such information, the covered entity must provide the individual with access to the protected health information in the electronic form and format requested by the individual, if it is readily producible in such form and format; or, if not, in a readable electronic form and format as agreed to by the covered entity and the individual.

(iii) The covered entity may provide the individual with a summary of the protected health information requested, in lieu of providing access to the protected health information or may provide an explanation of the protected health information to which access has been provided, if:

(A) The individual agrees in advance to such a summary or explanation; and

(B) The individual agrees in advance to the fees imposed, if any, by the covered entity for such summary or explanation.

(3) *Time and manner of access.* (i) The covered entity must provide the access as requested by the individual in a timely manner as required by paragraph (b)(2) of this section, including arranging with the individual for a convenient time and place to inspect or obtain a copy of the protected health information, or mailing the copy of the protected health information at the individual's request. The covered entity may discuss the scope, format, and other aspects of the request for access with the individual as necessary to facilitate the timely provision of access.

(ii) If an individual's request for access directs the covered entity to transmit the copy of protected health information directly to another person designated by the individual, the covered entity must provide the copy to the person designated by the individual. The individual's request must be in writing, signed by the individual, and clearly identify the designated person and where to send the copy of protected health information.

(4) *Fees.* If the individual requests a copy of the protected health information or agrees to a summary or explanation of such information, the covered entity may impose a reasonable, cost-based fee, provided that the fee includes only the cost of:

(i) Labor for copying the protected health information requested by the individual, whether in paper or electronic form;

(ii) Supplies for creating the paper copy or electronic media if the individual requests that the electronic copy be provided on portable media;

(iii) Postage, when the individual has requested the copy, or the summary or explanation, be mailed; and

(iv) Preparing an explanation or summary of the protected health information, if agreed to by the individual as required by paragraph (c)(2)(iii) of this section.

(d) *Implementation specifications: Denial of access.* If the covered entity denies access, in whole or in part, to protected health information, the covered entity must comply with the following requirements.

(1) *Making other information accessible.* The covered entity must, to the extent possible, give the individual access to any other protected health information requested, after excluding the protected health information as to which the covered entity has a ground to deny access.

(2) *Denial.* The covered entity must provide a timely, written denial to the individual, in accordance with paragraph (b)(2) of this section. The denial must be in plain language and contain:

(i) The basis for the denial;

(ii) If applicable, a statement of the individual's review rights under paragraph (a)(4) of this section, including a description of how the individual may exercise such review rights; and

(iii) A description of how the individual may complain to the covered entity pursuant to the complaint procedures in §164.530(d) or to the Secretary pursuant to the procedures in §160.306. The description must include the name, or title, and telephone number of the contact person or office designated in §164.530(a)(1)(ii).

(3) *Other responsibility.* If the covered entity does not maintain the protected health information that is the subject of the individual's request for access, and the covered entity knows where the requested information is maintained, the covered entity must inform the individual where to direct the request for access.

(4) *Review of denial requested.* If the individual has requested a review of a denial under paragraph (a)(4) of this section, the covered entity must designate a licensed health care professional, who was not directly involved in the denial to review the decision to deny access. The covered entity must promptly refer a request for review to such designated reviewing official. The designated reviewing official must determine, within a reasonable period of

time, whether or not to deny the access requested based on the standards in paragraph (a)(3) of this section. The covered entity must promptly provide written notice to the individual of the determination of the designated reviewing official and take other action as required by this section to carry out the designated reviewing official's determination.

(e) *Implementation specification: Documentation.* A covered entity must document the following and retain the documentation as required by §164.530(j):

(1) The designated record sets that are subject to access by individuals; and

(2) The titles of the persons or offices responsible for receiving and processing requests for access by individuals.

[65 FR 82802, Dec. 28, 2000, as amended at 78 FR 5701, Jan. 25, 2013; 78 FR 34266, June 7, 2013; 79 FR 7316, Feb. 6, 2014]

§164.526 Amendment of protected health information.

(a) *Standard: Right to amend.* (1) *Right to amend.* An individual has the right to have a covered entity amend protected health information or a record about the individual in a designated record set for as long as the protected health information is maintained in the designated record set.

(2) *Denial of amendment.* A covered entity may deny an individual's request for amendment, if it determines that the protected health information or record that is the subject of the request:

(i) Was not created by the covered entity, unless the individual provides a reasonable basis to believe that the originator of protected health information is no longer available to act on the requested amendment;

(ii) Is not part of the designated record set;

(iii) Would not be available for inspection under §164.524; or

(iv) Is accurate and complete.

(b) *Implementation specifications: Requests for amendment and timely action.* (1) *Individual's request for amendment.* The covered entity must permit an individual to request that the covered entity amend the protected health information maintained in the designated record set. The covered entity may require individuals to make requests for amendment in writing and to provide a reason to support a requested amendment, provided that it informs individuals in advance of such requirements.

(2) *Timely action by the covered entity.* (i) The covered entity must act on the individual's request for an amendment no later than 60 days after receipt of such a request, as follows.

(A) If the covered entity grants the requested amendment, in whole or in part, it must take the actions required by paragraphs (c)(1) and (2) of this section.

(B) If the covered entity denies the requested amendment, in whole or in part, it must provide the individual with a written denial, in accordance with paragraph (d)(1) of this section.

(ii) If the covered entity is unable to act on the amendment within the time required by paragraph (b)(2)(i) of this section, the covered entity may extend the time for such action by no more than 30 days, provided that:

(A) The covered entity, within the time limit set by paragraph (b)(2)(i) of this section, provides the individual with a written statement of the reasons for the delay and the date by which the covered entity will complete its action on the request; and

(B) The covered entity may have only one such extension of time for action on a request for an amendment.

(c) *Implementation specifications: Accepting the amendment.* If the covered entity accepts the requested amendment, in whole or in part, the covered entity must comply with the following requirements.

(1) *Making the amendment.* The covered entity must make the appropriate amendment to the protected health information or record that is the subject of the request for amendment by, at a minimum, identifying the records in the designated record set that are affected by the amendment and appending or otherwise providing a link to the location of the amendment.

(2) *Informing the individual.* In accordance with paragraph (b) of this section, the covered entity must timely inform the individual

that the amendment is accepted and obtain the individual's identification of and agreement to have the covered entity notify the relevant persons with which the amendment needs to be shared in accordance with paragraph (c)(3) of this section.

(3) *Informing others.* The covered entity must make reasonable efforts to inform and provide the amendment within a reasonable time to:

(i) Persons identified by the individual as having received protected health information about the individual and needing the amendment; and

(ii) Persons, including business associates, that the covered entity knows have the protected health information that is the subject of the amendment and that may have relied, or could foreseeably rely, on such information to the detriment of the individual.

(d) *Implementation specifications: Denying the amendment.* If the covered entity denies the requested amendment, in whole or in part, the covered entity must comply with the following requirements.

(1) *Denial.* The covered entity must provide the individual with a timely, written denial, in accordance with paragraph (b)(2) of this section. The denial must use plain language and contain:

(i) The basis for the denial, in accordance with paragraph (a)(2) of this section;

(ii) The individual's right to submit a written statement disagreeing with the denial and how the individual may file such a statement;

(iii) A statement that, if the individual does not submit a statement of disagreement, the individual may request that the covered entity provide the individual's request for amendment and the denial with any future disclosures of the protected health information that is the subject of the amendment; and

(iv) A description of how the individual may complain to the covered entity pursuant to the complaint procedures established in §164.530(d) or to the Secretary pursuant to the procedures established in §160.306. The description must include the name, or title, and telephone number of the contact person or office designated in §164.530(a)(1)(ii).

(2) *Statement of disagreement.* The covered entity must permit the individual to submit to the covered entity a written statement disagreeing with the denial of all or part of a requested amendment and the basis of such disagreement. The covered entity may reasonably limit the length of a statement of disagreement.

(3) *Rebuttal statement.* The covered entity may prepare a written rebuttal to the individual's statement of disagreement. Whenever such a rebuttal is prepared, the covered entity must provide a copy to the individual who submitted the statement of disagreement.

(4) *Recordkeeping.* The covered entity must, as appropriate, identify the record or protected health information in the designated record set that is the subject of the disputed amendment and append or otherwise link the individual's request for an amendment, the covered entity's denial of the request, the individual's statement of disagreement, if any, and the covered entity's rebuttal, if any, to the designated record set.

(5) *Future disclosures.* (i) If a statement of disagreement has been submitted by the individual, the covered entity must include the material appended in accordance with paragraph (d)(4) of this section, or, at the election of the covered entity, an accurate summary of any such information, with any subsequent disclosure of the protected health information to which the disagreement relates.

(ii) If the individual has not submitted a written statement of disagreement, the covered entity must include the individual's request for amendment and its denial, or an accurate summary of such information, with any subsequent disclosure of the protected health information only if the individual has requested such action in accordance with paragraph (d)(1)(iii) of this section.

(iii) When a subsequent disclosure described in paragraph (d)(5)(i) or (ii) of this section is made using a standard transaction under part 162 of this subchapter that does not permit the additional material to be included with the disclosure, the covered entity may separately transmit the material required by paragraph (d)(5)(i) or (ii) of this section, as applicable, to the recipient of the standard transaction.

(e) *Implementation specification: Actions on notices of amendment.* A covered entity that is informed by another covered entity of an amendment to an individual's protected health information, in accordance with paragraph (c)(3) of this section, must amend the protected health information in designated record sets as provided by paragraph (c)(1) of this section.

(f) *Implementation specification: Documentation.* A covered entity must document the titles of the persons or offices responsible for receiving and processing requests for amendments by individuals and retain the documentation as required by §164.530(j).

§164.528 Accounting of disclosures of protected health information.

(a) *Standard: Right to an accounting of disclosures of protected health information.* (1) An individual has a right to receive an accounting of disclosures of protected health information made by a covered entity in the six years prior to the date on which the accounting is requested, except for disclosures:

> (i) To carry out treatment, payment and health care operations as provided in §164.506;

> (ii) To individuals of protected health information about them as provided in §164.502;

> (iii) Incident to a use or disclosure otherwise permitted or required by this subpart, as provided in §164.502;

> (iv) Pursuant to an authorization as provided in §164.508;

> (v) For the facility's directory or to persons involved in the individual's care or other notification purposes as provided in §164.510;

> (vi) For national security or intelligence purposes as provided in §164.512(k)(2);

> (vii) To correctional institutions or law enforcement officials as provided in §164.512(k)(5);

> (viii) As part of a limited data set in accordance with §164.514(e); or

> (ix) That occurred prior to the compliance date for the covered entity.

(2)(i) The covered entity must temporarily suspend an individual's right to receive an accounting of disclosures to a health oversight agency or law enforcement official, as provided in §164.512(d) or (f), respectively, for the time specified by such agency or official, if such agency or official provides the covered entity with a written statement that such an accounting to the individual would be reasonably likely to impede the agency's activities and specifying the time for which such a suspension is required.

(ii) If the agency or official statement in paragraph (a)(2)(i) of this section is made orally, the covered entity must:

(A) Document the statement, including the identity of the agency or official making the statement;

(B) Temporarily suspend the individual's right to an accounting of disclosures subject to the statement; and

(C) Limit the temporary suspension to no longer than 30 days from the date of the oral statement, unless a written statement pursuant to paragraph (a)(2)(i) of this section is submitted during that time.

(3) An individual may request an accounting of disclosures for a period of time less than six years from the date of the request.

(b) *Implementation specifications: Content of the accounting.* The covered entity must provide the individual with a written accounting that meets the following requirements.

(1) Except as otherwise provided by paragraph (a) of this section, the accounting must include disclosures of protected health information that occurred during the six years (or such shorter time period at the request of the individual as provided in paragraph (a)(3) of this section) prior to the date of the request for an accounting, including disclosures to or by business associates of the covered entity.

(2) Except as otherwise provided by paragraphs (b)(3) or (b)(4) of this section, the accounting must include for each disclosure:

(i) The date of the disclosure;

(ii) The name of the entity or person who received the protected health information and, if known, the address of such entity or person;

(iii) A brief description of the protected health information disclosed; and

(iv) A brief statement of the purpose of the disclosure that reasonably informs the individual of the basis for the disclosure or, in lieu of such statement, a copy of a written request for a disclosure under §164.502(a)(2)(ii) or §164.512, if any.

(3) If, during the period covered by the accounting, the covered entity has made multiple disclosures of protected health information to the same person or entity for a single purpose under §164.502(a)(2)(ii) or §164.512, the accounting may, with respect to such multiple disclosures, provide:

(i) The information required by paragraph (b)(2) of this section for the first disclosure during the accounting period;

(ii) The frequency, periodicity, or number of the disclosures made during the accounting period; and

(iii) The date of the last such disclosure during the accounting period.

(4)(i) If, during the period covered by the accounting, the covered entity has made disclosures of protected health information for a particular research purpose in accordance with §164.512(i) for 50 or more individuals, the accounting may, with respect to such disclosures for which the protected health information about the individual may have been included, provide:

(A) The name of the protocol or other research activity;

(B) A description, in plain language, of the research protocol or other research activity, including the purpose of the research and the criteria for selecting particular records;

(C) A brief description of the type of protected health information that was disclosed;

(D) The date or period of time during which such disclosures occurred, or may have occurred, including the date of the last such disclosure during the accounting period;

(E) The name, address, and telephone number of the entity that sponsored the research and of the researcher to whom the information was disclosed; and

(F)   A statement that the protected health information of the individual may or may not have been disclosed for a particular protocol or other research activity.

(ii)   If the covered entity provides an accounting for research disclosures, in accordance with paragraph (b)(4) of this section, and if it is reasonably likely that the protected health information of the individual was disclosed for such research protocol or activity, the covered entity shall, at the request of the individual, assist in contacting the entity that sponsored the research and the researcher.

(c) *Implementation specifications: Provision of the accounting.* (1) The covered entity must act on the individual's request for an accounting, no later than 60 days after receipt of such a request, as follows.

(i)   The covered entity must provide the individual with the accounting requested; or

(ii)   If the covered entity is unable to provide the accounting within the time required by paragraph (c)(1) of this section, the covered entity may extend the time to provide the accounting by no more than 30 days, provided that:

(A) The covered entity, within the time limit set by paragraph (c)(1) of this section, provides the individual with a written statement of the reasons for the delay and the date by which the covered entity will provide the accounting; and

(B) The covered entity may have only one such extension of time for action on a request for an accounting.

(2) The covered entity must provide the first accounting to an individual in any 12 month period without charge. The covered entity may impose a reasonable, cost-based fee for each subsequent request for an accounting by the same individual within the 12 month period, provided that the covered entity informs the individual in advance of the fee and provides the individual with an opportunity to withdraw or modify the request for a subsequent accounting in order to avoid or reduce the fee.

(d) *Implementation specification: Documentation.* A covered entity must document the following and retain the documentation as required by §164.530(j):

(1) The information required to be included in an accounting under paragraph (b) of this section for disclosures of protected health information that are subject to an accounting under paragraph (a) of this section;

(2) The written accounting that is provided to the individual under this section; and

(3) The titles of the persons or offices responsible for receiving and processing requests for an accounting by individuals.

[65 FR 82802, Dec. 28, 2000, as amended at 67 FR 53271, Aug. 14, 2002]

§164.530 Administrative requirements.

(a)(1) *Standard: Personnel designations.* (i) A covered entity must designate a privacy official who is responsible for the development and implementation of the policies and procedures of the entity.

(ii) A covered entity must designate a contact person or office who is responsible for receiving complaints under this section and who is able to provide further information about matters covered by the notice required by §164.520.

(2) *Implementation specification: Personnel designations.* A covered entity must document the personnel designations in paragraph (a)(1) of this section as required by paragraph (j) of this section.

(b)(1) *Standard: Training.* A covered entity must train all members of its workforce on the policies and procedures with respect to protected health information required by this subpart and subpart D of this part, as necessary and appropriate for the members of the workforce to carry out their functions within the covered entity.

(2) *Implementation specifications: Training.* (i) A covered entity must provide training that meets the requirements of paragraph (b)(1) of this section, as follows:

(A) To each member of the covered entity's workforce by no later than the compliance date for the covered entity;

(B) Thereafter, to each new member of the workforce within a reasonable period of time after the person joins the covered entity's workforce; and

(C) To each member of the covered entity's workforce whose functions are affected by a material change in the policies or procedures required by this subpart or subpart D of this part, within a reasonable period of time after the material change becomes effective in accordance with paragraph (i) of this section.

(ii) A covered entity must document that the training as described in paragraph (b)(2)(i) of this section has been provided, as required by paragraph (j) of this section.

(c)(1) *Standard: Safeguards.* A covered entity must have in place appropriate administrative, technical, and physical safeguards to protect the privacy of protected health information.

(2)(i) *Implementation specification: Safeguards.* A covered entity must reasonably safeguard protected health information from any intentional or unintentional use or disclosure that is in violation of the standards, implementation specifications or other requirements of this subpart.

(ii) A covered entity must reasonably safeguard protected health information to limit incidental uses or disclosures made pursuant to an otherwise permitted or required use or disclosure.

(d)(1) *Standard: Complaints to the covered entity.* A covered entity must provide a process for individuals to make complaints concerning the covered entity's policies and procedures required by this subpart and subpart D of this part or its compliance with such policies and procedures or the requirements of this subpart or subpart D of this part.

(2) *Implementation specification: Documentation of complaints.* As required by paragraph (j) of this section, a covered entity must document all complaints received, and their disposition, if any.

(e)(1) *Standard: Sanctions.* A covered entity must have and apply appropriate sanctions against members of its workforce who fail to comply with the privacy policies and procedures of the covered entity or the requirements of this subpart or subpart D of this part. This standard does not apply to a member of the covered entity's workforce with respect to actions that are covered by and that meet the conditions of §164.502(j) or paragraph (g)(2) of this section.

(2) *Implementation specification: Documentation.* As required by paragraph (j) of this section, a covered entity must document the sanctions that are applied, if any.

(f) *Standard: Mitigation.* A covered entity must mitigate, to the extent practicable, any harmful effect that is known to the covered entity of a use or disclosure of protected health information in violation of its policies and procedures or the requirements of this subpart by the covered entity or its business associate.

(g) *Standard: Refraining from intimidating or retaliatory acts.* A covered entity—

(1) May not intimidate, threaten, coerce, discriminate against, or take other retaliatory action against any individual for the exercise by the individual of any right established, or for participation in any process provided for, by this subpart or subpart D of this part, including the filing of a complaint under this section; and

(2) Must refrain from intimidation and retaliation as provided in §160.316 of this subchapter.

(h) *Standard: Waiver of rights.* A covered entity may not require individuals to waive their rights under §160.306 of this subchapter, this subpart, or subpart D of this part, as a condition of the provision of treatment, payment, enrollment in a health plan, or eligibility for benefits.

(i)(1) *Standard: Policies and procedures.* A covered entity must implement policies and procedures with respect to protected health information that are designed to comply with the standards, implementation specifications, or other requirements of this subpart and subpart D of this part. The policies and procedures must be reasonably designed, taking into account the size and the type of activities that relate to protected health information undertaken by a covered entity, to ensure such compliance. This standard is not to be construed to permit or excuse an action that violates any other standard, implementation specification, or other requirement of this subpart.

(2) *Standard: Changes to policies and procedures.* (i) A covered entity must change its policies and procedures as necessary and appropriate to comply with changes in the law, including the standards, requirements, and implementation specifications of this subpart or subpart D of this part.

(ii)   When a covered entity changes a privacy practice that is stated in the notice described in §164.520, and makes corresponding changes to its policies and procedures, it may make the changes effective for protected health information that it created or received prior to the effective date of the notice revision, if the covered entity has, in accordance with §164.520(b)(1)(v)(C), included in the notice a statement reserving its right to make such a change in its privacy practices; or

(iii)   A covered entity may make any other changes to policies and procedures at any time, provided that the changes are documented and implemented in accordance with paragraph (i)(5) of this section.

(3) *Implementation specification: Changes in law.* Whenever there is a change in law that necessitates a change to the covered entity's policies or procedures, the covered entity must promptly document and implement the revised policy or procedure. If the change in law materially affects the content of the notice required by §164.520, the covered entity must promptly make the appropriate revisions to the notice in accordance with §164.520(b)(3). Nothing in this paragraph may be used by a covered entity to excuse a failure to comply with the law.

(4) *Implementation specifications: Changes to privacy practices stated in the notice.* (i) To implement a change as provided by paragraph (i)(2)(ii) of this section, a covered entity must:

(A)   Ensure that the policy or procedure, as revised to reflect a change in the covered entity's privacy practice as stated in its notice, complies with the standards, requirements, and implementation specifications of this subpart;

(B)   Document the policy or procedure, as revised, as required by paragraph (j) of this section; and

(C)   Revise the notice as required by §164.520(b)(3) to state the changed practice and make the revised notice available as required by §164.520(c). The covered entity may not implement a change to a policy or procedure prior to the effective date of the revised notice.

(ii)   If a covered entity has not reserved its right under §164.520(b)(1)(v)(C) to change a privacy practice that is stated in the notice, the covered entity is bound by the privacy practices as stated in the notice with respect to protected health information created or received while such notice is in effect. A covered entity may change a privacy practice that is stated in the notice, and the related policies and procedures, without having reserved the right to do so, provided that:

(A) Such change meets the implementation specifications in paragraphs (i)(4)(i)(A)–(C) of this section; and

(B) Such change is effective only with respect to protected health information created or received after the effective date of the notice.

(5) *Implementation specification: Changes to other policies or procedures.* A covered entity may change, at any time, a policy or procedure that does not materially affect the content of the notice required by §164.520, provided that:

(i) The policy or procedure, as revised, complies with the standards, requirements, and implementation specifications of this subpart; and

(ii) Prior to the effective date of the change, the policy or procedure, as revised, is documented as required by paragraph (j) of this section.

(j)(1) *Standard: Documentation.* A covered entity must:

(i) Maintain the policies and procedures provided for in paragraph (i) of this section in written or electronic form;

(ii) If a communication is required by this subpart to be in writing, maintain such writing, or an electronic copy, as documentation; and

(iii) If an action, activity, or designation is required by this subpart to be documented, maintain a written or electronic record of such action, activity, or designation.

(iv) Maintain documentation sufficient to meet its burden of proof under §164.414(b).

(2) *Implementation specification: Retention period.* A covered entity must retain the documentation required by paragraph (j)(1)

of this section for six years from the date of its creation or the date when it last was in effect, whichever is later.

(k) *Standard: Group health plans.* (1) A group health plan is not subject to the standards or implementation specifications in paragraphs (a) through (f) and (i) of this section, to the extent that:

> (i)   The group health plan provides health benefits solely through an insurance contract with a health insurance issuer or an HMO; and

> (ii)   The group health plan does not create or receive protected health information, except for:

>> (A)   Summary health information as defined in §164.504(a); or

>> (B)   Information on whether the individual is participating in the group health plan, or is enrolled in or has disenrolled from a health insurance issuer or HMO offered by the plan.

(2)   A group health plan described in paragraph (k)(1) of this section is subject to the standard and implementation specification in paragraph (j) of this section only with respect to plan documents amended in accordance with §164.504(f).

[65 FR 82802, Dec. 28, 2000, as amended at 67 FR 53272, Aug. 14, 2002; 71 FR 8433, Feb. 16, 2006; 74 FR 42769, Aug. 24, 2009]

§164.532 Transition provisions.

(a) *Standard: Effect   of   prior   authorizations.*   Notwithstanding §§164.508 and 164.512(i), a covered entity may use or disclose protected health information, consistent with paragraphs (b) and (c) of this section, pursuant to an authorization or other express legal permission obtained from an individual permitting the use or disclosure of protected health information, informed consent of the individual to participate in research, a waiver of informed consent by an IRB, or a waiver of authorization in accordance with §164.512(i)(1)(i).

(b) *Implementation specification: Effect of prior authorization for purposes other than research.* Notwithstanding any provisions in §164.508, a covered entity may use or disclose protected health information that it created or received prior to the applicable compliance date of this subpart pursuant to an authorization or other express legal permission obtained from an individual prior to the applicable compliance date of this subpart, provided that the authorization or other express legal permission specifically permits such use or disclosure and there is no agreed-to restriction in accordance with §164.522(a).

(c) *Implementation specification: Effect of prior permission for research.* Notwithstanding any provisions in §§164.508 and 164.512(i), a covered entity may, to the extent allowed by one of the following permissions, use or disclose, for research, protected health information that it created or received either before or after the applicable compliance date of this subpart, provided that there is no agreed-to restriction in accordance with §164.522(a), and the covered entity has obtained, prior to the applicable compliance date, either:

(1) An authorization or other express legal permission from an individual to use or disclose protected health information for the research;

(2) The informed consent of the individual to participate in the research;

(3) A waiver, by an IRB, of informed consent for the research, in accordance with 7 CFR 1c.116(d), 10 CFR 745.116(d), 14 CFR 1230.116(d), 15 CFR 27.116(d), 16 CFR 1028.116(d), 21 CFR 50.24, 22 CFR 225.116(d), 24 CFR 60.116(d), 28 CFR 46.116(d), 32 CFR 219.116(d), 34 CFR 97.116(d), 38 CFR 16.116(d), 40 CFR 26.116(d), 45 CFR 46.116(d), 45 CFR 690.116(d), or 49 CFR 11.116(d), provided that a covered entity must obtain authorization in accordance with §164.508 if, after the compliance date, informed consent is sought from an individual participating in the research; or

(4) A waiver of authorization in accordance with §164.512(i)(1)(i).

(d) *Standard: Effect of prior contracts or other arrangements with business associates.* Notwithstanding any other provisions of this part, a covered entity, or business associate with respect to a subcontractor, may disclose protected health information to a business associate and may allow a business associate to create, receive, maintain, or transmit protected health information on its behalf pursuant to a written contract or other written arrangement with such business associate that does not comply with §§164.308(b), 164.314(a), 164.502(e), and 164.504(e), only in accordance with paragraph (e) of this section.

(e) *Implementation specification: Deemed compliance.* (1) *Qualification.* Notwithstanding other sections of this part, a covered entity, or business associate with respect to a subcontractor, is deemed to be in compliance with the documentation and contract requirements of §§164.308(b), 164.314(a), 164.502(e), and 164.504(e), with respect to a particular business associate relationship, for the time period set forth in paragraph (e)(2) of this section, if:

> (i)   Prior to January 25, 2013, such covered entity, or business associate with respect to a subcontractor, has entered into and is operating pursuant to a written contract or other written arrangement with the business associate that complies with the applicable provisions of §164.314(a) or §164.504(e) that were in effect on such date; and

> (ii) The contract or other arrangement is not renewed or modified from March 26, 2013, until September 23, 2013.

(2) *Limited deemed compliance period.* A prior contract or other arrangement that meets the qualification requirements in paragraph (e) of this section shall be deemed compliant until the earlier of:

> (i)   The date such contract or other arrangement is renewed or modified on or after September 23, 2013; or

> (ii) September 22, 2014.

(3) *Covered entity responsibilities.* Nothing in this section shall alter the requirements of a covered entity to comply with part 160, subpart C of this subchapter and §§164.524, 164.526, 164.528, and 164.530(f) with respect to protected health information held by a business associate.

(f) *Effect of prior data use agreements.* If, prior to January 25, 2013, a covered entity has entered into and is operating pursuant to a data use agreement with a recipient of a limited data set that complies with §164.514(e), notwithstanding §164.502(a)(5)(ii), the covered entity may continue to disclose a limited data set pursuant to such agreement in exchange for remuneration from or on behalf of the recipient of the protected health information until the earlier of:

(1) The date such agreement is renewed or modified on or after September 23, 2013; or

(2) September 22, 2014.

[65 FR 82802, Dec. 28, 2000, as amended at 67 FR 53272, Aug. 14, 2002; 78 FR 5702, Jan. 25, 2013; 78 FR 34266, June 7, 2013]

§164.534 Compliance dates for initial implementation of the privacy standards.

(a) *Health care providers.* A covered health care provider must comply with the applicable requirements of this subpart no later than April 14, 2003.

(b) *Health plans.* A health plan must comply with the applicable requirements of this subpart no later than the following as applicable:

(1) Health plans other than small health plans. April 14, 2003.

(2) *Small health plans.* April 14, 2004.

(c) *Health clearinghouses.* A health care clearinghouse must comply with the applicable requirements of this subpart no later than April 14, 2003.

[66 FR 12434, Feb. 26, 2001]

Index